Deleuze and the Animal

Deleuze Connections

'It is not the elements or the sets which define the multiplicity. What defines it is the AND, as something which has its place between the elements or between the sets. AND, AND, AND – stammering.'

Gilles Deleuze and Claire Parnet, *Dialogues*

General Editor
Ian Buchanan

Editorial Advisory Board

Keith Ansell-Pearson

Rosi Braidotti

Claire Colebrook

Tom Conley

Gregg Lambert

Adrian Parr

Paul Patton

Patricia Pisters

Titles Available in the Series

Ian Buchanan and Claire Colebrook (eds), *Deleuze and Feminist Theory*
Ian Buchanan and John Marks (eds), *Deleuze and Literature*
Mark Bonta and John Protevi (eds), *Deleuze and Geophilosophy*
Ian Buchanan and Marcel Swiboda (eds), *Deleuze and Music*
Ian Buchanan and Gregg Lambert (eds), *Deleuze and Space*
Martin Fuglsang and Bent Meier Sørensen (eds), *Deleuze and the Social*
Ian Buchanan and Adrian Parr (eds), *Deleuze and the Contemporary World*
Constantin V. Boundas (ed.), *Deleuze and Philosophy*
Ian Buchanan and Nicholas Thoburn (eds), *Deleuze and Politics*
Chrysanthi Nigianni and Merl Storr (eds), *Deleuze and Queer Theory*
Jeffrey A. Bell and Claire Colebrook (eds), *Deleuze and History*
Laura Cull (ed.), *Deleuze and Performance*
Mark Poster and David Savat (eds), *Deleuze and New Technology*
Simone Bignall and Paul Patton (eds), *Deleuze and the Postcolonial*
Stephen Zepke and Simon O'Sullivan (eds), *Deleuze and Contemporary Art*
Laura Guillaume and Joe Hughes (eds), *Deleuze and the Body*
Daniel W. Smith and Nathan Jun (eds), *Deleuze and Ethics*
Frida Beckman (ed.), *Deleuze and Sex*
David Martin-Jones and William Brown (eds), *Deleuze and Film*
Laurent de Sutter and Kyle McGee (eds), *Deleuze and Law*
Arun Saldanha and Jason Michael Adams (eds), *Deleuze and Race*
Rebecca Coleman and Jessica Ringrose (eds), *Deleuze and Research Methodologies*
Inna Semetsky and Diana Masny (eds), *Deleuze and Education*
Hélène Frichot and Stephen Loo (eds), *Deleuze and Architecture*
Betti Marenko and Jamie Brassett (eds), *Deleuze and Design*
Hélène Frichot, Catharina Gabrielsson and Jonathan Metzger (eds), *Deleuze and the City*
Colin Gardner and Patricia MacCormack (eds), *Deleuze and the Animal*

Visit the Deleuze Connections website at
www.edinburghuniversitypress.com/series/delco

Deleuze and the Animal

Edited by Colin Gardner and
Patricia MacCormack

EDINBURGH
University Press

For Jane and Spiffy

Edinburgh University Press is one of the leading university presses in the UK. We publish academic books and journals in our selected subject areas across the humanities and social sciences, combining cutting-edge scholarship with high editorial and production values to produce academic works of lasting importance. For more information visit our website: edinburghuniversitypress.com

Edinburgh University Press Ltd
The Tun – Holyrood Road, 12(2f) Jackson's Entry, Edinburgh EH8 8PJ

Typeset in 10.5/13 Adobe Sabon by
Servis Filmsetting Ltd, Stockport, Cheshire,
and printed and bound in Great Britain by
CPI Group (UK) Ltd, Croydon CR0 4YY

A CIP record for this book is available from the British Library

ISBN 978 1 4744 2273 4 (hardback)
ISBN 978 1 4744 2275 8 (webready PDF)
ISBN 978 1 4744 2274 1 (paperback)
ISBN 978 1 4744 2276 5 (epub)

Contents

Acknowledgements

The editors would like to thank the contributors for their patience, their imagination and their fascinating lines of flight in expanding the animal without subsuming the nonhuman. We would also like to thank Carol Macdonald at EUP. Special thanks to renée c. hoogland for her kind permission to expand an earlier version of Chapter 8 from its original form as a book review for Wayne State University's *Criticism* journal. This book was collated with inspiration from all the tireless activists, from Jane, from Spiffy, from Louise Gardner and from James Fowler, and in memory of Nicky, Charlotte and Lizzie.

Introduction

Colin Gardner and Patricia MacCormack

In 'Your Special "Desiring Machines": What Are They?', a brief report on Pierre Benichou's 1970s inquiry into masochism, Gilles Deleuze paraphrases Karl Marx, stating: 'Your particular desiring machines: what are they? In a difficult and beautiful text Marx calls for the necessity to think human sexuality not only as a relation between the human sexes, masculine and feminine, but as a relation "between human sex and non-human sex". He was clearly not thinking of animals, but of what is non-human in human sexuality: the machines of desire' (Deleuze 2004: 243). Similarly, in the final lines of *What is Philosophy?* Deleuze and Guattari emphasise that philosophy needs non-philosophy, science needs non-science and art needs non-art (1994: 218). These ideas express an antithesis within a thesis, the alterity of difference within sameness that is expanded upon in *Difference and Repetition* and Deleuze's work on both Bergson and Spinoza. The ideas share an antagonism towards signifying structures which create binaries and attach values to the subjectification of any groups, by gender, race and particularly species, while testifying to the inherent unlikeness of anything within itself that is its own internal difference for itself – even within the repetition of its behaviours.

Any claim towards a thing's own 'thingness' is tactical. When a thing is named by another, the affects of power are foregrounded and the capacity for the named being to be able to express itself freely is diminished because the other's difference exists now only in isomorphic relation with the one who names, the one who evaluates and signifies. For humans this can result, as *A Thousand Plateaus* tells us, in being depraved, deviant or a tramp (Deleuze and Guattari 1987: 159). For minoritarians who were never signified enough to resist from an equal standing, gender, race, sexuality, ability and so forth already reduce us to 'different to' without our difference being a positive haecceity.

The logic of signification, even of apparent difference, if it operates by the organising principles Deleuze and Guattari critique, is inherently anthropomorphic. Creating a relation of knowledge as a relation of comparison forms a monodirectional mode of apprehension that both imposes meaning upon the other and diminishes the other's freedom, which Spinoza would critique as negative ethics.

No group of organisms suffers more from this human tendency than do nonhuman animals. Animal studies, ethology, vindicators of the murder and torture, incarceration for entertainment and other exploitations of nonhuman animals, even many animal 'rights' advocates, operate under this anthropocentric system. The vast majority of encounters humans have with nonhuman animals are 'for' humans, always by humans and ultimately to the advantage of humans. From the most sympathetic attempts at understanding to the hourly holocaust of nonhuman animal lives there is an impasse which prevents the nonhumans with which we share this planet (albeit, from our side, greedily and selfishly) from figuring as their own agents, as having the capacity to express their own haecceities without subsumation, due to the anthropocentric signifying voracity of human 'knowledge', 'representation', 'understanding', which ultimately comes down to use in all its manifestations – from the actual use of the physical flesh of nonhuman animals, to their use in contemporary philosophy as offering trendy models for thinking human interactions alternatively, or using observation of their being to vindicate their preservation and our no longer imposing upon them. Wherever a human's sympathy lies with the ethical status of the animal in contemporary society, all parties are forced to negotiate via this singular playing field of discourse, which is the anthropocentric, signifying, subjectifying and absolutely human mode of knowledge and representation. In this game, the nonhuman animal or their allies can never win. Speaking the animal requires an 'about' or an 'of'. Emphasising the social field to which such speaking belongs, as antagonistic to the natural nonhuman world (by which we mean an ecosophical world of relationality, not one which reverses the binary of nature and culture), Deleuze states:

> Difference is not and cannot be thought in itself, so long as it is subject to the requirements of representation. . . . In any case, difference in itself appears to exclude any relation between different and different which would allow it to be thought. It seems that it can become thinkable only when *tamed* – in other words, when subject to the four iron collars of representation: identity in the concept, opposition in the predicate, analogy in judgement and resemblance in perception. (1994: 262, our emphasis)

Minoritarians have fought against difference being reducible to being different from majoritarians, but our modes of resistance have been limited to fighting as majoritarians to achieve equality by enacting (but never becoming, for there is no becoming-majoritarian) dominant modes of expression which reduce all difference to a masquerade of 'different from', never difference for itself or difference within itself. Should these last two differences flourish, ecosophical ethics would expand within and between all lives and collectives. Gender, race, sexuality would become defunct, along with the former singularities of identity and subjectivity. Packs would be created with the unlike, both politically and as deterritorialising desiring machines. Further and most crucially for this collection, in reference to nonhumans we would cease using concepts such as species (identity), seeing human and animal as binaries (opposition – this would also include becoming-nonhuman or ahuman), or the isomorphic evaluation and treatment of nonhuman animals based on their anthropocentric values (judgement and perception). Judgement and perception are instruments for seeing pets Oedipalised, 'exotic' non-humans incarcerated in zoos, great apes privileged by animal rights advocates and the fly on a human's arm slapped as inconsequential.

Even the maintenance of species in these examples continues to refuse the rights of a specific individual life and its own differentiating multi-plicity. The signifying and subjectifying principles of the organised body which Deleuze and Guattari decry as exemplary of Artaud's critique of the Judgement of God are precisely mirrored in the human as God-Man, evaluating nonhumans through an anthropocentric understanding of their uniqueness as lives. Speaking about animals at all inserts them into a form of discourse in which they have no consent or voice. Discussing animals reduces them to objects discussed between humans. For Michel Serres this is the social contract which overwrites the natural contract – opinion become judiciary fact. For Jean-François Lyotard it is the victim denied their victimhood because they cannot navigate the language of the master – the *différend*. For Deleuze, through his reading of Spinoza, the element of Nature in the philosopher (which he sees as solitude, humility, poverty) is essential to a good society, and 'the best society, then, will be one that exempts the power of thinking from the obligation to obey' (1988: 4).

Animals are often given rights when their qualities obey our index of requirements for moral consideration. Ethically, to think the animal would be to make them unthinkable if both humans and nonhuman animals are liberated from the obligation to obey in their ethical con-templations, expressions and affects. According to Deleuze, Spinoza's celebration of life is antagonistic to the world of Man, which is merely a world of semblances (1988: 12), and, importantly, 'animals are defined less by the abstract notion of genus and species than by a capacity for being affected, by the affections of which they are "capable", by the excitations to which they react within the limits of their capability' (1988: 27). Unlike Spinoza, Deleuze includes the human in the category of animal (as a sketch of 'life'), and claims that the '*Ethics* is an *ethology*' (1988: 27). Deleuze's critique of the abstract semblances Man makes upon the world as a teeming series of relations of expression and affects shows anthropocentric discourse as both unethical and a denial of the affirmation of life.

Denying species continues this point, where Deleuze shows that within each life each organism's own affects and expressions already teem with each other, so his reading of Spinozan ethics emphasises the ecosophical nature of what philosophies of ethics take into account – all relations, all affects, all expressions and ways in which to increase rather than diminish each life as a haecceity free to express. For contemporary animal studies, ethology, philosophies of the posthuman and digital media, the categories of genus and species are ripe for co-option. Denying difference (and the difference within the repetition of each individual organism) in favour of semblance means the only way in which animals are able to be present is as re-presented via the discourse of Man, or as a symbol of Man's postmodern crisis of identity in the face of the unknowable other. Once again, the nonhuman remains for its use value rather than simply being allowed to be.

At this point the reader will no doubt recognise the nonhuman becomings Deleuze and Guattari advocate as belonging to this ethological turn in what remains anthropocentric philosophy, becomings on which this collection relies heavily. Deleuze and Guattari's 'examples' of becoming-animal do not exemplify anything animal per se (either of an individual or a species), but human apprehensions of affects of animality or intensities divested of human anthropocentric modes of perception. Knowledge of the rat, the dog, the wolf, the spider, the wasp, the whale, the cockroach and other referents utilised in examples of becomings is not knowledge of a breed, a myth, an icon or a symbol. Entering into the movement, the affects of imagined molecular alterities, vague and material – furriness, hunger, howling, scuttling – are where we find becomings without emulation. The further Deleuze and Guattari venture into becomings, the more abstract and fabulated the terms are, and while woman-to-animal-to-vegetal-to-*x* has a dubious devolutionary trajectory, the animal in their becomings is always a constellation of unlike individual examples of species in packs ultimately becoming the human abject fabulations of werewolf, vampire, fog, music and imperceptible.

Deleuze and Guattari have been extensively critiqued for their fetishisation of alterity, particularly for their idea of becoming-woman. While we are sympathetic to these critiques and acknowledge that they hold for the nonhuman animal in many ways, this book has been developed with two motives, which may seem incompatible. The first motive concerns animal theory and the question/concept/problem of the animal emerging as fashionable in contemporary philosophy: we hoped to redeem the animal from its current position of being used as co-opted concept or fetish. We wanted what Deleuze can do for ethical thinking about nonhumans to appear simultaneously with the becomings that seem so immediately applicable. From an abolitionist's perspective (rather than that of 'rights') we wanted to produce a volume that would place nonhuman abolitionist activism side by side with the fabulations Deleuze and Guattari's becoming-animal affords.

Our second motive was driven by wanting the book to emphasise the imperative to break down anthropocentric understandings of *anything*, but especially of human subjectivity. In order for the world to be a more open series of ethical relations of haecceity we need not think animals differently. Rather, while not thinking them at all via anthropocentric representation, we also need to unthink ourselves. Here is where Deleuze and Guattari's becomings-animal are so liberatory. They have never been about animals. They have always been about escape routes – the becoming ahuman of Man. If we humans are the problem with the world then attempts to treat nonhuman animals well or differently within this world is trying to force an eternal victim into an unresolvable problem. Better to unravel the problem itself, for

> To become animal is to participate in movement, to stake out a path of escape in all its positivity, to cross a threshold, to reach a continuum of intensities that are valuable only in themselves, to find a world of pure intensities where all forms come undone, as do all the significations, signifiers, and signifieds, to the benefit of an unformed matter of deterritorialized flux, of nonsignifying signs. (Deleuze and Guattari 1986: 13)

What we 'learn' from animals in how we select our intensities and vibrations from the nonhuman other does not necessitate taking from them. We need not observe, interact or encounter, for these all potentially lead to knowledge and representation via anthropocentric signification and subjectification. Our thinking of animal intensities demands human imagination becoming ahuman, which is why it is not parasitic on nonhuman animals, but only debilitates human understandings of species, ethology, the animal as other. We are of and belong to a natural world (whatever that means when we no longer have signification), so whatever is unthinkable within anthropocentrism is a becoming with nature, with the nonhuman. We do not mean to suggest that nonhuman animals either have or do not have their own modes of signification or perception, but *they are not ours to know*. Deleuze and Guattari repetitively confirm that becomings are not imitations, filiations or copies (all of which involve the idea of a representation, no matter how domestic), but so too they are not the animal converted to myth, icon, god or any other representation as human idea or human mode of expressivity. The animal is the entirely unknowable other, hence the unthinkable itself within ourselves, the difference within the self that cannot be expressed through Man's signifying regimes. 'There is no subject of the becoming' (Deleuze and Guattari 1987: 292) is the position from which what we offer here as a volume all about something called animal is also nothing that describes, codes or captures any nonhumans. This is not a collection 'about' animals. It is about humans and how to get outside of the represented human towards the asignified ahuman, using the tentative virtualisation of what a nonhuman human could be while also thinking about how to be more graciously ethical towards actual nonhuman animal lives.

We have deliberately kept the definition of 'the animal' open to a multiplicity of interpretations, partly because it is a contentious term in nonhuman and ahuman theory (where the human is considered, by turns, animal and not animal), but also because its usage varies as Deleuze and Guattari themselves move towards a more machinic model of deterritorialised becomings, culminating in Guattari's own ecosophical agenda in his individual writings. In light of this we have divided the book into five relatively loose thematic sections that trace these different becomings and the important role that animality plays in each sphere, both material and ontological.

Thus in Part I, chapters by Patricia MacCormack, John Ó Maoilearca and Joanna Bednarek employ different strategies to 'undo' anthropocentrism. In MacCormack's chapter, this takes the form of ahuman abolitionism, an ethical, activist principle of 'leaving be', or what Serres calls a gracious stepping aside. MacCormack grounds her discussion in Spinozan ethics, a speculative, practical mode of *living*, a joyful autoaffection involving an enquiry into what a body (and therefore thought) can do in terms of its ability to affect – in the form of compositions and decompositions –and be affected in turn. Ultimately, this is a question of coherence (as opposed to unity), for ethically positive interactions encourage organisms to grow, metamorphose and generate new relations with other bodies. However, we can never really know what our body is capable of doing (and, by extension, our mind's intent) due to our tendency to impose unitary limits, which naturally circumscribes our ability to create truly activist schema.

On the other hand, with (self) knowledge inherently forestalled, we have the ability to discover how *thought* might surpass the consciousness we have of it, so that abolitionist attitudes towards nonhumans might open up an outside beyond our delimiting 'compulsion to know'. In this sense, abolitionist activism is always an excessive corporeal activity and therefore as much unconscious as conscious, corresponding to Deleuze and Guattari's crucial difference between human sex and 'nonhuman' sex (that is, large aggregates of molecular desiring machines). In both abolitionism's relationship to welfarist animal rights and desire's relation to sexuality, the common enemy is anthropomorphism. MacCormack concludes with a post-Oedipal return to the unconscious through which connections between all organisms can be manifested without hierarchy, limits or borders. However, she retains the necessary form of *absolute* opposition that manifests as a creative 'wonderment' at alterity rather than perpetuating the dialectic between human and nonhuman animals, which tends to subsume both within the hegemonic field of human discourse. In this sense, MacCormack ludically utilises Spinoza's common notions not to promulgate a sympathy between species (manifested through becoming-animal) but rather through 'common enemies' – namely the nonhuman, the ahuman and the human.

Working on similar lines, Ó Maoilearca appropriates François Laruelle's principle of non-philosophy as well as Deleuze and Guattari's becoming-animal to deconstruct the duality of apparent wisdom (the exclusive province of *homo sapiens*) and ignorance (the imperfect, unwise animal) in order to elaborate an infinite thought outside philosophy itself. At first glance, Laruelle and Deleuze would seem to have much in common, for as Ó Maoilearca and Anthony Paul Smith point out, 'Laruelle's idea that thought should think of itself as immanent to the Real, rather than as a representation that transcends it, looks like something that Gilles Deleuze might say' (Mullarkey and Smith 2012: 3). However, Laruelle insists that Deleuze says it in the name of *his* (Deleuzian) philosophy – *he* explains the Real, in other words he necessarily conceptualises it within the circumscribing framework of philosophical thought itself. 'For Laruelle, however, there is no explaining the Real, because *every thought, Deleuzian or not, philosophical or not*, is as good or as bad an explanation as any other – for they are all (non-summative) material parts' (Mullarkey and Smith 2012: 3). This explains why Laruelle strives to de-philosophise the human and nonhuman and the duality of apparent wisdom and ignorance that goes along with them.

Rejecting Deleuze's own theory of stupidity in *Difference and Repetition*, whereby the idiot becomes a kind of philosopher's stooge – 'Cowardice, cruelty, baseness and stupidity are not simply corporeal capacities or traits of character or society; they are structures of thought as such' (Deleuze 1994: 151) – Laruelle re-situates the issue as a *nonhuman* matter. The problem then becomes, can we generate an 'outside-philosophy' of thought, whereby the Real constitutes an 'unlearned knowledge', rather than a 'learned ignorance'? Following Laruelle, Ó Maoilearca makes the case for an 'unlearned' thought that is no longer the singular province of humans (which, in conventional philosophical terms defines their essence), but rather becomes a universal milieu, not unlike Spinoza's third level of (intuitive) knowledge where we attain a grasp of the finite body as it inheres in nature – the infinite – an understanding of its essence through an immanent chain of causes. It is only the third level that produces pure joy and necessitates a move from individuality to singularity, from culture to universe, which would allow us to treat animality and humanity on an equal footing. The question then becomes, in relation to Deleuze and Guattari, can their notion of becoming-animal be understood and used practically outside of its Deleuzian philosophical context so that it can blur the differences between philosophy, science and art? Ultimately, for Laruelle and Ó Maoilearca, this must be a performative act, for 'Non-philosophy performs re-descriptions on the raw-material of philosophy, *and, in doing so, it is performative – producing real effects on how the texts are seen*' (Mullarkey 2012: 143).

Finally, Bednarek builds upon Donna Haraway's critique of Deleuze and Guattari's anti-Oedipal wolf/dog, wild/domestic binarism in *A Thousand Plateaus*, with its minoritarian/majoritarian implications, to construct a more asymmetrical, reciprocal relation that she calls 'becoming-with'. In particular, Bednarek asks the key question: what is the position of empirical, 'molar' nonhuman animals in Deleuze and Guattari's philosophy? By concentrating on one specific example – the dog ('the Oedipal animal *par excellence*') – Bednarek shows how the wolf/dog opposition in *A Thousand Plateaus* does little more than employ conventional imagery of domestic and wild animals to privilege one half of an already dubious binary, whereby only 'demonic' animals are connected with true becoming. Even then, the animal merely functions as the second, subordinated term of becoming, which is understood as a specifically human deterritorialisation. Moreover, it is a *molecular* animal, for 'all becomings are already molecular. That is because becoming is not to imitate or identify with something or someone. Nor is it to proportion formal relations. . . . Becoming is to emit particles that take on certain relations of movement and rest because they enter a particular zone of proximity' (Deleuze and Guattari 1987: 272–3). In other words, as Bednarek argues, the molecular animal not only doesn't have to be real, but *can't* be real.

Bednarek's solution is to transform the concept of becoming so that the asymmetry between major and minor terms gives way to a reciprocal relation by stressing the molar dimension of the minor term of becoming (in this case, dog), and to explore how the molecular transformations in the process of becoming affect it. This is a difficult undertaking because molecular, affectual animals have no direct connection with molar (that is actual, empirical) animals. Their only connection to a molar dimension is through the molar human being that is the subject of becoming itself. Their 'molarity' can only be constituted through a human corporeality that enters a state of becoming by emitting molecules of animality. Bednarek's ultimate conclusion then is that only humans can give pure expression to the natural force of deterritorialisation, taking it to its absolute limit.

However, in their defence, one should acknowledge that for Deleuze and Guattari becoming-animal is always a question not of individual subjects (whether animal or human) but of deterritorialised machinic subjectivities, a question of pack-like multiplicities rather than Oedipal dogs or totemic lone wolves. In this respect, becoming-animal is part of a larger vector that starts with becoming-woman (in effect a becoming-minoritarian from the majoritarian patronymic) and culminates with becoming-imperceptible, a shift from the finite to the infinite. The chapters in Part II explore these vectors through a variety of interconnected media.

Thus Colin Gardner analyses the molecular assemblage that constitutes the Kleistian war machine in *Penthesilea* via its stratigraphic application as an affective 'climate of infection' in Louis Malle's surrealist fable, *Black Moon* (1975), where one multiplicity of bodies is invaded by another to create a non-hierarchical line of flight. Kleist radically rewrites the Homeric war between the Greeks and the Amazons by having Achilles and Penthesilea betray their respective States rather than fulfil their fated destiny as combative foes. Achilles disobeys Agamemnon by throwing in his lot with the enemy, while Penthesilea contravenes Amazon law by choosing her Greek opponent, allowing them to become lovers rather than bitter foes. Together, they form a new assemblage of *affective* rather than combative war, 'Achilles in the act of becoming-woman, Penthesilea in a becoming-dog' (Deleuze and Guattari 1987: 278). Although their revolt ends in a tragic *liebestod*, their brief liaison heralds the utopian promise of a deterritorialised, intensive love: the culmination of what Mathieu Carrière calls 'Kleist's great desire – to live as two in madness' (cited in Bogue 2003: 123).

In Malle's *Black Moon*, the battle of the sexes forms the backdrop to a form of waking dream, as a nomadic teenage fugitive, Lily, is lured by a strange unicorn to a secluded Dordogne farm where Kleist's utopian 'mad duality' is already established in the form of a non-Oedipal family dynamic. Androgynous male and female siblings, both called Lily (who represent becoming-woman and becoming-animal respectively), oversee their bedridden mother – whose sole companion is a talking rat – and an assorted gaggle of naked children and poultry. The farm has no ostensible hierarchy between adults and children, humans and animals: this is an advanced multiplicity of the pack, a pure war machine that envelops both protagonists and spectators alike in a transformed zone of indiscernibility. Although Brother and Sister Lily ultimately become ensnared by the ravages of the ongoing gender war, teenage Lily inherits the film's Kleistian deterritorialised velocity of 'vitality affect' by adopting the role of the breastfeeding mother to the unicorn. In effect she has become Deleuze and Guattari's 'Anomalous', an unclassifiable, contagious, 'supernormal' role that defies conventional borders between human and animal but at the same time acts as a vector for creating further multiplicities. In short, Lily comes to manifest pure affect as an eternal flow of becomings, unleashing *Black Moon*'s moment of radical immanence.

In 'Ant and Empire', Zach Horton works from the other extreme, starting with the already multiple and molecularised ant as a limitless, processual and colonising limit case but which also has innate tendencies towards imperial hierarchisation, in short, a regressive becoming-human. In other words, ants deterritorialise their inherent molecularity in order to become-molar, not to create a supernormal 'surplus value' of life but to enslave. Horton takes his cue from two literary sources. Firstly, he analyses H. G. Wells's 1905 story, 'The Empire of the Ants', which raises the question of 'what can a species do?' by exploring ants as a form of contagious vector in the context of settler colonialism in the Amazon jungle: a case of the imperialist Europeans getting a taste of their own medicine. Secondly, he explores Bernard Werber's 1991 novel, *Les Fourmis,* a postcolonial narrative where interspecies communication plays out on multiple levels of becoming-ant. Here, ant and human territories become co-extensive and multi-vectored, but of course the discrepancy in scale makes for an ever-shifting topography of both space and power. As Horton puts it, 'whose territory is inside whose?'

Then, using the Google Glass game *Swarm!* as a model, Horton suggests ways that we might construct a non-imperialistic becoming that would engage the dynamics of other scales rather than simply 'scaling up or down' on a consistent continuum. The game engages the movements and perceptions of its participants by tracing on the Google Glasses the virtual pathways and tracks of all the ants that have 'passed this way before', thereby superimposing them on the player's field of vision. Rewards are given for following certain paths (which of course reinforces their 'striating' import) and obeying certain instructions. In this respect, *Swarm!* encourages the participant/spectator to simulate becoming-ant as a becoming-human but at entirely new scales, creating, in effect, a molecularisation and reconfiguration of corporeal assemblages. The dynamic of scale – in addition to Deleuze and Guattari's habitual focus on time and movement – thus becomes an essential component of reterritorialising molar identity, less as a continuum or smooth line of flight than as 'a leaping, trans-scalar vector'.

Such non-hierarchical becomings are central to Edward Campbell's discussion of musical works by Gérard Grisey, Michaël Levinas and Georges Aperghis, whose compositions create 'hybridisations' between vocal, instrumental and animal sound worlds to the extent that their musical resonance is neither completely human nor perfectly animal. In short, music no longer evokes animality but rather *becomes* animal as a form of Deleuzo-Guattarian diagram. Throughout *A Thousand Plateaus,* Deleuze and Guattari show a keen interest in Olivier Messiaen's use of birdsong as a melodic and rhythmic stimulus for a number of works – most notably the *Catalogue d'oiseaux* for piano (1956–8). At one point, discussing the deterritorialisation of the refrain, they go so far as to state that 'it is not certain whether we can draw a dividing line between animals and human beings: Are there not, as Messiaen believes, musician birds and nonmusician birds? Is the bird's refrain necessarily territorial, or is it already used for very subtle deterritorializations, for selective lines of flight?' (1987: 301–2).

In his richly illustrated chapter, Campbell cites Levinas's use of sonic hybridisations in both the *Ouverture pour une fête étrange* (1979) – where sound is amplified to the point that it becomes 'an almost animal living mob' – and the Kafka-based opera *La Métamorphose* (2011), where Gregor's lament is 'neither totally human nor perfectly animal'. In contrast, in Aperghis's experimental music theatre piece *Avis de tempête* (2004), based on a 'fetish reading' of *Moby-Dick*, although the great whale never appears either visually or sonically, his virtual trace does, causing a fragmented subjectivity throughout the piece. Finally, Grisey uses varying temporalities in *Le Temps et l'écume* (1989) to create different aspects of animality: 'normal', extremely compressed and extremely slow indicate the varied temporal frames of humans, birds and whales. These should not be read as representational or imitative qualities, notes Campbell, but rather as a becoming-animal diagram.

In the concluding chapter in this section, renée c. hoogland uses the autobiographical writings and photographic self-portraits/self-stagings of Claude Cahun (1894–1954) to explore the multiplicitious nature of 'performed' identity as a shifting configuration of fragments and collages that constitute so many masked selves, in effect a pack rather than a coherent subjective identity, where the individual artist herself becomes an indiscernible, even outlandish *oeuvre* that defies categorisation and representation. Cahun's protean ability to become anew without reaching a final form allows hoogland to make a key observation that for Deleuze and Guattari, becoming-animal doesn't actually require an endpoint, that it can remain open-ended enough to undo any attempts to reduce it to a stable artistic or philosophical canon. In Cahun's case, her 1930 *faux* autobiography, *Aveux non avenus* (*Disavowals, or, Cancelled Confessions*), a book of essays and recorded dreams illustrated with photomontages, caused her to be quickly claimed as an artistic fellow traveller by both the Surrealist movement and the avant-garde. The subsequent discovery of her staged photographic self-portraits (ranging from youth to old age) in the late 1980s made her an obvious candidate for appropriation (or, as hoogland argues, 'domestication') by an affirmative gender/identity politics.

Ultimately, Cahun defies such discursive colonisation because her agency of becoming is constituted through a combination of subtle shifts – such as shaving off half an inch of hair between seemingly contiguous shots – and often imperceptible 'micro-cracks', which are usually associated with the aging process, or, as in the case of Deleuze and Guattari's chosen example, F. Scott Fitzgerald's 'The Crack-Up', provide an answer to the question, 'What happened?' As they explain, 'This molecular line, more supple but no less disquieting, in fact, much more disquieting, is not simply internal or personal: it also brings everything into play, but on a different scale and in different forms, with segmentations of a different nature, rhizomatic instead of arborescent. A micropolitics' (1987: 199). Through an enfolding of affect, love and destruction, Cahun and hoogland invite us to join their multiplicitous pack as a nomadic assemblage where both artist and audience enter the 'discontinuity of the un/becoming self' as a new form of aesthetic 'peopling'.

In Part III – 'Animal Politics, Animal Death' – chapters by Colin Gardner, Nur Ozgenalp, Charles Stivale and Laurence Rickels exploit the transverse nature of animal-human connectivities to forge an immanent ethics (in a Spinozan sense) that fully exploits what each body (and therefore thought) is capable of producing in terms of its ability to affect and be affected in turn (affirming both life *and* death). Gardner turns specifically to the seminal work of the English anthropologist/cyberneticist, Gregory Bateson (1904–80), as a crucial ecological and ludic foundation not only for the work of Deleuze and Guattari – the pair borrowed the term 'plateau' as a continuous, self-vibrating region of intensities from Bateson's study of Balinese culture – but also for Brian Massumi's more recent exploration of the supernormal tendency in animal play as a metacommunicative model for a new form of political metamodelisation based on Guattari's advocacy of an ethico-aesthetic paradigm.

Drawing heavily on Bateson's 1955 essay, 'A Theory of Play and Fantasy', Massumi stresses how, for example, a play fight between wolf cubs entails the staging of a paradox, whereby a cub bites and at the same time says 'This is not a bite, this is not a fight, this is a game', such that the ludic stands in for the suspended analogue: real combat. Massumi calls this level of abstraction the game's '-esqueness', its metacommunicative level which self-reflexively mobilises a vitality affect that generates a trans-situational process that moves across and between intersecting existential territories. The latter entails the construction of a third dimension, the 'included middle' of play and combat's mutual influence, which Massumi calls 'sympathy'. Expanding on Massumi while avoiding using 'the animal' as template, Gardner extrapolates the political import of this ludic territory of becoming-ahuman through two filmic case studies – *Dr. Cyclops* (1940) and *The Incredible Shrinking Man* (1957) – where humans are shrunk to microscopic size and pets and spiders become life-threatening monsters. In the case of the former, the middle is excluded and there is no reciprocal meeting ground between species (which befits a film whose primary objective is to demonise megalomaniacal dictators all the better to reinforce a 'good vs. bad science' binarism). In the latter, the *included* middle expands far beyond simple animal-human relations and instead takes on radical ontological repercussions as the film's ostensible 'action hero' shrinks to microscopic proportions, becoming one with the infinite and achieving the ultimate deterritorialised becoming: pure immanence.

Through a discussion of television's re-vamping of the Little Red Riding Hood story in the 2012 'Red Handed' and 'Child of the Moon' episodes of ABC's *Once Upon a Time* (2011–present), Ozgenalp connects becoming-animal with becoming-woman to explore what kind of micropolitical transformation might occur (and by extension, what new affects might be born) when the wolf is placed inside the girl rather than the reverse (where traditionally Red cuts her way out of the wolf's stomach in an overt act of defiance). Taking her lead from Deleuze's declaration that 'The brain is the screen', Ozgenalp treats televisual images less as cultural signifiers or representations of personal or collective memory than as 'dynamic manifestations of cultural and political activities in contemporary digital networked screen culture', specifically as they relate to post-feminist theory and posthumanist studies. Moving well beyond traditional psychoanalytic paradigms, Ozgenalp instead positions the show's becomings as an inherently collective enterprise.

Thus, in addition to Red/Ruby and her friend Belle, male characters such as David also become-shewolf, since becoming is not a question of resemblance or imitation but rather one of transforming in relation to others as a form of pack or multiplicity. As Ozgenalp notes, becoming-shewolf is not exclusively a 'she becoming' reserved to females, just as becoming-woman is not confined to women. In this respect she follows Claire Colebrook's observation that becoming-woman doesn't entail perceiving 'as a woman' but *perceiving itself* is now reformulated as a form of becoming. In other words, the whole question of point of view is desubjectified and de-gendered as a collective set of singularities. Becoming-shewolf in *Once Upon a Time* is thus a post-anthropocentric and post-gender solidarity in practice.

Stivale also turns to television – in this case Mads Mikkelsen's characterisation of Hannibal Lecter in Bryan Fuller's adaptation of the Thomas Harris novels (which also gave us Jonathan Demme's *The Silence of the Lambs*) – to explore the innate link between creativity, thinking and animality through the practice of 'être aux aguets' (being on the lookout) for *rencontres* (encounters) that span transversally across different space-times, creating new 'refrains'.

Deleuze discusses the concept in *L'Abécédaire de Gilles Deleuze*, a video interview with Claire Parnet that was originally produced in 1988–9 (transmitted 1994–5). Here, Deleuze makes a direct link between creativity, thinking and animality through a kind of transverse sideways glance that can generate new connectivities and concepts, as if peripheral vision has a greater power of perception (and, in Hannibal's case, seduction) than the more directly focused hypnotic 'gaze' employed, say, in *Dr. Cyclops*.

Hannibal is similarly always 'on the lookout' as part of his very being as a (usually frightening and ominous) creative assemblage, as much concerned with death as with life. Of course Hannibal rarely comes across as an evil predator (in many ways he enacts his appetites as a form of gourmet-like '-esqueness'), and although the viewing audience is always in on the act, his carefully chosen guests are usually blissfully unaware that Hannibal's mouth-watering menu includes themselves. At the same time, Hannibal has highly refined instincts (especially olfactory), which mean he can not only sense the presence of a nearby threat but is also able to categorise, store and subsequently recall any such scents and essences through his Memory Palace, which is far more akin to a 'databank of death'.

In contrast to Stivale's 'dark pedagogy', it is the unmournable nature of animal death that is the subject of Rickels's chapter, which turns to Heidegger, Freud and Melanie Klein (as advocates of both successful and unsuccessful mourning, first and second deaths) as entry points for an analysis of Émilie Deleuze's 2003 film, *Mister V*. The film tracks the changes in relationality incurred when the eponymous psychotic horse escapes and tests not only the boundaries of the film's diegesis but also its own discursive fabulation. Like Bednarek in her chapter on companion species and becoming, Rickels notes that man, as majority figure, is not an option for becoming. Man must be divested of his majoritarian status before he can become other. In this regard, 'becoming-animal' is the missing link between man and 'becoming multiple', so that the metamorphosis necessarily entails a 'loss' as initiation so that we can enter the substitutive order of becoming-other.

Significantly, Rickels makes a key point that this is not necessarily incompatible with Freud. Indeed, the two main trajectories of the latter's thought: 1) totemic identification and 2) castration (as an initiation into the 'management' of loss or lack) also separate out as tendencies of unmourning and 'successful mourning', of first and second deaths, respectively. Both, according to Rickels, are compatible with the anti-Oedipal momentum of Deleuze and Guattari's schizoanalysis. Indeed, Deleuze and Guattari's philosophy of becoming supplies many 'metabolic features' in the crack of psychosis that might otherwise be unavailable in a strictly Freudian reading. Moreover, 'becoming-animal' doesn't necessarily invalidate Freud either: it is in many ways compatible with a contradiction internal to Freud's thought on mourning. Yes,

Deleuze and Guattari contemptuously dismiss companion and domesticated animals as the Oedipal equivalent of neurotic props, but, argues
Rickels, isn't 'becoming-animal' just another way to negate and avoid
the responsibility to the other that is fundamental to mourning? In other
words, why opt for the demonic animal – the minoritarian vector for
true becoming – rather than acknowledge the equally wild multiplicity
of grief that is manifested through a first or second death?

Rickels's narrative provides a neat lead-in to the next section, which
self-reflexively explores the de- and reterritorialising role of animal
becomings in the narrative and representational structures of art and
film. Like Stivale, Gregg Lambert turns to Deleuze's series of interviews
with Claire Parnet – *L'Abécédaire* – to extrapolate the philosopher's
comments in 'A is for Animal' on the relation between a distinctive territory and art that often bears on the animal's extraction of singularities
from a specific milieu (a captivation by an environment as opposed to the
human's more generalised relation to a world). In other words, while the
animal has a relation to its world that is produced via a relation to a distinctive territory, the human has a relation to world, but none to a proper
territory that it can call its own. However, for Deleuze, notes Lambert,
there is another possibility for territory creation through the media of art
and writing (and their necessary becomings). Here, the individual loses
his/her identity as a subject and instead becomes a singularity, entering
into a deterritorialising process similar to that of the animal's 'captivation' by an environment.

We have already noted, through reference to Messiaen, the territorial importance of birdsong in this regard. Here, 'The refrain is rhythm
and melody that have been territorialized because they have become
expressive – and have become expressive because they are territorializ-
ing' (Deleuze and Guattari 1987: 317). In contrast, from the perspective
of the artist and the resulting work of art, the territorialising factor isn't
innate but must be produced, it 'must be sought . . . in the becoming-
expressive of rhythm or melody, in other words, in the emergence of
proper qualities (color, odor, sound, silhouette. . .). Can this becoming,
this emergence, be called Art? That would make the territory a result of
art. The artist: the first person to set out a boundary stone, or to make a
mark' (Deleuze and Guattari 1987: 316).

Dennis Rothermel connects these distinctive animal territories to
specific uses of film language through a series of case studies, most
notably Robert Bresson's *Au hasard Balthazar* (1966), Michelangelo
Frammartino's *Le Quattro Volte* (2011), Bela Tarr's *The Turin Horse*
(2011), and Ang Lee's *Life of Pi* (2012). Significantly, becoming-animal

cannot be represented by conventional point-of-view and shot-reverse-shot editing (the structural mainstay of filmic suture), because it ties the animal to the conventional (and thus delimiting) human vectorial space of Deleuze's action-image. Instead, inspired by Pier Paolo Pasolini's seminal essay, 'The "Cinema of Poetry"', Rothermel notes that his four filmmakers all resort to a form of free-indirect discourse, whereby animality fills up the film from the inside 'as formative of the representation rather than rendering the subject within the structure of representation'.

Not unlike T. S. Eliot's objective correlative, where the character's subjectivity is presented objectively in and through the *mise-en-scène* as well as individual focalisation (in this case the character is also on-screen), animal perception is able to be expressed by a form of camera self-consciousness (what Rothermel calls his filmmakers' 'cinema sorcery'). 'We are no longer faced with subjective or objective images', notes Deleuze, 'we are caught in a correlation between a perception-image and a camera-consciousness which transforms it (the question of knowing whether the image was objective or subjective is no longer raised). It is a very special kind of cinema which has acquired a taste for "making the camera felt"' (1986: 74). In contrast to Direct Discourse (which, for Pasolini, is the point-of-view shot, where the director stands aside and cedes the act of speech to his character), the Free Indirect gives us something much closer to a pure perception-image, with its specific roots in bodily and vitality *affect*. In the four films, for example, Rothermel notes 'a donkey as the on-screen operative, the wind as the sorcerer's operative, a dog as a sorcerer, and a young man who applies sorcery to himself and finds himself externalized in the accompanying tiger'. Pasolini recognises the import of this 'sorcery', arguing that if the director 'immerses himself in his character and tells the story or depicts the world through him, he cannot make use of that formidable natural instrument of differentiation that is language. *His activity cannot be linguistic; it must, instead, be stylistic*' (1988: 177–8).

Concluding Part IV, Ronald Bogue's chapter on Jean-Luc Godard's experimental 3D outing, *Adieu au langage* (2014) equates becoming-animal (manifested through Godard's dog, Roxy) with the time of the intolerable, another crisis in the action-image which precludes any absorption of affect within the sensory-motor schema. In this sense, Roxy becomes an immanent, animistic force that remakes the world (and by extension, as in all of Godard's films, cinema itself) into a protean force of becoming, where even 3D bifurcates and deterritorialises as a new form of machinic fabulation. Throughout the film, Godard includes multiple shots of Roxy, juxtaposing images of the dog in a fragmented fashion that allows him to question both the animality of humans and the bestial sub-animal cruelty of human war and violence.

As Deleuze points out in *Cinema 2: The Time-Image*, the key to understanding Godard's *oeuvre* is not so much montage (that is, rational cuts) as the invisible building blocks for the creation of a sequential and teleologically driven causal narrative, but rather a series of self-reflexive images formed by irrational cuts (interstices) and a corresponding false movement, a form of 'montrage' or *showing* as opposed to interpreting or explaining. In the case of the intolerable, where our sensory-motor schema is allowed to jam or break, a different type of image appears, what Deleuze calls a pure optical-sound image: 'opsigns' and 'sonsigns', images where the seen and heard no longer extend into action. In *Adieu au langage*, Bogue notes that Godard's use of 3D also offers a new kind of time-image, a lectosign (a visual image which must be 'read' as much as seen) that requires the eye's negotiation of conflicting points of attention within the shot, thereby inducing crisis and the intolerable within the image itself.

Finally, in Part V, we expand the transverse nature of animality into a more ecosophical and ethological series of becomings, inspired by Guattari's *What is Ecosophy?* and *The Three Ecologies*. Gary Genosko, for example, focuses specifically on alcohol (in its pure form of ethanol) as a mechanism (or more accurately, machinic unconscious) to move beyond anthropocentrism into an interspecies series of connectivities that move across assemblages and their confining western-centric paradigms. Genosko notes, for example, that alcohol sets up 'relations of exteriority' that can encompass water, plant matter and fermentation. In addition, it can move across different species in the context of controlled scientific experiments as well as through natural fermentations. In research into inter-generational alcoholism, fruit flies have been known to imbibe towards a state of complete drunkenness, while in the wild, birds are capable of bingeing on fermented berries before reaching a state of utter stupor. In addition, the exploitation of ethanol fermentation exists across species.

Genosko also explores the recent Japanese trend in developing 'wine' for cats. This is, as one might expect, a case of overcoded anthropomorphism where interspecies companionship requires a simulacrum of human domesticity through a shared 'connoisseurship'. It turns out that the 'wine' is a non-alcoholic liquid catnip. Genosko explores this tendency towards 'shared pleasures' between animal and human through a Guattarian lens, noting a deterritorialisation from deterministic biological factors to their modification through the machinic unconscious.

Alcohol's passage is thus traceable across and between assemblages (both material and socio-cultural) while at the same time avoiding a delimiting anthropocentrism. More importantly, Genosko also accommodates animal desire itself in the equation, noting for example that elephants use alcohol to cope with their own specific traumas in response to shrinking territories, deforestation, and so on. In such cases, animals and alcohol recorporealise in response to each other. As Genosko puts it, 'Desire flows as much as alcohol within the assemblage and together they build complex relations and milieus, rearranging ethograms and ecologies across species.'

Finally, Serazer Pekerman gives this ecological trajectory a directly political agenda by focusing on the brutal police suppression of the unarmed 'tree huggers' who participated in the May 2013 anti-government 'Gezi Park Resistance' movement in Turkey. The protest, which resulted in twenty-two deaths, was in direct response to a February 2012 meeting of the youth wing of the Justice and Development Party, where the then prime minister (now president) Recep Tayyip Erdoğan declared in favour of raising 'pious and vengeful generations'. Of particular note is that many of the protesters and police had no recall of the actual details of the events, in many cases unable to acknowledge acts of violence despite video and photographic evidence to the contrary. Pekerman explores direct analogies with the werewolves of myth and fiction to show how becoming-animal as multiplicity can open up places and spaces of resistance to create a 'people yet to come', as much an unstoppable and incommensurable animal pack as a deliberate and wilful strategic deployment. Her aim is to try to understand the government's brutal response and how these resemblances might also help us understand the original resistance.

In addition to exploring the concept of becoming (specifically 'becoming-animal'), she also relates Freud's Wolf-Man case study (a key part of the '1914: One or Several Wolves?' plateau of *A Thousand Plateaus*) to documented events during the Gezi Park protests. As Pekerman notes in her conclusion, more than half the protesters were women attempting to call attention to the culture of misogyny that is all pervasive under Erdoğan's regime. Inevitably, their protest was silenced 'in the name of the father', so that the werewolf's desire (as multiplicity) was sacrificed to conform to patriarchal (read: Freudian) norms and values. 'Freud tried to approach the crowd phenomena from the point of view of the unconscious,' argue Deleuze and Guattari, 'but he did not see clearly, he did not see that the unconscious itself was fundamentally a crowd' (1987: 29). The schizo-wolf had indeed become a State-fed dog.

Each of these chapters grapples with impossible tasks. These tasks coalesce as both the zenith of this so-called Anthropocene Age and the imperative by which we must escape it. We must open ethical affective relations with nonhuman lives without knowing or schematising them within the relation. We must act materially and accountably without being a signified subject who acts. Deleuze and Guattari state, 'It is no longer a question of graduating resemblances, ultimately arriving at an identification between Man and Animal at the heart of a mystic participation. It is a question of ordering differences to arrive at a correspondence of relations' (1987: 236). When Deleuze and Guattari invoke nature and ecosophical relations, they frequently see these as territories teeming with thought but without structure, planes upon which becomings thrive without reified identities, individual or collective. They call becomings 'Unnatural participation' (1987: 240) because, for the signifying human systems in place, participation without identification, perception, judgement and representation seems unnatural. Those are relationships between nature and culture, monodirectionally imposed by culture. Ethical relations are unnatural because they produce different affects, opening the differences within organisms to expression in novel creative ways. They are both becoming-imperceptible and allowing the perceptibility of the nonhuman animal to also remain imperceptible via human logic. Affect is both an event in Spinozan ethics and the conversion from relation as comparison to relation as creative production which forms the foundation of all becomings. 'For the affect is not a personal feeling nor is it a characteristic; it is the effectuation of a power of the pack that throws the self into upheaval and makes it reel . . . which uproot[s] one from humanity' (Deleuze and Guattari 1987: 240).

Entering into becomings that explore the unnatural within nature opens potentials of ahuman trajectories but ethically also opens the world to itself, the world humans have turned into an anthropocentric territory only. The nonhuman animal gifts us the option of thinking otherwise, outside of thought, without meaning to. We have taken so much materially, physically, actually, from nonhuman animals. While we can acknowledge our affects and attempt ethical relations with nonhuman animals through, for example, abolitionist activism, Deleuze may also encourage us to take this gift they give without knowing in order to create new trajectories that will form what Guattari calls an ecosophic cosmos:

> to bring into being other worlds beyond those of purely abstract information, to engender Universes of reference and existential Territories where

singularity and finitude are taken into account by the multivalent logic of mental ecologies and by the group Eros principle of social ecology; to dare to confront the vertiginous Cosmos so as to make it inhabitable; these are the tangled paths of the tri-ecological vision. (Guattari 2000, 67)

References

Bogue, R. (2003), *Deleuze and Literature*, New York and London: Routledge.

Deleuze, G. (1986), *Cinema 1: The Movement-Image*, trans. H. Tomlinson and B. Habberjam, Minneapolis: University of Minnesota Press.

Deleuze, G. (1988), *Spinoza: Practical Philosophy*, trans. R. Hurley, San Francisco: City Lights.

Deleuze, G. (1989), *Cinema 2: The Time-Image*, trans. H. Tomlinson and R. Galeta, Minneapolis: University of Minnesota Press.

Deleuze, G. (1994), *Difference and Repetition*, trans. P. Patton, New York: Columbia University Press.

Deleuze, G. (2004), *Desert Islands and Other Texts 1953–1974*, trans. M. Taormina, New York: Semiotext(e).

Deleuze, G. and F. Guattari (1986), *Kafka: Toward a Minor Literature*, trans. D. Polan, Minneapolis: University of Minnesota Press.

Deleuze, G. and F. Guattari (1987), *A Thousand Plateaus: Capitalism and Schizophrenia*, trans. B. Massumi, Minneapolis: University of Minnesota Press.

Deleuze, G. and F. Guattari (1994), *What is Philosophy?* trans. H. Tomlinson and G. Burchell, London: Verso.

Guattari, F. (2000), *The Three Ecologies*, trans. I. Pindar and P. Sutton, London: Athlone.

Mullarkey, J. (2012), '1 + 1 = 1: The Non-Consistency of Non-Philosophical Practice (Photo: Quantum: Fractal)', in J. Mullarkey and A. P. Smith (eds), *Laruelle and Non-Philosophy*, Edinburgh: Edinburgh University Press, pp. 143–68.

Mullarkey, J. and A. P. Smith (2012), 'Introduction: The Non-Philosophical Inversion: Laruelle's Knowledge Without Domination', in J. Mullarkey and A.P. Smith (eds), *Laruelle and Non-Philosophy*, Edinburgh: Edinburgh University Press, pp. 1–18.

Pasolini, P. P. (1988), 'The "Cinema of Poetry"', in *Heretical Empiricism*, trans. B. Lawton and L. K. Barnett, Bloomington and Indianapolis: Indiana University Press, pp. 167–86.

PART I

UNDOING ANTHROPOCENTRISM: BECOMING-ANIMAL AND THE NONHUMAN

Chapter 1

Ahuman Abolition

Patricia MacCormack

Spinoza said that there was no telling what the human body might achieve, once freed from human discipline. (Deleuze 1988a: 93)

Deleuze's work on Foucault is a work on knowledge as a stratum of great status, where status trumps content and closes thought. Knowledge as power is both constitutive of and a vindication for the status of the organism that believes it discovered but actually invented knowledge as disclosure of truth or reality and thus has a monopoly on it – the human. Knowledge precludes the human from access to Outside, where potential, organic folding of unlike elements, thought beyond signification, and even ethical relations, are experienced. Knowledge is the bio-power that privileges power over life by claiming scientific comprehension of life – all life as subject but not individual lives as entities – that affords control over the way life occurs and is manipulated in the world. Man is not so much a living thing among a taxonomy of other living things, but the idea that decides what living things are and their place in the world, which is essentially their place in reference to Man. 'But when power in this way takes life as its aim or object, then resistance to power already puts itself on the side of life, and turns life against power . . . Contrary to a fully established discourse, there is no need to uphold man in order to resist . . . it is in man himself that we must liberate life, since man himself is a form of imprisonment for man' (Deleuze 1988a: 92). Deleuze's Nietzschean reading has two reverberating effects which are crucial in the ways philosophy mediates nonhuman life. First, man must liberate himself from the knowledge of being man in order to be able to think outside – that is, to think nonhuman life. Second, the upholding of the category of man and its associations with knowledge and power are against life. The first effect must be qualified however. For Foucault and Deleuze, to think belongs to the folds and dissipative trajectories without established pathways or a language of the outside. Thought is not related to knowledge as it is power belonging to vitalistic potential rather than power belonging to imposition of oppressive force, a side-effect of discursive knowledge as a form of bio-power. Thus to 'think' the nonhuman ethically, we must think in a way which acknowledges our forces and impacts upon nonhumans, but never are we actually discursively constructing knowledge about them. Nothing of their qualities is imposed upon them by humans, no matter how attentive we may believe ourselves to be, because the moment the human claims to think in order to know a nonhuman organism, we have already slaughtered that organism by placing it within the taxonomical bio-powers which relegate it to a certain fate of being below, and ultimately under the control of, the human. In a way then, thinking 'the' nonhuman is about inverting the question to ask the human how to un-know itself, to forsake the powers implicit in being human. This is the ethical element of becomings and their departure from fetishisation or imitation – to get away from the irredeemable human in order to effectuate a more gracious actual present for nonhuman life, and the first task is implicit in the second.

The majority of philosophical writing on nonhumans is 'about' nonhuman animals. In animal rights, it is about why (usually only certain) animals deserve to be granted a similar capacity for liberty and freedom from pain as humans. Exhaustive torturous tests are undertaken to 'prove' whether certain species – itself a bio-power term – are enough like humans to suffer under our discourses and our technologies. The banality of the eternal holocaust of murder for food is rarely included, but when it is, the spectre of species again emerges, the Oedipal dog is not for consumption, the pastoral cow is so. Speciesism is increasingly critiqued by new generations of animal activists, because the very concept of species is against life as it belongs to the same operation of power through (claimed or perceived) knowledge of collectives of things who have nothing in common except a failure to be human and are thus at the mercy of human bio-powers of knowledge. What is a species? A tactical management of the accepted and unaccepted acts of oppression which are distributed according to the worthiness of the life, but the life which is never one life, this life, a unique singular example of life, but rather an exemplar of a species and thus a symbol emptied of their material reality in order for humans to know what they can and cannot do with them or get from them. 'When power becomes bio-power resistance becomes the power of life, a vital power that cannot be confined within species, environment or the paths of a particular diagram' (Deleuze 1988a: 92). Power becomes bio-power when a claim to know a life occurs and homogenises it with other lives primarily in relation with the isomorphic superior status of those who name lives. Ethology is the biopolitical practice that prevents actual lives living. The making invisible of the scientist is a technique which conceals 'objective' analysis behind bio-power's capacity to slaughter through knowledge, as knowledge of nonhumans is inevitably always deferred to a project which demarcates the nonhuman's capacity to vindicate its right to live. The nonhuman is drawn into a contract of proving its worth as a life, a contract it has neither agreed to nor can ever benefit from. Increasingly humans are not having to prove their worth as their resemblance to the imagined deity Creator is relegated to a defunct myth, but through ethology humans are creating the world in their own image still, and the image privileges power within knowledge without accessing thought or imagination, found in the singularities of life beyond species and intervention into nonhuman lives.

Here is a conundrum: in our ethical becomings we must relinquish the human in order to free all lives from bio-power imposed through human knowledge, systems of signification, and the abuse to which they lead, yet simultaneously the most ethical way to navigate the world teeming with its many nonhuman lives is to leave them alone. But this conundrum is workable in that certain abolitionist viewpoints automatically liberate the self from systems and signifying operations. Abolitionism, unlike animal welfarism and animal rights, sees the only way to truly allow nonhuman animals liberty as coming from leaving animals alone, avoiding all intervention unless absolutely necessary (in the case for example of domesticated animals), and ultimately seeks a world where animals are left entirely without human intervention. Base level abolitionist activism occurs through rescue, veganism, ALF-type acts of liberation, boycott of tested products, funding of alternatives in medicine and vegan products for domesticated obligate carnivores, cessation of use of animals in entertainment, from zoos and circuses to wildlife documentaries. Many abolitionists include being child-free as part of the greater aim towards a world where animals are freed from human oppressive regimes. Abolitionists critique the focus in activism on single-issue campaigning. What abolitionists seek is not the one-by-one reduction of single issues of murder and torture of nonhuman animals – vivisection, circuses, the meat industry. These issues rely on the maintenance of species and return the onus of liberty onto the nonhuman who never agreed to the relation in the first place. The 'why' of single-issue campaigning is a desperate plea to bio-power but is forced to use bio-power to argue against its effects – scientific 'evidence', objective logocentric arguments. There is no paradigm shift here. Man remains supreme as the zenith of the pyramid of life and the one who designed the pyramid and thus has sole access to its manipulation.

Abolitionists advocate the 'leave be' principle, or what I have elsewhere termed, after Serres, gracious stepping aside. In a perverse postmodern turn, the most active activism we can perform, in reference to intervention into nonhuman life, is to *not* act. One must, that is, adopt a veganism that refuses to consume any animal products, boycott cosmetics and household products by refusing to purchase those tested on animals or without fixed cut-off dates, abandon circuses and zoos, and refuse to benefit commercially from animal incarceration and torment. The act is a non-act. Of course certain activisms involve acting, such as the ALF's admirable 'until every cage is empty' campaign; however, the fact that this is still illegal shows to what extent bio-power both criminalises gracious acts of mercy and converts 'life' into property when those prosecuted are charged with vandalism and theft. In this sense, non-act activism is beautiful in its banality – it is easy and available for all right now, and returns the onus onto the human to vindicate how they could possibly see torture and murder for consumption and science as viable. Following such logic, nonhumans would have to be left be until the constituted man completes his argument with the ahuman activist, and as we know, this resolution will never happen because of the incommensurability of discourse versus non-discourse. But at least the default position of harm until the nonhuman proves worthy is reversed to until the human proves worthy. Halcyon perhaps, but the *not* has great power in an apathetic world. Deleuze and Guattari state:

> Such pedagogies are only possible if each of the disciplines is, on its own behalf, in an essential relationship with the No that concerns it. The plane of philosophy is prephilosophical insofar as we consider it in itself independently of the concepts that come to occupy it, but the nonphilosophy is found where the plane confronts chaos. *Philosophy needs a nonphilosophy that comprehends it; it needs a nonphilosophy just as art needs nonart and science needs nonscience.* (Deleuze and Guattari 1994: 218, original emphasis)

The inherent necessity of alterity in this claim is crucial for thinking ethics and activism from an abolitionist position. Primarily, to return to man and knowledge, man needs nonman to think. By this I do not mean man needs the nonhuman animal, but rather, man needs the becoming-ahuman of man as a catalyst to unravel the oppressive affects of bio-power and to liberate self and world from discourse. Man needs nonman to achieve the access to life that discourse prevents, because life is the chaos that discourse represses but philosophy, art and ethics maps in singular events in order to harmonise the world as it teems with unlike entities. Harmony does not mean homogeneity, dissymmetry or taming, but rather a way of organising the plane which allows man/ nonman access to tactics of experimental activism and creative ethics that make the human entity one life among many and always travers- ing between interactions, without imposing his life as the only worthy one, which essentially is what human discourse does in describing the world. Simple activisms such as veganism undo presumptions about necessity and right for man and show there is an option for not-doing in habitual doing. It also acknowledges the affect of actions without the capitalist benefit of immediate satisfaction of causality by changing the concept of activism equalling immediate change. It trains us to alter our habitus from capitally satisfying to altering the human territoriali- sation of the world in ways we may not perceive, but which are forces for affective ethics nonetheless. Most importantly, it shows the ethical paradox of the common notions of which Deleuze speaks in relation to Spinoza, as the commonality which does not make us the same, and the expressions of acts which can open up the liberty for other lives to express, which we may never encounter. Like certain kinds of boycott activism, ethology needs to not-do – knowing animals invalidates their alterity, drawing them into a system in which they can never survive. The nonhuman is what we must become, not what we should seek to know. On becoming-animal Deleuze and Guattari quote Schèrer and Hocquenghem as describing *'an inhumanity immediately experienced in the body as such'* (1987: 273, original emphasis). While Deleuze and Guattari adamantly and repetitively remind us that becoming-animal is neither imitation nor metaphor, the problem of species remains (even when we are told we can enter becoming-dog with a cat or becoming- monkey with a horse). What this quotation shows is that it is the not which is more important than the newly formed and forming becoming entity. In becomings it is what we are no longer that leads to life, both our own and the acknowledgement of the pure alterity of other living organisms – no longer human, signified, stratified, organised, facialised. What we are becoming is important in that it is the launching onto life away from bio-power, so it is activism and resistance simultaneously, but the forsaking of discourse is what evinces our becoming inhuman (or what I call ahuman) and opens up the world for nonhuman lives to have freedom of expressivity. Becoming-ahuman is about extending or expression but also diminishing our negative affects, so the ethical relation it creates with nonhumans is beneficial not because of empathy, sympathy, intimacy or understanding but because of distance, the grace of avoidance, the liberation of leaving be.

Abolitionist ahumanity is as creative a project as it is a commitment to leaving be. While leaving the nonhuman animal be, we are simultaneously forced to rethink the modes of production which generate the forces of the (now residually) human organism. In *Anti-Oedipus* Deleuze and Guattari explore Samuel Butler's notion of the dispersed organism, stating that the organism is never a singular unity in opposition to the aggregate animal collective, but that each organism creates unique collective assemblages with its many parts with unlike entities, so that any one organism is only understood as a machine that one or more of its features or elements create with another. Deleuze and Guattari extend Butler's argument by claiming that far from animals (including human animals) being machines, machines are created through the extensive dispersion of all organisms that is necessary for their operation in the world – put simply, we are always in a machinic connection with elements in the world as we operate, and this is what it means to be a vitalistic-as-productive/extensive (rather than as a unified closed circuit) living organism. To be an organism is *not* to be one, to be a life is *not* to be separate from other lives: '[Butler] *shatters the vitalistic argument by calling into question the specific or personal unity of the organism, and the mechanist argument even more decisively by calling in question the structural unity of the machine*' (Deleuze and Guattari 1996: 284, original emphasis). While the abolitionist approach to ethical human/ nonhuman animal co-existence may seem to alienate interspecies interaction (remembering that generally speaking this is usually for the benefit of the nonhuman animal, very few human interventions are beneficial), here Deleuze and Guattari show that understanding the divide between the nonhuman and human is always tactical and a sketch or plan to catalyse activism. No matter how physically or conceptually extricated the human is from the nonhuman animal, the affects of human action are always part of an ecological network. Abolition finds its doing in this sense, in reference to an active rectification of the human destruction of the world, alongside its not doing, in the boycott of the murder, torture and incarceration of nonhuman animals. The ahuman becomings abolition can inspire emphasise the dispersive nature of the human organism whether it seeks to disperse or not; the fact that the human as a conceptual unity and as an actual global parasite of the Earth as a holistic machine has made its dispersal known to catastrophic effects is undeniable. At the heart of ethics is being accountable for the affects we may not be able to predict that often come – well-meant or in the name of capital – from the dispersive nature of our organism. While our idea of being a hermeneutic organism with intentional acts supports humanist phantasies of integrity and unity, it denies the real reverberating waves and alterations human activity intentionally and unintentionally effects on the nonhuman world. Just as this chapter began with Deleuze stating we can never know what our body is capable of doing, due to our limitation of its potential through phantasies of integrated limit and unity, so too we are incapable of knowing our mind's intent (in a non-Cartesian non-bifurcated manner) when creating activist schema. 'It is a matter of showing that the body surpasses the knowledge that we have of it, *and that thought likewise surpasses the consciousness that we have of it*' (Deleuze 1988b: 18). When forsaking knowledge as a human discursive bio-political impulse for abolitionist attitudes towards nonhumans, leaving be the compulsion to know, thought necessarily opens up as there are no longer directed routes for 'logical' default established trajectories. Abolitionist activism is an irrefutably corporeal activism – from entirely altering one's eating habits to altering one's social activities and altering one's legal standing through various liberation activities. However, as the human default position is one which places the onus on nonhumans, when this onus is lifted and shifted towards the human, in abolitionist activism one's status as a habitual human is altered and so too is knowledge of self and world. Ironically perhaps, when abolitionism is welcomed and animal interaction is radically decreased, one's unity as part of the greater ecological aggregate is exacerbated in terms of awareness and the need to be imaginative when attempting to think new modes of being part of the aggregate without causing harm. There is, therefore, a need for the unconscious in abolitionist activism, just as all becomings tap into the unconscious to discover the 'what next' on unpredictable journeys without genesis or destination.

Abolitionist activism shares many qualities in this sense with the very terms Deleuze and Guattari privilege in their becomings – the germinal non-established potentiality of the little (girl) child, the metamorphic adaptability of fabulated animals such as the transformative werewolf and vampire, and the refusal of logic based on a singular valued mode of thinking denigrated in phallogocentrism but celebrated in feminism in becoming-woman. Abolitionist activism welcomes many elements repudiated by the rights or welfare arguments of those who see nonhuman animals as viable only to the extent they reflect or adhere to certain human qualities, which leads to the pyramid of speciesism that Deleuze and Guattari invert in becomings. In Spinozan ethics, 'as conscious

beings, we never apprehend anything but the *effects* of these compositions and decompositions [when two bodies encounter one another]:
we experience *joy* when a body encounters ours and enters into composition with it, and *sadness* when, on the contrary, a body or an idea
threatens our own coherence' (Deleuze 1988b: 19). Deleuze emphasises
the passions within the organism, which truly constitute the organism's
well-being, rather than external reasons or observable objective effects.
No amount of observation or scientific study, beyond the irredeemable
suffering these studies have hitherto caused for nonhuman animals,
can ever access nonhumans' joy and sadness, because imposing human
apprehension as the one true mode of understanding is its own form of
torture. Joy and sadness are not shared between any two organisms,
let alone between 'species', so attempts to evaluate the joy and sadness
of nonhuman animals under the unforgivable conditions into which
humans force them is simply a way humans maintain their excuses in
order to vindicate what they already know to be unnecessary acts of
murder, torture and incarceration.

Coherence in Spinoza is very different to unity. Interactions which
are ethically positive allow an organism to continue to grow and extend
in their capacity to express, so coherence is inherently defined by metamorphosis and freedom by novelty of encounter which produces new
relations. The repetitious nature of human and nonhuman animal interactions in contemporary society in our murder and enslavement of nonhuman animals prevents liberty both actually and in the capacity for
another organism to 'be' themselves by extending themselves. Here again
we see an example of non-interaction being positive joyful interaction,
and human/nonhuman animal interaction being one which usually produces sadness and limits the nonhuman animal's capacity for coherence
through expression and extension. Obviously even some sympathetic to
veganism and abolitionist activism will respond with claims that some
nonhuman interactions with humans are 'beneficial' or 'enriching'. With
the possible exception of rescuing domesticated nonhuman animals, for
whom we have made ourselves responsible (tragically in the case of cats
and snakes for whom the murder of other animals in the pet food industry persists in a continuation of Oedipal speciesist privilege), the massively overwhelming reality is that humans are far more devastatingly
detrimental in their interaction with nonhuman animals than they are
beneficial. At best, nonhuman animal curiosity towards humans is delu-
sionally converted by anthropocentric interpretation as seeking interaction (usually as a result of humans imposing themselves forcefully into
nonhuman territories); at worst, insidious arguments for 'welfare' and

'conservation' perpetuate zoos and the breeding of endangered species, where species are privileged over individual nonhuman lives as fetishes so human future generations may be entertained by nonhuman diversity. The individual lives of singular nonhumans is never acknowledged in these all-too-anthropocentric human modes of perception.

Without an isomorphic opposition to the human (i.e. the nonhuman) the ahuman is an organism with a unique appetite. Deleuze defines Spinoza's understanding of appetite thus: 'Now the appetite is nothing else but the effort by which each thing strives to persevere in its being, each body in extension, each mind or each idea in thought (*conatus*)' (1988b: 21). Because for Deleuze and Guattari desire is neither for an object nor an outcome, this striving is the flow which runs through all organisms. Perseverance is a wonderful term in the way it resonates with 'living' (but not necessarily being a life) in that the organism does not wish necessarily to persevere as itself – nor, as Spinoza tells us, is anything ever aware of its own consciousness of thought nor its own capacity as a body – but simply to extend, connect, continue as a consistency within the multiple inevitable connections it enters into as an organism in the ecological mesh. There is something devastatingly simple and full of potential in the idea of perseverance as, like abolitionist activism, it suggests a form of 'what next' rather than a reification of the I which attempts to persevere as the I it perceives itself to be in thought and flesh (a thoroughly human tendency). If any organism simply perseveres to be itself, a self it cannot know (and here I am not imposing Spinozist claims onto nonhumans, but speaking of humans outside humanist traditions of metaphysical reflections on existence), then every organism neither knows itself nor can know another, so all organisms are entirely unique while simultaneously inextricable from the extensions and connections of which they are a part in the ecological cosmic machine. Appetite here is a form of desire. As Deleuze and Guattari emphasise:

> The true difference is not the difference between the two sexes but the difference between the human sex and the 'nonhuman' sex. It is clearly not a question of animals, nor of animal sexuality. Something quite different is involved ... Desiring machines are the nonhuman sex, the molecular machinic elements, their arrangements and their syntheses, without which there would neither be a human sex specifically determined in the large aggregates, nor a human sexuality capable of investing these aggregates. (1996: 295)

Tentatively then, abolitionism is to welfarist animal rights what desire is to sexuality, as Deleuze and Guattari accuse psychoanalysis of anthropomorphising sex (1996: 295) and abolitionists accuse rights reformists of anthropomorphising animals in order for nonhuman animals to justify their liberation. Just as minoritarians, especially women, cannot win in phallic Oedipal sexual structures, so too nonhuman animals have no chance in anthropomorphic structures. Further, one could argue that what the phallus is to sexuality, ethological 'knowledge' is to the continued abuse of animals, from pro-murder to welfarism and rights. Deleuze and Guattari state: 'We maintain, therefore, that *castration is the basis for the anthropomorphic and molar representation of sexuality*' (1996: 296, original emphasis). Knowledge 'of' nonhuman animals, which persistently makes they who need not account accountable for our abominable acts, creates the whole world in the image of man, just as the phallus and its possible lack creates sexuality in the image of the masculine alone. The role of representation is shared in both systems. Representing animals denies them their specificity and reveals our absolute incapacity to ever access their modes of negotiating themselves in and as part of the world. It is a fatally human project and human projects of knowledge all too often prove actually fatal to nonhumans. Representing the phallus creates a single point of reference against which all other references fail or cannot be recognised, so the concept of one – the human or the phallus – is the only concept rather than part of the ecology of concepts which are themselves in flux in ethical relations. Both the phallus and the human close off relationality entirely in their refusal to recognise anything except the one, measuring all else only against that singular template. Hence both operate a degenerative or bad ethics. 'Making love is not just becoming as one, or even two, but becoming as a hundred-thousand. Desiring machines, or the nonhuman sex: not one or even two sexes, but *n* sexes' (Deleuze and Guattari 1996: 296). If we take ethics as a form of love (which I would say it most definitely is), then abolitionist activism entails entering into the becoming *n* with the myriad organisms, human and nonhuman, with which we share the planet. What makes abolitionist activism unique in its abstraction is that it enters into a loving ethical relation with organisms or entities it will likely never encounter, and specifically seeks not to encounter, as in the example of boycotts. It is becoming *n* with the imperceptible world, a form of becoming-imperceptible which is simultaneously overtly corporeal and fleshly and vitalistic in its impact on all actual bodies, from the abolitionist's to those it seeks to affect (through presence as absence and vice versa).

The abstract machine of abolitionist activism delivers the human towards their own becoming-imperceptible while making them the nonhuman to the human who persistently reiterates the problematic violence perpetrated on nonhuman animals. Humans *need* the nonhuman ahuman (that is, the formerly human ahuman) in the same way philosophy needs non-philosophy and art non-art, ultimately in order to open thought to the outside and relegate the human, with its petrified hierarchies and arboreal structures of knowledge, to a memorial which reminds us of the violence knowledge of the other perpetrates, both in its inevitable failure to know the other and in its incapacity to apprehend the mode of knowing as a reflection entirely upon the self who claims to know. Welfarism and rights, though they have saved many individual animal lives and should be applauded for doing so, belong with the human, they fail at non-knowledge and non-philosophy because they work within the limits of the arguments human logocentrism allows. While strategies and outcomes for a 'better' life undeniably save lives, opposition, speciesism and the ablation of all modes of discourse other than the human are revalidated. There is no outside, unfortunately, for the nonhuman animal, who resides only outside. 'Here again', writes Guattari,

> we find the problematic of the alternative between subject-groups/subjugated groups, which can never be taken as an absolute opposition. The relations of alienation between fields of competence always suppose a certain margin which it falls upon pragmatics to locate and exploit: in other words, within *any situation whatsoever, a diagrammatic politics can always be 'calculated'*, which refuses any idea of fatalism, whichever name it may take on: divine, historical, economic, structural, hereditary or syntagmatic, a politics which thus implies, in the first place, an active refusal of any conception of the unconscious as a genetic stage or structural destiny. (2011: 174)

Guattari claims desire occurs before the crystallisation of the body via subjectification and stratification. Myriad arguments played out within human consciousness defer to all of the above fatalistic sources – religion, tradition, even necessity. Abolitionist politics arrives before the crystallisation of the use and abuse of nonhuman animals as part of normalised human operations, yet it occurs as a decisive refusal after the forsaking of the position of human with its benefits of oppression; it thus belongs to Guattari's plea for a post-Oedipal return to the unconscious as a means by which the connections between all organisms can manifest, without margins or borders but also with a form of absolute opposition that could be described as wonderment at alterity, rather than the subsuming isomorphic opposition between human and nonhuman animals which always relegates both entities within the field of human discourse. Guattari calls for an ecosophy based on an abstract machine that comes from the unconscious, which he opposes to arboreal structures and to logos, and in which he explicitly critiques language. This returns us to the crucial Spinozist idea of common notions but, via Deleuze on Foucault, without common discourse. Perhaps a more cynical understanding would be that abolitionist activism's common notion with nonhuman animals is not found in becoming-animal, nor in empathy, but in the common enemy of the nonhuman and the formerly human ahuman which is the human.

References

Deleuze, G. (1988a), *Foucault*, trans. Sean Hand, London: Athlone.

Deleuze, G. (1988b), *Spinoza: Practical Philosophy*, trans. Robert Hurley, San Francisco: City Lights Books.

Deleuze, G. and F. Guattari (1987), *A Thousand Plateaus: Capitalism and Schizophrenia*, trans. B. Massumi, London: Athlone.

Deleuze, G. and F. Guattari (1994), *What is Philosophy?*, trans. Hugh Tomlinson and Graham Burchell, New York: Columbia University Press.

Deleuze, G. and F. Guattari (1996), *Anti-Oedipus*, trans. R. Hurley, M. Seem and H. R. Lane, Minneapolis: University of Minnesota Press.

Guattari, F. (2011), *The Machinic Unconscious*, trans. Taylor Adkins, New York: Semiotext(e).

Chapter 2

Brutal Thoughts: Laruelle and Deleuze on Human Animal Stupidity

John Ó Maoilearca

Introduction

François Laruelle's non-philosophy of definitional mutation involves reconfiguring not only what we mean by philosophy but also what we mean by *homo sapiens* as the thinking, 'wise' animal. Of course, *philosophia* itself is understood by many as the 'love of wisdom', which is presumably one reason why Laruelle characterises the philosopher's self-description, with no little irony, as 'the human par excellence in speaking, knowing, acting' (2012c: 40). The contrast, by implication, is with the imperfect, unwise animal, that is, with the non-philosophical individual (whatever he, she, or 'it' may be). This is precisely why Laruelle does *not* follow philosophy's definitions – of itself, of the human, or of the nonhuman. Quite the contrary: de-philosophising the human and nonhuman is what is needed most. This duality of apparent wisdom and ignorance allows a new stark formulation of Laruelle's project – 'how to elaborate an outside-philosophy thought. . . ?', as he puts it (2012a: 3). At one still recognisably human and even philosophical level, the elaboration of such an 'outsider thought' or *philosophie brute* requires a kind of unlearning: 'the Real is an unlearned knowledge, rather than a "learned ignorance". Unlearned means that it is neither an expert knowledge nor a taught knowledge. It is non-taught knowledge' (Laruelle 2014b: 44).

Admittedly, the commendation of any form of ignorance (even as a Keatsian 'negative capability') can strike some as churlish and even duplicitous. Certainly, Laruelle finds Gilles Deleuze's own theory of stupidity (in *Difference and Repetition*) a rather disingenuous move. Despite its being offered in place of the standard image of error in representationalist philosophy,

> we find here once again, under the mitigated form of an unlimited becoming, the distinction between man and philosopher, their hierarchy in spite of all: the philosopher who constructs the system and the idiot whom he talks about and who doubtless stumbles through the windings of the system do not adequately coincide. Once again the philosopher does not really want idiocy, he limits it. (Laruelle 2012a: 42)

Merely playing the idiot will not suffice for Laruelle: if there is anything like a 'transcendental idiot' who is not merely a philosopher's stooge, then he, she, or it will exist in a much more *nonhuman* manner. Indeed, at another level, non-philosophical 'unlearning' involves something more radical again, the idea that

> thought is not the intrinsic property of humans that must serve to define their essence, an essence that would then indeed be 'local'; it is a universal milieu. If we tend now to emphasise animality, bringing it within the sphere of culture, then why not emphasise the most elevated humanity, so as to bring it into the universe; and, through a paradoxical example, why not reexamine its links with animality, of which it will then be a matter of knowing whether it, also, is universal? (Laruelle 2012b: 340, translation altered)

Indeed, this 'most elevated humanity' may well be something far more nonhuman *and* non-philosophical – in the Deleuzo-Guattarian sense (animals are not instruments of human writing) – than either Deleuze or Laruelle might have imagined. It is the purpose of this chapter to explain why.

Philosophy and the Animal

Before we go any further we must enquire into the perplexing role of the human – as well as the nonhuman – in Laruelle's non-philosophy. What of the human in non-philosophy? This is particularly important given Laruelle's repeated contention that 'non-philosophy is fully and simply human. Non-philosophy is the philosophy of man' (Laruelle 2013b: 200). In fact, the question of anthropomorphism, which assertions like this surely raise, is linked here to the issue of the (non)human too. Philosophy, according to Laruelle, not only anthropomorphises the Real, it also *anthropomorphises Man* (or as we will say, it 'philosomorphises' both after its own image – see Mullarkey 2013).

Despite its protestations to the contrary, to many readers non-philosophy still seems idealist, and hence philosophical, in virtue of this nomination of the Real as 'Man' or 'human' (Laruelle uses each term interchangeably). As Ray Brassier writes, the 'privileging of the nomenclature "man" to designate the real cannot but re-phenomenologize and re-substantialize its radical in-consistency' (2007: 137). Ian James echoes Brassier's point and also questions Laruelle's apparent contradiction in humanising the Real while also declaring not to define it (2012: 179). So what exactly is Laruelle doing with such a humanisation? Anthony Paul Smith and Nicola Rubczak, on the other hand, offer a positive interpretation of the issue:

> what we find here is not typical philosophical humanism, represented in everyday culture as a privileging of some claimed universal human being that is in reality taken as a hetero-normative, white, healthy male. But instead the question of the human is open in non-philosophy, even as the human or what he comes to call Human-in-person is also the name of the Real. It is not the Real that is impersonal, but rather the Real is foreclosed to philosophy, represented not in some anti-humanist hatred or indifference towards human beings, but in the maxim that, 'Philosophy was made for man, not man for philosophy.' (2013: xv)

Indeed, this apparent anthropomorphism of the Real actually lies at the heart of non-philosophical research. It is not only central on account of its endeavour to re-orient thought – from going from philosophy to the Real to going from the Real to philosophy – but also on account of the maxim that Smith and Rubczak refer to above, which actually accompanies this shift. The non-philosophical maxim is that philosophy should be made for the human rather than (as is the case in standard philosophical thought) that the human be made for philosophy: 'we must change hypothesis and even paradigm: break up the mixtures, found philosophy on man rather than the inverse' (Laruelle 2012c: 46). Man has been described, defined, categorised, quantified and normalised by philosophy since its beginning, and it is the task of non-philosophy to invert this mediation of the human through philosophy.

This double re-identification of both the human and the Real over philosophy carries with it this new identity of the Real with the human. But with that we also have two opposed 'subspecies' of anthropomorphism: alongside the idealisations of man through philosophy (the human modelled on philosophical anthropology – 'philosomorphism'), there is the Laruellean inversion that realises man through non-philosophy. This realisation (or de-idealisation) does not *define* man, however, but simply subtracts two and a half millennia of philosophical mediation (exploitation, harassment, racism, sexism, inequalities of all kinds) from the image of the human.

Here, then, anthropomorphism – the transformation of animals and inanimate objects into an image of the human – is reframed by this new, more *radical* form that equates the human and the Real. This re-articulation is not without connection with traditional analyses of anthropomorphism, though, as we can see in what Lorraine Daston and Gregg Mitman say here:

> 'anthropomorphism' is the word used to describe the belief that animals are essentially like humans, and it is usually applied as a term of reproach, both intellectual and moral. Originally, the word referred to the attribution of human form to gods, forbidden by several religions as blasphemous. Something of the religious taboo still clings to secular, modern instances of anthropomorphism, even if it is animals rather than divinities that are being humanized. (2005: 2)

What religion forbids, the 'heresy' of non-philosophy performs. In this secular, *affirmative* anthropomorphism, however, identifying the human with the Real allows the human image to be multiplied as a consequence (without any definition, nor synthesis of definitions).

So, what is the human for non-philosophy? Is Laruelle's resistance to any definition of man a token of Sartrean existentialism – placing existence before any essence? Even this is no doubt too philosophical for Laruelle (being predicated on an ontology of negation). By contrast, Sartre himself certainly knew what a human was by the time he wrote the first volume of the *Critique of Dialectical Reason*:

> This is the contradiction of racism, colonialism and all forms of tyranny: in order to *treat a man like a dog*, one must first recognize him as a man. The concealed discomfort of the master is that he always has to consider the *human reality* of his slaves (whether through his reliance on their skill and their synthetic understanding of situations, or through his precautions against the permanent possibility of revolt or escape), while at the same time refusing them the economic and political status which, *in this period*, defined human beings. (2004: 111)

The inserted qualification, 'in this period', is *not* what gives Sartre's essentialism away, however (*that* actually points to his consistency – man is what he makes of himself in each situation). The real point is that, in recognising 'human reality', the slave-owner must recognise a different *nonhuman* reality *as inferior*. In order to mistreat his slave, the slave-owner must already (think that) he knows what a dog is, and so also what it is to *treat a dog like a dog*. This 'human reality' is what *should not be treated like a dog's reality*. Sartre's humanist essentialism is vicarious, but an essentialism nonetheless. Indeed, this corollary is hard to avoid, and is something that the master's politics shares with Sartre's politics. After all, being both a humanist and a Marxist allowed Sartre to declare that 'every anti-communist is a dog' (albeit that Sartre could presumably see the potential for even an anti-communist or slaver to recognise himself or herself eventually as something non-dog, i.e. a human).

Laruelle, by contrast, has no recourse to nothingness or any other philosophical concept to account for the human (be it an ontology of the void, like Badiou's, or the negation of dogs, like Sartre's). As Alexander Galloway states, 'the primary ethical task' is clear for Laruelle: 'to view humanity as indivisible, without resorting to essence or nature' (2013: 105). Negation is just one more philosophical essence – be it attributed to the human or anything else. For here is the thing: Laruelle will not account for the nonhuman either, *especially* should the 'non-' be understood as negation. The question of the human *and* animal, then, is equally live for non-philosophy and sets up the possibility of the animal as *non-standard* (the 'animal-in-person') alongside the human or 'Man-in-person'. It will also raise the question of animals as non-standard, or extended, humans.

In as much as the influence of Marx on Laruelle's thought might also be credited with the latter's 'humanisation' of the Real, we should introduce an important distinction here. Marx's elaboration of the concept of 'species-being' (*Gattungswesen*) envisages *homo sapiens* as unique amongst animals, not only on account of its exceptional mental powers, but because 'man' alone freely and consciously produces both himself and the natural world through his material labour. It is this labour that constitutes man's species-being:

> In creating an objective world by his practical activity, in working-up inorganic nature, man proves himself a conscious species being . . . Admittedly animals also produce . . . But an animal only produces what it immediately needs for itself or its young. It produces one-sidedly, while man produces universally . . . An animal produces only itself, whilst man reproduces the whole of nature . . . An animal forms things in accordance with the standard and the need of the species to which it belongs, whilst man knows how to produce in accordance to the standards of other species. (Marx cited in Viveiros de Castro 2012: 101)

Marx's 'primitive narcissism' here ('man reproduces the whole of nature') has been criticised by, amongst others, Brazilian anthropologist Eduardo Viveiros de Castro. However, in Viveiros de Castro's glossing of this passage from Marx's *1844 Manuscripts*, a distinction emerges that pertains to non-philosophy as well as Viveiros de Castro's own research on Amerindian perspectivism:

> While apparently converging with the Amerindian notion that humanity is the universal form of the subject, Marx's is in fact an absolute inversion of it: he is saying that humans can 'be' any animal – that we have more being than any other species – whilst Amerindians say that 'any' animal can be human – that there is more being to an animal than meets the eye. 'Man' is the universal animal in two entirely different senses, then: the universality is anthropocentric in the case of Marx, and anthropomorphic in the Amerindian case. (2012: 101)

Marx, following Hegel's post-Kantian thought, remains anthropocentric. Indeed, Laruelle's non-Kantian humanisation of the Real is a kind of (radical) anthropomorphism and looks similar to this Amerindian perspectivism that sees all animal beings as 'human'. In places, Laruelle can indeed sound like Marx, writing with an almost cosmic optimism of humans as 'perhaps an imitation, itself inventive of the universe' (2010: 320). Yet Laruelle's anthropomorphism is one that also mutates the human and the animal, not in a metaphysics of becoming, but in a continual 'indefinition' of both human and animal that allows both to escape philosophical domination.

Pet Theories: On Philosomorphism

Clearly, what Laruelle says of anthropology – that it uses Man *for* philosophy – can also be said of any philosophy (or representation) of the animal: if the animal appears by name at all, it is as a proxy for one or other philosopheme of what the animal means to (human) philosophy. Traditionally and in separatist mode, these appearances have only been to inflate the human at the animal's expense. The human is defined in wide-ranging ways, with some depictions simply opposing properties attributed to 'animals' (man as the non-animal, the immaterial, the preternatural, and so forth), while others offer continuist images of humans as sentient animals, conscious animals, rational animals, linguistic animals, political animals, temporal animals. . . . Hence, man is described by Aristotle as exclusively political, by Descartes as exclusively conscious, by Kant as exclusively rational, by Heidegger as exclusively temporal, by Davidson as exclusively linguistic, and so on. This positive account consequently provides us with another list of attributes for the animal: the non-political, the non-conscious, the non-rational, the non-temporal, the non-linguistic, etc. And alongside these prosaic descriptions one can line-up all the more fanciful ones – of man as the animal who has the right to make promises (Nietzsche), or who is what he is not and is not what he is (Sartre), or even who goes to the movies (Agamben). All of this is simply the flip-side of Laruelle's anthropological harassment of Man, which harasses animals to an even greater extent.

Indeed, it is pack animals, animals as assemblages of other, smaller (molecular) animals, that precisely also marks out the Deleuzian philosomorphic approach that is predicated on a metaphysics of becoming. Wolves, cockroaches and rats are the stars of this menagerie, especially rats:

> We think and write for animals themselves. We become animal so that the animal also becomes something else. The agony of a rat or the slaughter of a calf remains present in thought not through pity but as the zone of exchange between man and animal in which something of one passes into the other. This is the constitutive relationship of philosophy and nonphilosophy. (Deleuze and Guattari 1994: 109)

Pity, of course, would be a *reactive* relation that does neither the dying animal nor the thinking philosopher any good. Jacques Derrida's compassion for the animal, for instance, is a morbid response that Deleuze's (and Guattari's) vitalist thinking cannot stomach. Where Derrida focuses on the suffering and death of the animal, Deleuze concentrates on (its) life. And if there is an ethics in our relationship with the animal, it is strictly affective, concerning forces, or degrees of motion and rest. It is also asymmetric – not in the Levinasian mode of being *for* the other – but in the philosophically *aristocratic* mode of being for the greater good of a healthier, more joyful relation. It is *the relation* that is the end in itself: 'Man does not become wolf, or vampire, as if he changed molar species; the vampire and werewolf are becomings of man, in other words, proximities between molecules in composition, relations of movement and rest, speed and slowness between emitted particles' (Deleuze and Guattari 1984: 107).

Admittedly, Luce Irigaray famously took Deleuze and Guattari to task for also insisting upon a 'becoming-woman' that would incorporate both 'molar' women *and* men within a greater molecular process, to the neglect of any actual identitarian politics (whose achievements had been hard-won by molar women – see Irigaray 1985: 141). Indeed, the fact that Deleuzian men can piggyback on becoming-woman (as the 'key to all the other becomings') smacks of an opportunistic avoidance of political responsibility. Might not the same be said of this 'becoming-animal'?

Pace Deleuze and Guattari's assertion that they think and write '*for* animals' and even become animal '*so that* the animal also becomes something else' – it is arguable that it is only *human* becoming that really interests them. The animals' part in this pact most often appears as only a means to an end: 'the becoming-animal of the human being is real, even if the animal the human becomes is not' (Deleuze and Guattari 1987: 238). Indeed, if becoming-woman were the key to *all* other becoming, then every *nonhuman* becoming would be seemingly impossible, and Deleuzian thought would reduce to a type of Heideggerian anthropocentrism, with only gendered humans being 'rich-in-becoming' and animals being 'poor-in-becoming'.

Perhaps we should not be so hard on Deleuze (and Guattari), however: much of what they say has a relevance for a proto-Laruellean stance on animal philosophy. On the one hand, it is doubtless that the commendation of process over product is part of an anti-representationalist, anti-mimetic, tendency in Deleuzian thought specifically. In order to 'be the Pink Panther', one must imitate and reproduce 'nothing'; but like that big cat, one 'paints the world its colour, pink on pink; this is its becoming-world' (1987: 11). Deleuze's 'animal philosophy' (as Badiou dubs it) is a philosophy of life that, like its forbear in Bergson, is utterly immanentist – there is no *state* outside of becoming to become. Molarity, be it of the human or the nonhuman, is not to be imitated; even further, it *cannot* be imitated (hence, what looks like reproduction is always a new production, a productive repetition). The fact remains, though, that there are kinds of animal that Deleuze prefers over others in this all-encompassing molecular becoming: domesticated (pitied) and individuated (molarised) animals are unhealthy, reactive and sad – this being the motive behind the infamous proclamation that 'anyone who likes cats or dogs is a fool' (Deleuze and Guattari 1987: 239). Likewise, State animals (the lions, horses and unicorns of empires, myths and religions) are to be disavowed. It is the 'demonic' or pack animal that is the Deleuzian favourite, the *philosopher*'s pet. So, *qua animal* becomings (rather than the becoming-animal of humans), the true animal is always a multiplicity (as in a wolf pack) and a process (every such pack is a *wolfing*).

On the other hand, however, *qua* becoming-animal, what should be (at least) a two-sided process involving active becomings for all participants, does indeed invariably only profit the human. For example, in the plateau on the 'War Machine' in *A Thousand Plateaus*, the nomad invention of the stirrup involves a human becoming-animal within a 'man-horse-stirrup' assemblage. Similarly, the bridle used in masochistic practice is itself derivative of a human 'becoming-horse' (1987: 399; 260). It seems that, as a State animal, the horse can only serve a Deleuzian becoming when participating in *human* enhancement. Obviously, Deleuze and Guattari are fully alert to the danger here of 'becoming-animal' manifesting itself as merely an imitation of a 'molar' image (*playing* 'horsey'), or as a form of abstract 'horseness', or as a part-object fetish. This is supposed to be a process of recreating certain speeds and slownesses – a metamorphosis rather than a representation. Yet they seem oblivious to the politics of their own examples, horses in particular. How can a stirrup involve any kind of *becoming* for the horse when we remember that Deleuze's (Nietzschean) conception of genuine becoming must be *active* and not *reactive*? The stirrup is a control device and so cannot be part of anything affirmative (in Deleuze's sense). A domesticated horse may take pleasure in fulfilling some of its functions, but that is only because it has been broken in, made into a sad animal (no less than a dog is a sad wolf, according to Deleuze). The technology itself is reactive – a policing, disciplining and controlling of life rather than its further production. And as for the agony of a dying rat or slaughtered calf, the technologies involved in 'pest' control and factory-farming can hardly be deemed life-affirming, at least *from the point of view of the animal lives involved.*

There seems little place for the animal's *own* 'becomings', therefore, in the alter (animal)-side of a human becoming-animal. What can be said of *its* or their 'becoming-human'? Can it only ever be a token of domestication and anthropomorphism – a matter of 'our' projection, sentimentality and pity? Where is the example of human and animal change as a real co-becoming, such as the wasp and the orchid enjoy in *A Thousand Plateaus*, that is, as an active, joyful 'deterritorialisation' for *both* creatures (Deleuze and Guattari 1987: 293)? As things stand, the animal, demonic or domestic, appears to be a philosophical myth in Deleuze's thought, a philosomorph that must play a lesser part in the architecture of becoming, for any such process is always evaluated from the perspective of the human alone (of one defined kind, moreover). Indeed, such is the immanence of Deleuzian thought it is even arguable that the animal *must* remain the outsider of genuine becoming if, as he says, its agony and slaughter is constitutive of a zone of exchange between human and animal as well as philosophy and non-philosophy. The dying animal is here the permanent outsider of thought too, the shock to thought, and so the non-philosophical as such (in the negative rather than Laruellean sense of the term). To be allowed its own life and vital becoming would be to allow the animal too much philosophy, too much thought for itself. And yet this very withdrawal of privileges is itself a token of the philosomorphic use of the animal pervasive in Deleuzian thought.

Transcendental Idiocy, or, the Insufficient Animal

We referred earlier to the possibility of a more *radical* anthropomorphism – wherein the 'human' (philosophy's 'the-man' as Laruelle puts it) is also altered and multiplied by the Real. In Laruelle's words, this would be a 'simplified and unfolded Humanity . . . a hyper-philosophical general-ity . . . We call this universal Humanity.' He then continues: 'Man is this Idiot who exists also as universal Humanity of Stranger.' He, or she, or it, then, is certainly not the 'wise one', the master, but the Idiot or, we might add, the 'stupid beast' (*bête bêtise*). This turn to what Laruelle also calls the 'transcendental Idiot of an ante-decisional simplic-ity' would, nonetheless, be a 'non-rousseauian mutation' – that is, it is not supposed to be a return or mere reversal to an idealised past of noble savagery (Laruelle 1995: 78, 110, 96, 160). The question of the clever philosopher versus the simply human, the naïf, or ordinary idiot, was mentioned at the outset. So, we need to ask, what does *Laruelle* mean by transcendental idiocy or *'transcendental naïvety'*, and does it have any connection with what we have seen of Deleuze's philosomorphism (Laruelle 2012c: 54)?

The second part of this question is pertinent inasmuch as part of the meaning of idiocy or stupidity emerges from Laruelle's reaction against Deleuze's *Difference and Repetition* and its attempted appropriation of a theory of stupidity (that we cited in our introduction). Deleuze there forwards a theory of stupidity over a theory of error (standard within the traditional 'image of thought' in philosophy). Error is a matter of actual facts, according to Deleuze:

> Who says 'Good morning Theodorus' when Theaetetus passes, 'It is three o'clock' when it is three-thirty, and that 7 + 5 = 13? Answer: the myopic, the distracted and the young child at school. (1994: 150)

Empirical idiocy, that involving mere actual facts, stems from the poor-sighted, the absent-minded and the uneducated. Then, in an apparent gesture of humility, Deleuze wonders whether 'Philosophy could have taken up the problem [of error] with its own means and with the nec-essary modesty, by considering the fact that stupidity is never that of others but the object of a properly transcendental question: how is stu-pidity (not error) possible?' (1994: 151).

It is interesting to note that Bernard Stiegler reads Deleuze's transcendental magnanimity here quite 'personally': 'One would clearly understand nothing . . . if one did not posit . . . that "stupidity [*bêtise*] must be understood as my stupidity [*ma propre bêtise*]"' (Stiegler 2013: 161–2). Moreover, this self-attribution of stupidity concerns the *transcendental* conditions of *human* perception – it does not concern the superiority of human intelligence over that of the animal:

> Between *being* (stupid), *doing* (stupid things), *and saying* (stupid things), the question of stupidity would be at the same time older, deeper and lower than the *question of being and of spirit*, including in *Of Spirit: Heidegger and the Question*, where Derrida *approaches* the question of the animal 'poor in world.' The *default* of spirit, that is, the *feeling* of *not having any*: such would be the commencement of spirit starting from that which is stupid . . . (Stiegler 2013: 172n11)

As Stiegler has it, Deleuze is following Gilbert Simondon in trying to think stupidity from out of the 'pure ground' of 'individuation': 'it is in relation to this inseparable ground [*fond*] that stupidity takes place as a transcendental structure of thinking' (2013: 172n11). Moreover, Deleuze himself makes it clear that stupidity is not the same as animality, despite their shared French etymology: 'stupidity [*bêtise*] is not animality. The animal is protected by specific forms which prevent it from being "stupid" [*bête*]' (Deleuze 1994: 150). In other words, animals are too animal (*bête*) to be stupid (*bête*). They lack the 'individuation as such' that is 'inseparable from a pure ground'. In this respect, animals are protected because they are beyond cleverness *and* stupidity. For, as Deleuze says:

> Animals are in a sense forewarned against this ground, protected by their explicit forms. Not so for the I and the Self, undermined by the fields of individuation which work beneath them, defenceless against a rising of the ground which holds up to them a distorted or distorting mirror in which all presently thought forms dissolve. Stupidity is neither the ground nor the individual, but rather this relation in which individuation brings the ground to the surface without being able to give it form (this ground rises by means of the I, penetrating deeply into the possibility of thought and constituting the unrecognised in every recognition). (1994: 152)

Stupidity is a matter of the (transcendental) faculties, which belong to the human (Kantian) I and Self. The ground interferes with the surface, and stupidity emerges.

Laruelle, however, is suspicious of Deleuze's moves here, not so much vis-à-vis the animal, but as regards the human, especially the human philosopher as transcendentally stupid versus those ordinary humans ('nondescript' men) who are only empirically stupid (the distracted, the child, the short-sighted, or perhaps even the 'fool' who likes cats or dogs):

> if man is re-submerged into pure immanence, then one turns him into what Deleuze calls an idiot. But since there are (at best) two kinds of immanence or real, there will be two idiocies. If immanence is absolutely devoid of transcendence, the ego or man will be a transcendental idiot. If, on the contrary, as in Spinoza and Deleuze, it includes the pure form of transcendence, then man will be at once a transcendental and a transcendent idiot, which is to say, half-idiot and half-philosopher – a concept which, from our point of view, is rather transcendent. (Laruelle 2012a: 61)

This, of course, begs the question as to what an ordinary idiocy looks like from within non-philosophy, one that, should it retain the name 'transcendental idiot', is nonetheless *not* a philosophical projection.

If the idiot needs to be 'educated', then it was Plato who first discussed this necessity in the *Republic* under the title 'The Education of the Philosopher' (see Plato 1984: 523–4). Here Socrates teaches Glaucon (Plato's brother) about those 'contradictory' perceptions that 'call for thought' (a passage Deleuze addresses just before his discussion of stupidity in *Difference and Repetition* – see Deleuze 1994: 141). Even when looking at the fingers of my own hand, I need *thought* to 'distinguish properly whether they are large or small', that is, 'to investigate whether one object has been reported to it or two'. Sight alone 'perceives large and small as qualities which are not distinct but run into each other' says Socrates, and hence 'to clear the matter up thought must adopt the opposite approach and look at large and small as distinct and separate qualities – a reverse process to that of sensation'. 'True' replies Glaucon. The educated philosopher reverses perception in order to create the represented object – it forces the anthropocentric perspective that measures the Real object according to a human measure. The non-philosopher, by implication, would invert or reorient that reversal in order to restore the Real. Or rather, he or she would destroy that distance, his or her own withdrawal. *Philosophy cannot perform this task as it is itself the phenomenon at issue*: the distance created by 'intelligence', by the clever animal.

When, in *Difference and Repetition*, Deleuze discusses Socrates' education of Glaucon on sameness and difference (between large and small fingers), he refers to Plato's need to interrupt any *'mad-becoming'* (1994: 159). In his essay, 'Touched by Madness: On Animals and Madmen',

René ten Bos begs to differ with Deleuze here. While noting that Deleuze distances the animal from this madness completely, he prefers to place the folly of animal madness in and as the background to human, moral madness (especially as studied by Michel Foucault):

> One might argue therefore that an animal madness (*folie*) opposes a moral madness (*déraison*), but Foucault's entire point is that the first kind of madness, that is, the animal form, is the background of the moral form. What heretics, witches, and fornicators are doing, is opening the door to animality and this alone justifies the severest measures imaginable. The madness of a heretic, witch, or fornicator does not only reveal moral degeneration but also the abysmal freedom of the animal in each human being. (ten Bos 2009: 438–9)

Laruelle, of course, is the archetypical philosophical heretic. In a lecture entitled 'Life in-the-Last-Humanity: On the "Speculative" Ecology of Man, Animal, and Plant', he speaks about his latest ideas concerning the quantum nature of non-standard philosophy. In the final section, he concludes:

> man has no exorbitant or metaphysical privilege in quantum thought, even when it is about life, it is an *a priori* of the lived like the other combined variables. We obtain inverse products, MA (man as animal) and AM (animal as Man), but also MP (Man as Plant) and PM (Plant as Man) which form unequal and above all non-commutative products for the knowledge of life. (2014c: n.p.)

Man has no 'exorbitant or metaphysical privilege': the human is, rather, an '*a priori* of the lived'. This is why, in our introduction to this chapter, we conjectured whether what Laruelle refers to as the 'most elevated humanity' may well be something more nonhuman than something (philosophically, anthropologically) 'human'. In summation, we should now say that seeing X '*as* human' is a specific kind of seeing-as, an honorific seeing. It is also an axiomatic seeing, an *a priori* of the lived, that is equally axiological. Seeing-as-human is an attribution of value *before* it attributes any specific essence, properties or perfections (which will always be cut to size depending on the contingent philosophical definition of 'human' and 'nonhuman' at play in that moment). Before X *is* human, X is *as* human (the details of 'is' can be filled in later). Being human is value-creating, not in the Sartrean ontological sense of *bringing* value (qua nothingness) into Being, but in the sense that being-human is value per se, the withdrawal from the 'rest' – animals, plants, objects – who must now fall back into the background as lower in value – whatever that may entail.

A non-standard philosophy, that is, a non-philosophy *already* 'written' by the nonhuman Real (rather than by the human philosopher *becoming*-animal) thereby amounts to a radical inversion of this withdrawal. The human here is neither eliminated nor extinguished in favour of a new technology (A.I.) or a world-without-us – either of which operate on the presumption of a given image of what the human is that is being superseded – but is expanded (via mutation) and so restored to those 'other' humans lost from view. If it is true that one is not born, but rather becomes an animal (in a sense more akin to de Beauvoir's becoming than Deleuze's), then it is possible to reverse that becoming and see those called 'animals' become the human they always were (Ó Maoilearca 2015).

References

Brassier, R. (2007), *Nihil Unbound: Enlightenment and Extinction*, Basingstoke: Palgrave Macmillan.

Daston, L. and G. Mitman (2005), 'The How and Why of Thinking With Animals', in Daston and Mitman (eds), *Thinking With Animals: New Perspectives On Anthropomorphism*, New York: Columbia University Press, pp. 1–14.

Deleuze, G. (1994), *Difference and Repetition*, trans. Paul Patton, London: Athlone Press.

Deleuze, G. and F. Guattari (1984), *Anti-Oedipus*, trans. Robert Hurley, Mark Seem and Helen R. Lane, London: Athlone.

Deleuze, G. and F. Guattari (1987), *A Thousand Plateaus*, trans. Brain Massumi, London: Athlone.

Deleuze, G. and F. Guattari (1994), *What is Philosophy?* trans. Hugh Tomlinson and Graham Burchell, London and New York: Verso.

Derrida, J. (2011), *The Beast and the Sovereign*, Vol. 1, trans. Geoff Bennington, Chicago: University of Chicago Press.

Galloway, A. (2013), 'Review of François Laruelle, *Théorie générale des victimes*', *Parrhesia*, No. 16, pp. 102–5.

Irigaray, L. (1985), *This Sex Which is Not One*, trans. Catherine Porter with Carolyn Burke, Ithaca, NY: Cornell University Press.

James, I. (2012), *The New French Philosophy*, London: Polity.

Laruelle, F. (1995), *Théorie des Étrangers: Science des hommes, démocratie, non-psychanalyse*, Paris: Kimé.

Laruelle, F. (2010), *Philosophie non-standard: Générique, quantique, philo-fiction*, Paris: Kimé.

Laruelle, F. (2012a), '"I, the Philosopher, Am Lying": Reply to Deleuze', in *The Non-Philosophy Project: Essays by François Laruelle*, ed. Gabriel Alkon and Boris Gunjevic, New York: Telos Press Publishing, pp. 40–74.

Laruelle, F. (2012b), 'The Degrowth of Philosophy: Towards a Generic Ecology', trans. Robin Mackay, in F. Laruelle, *From Decision to Heresy: Experiments in Non-Standard Thought*, ed. Robin Mackay, Falmouth: Urbanomic/Sequence Press, pp. 327–49.

Laruelle, F. (2012c), 'A Rigorous Science of Man', in F. Laruelle, *From Decision to Heresy: Experiments in Non-Standard Thought*, ed. Robin Mackay, Falmouth: Urbanomic/Sequence Press, pp. 33–73.

Laruelle, F. (2013a), *Anti-Badiou*, trans. Robin Mackay, London: Bloomsbury.

Laruelle, F. (2013b), *Philosophy and Non-Philosophy*, trans. Taylor Adkins, Minneapolis: Univocal.

Laruelle, F. (2013c), *Principles of Non-Philosophy*, trans. Nicola Rubczak and Anthony Paul Smith, London: Bloomsbury Academic.

Laruelle, F. (2014a), 'L'Impossible foundation d'une écologie de l'océan' (2008), at http://www.onphi.net/lettre-laruelle-l-impossible-fondation-d-une-ecologie-de-l-ocean-27.html (accessed 6 June 2014).

Laruelle, F. (2014b), *Intellectuals and Power: The Insurrection of the Victim. François Laruelle in Conversation with Philippe Petit*, trans. Anthony Paul Smith, London: Polity.

Laruelle, F. (2014c), 'Life in-the-Last-Humanity: On the "Speculative" Ecology of Man, Animal, and Plant', paper given at London Graduate School, 13 June.

Lawlor, L. (2008), 'Following the Rats: Becoming Animal in Deleuze and Guattari', *SubStance*, Vol. 37, No. 3, pp. 169–87.

Mullarkey, J. (2006), *Post-Continental Philosophy: An Outline*, London: Continuum.

Mullarkey, J. (2013), 'Animal Spirits: Philosomorphism and the Background Revolts of Cinema', *Angelaki*, Vol. 18, No. 1, pp. 11–29.

Ó Maoilearca, J. (2015), *All Thoughts Are Equal: Laruelle and Nonhuman Philosophy*, Minneapolis: University of Minnesota Press.

Plato (1984), *The Republic*, trans. B. Jowett, London: Penguin.

Sartre, J-P. (2004), *Critique of Dialectical Reason*, Vol. 1, trans. Alan Sheridan-Smith, London: Verso.

Smith, A.P. (2013), *A Non-Philosophical Theory of Nature: Ecologies of Thought*, Basingstoke: Palgrave Macmillan.

Smith, A.P. and N. Rubczak (2013), 'Cloning the Untranslatable: Translators' Introduction', in Laruelle, 2013c, pp. xi–xix.

Stiegler, B. (2013), '"Doing and Saying Stupid Things in the Twentieth Century": *Bêtise* and Animality in Deleuze and Derrida', trans. Daniel Ross, *Angelaki*, Vol. 18, No. 1, pp. 159–74.

ten Bos, R. (2009), 'Touched by Madness: On Animals and Madmen', *South African Journal of Philosophy*, Vol. 28, No. 4, pp. 433–46.

Viveiros de Castro, E. (2012), 'Cosmologies: Perspectivism', in *Cosmological Perspectivism in Amazonia and Elsewhere*, Vol. 1, Manchester: HAU Network of Ethnographic Theory, pp. 45–168.

Chapter 3

The Oedipal Animal? Companion Species and Becoming

Joanna Bednarek

Deleuze and Guattari's philosophy is generally (and duly) regarded as a theory that, unlike many twentieth-century philosophical systems, removes 'man' in his various guises (as phenomenological pure consciousness, *Dasein* or Lacanian subject)[1] from the centre of its ontology. Because of this it was granted the status of a thought capable of helping us get beyond anthropocentrism (Braidotti 2006; Haraway 2008). Those aspects of Deleuze and Guattari's theory that are praised for their non-anthropocentric qualities are mostly the general traits of their ontology. The category of immanence/a life abolishes divisions used in attempts at the classification of beings: organic vs inorganic, biological vs cultural, animal vs human. Forms of organisation of being, such as strata or the molar and the molecular dimensions, are present in all kinds of beings: inorganic, organic as well as social/cultural. There is no place for the specificity of the human world – the social, consciousness or the subject – or for its elevation to the role of the agency endowing being with meaning. This makes Deleuze and Guattari's ontology a basis for the development of such theoretical endeavours as posthuman theory and the new materialism (Dolphijn and van der Tuin 2012).

The Deleuzian perspective also makes an important contribution to animal studies; it helps us to overcome the difficulties faced by this discipline, such as its tendency to remain too close to animal rights discourse with its liberal, Oedipal vision of the subject, which results in thinking about nonhuman others in terms of validating them by proving that animals, too, can think or feel (Wolfe 2003: 169). Deleuzian analyses of animality concentrate not on nonhuman animals regarded statically, in isolation, but on nonhuman forces present in different forms of organisation of organic and non-organic life (Grosz 2011; Lingis 2003; Massumi 2014). At stake in these analyses is the invention of practices that allow us to dismantle the human standard of subjectivity and come into contact with ahuman forms of organisation that constitute us and go beyond us: to find 'escape routes from humanism' (MacCormack 2014: 2).

On the other hand, certain elements of Deleuze and Guattari's theory – precisely those concerning the practices mentioned – are disturbingly anthropocentric (and androcentric as well); among them the most visible, and triggering the most severe critique, seems to be the notion of becoming (Haraway 2008; Jardine 1984; Shukin 2000). For this reason I have decided to approach the question of Deleuze and Guattari's anthropocentrism from the perspective of becoming. It is crucial to do so, because this is the point in their *oeuvre* at which the danger of treating nonhuman nature as a means for human ends, overcome at the level of ontology, threatens to return.

I will thus reconstruct the notion of becoming-animal in order to identify the elements responsible for its anthropocentric dimension. This also means that the second issue important to me will be Deleuze and Guattari's view of domestic animals – the fact that all the passing remarks on domestic animals, especially dogs, that appear in *A Thousand Plateaus* are consistently scornful and negative, and that this is not merely a question of rhetoric. They figure in two contexts: the first is the critique of psychoanalysis, in the 'One or Several Wolves?' plateau, where the dog, associated with Freud, Oedipality, castration, the molar dimension and so on, is the opposite of the wolf (molecular dimension, multiplicity, field of impersonal affects). The dog, as 'Oedipal animal par excellence' (Deleuze and Guattari 1986: 15), embodies all the traits regarded as undesirable in humans as well as nonhumans:

> Freud knew nothing about wolves, or anuses for that matter. The only thing Freud understood was what a dog is, and a dog's tail . . . Who is ignorant of the fact that wolves travel in packs? Only Freud. Every child knows it . . . Freud only knows the Oedipalised wolf or dog, the castrated-castrating daddy-wolf, the dog in the kennel, the analyst's bow-wow. (Deleuze and Guattari 2008b: 30, 32)

The second context in which dogs appear is the question of becoming (the 'Becoming-Intense, Becoming-Animal, Becoming-Imperceptible' plateau); here, the domestic animals (dogs among them) are again classified as Oedipal animals and contrasted with demonic animals, the ones connected with becoming: 'Are there Oedipal animals, with which one can "play Oedipus," play family, my little dog, my little cat, and then other animals that by contrast draw us into an irresistible becoming?' (2008b: 257). We should of course note that the examples mentioned above don't have to refer at all to empirical dogs or wolves. Wolves are the central element of the Wolf-Man's desiring assemblage; animals of becoming and of Oedipal regression can be empirical or not – depending on the role assigned to them by the human – even when 'inhuman' – desire. The negative attitude towards dogs and cats touches here only on the cultural meanings associated with them; the role fulfilled by actual animals depends on the case, that is, on the way they function in the assemblage. That's why our authors grant even the Oedipal animals the privilege of being able to gain the status of 'demonic' animals of becoming: 'Can the same animal be taken up by two opposing functions and movements, depending on the case? . . . it is . . . possible for any animal to be treated in the mode of a pack or a swarm . . . Even the cat, even the dog' (2008b: 258, 266).

We may thus say that Deleuze and Guattari are never 'against' real cats or dogs, but only against certain human modes of relating to them (Massumi 2014: 116). Any animal, cats and dogs included, can function in the mode of a pack or a swarm (Williams 2009: 51). But this, in my opinion, is not enough. The very distinction between the Oedipal and demonic mode is problematic and indicates the existence of certain difficulties inherent to the notion of becoming.

Becoming-animal: Flight From the Ordinary?

First, we have to answer the question: what is becoming? Who, or what, becomes, or, how do we identify the subject of becoming? As we will see, these questions have profound consequences for the status of animals in becoming-animal. The notion of becoming is eleborated most fully in the 'Becoming-Intense, Becoming-Animal, Becoming-Imperceptible' plateau in A Thousand Plateaus. In the course of developing this concept, Deleuze and Guattari undertake an intervention into the interpretations of evolutionary theory, structural anthropology and Jung's theory of archetypes (among others). Here, I reconstruct only the basic structure of becoming, at the price of losing some of the complexity and richness of the category.

A provisional definition would thus be the following: becoming is the process of intense, experimental transformation taking place in the (impersonal) unconscious. Although it always exceeds rational calculations, it may be initiated by conscious decision (as in becoming that takes place in artistic creation) or may be entirely independent of the conscious, rational will, as in processes triggered by social or political forces or by erotic encounters. The transformation that takes place is always a flight from established identity – especially from its Oedipal components. It takes the subject beyond limits of the structures that constituted it – it displaces and puts into movement our identifications, phantasmatic and symbolic structurations or previous libidinal cathexes (Deleuze and Guattari 2008a: 1–9). Because the unconscious is, according to Deleuze and Guattari, impersonal and structured primarily not by the logic of the signifier (as in Lacan), but by the machinic processes of flows and cuts of desiring production (Deleuze and Guattari 2008a: 3; Buchanan 2008: 21–5, 95), becoming as the process of dismantling Oedipal structures brings the subject into contact with the material forces that underlie and condition its functioning.

As becoming is the process of the deterritorialisation (or dis-identification) of the subject, it seems to be a process that only a human being can undergo – it needs a human, Oedipally structured subject in the first place, as its departure point. Which leads us to the question: can an animal be the subject of becoming? Or can it only function as the means or medium of becoming for a human subject? Donna Haraway's critique of becoming-animal in *When Species Meet* addresses precisely this issue. Both contexts of the appearance of dogs – the critique of psychoanalysis and the question of becoming – in Deleuze and Guattari's *oeuvre* are important for Haraway's critique (although she concentrates explicitly only on the fragments concerned with becoming-animal). Although, in her words, the two authors try very hard to get beyond the Great Divide between humans and other animals, they end up with nothing other than a version of anthropocentric theory, distinguished merely by the abundant use of animal imagery – metaphors, literary tropes or symbols – for purely 'human' purposes. There is no concern for real, empirical, 'molar' nonhuman animals in all their diverse characteristics in Deleuze and Guattari. As Haraway states with regard to the way they deal with the bonds between humans and domestic animals:

> Here I find little but the two writers' scorn for all that is mundane and ordinary and the profound absence of curiosity about or respect for and with actual animals . . . Derrida's actual little cat is decidedly not invited into this encounter . . . No reading strategies can mute the scorn for the homely and the ordinary in this book. (2008: 27–8, 29)

The opposition of dog and wolf in *A Thousand Plateaus* is, according to Haraway, a 'symptomatic morass for how not to take earthly animals – wild or domestic – seriously' (2008: 29). What is more, as the author of *When Species Meet* notes, this opposition succumbs to the rather conventional 'call of the wild' theme: domestic, tame animals are a metaphor for Oedipal subjectivity, whereas wild animals (wolves in particular) are a metaphor for becoming, molecular sexuality and the multiplicity of affects. The way Deleuze and Guattari regard dogs might be treated as an example of the 'fear of the familiar' (Baker 2000: 166) displayed by poststructural thought in addressing animals. This has, of course, nothing to do with either actual, empirical dogs or wolves, or the way they are inserted in naturecultures. This reliance on the traditional opposition of nature and culture (domestication as the way of making an animal a part of the human world) is all the more disappointing and strange because it is precisely this distinction that is being abolished by Deleuze and Guattari's concepts of the machinic and the strata. The division of being into natural and artificial, the distinction between organic and mechanic totality, and, what is most important for us here, the distinction between living being uncontaminated by human intervention and one transformed or produced with the aim of meeting human needs – all become disassembled in Deleuzo-Guattarian ontology. Unfortunately, the last of them sneaks back in with the dog-wolf opposition.

Of course, as Charles J. Stivale and Alain Beaulieu observe, this critique leaves much to be desired (Stivale 2014; Beaulieu 2011). It is based on a very fragmentary reading of Deleuze and Guattari and as such may appear quite unsubstantiated. But I'm not sure if referring to the broader context of these infortunate remarks on dogs and their humans can simply cancel them out, as both authors seem to state. Haraway's critique, though obviously biased and unfavourable to its subject, can nevertheless help us see becoming in a different light (which distinguishes it from critical statements based on projections and insinuations) (Iveson 2013; Vitamvor 2009). It is worth mentioning here that the source of her bias is the fact that she has different premises and priorities than the authors of *A Thousand Plateaus*. At least as important in the field of critical animal studies and posthuman theory as Deleuze and Guattari, Haraway introduced an interdisciplinary theory combining the insights of biology, science studies and feminist theory. Her empirical analyses of the development of primatology (Haraway 1989) or the impact of technoscience on our lives (Haraway 1997), carried out using concepts such as naturecultures and co-evolution, are key lessons in non-anthropocentric thinking – definitely less philosophical than Deleuze and Guattari's, but more attuned to the particularities of connections between different beings (Vanderwees 2009). I think this perspective is valid in itself and needs to be introduced, at least partially, into Deleuzian analyses of (human and nonhuman) animality.

This is not to say that paying attention to 'real' animals must in itself result in increased sensitivity about the way we treat them. As Zipporah Weissberg proves, Haraway's approach 'reveals disturbing collusion with the very structures of domination she purports to oppose' (2009: 23), which is evident in the rather tolerant way she approaches the question of laboratory animals' status or the disciplinary practices that dogs are subjected to. Nevertheless, her conceptual interventions allow us to question these solutions, as well as those provided by Deleuze and Guattari.

Haraway makes two serious charges against the authors of *Capitalism and Schizophrenia*: 1) they despise the ordinary; 2) they are not interested in real animals.

The first charge, although to some extent justified by the particular fragments of the text to which Haraway refers, can nevertheless be refuted if we look at the totality of their work. The distinction between the ordinary and the transgressive, although we could say Deleuze and Guattari make use of it to some degree, is complicated and ambiguous. First of all, the distinction between the territorialised and the deterritorialised is not the same as the distinction between ordinary and extraordinary in the common sense of the terms. All activity, human and nonhuman alike, of species and societies as well as individuals, is a kind of balancing or oscillating between movements of territorialisation and deterritorialisation, creating a territory and leaving it. Which one prevails in the activity of a particular being at any particular moment is a question of the composition of its forces. Territory brings beings into existence and provides them with the necessary basis; deterritorialisation changes the mode of this existence and transforms a previously established identity. A being (or more precisely an assemblage underlying it) is composed of lines responsible for the tendency towards territorialisation or deterritorialisation. Generally, molar or segmentary lines are responsible for reterritorialisation, whereas with lines of flight – for deterritorialisation – the role of molecular or supple lines is more ambiguous, as they underlie molar segments and displace their rigid boundaries. Each assemblage – human naturalcultural practice, for instance – is consequently a composition of various lines; its 'normality' (conformity to a majoritarian, segmentary standard) is simultaneously both constituted and undermined by molecular lines and constantly (although to a different extent), carried away by lines of flight.

The way Deleuze and Guattari approach the question of experiments in deterritorialisation in the 'How Do You Make Yourself a Body Without Organs?' plateau is testimony to the complexity of the problem of the normal and the extraordinary. Experiments with sexuality, identity, perception (for example, experiments with drugs) can be an opportunity for constructing a BwO, but in themselves they don't guarantee a positive outcome of the process. Ostensibly transgressive practices can be reterritorialised and reduced to the role of a distraction (the sad fate of many experiments and extremities in capitalism). The most radical deterritorialisation, on the other hand, amounts to simple destruction. That's why genuine experiment requires an art of caution. It consists not in what happens on the molar level, but in molecular displacements and in the liberation of a line of flight in a way that won't be destructive for the organism. As the two philosophers say, what is important is to 'reach the point where "to get high or not to get high" is no longer the question' (Deleuze and Guattari 2008b: 315). Deleuze and Guattari are not the prophets of Bataillean-style transgression; their ultimate conclusion would rather be that the difference between the apparently extraordinary and the apparently ordinary can be misleading; for these are molar differences, and what defines the experiment are the molecular differences, the movements, the affects involved.

The account of territorialisation from the beginning of the 'Of the Refrain' plateau can also serve as testimony against Deleuze and Guattari's alleged disregard for the ordinary. The descriptions of the gesture of creating a territory as the basis for the development of the everyday activity of people and other animals carry within themselves a sense of the importance of this crucial, though most elementary and ordinary, gesture. Spatial or sonic territory, the minimum of order, is necessary for all further processes – deterritorialisations, reterritorialisations – to take place. This simple gesture also contains the minimal internal difference required for it to be creatively plastic and dynamic. Because of that it constitutes, as Brian Massumi notes (when analysing animal play), the origin of art, language and politics (2014: 8–25).

Deleuze and Guattari are thus quite sensitive to the experimental molecular dimension of ordinary, everyday practices. So, we may ask, why do they appear to be so insensitive when it comes to domestic animals and people's relations with them, and start to employ conventional oppositions like wild vs domestic? We could of course say that this opposition is only rhetorical and has no intrinsic philosophical content; in other words, that it is not an outcome of conceptual invention. We can limit our analysis to the purely philosophical, abstract problems of de- and reterritorialisation and cast aside the animal imagery. Deleuze and Guattari would thus be guilty merely of employing bad rhetoric. But my thesis here is that there is a connection between all these rhetorical equations (dog–Oedipus–psychoanalysis) or oppositions (dog–wolf) and the internal limitations of the two authors' account of becoming. The way they approach this conventional distinction is a symptom of their general carelessness towards the problem of human–animal relations; they seem not to be concerned with the problem of the real existence of an agency different than the human agency.

Three Kinds of Animals and Their Relation to Becoming

The 'Becoming-Intense ...' plateau introduces us to three kinds of animals. Animals of the first kind are personal and familial; they function (or, more importantly, make *us* function) in the realm of Oedipal affects. They are

> individuated animals, sentimental, Oedipal animals, each with its own petty history, 'my' cat, 'my' dog. These animals invite us to regress, draw us into narcissistic contemplation, and they are the only kind of animal psychoanalysis understands, the better to discover a daddy, a mommy, a little brother behind them (when psychoanalysis talks about animals, animals learn to laugh); anyone who likes cats or dogs is a fool. (Deleuze and Guattari 2008b: 265)

Oedipal animals make us 'play Oedipus' (257) – mock, and at the same time extend and enforce Oedipal patterns of subjectivity.[2] The second kind of animal, State animals (symbolic, mythical, archetypal ones), are of no great interest for us here – although later we will see their shadow suddenly emerging in a dimension where they are least expected. Finally, the third kind of animals are demonic animals: 'pack or affect animals, that form a multiplicity, a becoming, a population, a tale ...' (265) – animals we enter into becoming with, the only ones worth 'our' consideration. (We should notice the limited perspective: what is continually at stake is once again 'our' – human – becoming). What is the status of these demonic animals, animals of becoming?

First of all, they are never individual, always a multiplicity, that is, a pack: 'a troop of monkeys, a school of fish ... We do not become animal without a fascination for the pack, the multiplicity' (2008b: 264). Deleuze and Guattari underline that their notion of the pack doesn't bear affiliations with the biological notion of the molar animal pack: 'We do not wish to say that certain animals live in packs' (264). This means that a pack has nothing to do with filiation, or biological descent (266), as it multiplies by means of contagion and not sexual reproduction. Another aspect of the disconnection with biological discourse is Deleuze and Guattari's critique of Konrad Lorenz's view of the pack as, in his evolutionary hierarchy, the lower state of socialisation. The pack is not a social structure organising the lives of molar, empirical animals or humans, but the point at which 'the human being encounters the animal' (264). To become is, for both the human and the animal, to become molecularly many, a multiplicity. Or, to be more precise: becoming means for a human to become many by contact with the molecular animal pack. Deleuze and Guattari have good reason to distance themselves from biology and ethology here (at least from Lorenz's version of it); but this strategy also entails a distancing from the biological concept of the pack altogether. This has serious consequences: it means that there can be no connection between the molar and the molecular animal pack. We should bear in mind that the strategy is by no means something general in Deleuze and Guattari: in the 'Of the Refrain' plateau, for example, the discourse of biology and its findings on the practices of territory marking by animals (mostly birds) is a crucial part of their argument.

Deleuze and Guattari also want to differentiate becoming as production from imitation by means of analogy and structural resemblance. The unplanned outcome is again the introduction of an opposition between the demonic animal and the molar animal: 'do not look for a resemblance or analogy to the animal, for this is becoming-animal in action, the production of the molecular animal (whereas the "real" animal is trapped in its molar form and subjectivity' (2008b: 303). What is important for our argument is that only the third kind of animals, demonic animals, are a proper part of becoming. Equally crucial is that only the becoming is real; the animal one becomes doesn't have to be: 'The becoming-animal of the human being is real, even if the animal the human being becomes is not; and the becoming other of the animal is real, even if that something other it becomes is not' (262).

Becoming-animal involves neither imitating nor entering into a relationship with some molar, actual animal (although it may, we can speculate, also mean that, but purely accidentally – an encounter with an empirical animal is neither necessary nor sufficient). The essence of the process, as the two authors describe it, is the production of a molecular animal (just like becoming-woman means to emit molecules of femininity, not to impersonate molar woman). From the perspective of one term of becoming the process is thus quite clear: a molar human being enters (or is carried away by) the process of becoming and is transformed, becomes a molecular animal that is being produced in the becoming. But what happens to the second term, the animal? Deleuze and Guattari stress that in becoming both engaged terms are transformed – if so, what does it mean if the animal that is being transformed is a molecular one? Can a molar animal be at the same time a molecular one? Is there a molar animal in becoming? And, can an Oedipal animal really be at the same time an animal of becoming, as our authors state? (2008b: 258). The answers to all these questions require a reconstruction of the structure of becoming.

Becoming – human, all too human?

Becoming is a kind of deterritorialisation; what then are the laws governing deterritorialisation? The most interesting from my perspective will be five chosen theorems (1, 3, 5, 6 and 7) of simple and double deterritorialisation (I omit theorems 2, 4 and 8, although they perform an important function in the reconstruction of deterritorialisation, because I view this function as mostly intermediary or not relevant for my line of argumentation):

Simple deterritoralisation ('Year Zero: Faciality' plateau, 2008b: 193–4):

Theorem 1: one never deterritorialises alone; there are always at least two terms ... And each of the two terms reterritorialises on the other ... Thus there is an entire system of horizontal and complementary reterritorialisations ... [first system]

Theorem 3: the *least* deterritoralised [element] reterritorialises on the *most* deterritorialised. This is where the second system of reterritorialisation comes in, the vertical system running from bottom to top [second system].

Double deterritorialisation (becoming) ('Becoming-Intense ...' plateau, 2008b: 338):

Theorem 5: deterritorialisation is always double, because it implies the co-existence of a major variable and a minor variable in simultaneous becoming (the two terms of a becoming do not exchange places, there is no identification between them, they are instead drawn into an asymmetrical block in which both change to the same extent and which constitutes their zone of proximity).

Theorem 6: in non-symmetrical double deterritorialisation it is possible to assign a deterritorialising force and a deterritorialised force, even if the same force switches from one value to the other depending on the 'moment' or aspect considered; furthermore, it is the least deterritorialised element that triggers the deterritorialisation of the most deterritorialising element ...

Theorem 7: the deterritorialising element has the relative role of expression, and the deterritorialised element the relative role of content . . .

We can see that theorems 5 and 6 repeat and confirm to a significant extent the prescriptions of theorems 1 and 3, although on the level of increased complexity and precision. Becoming functions within two systems: a horizontal one and a vertical one. The horizontal system merely prescribes the *existence* of two terms, whereas the vertical system assigns different *functions* to them. In simple deterritorialisation, differentiation of functions occurs in theorem 3, which introduces the vertical system; but in double deterritorialisation, at the more advanced and complex level of deterritorialisation that constitutes becoming, differentiation takes place as early as in the first system. This is possible because the terms are not deemed to reterritorialise each other, as in the case of simple deterritorialisation. Note that theorem 1 is the only place where Deleuze and Guattari don't take into account the specification of functions of the two terms and its elements (other fragments of *A Thousand Plateaus* that offer a different, less hierarchical vision of becoming will be dealt with later). In becoming-animal, we can thus assume that 'Man' is the term containing the least deterritorialised element, and 'animal' the term containing the most deterritorialising element; the relation between these elements is, according to theorem 7, identical with the relation of content and expression.

The block of becoming is thus structured in the following way:

Subject	Medium
Major variable	Minor variable
Least deterritoralised element	Most deterritorialising element
Content	Expression
(Man)	(animal)

The consequence of these theorems is not only the asymmetry, but also the hierarchy involved in each becoming. Two terms together forming a block of becoming have different functions: the subject and the medium, with the function of the medium clearly taking a subordinate role within the whole process. Although the medium is of course indispensable, it functions only as a tool, an instrument of becoming. Its becoming is secondary and instrumental: its essence is to enable the subject to become.

The hierarchical nature of the structure of becoming comes to light with exceptional clarity in the case of becoming-woman. It is primarily man who becomes woman, but, as Deleuze and Guattari add with their quasi-egalitarian, 'add women and stir' approach, women also can, and even must, become women (2008b: 304). They seem to imply by this that women also have a molar, universally human/masculine subjectivity that they have to abandon. This alone is questionable, if not in the light of numerous feminist attempts to demonstrate the specificity of woman's symbolic position as 'other' in phallogocentric culture (de Beauvoir 1972; Braidotti 1991; Irigaray 1985), then in the light of Deleuze and Guattari's own assumptions of the existence of the hierarchy of the major standard and minor deviations from it (2008b: 320–3). The trouble with becoming-woman is even more significant because of what Deleuze and Guattari exactly say on the topic (the second part of this sentence is often omitted): 'the woman as a molar entity has to become-woman in order that the man also becomes- or can become-woman' (2008b: 304).

The one and ultimate goal of becoming is set as the becoming-woman of its subject (symbolically male). Women's politics, termed 'molar', is not a part of the process of becoming. However, such a designation seem to be arbitrary: can't there be a molecular women's politics, a women's micropolitics? The answer appears to be 'no'. Women's politics, as a necessarily molar, majoritarian enterprise, has nothing to do with becoming-woman; as Deleuze and Guattari remark, it can even be dangerous, limiting the opportunity of Man/men to become-woman: 'The song of life is often intoned by the driest of women, moved by *ressentiment*, the will to power and cold mothering' (2008b: 304). Molecular woman can only be a product of the second term of becoming, whose subject is symbolically male. There is no special need for empirical, molar women in becoming-woman (not to mention feminists). It follows as much from our authors' personal prejudices as from the abstract structure of becoming instituted in theorems 2–6, in which the medium is necessarily subordinated to the subject and has no autonomous molar existence. Only theorem 1, the most basic one, that founds the first system of deterritorialisation, avoids establishing this hierarchy.

The animal in becoming is, as the starting point, molar being – but understood not as a particular individual, but as an abstraction, an animal of a given species in general, an animal-form (maybe a kind of State animal), that is to dissolve gradually in the process of becoming. The existence of this molar animal that is to become-other is rather spectral; it has no grounding in an individual molar body. This is the way both terms become something other; becomings can thus be described as 'rapid acts by which a human becomes animal at the same time as

the animal becomes . . . (Becomes what? Human, or something else?)'
(2008b: 262).

The molar animal can only become-animal in order that the man can
become-animal . . . and if, as an animal-form, it becomes something
other, this other and its becoming is still subordinated to the subject's
becoming. Or, what amounts to the same, animal becomes-human – but
only in the sense of a reterritorialisation of the major term. If an animal
became human in a sense other than this reterritorialisation, becoming
would be reciprocal, though still asymmetrical, and this is what Deleuze
and Guattari don't want to allow here. Moreover, the animal can only
be reterritorialised as a 'human' animal, the property (in both senses of
the word) of Man.

What exactly is the status of Ahab's white whale or D. H. Lawrence's
tortoise, or the Wolf-Man's pack of wolves? They are all 'molecular
animals' – remember, becoming-animal means producing a molecular
animal. Doesn't becoming in general mean freeing molecular dimensions
and setting molecules into movement by a line of flight towards absolute
deterritorialisation as a limit that can't be reached? And are the terms of
becoming not mostly abstract categories, bearing only contingent reference to bodies or individuals? Yes, but becoming does affect a molar
being that enters into a becoming: this being starts to produce molecular
affects and follows a line of flight. If a molar being enters into becoming-
animal, it can only enter it as the subject, that is, Man – understood not
only as Man-form, but also as a particular human being, an individual
undertaking the experiment: 'In a way, the subject in becoming is always
"man," but only when he enters a becoming-minoritarian that rends
him from his major identity' (Deleuze and Guattari 2008b: 321).

The molar animal, on the other hand, can only appear as a form
which doesn't have autonomous existence. The essential, not only contingent or optional, feature of molecular animals is their lack of connection with molar (actual, empirical) animals. Being molecular, affectual
animals, they can't have a molar dimension other than the molar human
being that is the subject of becoming; their molar body can only be a
human body, entering into becoming and emitting molecules of animality. One can even risk the statement that demonic animals can be so
unfamiliar, completely other (having nothing to do with molar wolves,
tortoises, dogs and so on), because they sometimes tend to be imaginary in the worst meaning of the term. Their constitution takes place
between the realm of State animals (abstract forms and symbols) and the
realm of molecules of animality, both rigorously disconnected from any
molar individual animal and connected with molar individual human

being. The ultimate conclusion then, would be that in becoming-animal, demonic animals don't have to be real, but in addition that they can't be real.

Why is this the case? Because it is only the human that can give pure expression to the natural force of deterritorialisation, can take it to its absolute limit. This is, we may say, a uniquely human task. Humans can effectuate absolute deterritorialisation, whereas animal deterritorialisation is always merely relative (Massumi 2014: 56–8). Becoming-animal requires the subtraction of the molar, real animal, because 'it subtracts the actual animal in play in nature, in order to put the very nature of the animal into play' (Massumi 2014: 63). The stake of the Deleuzian anthropocentric endeavour is to tap into inhuman forces and take them to the limit; and it is effectuated by activities traditionally considered to be the most prestigious and sublime, mostly by writing (Massumi 2014: 59; Colebrook 2014). It's a different type of human exceptionalism than the one we are accustomed to, but in the end it is yet another example of the narrative about something that only humans can do – this time it is not simply art (because animals can make art too), but absolute deterritorialisation.

What Can We Do to Transform the Notion of Becoming into 'Becoming With?'

Becoming-animal in its primary, orthodox version doesn't allow its terms to enter into any relation other than a functional and hierarchical one; moreover, the only agency necessary and sufficient for becoming is human being. Becoming-animal is therefore hardly the ideal notion allowing for a reformulation of human-animal relations in a direction leading from anthropocentrism towards different approaches to agency and subjectivity. 'Animal' in becoming is entirely a human product, a means to human ends (the fact that these ends involve bringing natural deterritorialisation to its limit changes little). Assuming our goal is to change the anthropocentric angle of thought and social practice and the prevailing view of human-animal relations as subject-object or means-end relations, is there anything we could do with the concept of becoming so that it serves this goal?

One possibility would be to apply unchanged the category of becoming to molar subjects other than that of standard or majoritarian Man – to place women/children/ animals in the position of the subject/major variable, and in consequence to allow their agency. Deleuze and Guattari themselves provide us with examples of becoming from the plant and animal kingdom in the 'Rhizome' plateau: a wasp-orchid becoming and *a* 'becoming-baboon of the cat' (Deleuze and Guattari 2008b: 11). In the first case, certain species of orchids imitate the appearance and sexual pheromones of the female wasp; the male wasp 'copulates' with the flower and then transports its pollen to another flower, enabling reproduction of the orchids. In the second, a virus moving from one host (baboon) to another (cat), carries within itself the genetic information of the previous host. The most striking thing in these examples is their difference from the model of becoming prescribed by theorems 4–7.

First, becomings from the 'Rhizome' plateau involve two distinct entities – both are 'real' on the molar level and both undergo in-depth changes in their molar being and functioning. Second, becoming is described as asymmetrical, but engages both terms in the same way and to the same extent: 'becoming-wasp of the orchid and a becoming-orchid of the wasp' (Deleuze and Guattari 2008b: 11). The wasp-orchid example is more interesting from our point of view: its structure doesn't show the signs of asymmetry and instrumentality seen in the case of becoming-animal and becoming-woman:

> The orchid deterritorialises by forming an image, a tracing of a wasp; but the wasp reterritorialises on that image. The wasp is nevertheless deterritorialised, becoming a piece in the orchid's reproductive apparatus. But it reterritorialises the orchid by transporting its pollen. (2008b: 11)

Both terms deterritorialise and reterritorialise each other; both undergo transformation, both are infected with the other's affects and intensities – though the way of becoming is not the same for both. The orchid deterritorialises itself in order to make the wasp part of its own reproductive apparatus – and therefore, eventually, reterritorialises itself (the instrumentalisation of the wasp by the orchid is not connected with becoming-other, but with reterritorialisation). The wasp's reterritorialisation, enabled by the becoming-wasp of the orchid, is more complicated. The wasp's sexual behaviour, unconnected to reproduction, is as much deterritorialised as reterritorialised. We cannot say, however, that the wasp is merely a means for the orchid's becoming.

The case of the cat and the baboon is different from the previous example and bears more similarity to becoming-other. The cat becomes baboon as the 'major' term, by being deterritorialised, and the baboon becomes cat as a 'minor' term (the reterritorialised one):

cat	baboon
Deterritorialised	Deterritorialising

Major term   Minor term
Content   Expression

The structure of becoming is the same in 'Rhizome' as in 'Becoming-Intense . . .' – one entity assumes the role of the major, the other of the minor term. The only real difference is that both terms have an autonomous molar dimension that undergoes transformation.

What is the origin of these differences? One may have the impression that the specification of functions starts to signify a loss of molar existence of the minor term when Man as a majoritarian standard is established as one of the terms of becoming. It seems that even in the process of losing his identity he subordinates the whole process to his needs and causes the major term to lose its molar reality and autonomy. The structure of becoming assigns to its variables mutually exclusive roles of deterritorialising and deterritorialised force; when applied to 'Man' and 'animal' it can only effectuate total subordination of the goals (and the very being of the latter) to the goals and being of the former.

The notion of becoming doesn't provide the ground for thinking human-animal relations as asymmetrical but reciprocal, mutually enriching and transforming deterritorialisation. Would it then be possible to modify the structure of the concept of becoming itself, so that becoming entails two subjects, engaged in asymmetrical but reciprocal experiments with identity – that is, to transform becoming into *becoming-with*? The term is Donna Haraway's invention and refers to the way living creatures (or, in her words, *critters*) function on a daily basis. This, as we have seen, entails deterritorialisation; but maybe it would be good to abandon the distinction between the relative and the absolute, or between deterritorialisation in general and becoming? The existence of a living being, as well as its identity, would thus always be the outcome of the interaction and intersection of multiple forces, identified both on a temporal and on a spatial axis. What is more, it would entail constant transformation – deterritorialisation – stemming from the complexity of day-to-day interaction of multiple evolutionary, social and technical factors, referred to as naturecultures. Becoming would present itself as less experimental, more ordinary, an almost daily matter, more entangled in social and technical contexts; it is therefore, from the structural point of view, closer to simple deterritorialisation. As Haraway says, 'to be one is always to become with many' (2008: 4). Or, as Massumi states, becoming 'doesn't sweep up one without sweeping up at least two. It marks an instantaneous transformation-in-place that is immediately transindividual in nature' (2014: 42).

The elements of a similar approach to becoming can be traced in Deleuze and Guattari's writings, although the theorems of becoming that define the notion seem to contradict it. The wasp-orchid example from 'Rhizome' indicates, unequivocally, that becoming can be something other than the existential quest of Man. This will demand modifications directed at the structure of becoming. (What follows is, of course, only a preliminary sketch – I don't intend to offer a full theory of becoming-with or non-hierarchical becoming).

The first step would be to reduce the notion of becoming to its most basic features – one should eliminate theorems 3, 5 and 6, because they prevent double deterritorialisation from being the reciprocal, mutual, non-hierarchical transformation of two terms or variables. We should also focus on the molar dimension of the minor terms of becoming (this applies to becoming-animal, as well as to becoming-woman, child, and so on). This is important because it is the molar dimension of both terms that is always affected by molar modifications and the line of flight of becoming – and our goal would be to elaborate, with regard to assemblages that enter becoming, how exactly it happens. Three lines of an assemblage should thus be viewed as intertwined – entangled, as Haraway would say. It is important to take a close look at molar segments (of species in the case of becoming-animal) to see if they don't contain unexpected molecular transformations; in other words, how might humans and animals function in naturecultures and what molecular transformations are responsible for the dynamics of these naturecultures?

In *Kafka: Toward a Minor Literature*, Deleuze and Guattari mention briefly (more in the context of writing than molar animals) the 'becoming-dog of the man and the becoming-man of the dog' (Deleuze and Guattari 1986: 22). This is exactly what happened to dog and human – for better or for worse. From this perspective, we can regard the supposedly Oedipal domestic dog (*Canis lupus familiaris*), due to its co-evolution (Haraway 2003) with *Homo sapiens*, as the most deterritorialised of the *Canidae* family. In order to back up this statement, I will present some brief remarks on the social behaviour of dogs. I think it's important to descend to the level of such literalities, as they will help us see that our relations with dogs are not all about Oedipality. Among the genera and species that are the members of the *Canidae* family one can identify various types of pack structure. For example, Ethiopian wolves hunt alone, but form packs in order to defend their territory; the groups usually consist of related males (who stay in the pack they were born into) and unrelated females, migrating between packs (Sillero-Zubili and Marino 2004).

The wolf pack appears in this context as the least interesting example of pack structure, because it is nothing other than a nuclear family, consisting of breeding ('alpha') pairs and their offspring (Ursula LeGuin's *The Wife's Story*, in a reversal of the werewolf theme, confirms this in a brilliant way (LeGuin 2005)). There are exceptions to this rule, as there have existed packs with more alpha pairs and more 'families', but they are quite rare (Mech 1999).[3] This seems unrelated to the notorious status of the wolf pack in Deleuze and Guattari, as the latter refers more to the schizoanalytic reinterpretation of the Wolf-Man case (Deleuze and Guattari 2008b: 29–44) than to the actual social behaviour of the molar animal species – although it may be noticed that the example raises at least some associations with the animals mentioned and because of this the connection is somewhat unfortunate. Packs of molar wolves, in contrast to the locust or the rat pack, do not provide a good illustration of a molecular, deterritorialising swarm.

The domestic dog and the grey wolf are genetically very closely related (Lindblad-Toh et al. 2005),[4] but it is a mistake to extrapolate the results of research into the wolf's social behaviour to explain a dog's social behaviour (Kubinyi et al. 2007; Kerkhove 2004).[5] Forty thousand years of co-evolution are responsible for the uniqueness of their social and communication skills. Dogs display greater ease in developing a preference for other species – not only humans, but rabbits or cats, as well as greater flexibility in social learning (Hare 2002; Kubinyi et al. 2007; Smuts 2006).[6] 'They are able to learn from (members of) another species and do so without food or any other causal reinforcement, even in cases where the goal or the result of the action is not clear'; in addition, 'some evidence has been obtained that dogs could be capable of using a human behavior action as a cue for showing a functionally similar behavior ... and follow social rules in the context of interacting with humans' (Kubinyi et al. 2007: 35–6).

We can't even say for sure whether dogs are pack animals, since there is no 'natural' state of their socialisation that could serve as a normative standard against which we could compare all the 'deviations' such as domesticity. Dog is the animal that became human, which means that its nature – more than the nature of other animal species – always was and is natureculture. Biologist Andrei Poyarkov, who has been doing research on Moscow's stray dogs since 1979, says that the dogs' adaptation to the urban environment caused specific changes in their behaviour and social organisation (Sternthal 2010). They form packs or live alone depending on the way they obtain food and the way they fit a naturalcultural territory dominated by humans. Guard dogs, casting their lot with human institutions such as hospitals or factories, are almost always solitary: 'Their territories tend to be garages, warehouses, hospitals and other fenced-in institutions, and they develop ties to the security guards from whom they receive food and whom they regard as masters' (Sternthal 2010).

Beggar dogs, whose source of food is compassionate humans, tend to live in small packs. Scavenging or hunting dogs also form packs, but it's impossible to compare them to the social structures created by canids that live in the state we are accustomed to call 'natural'. As Wendy van Kerkhove states, 'feral dogs do not exhibit the classic wolf-pack structure' (Kerkhove 2004). Dog packs are not the equivalent of wild canids' packs; they are not stable, lasting social structures. The packs usually gather around food resources; they disperse quickly, and the individuals often migrate between packs. Fights for dominance occur, but the dominance established usually doesn't last long; and there is no connection between hierarchy and kinship (the animals are usually unrelated) (Sternthal 2010).

Dogs don't function in the structures of kinship; they make connections. Their socialisation is based on alliance rather than on filiation. As Haraway demonstrates brilliantly in *The Companion Species Manifesto*, the relationships of dogs and people are not ones of imitation of Oedipal, familial ties, but ones of *significant otherness*: 'co-constitutive relationships in which none of the partners pre-exists the relating, and the relating is never done once and for all' (Haraway 2003: 12). Seen in this light, even the classical pet-keeping practice, viewed by Deleuze and Guattari as the epitome of familial territoriality, can appear in a different way. The inclusion of a dog as a family member, if it is serious, and not based on sentimental 'playing the family', effects more in a queering of the family than in reterritorialising the animal (Kuzniar 2006: 107–35).

Finally, I would like to invoke the following two singularities, individualised by name and the knot of molecular affects involved, which are taken from the long history of co-constitution taking place in naturecultures and which act as the proof of the complexity of this relationship. The story of Hachikō, an Akita dog who waited for his human significant other, Professor Ueno Hidesaburō, for ten years, is supposedly the most sentimental and Oedipal of all. But if we decide to look at it from a slightly changed perspective, focusing not on its tear-jerking qualities (responsible for two movies on Hachikō: one Japanese from 1987, the other American, from 2009), but on the affects involved, it may seem more interesting than it is conventionally perceived. It is surely a case of proverbial canine 'fidelity' – but we must remember that this fidelity is more a human construct than an actual trait of canine behaviour. Hachikō's story became very popular in pre-Second World War Japan, and the dog was elevated to the status of the symbol of loyalty (familial and national, first and foremost). The fact that the statue of Hachikō was erected in 1934, while he was still alive, is a clear signal of disregard for the actual, singular dog and his affects, and also for the personal bond between a human and a dog. But Hachikō's stubborn waiting, devoid of the symbolical layers thrust upon it, appears to be somewhat excessive and arouses uneasiness. He was only two years old when Professor Ueno died, so he had devoted the vast majority of his life to a futile waiting at the exit from the Shibuya metro station. What could it mean to reduce a whole life to the sole activity of waiting, at the same time contracted and endless? We cannot tell; but waiting definitely carried Hachikō beyond the limits of normality, whether defined as a standard for human or for canine subjectivity.

The second singularity I'd like to deal with was also celebrated with a monument – and also has connections with the metro; it is the story of Malchik, one of the stray dogs inhabiting the Moscow subway. They are a small minority of the general population of Moscow's free-ranging dogs, which numbers about 35,000, and are unique in their ability to adjust to this special naturalcultural milieu consisting of stations, trains and millions of commuters. According to dog behaviourist Andrei Neuronov, about twenty of them have been confirmed to actually travel:

> They orient themselves in a number of ways. They figure out where they are by smell, by recognising the name of the station from the recorded announcer's voice and by time intervals. If, for example, you come every Monday and feed a dog, that dog will know when it's Monday and the hour to expect you, based on their sense of time intervals from their biological clocks. (Sternthal 2010)

Malchik lived on Mendeleyevskaya station and treated it like his territory. In 2001, he was killed by Yulia Romanova, a model, who encountered him when going home with her pet dog. Malchik started to bark, defending his territory, and the woman pulled a knife out of her handbag and stabbed him to death. Though *metrodogs* meet with a range of different feelings, from abomination to affirmation (testimony of which is the webpage devoted to them: www.metrodog.ru), Malchik's death was met with general public outrage and Romanova was sentenced to one year of psychiatric treatment. His statue, now standing on Mendeleyevskaya station, was quickly funded from public donations.

The stories of Hachikō and Malchik definitely display a peculiar mix of cruelty and sentimentality present in our approach to domesticated animals, particularly dogs (Kuzniar 2006: 34, 101–3). But they don't exhaust all the affects that contribute to them. 'This is a story of bio-power and biosociality, as well as of technoscience' (Haraway 2003: 5), of abuse and Foucauldian *asujettissement,* but also of deterritorialisations and mutual transformations – always relative and followed by reterritorialisations, but no less radical for that. There's always something more: a queerness lurking behind Oedipal propriety. We may be blind to it, but that is our, not our dogs', failure.

Notes

1. I see the division between humanism and anti-humanism as secondary here; both humanist (existentialism) and anti-humanist (Lacanian psychoanalysis, Alain Badiou's ontology) theories state the necessity of an agency (whether it is called man, *Dasein,* or the subject is less important) organising and actualising being, fulfilling the role of its constitutive moment (often in the form of constitutive negativity – a cleavage, chasm or lack).
2. Deleuze and Guattari don't take into account the possibility that this kind of play may generate a subversion or displacement – in the manner of Judith Butler's displacement of the heterosexual matrix – of Oedipality. What would it mean to seriously include an animal in family structures? The real centre (unnoticed by the authors of *Capitalism and Schizophrenia*) of the issue of 'playing Oedipus' is that humans are almost always aware of the difference between this play and real (human) family relations and responsibilities. The average amount of time the animal stays with the family in the US is two years; dogs or cats are then, in most cases because of 'bad behaviour', removed to the animal shelter and killed (Palmer 2006).
3. This pack structure occurs also in other canids, for example black-backed jackals.
4. 'Grey wolf and dog are most closely related (0.04% and 0.21% sequence divergence in nuclear exon and intron sequences, respectively), followed by a close affiliation with the coyote, golden jackal and Ethiopian wolf, three species that can hybridize with dogs in the wild' (Lindblad-Toh et al. 2005: 815).
5. Such extrapolation was, as 'the dominance model of pet dog behaviour', popular in dog training discourse and practice from the 1960s until recently. It was not only based on erroneous extrapolation, but also on an incorrect interpretation of wolves' social behaviour (Ryan 2010).
6. This is, of course, not the whole story. Other research indicates that dogs are much worse than wolves at problem-solving tasks that involve learning from other members of their species (Range et al. 2015; Range and Viranyi 2014). This shows that co-evolution with humans involved an evolutionary trade-off: dogs may be better than wolves at reading human body language, but they fail when it comes to cooperating with each other. We may say their deterritorialisation from a previous wolves' form of life involved a reterritorialisation (an excessive one, maybe) on the human (Ward et al. 2008).

References

Baker, S. (2000), *The Postmodern Animal*, London: Reaktion Books.

Beaulieu, A. (2011), 'The Status of Animality in Deleuze's Thought', *Journal for Critical Animal Studies*, Vol. IX, Nos 1–2, pp. 69–88.

Braidotti, R. (1991), *Patterns of Dissonance: A Study of Women and Contemporary Philosophy*, Cambridge: Polity.

Braidotti, R. (2006), 'Posthuman, All Too Human: Towards a New Process Ontology', *Theory, Culture and Society*, Vol. 23, Nos 7–8, pp. 197–208.

Buchanan, I. (2008), *Deleuzism: A Metacommentary*, Durham, NC: Duke University Press.

Colebrook, C. (2014), 'Suicide for Animals', in P. MacCormack (ed.), *The Animal Catalyst: Towards Ahuman Theory*, London and New York: Bloomsbury, pp. 133–44.

de Beauvoir, S. (1972), *The Second Sex*, trans. H. M. Parshley, Harmondsworth: Penguin.

Deleuze, G. and F. Guattari (1986), *Kafka: Toward a Minor Literature*, trans. D. Polan, Minneapolis: University of Minnesota Press.

Deleuze, G. and F. Guattari (2008a), *Anti-Oedipus: Capitalism and Schizophrenia*, trans. R. Hurley, M. Seem and H. R. Lane, London and New York: Continuum.

Deleuze, G. and F. Guattari (2008b), *A Thousand Plateaus: Capitalism and Schizophrenia*, trans. B. Massumi, London and New York: Continuum.

Dolphijn, R. and I. van der Tuin (2012), *New Materialism: Interviews and Cartographies*, Ann Arbor: Open Humanities Press.

Grosz, E. (2011), *Becoming Undone: Darwinian Reflections on Life, Politics, and Art*, Durham, NC: Duke University Press.

Haraway, D. (1989), *Primate Visions: Gender, Race and Nature in the World of Modern Science*, New York and London: Routledge.

Haraway, D. (1997), *Modest_Witness@Second_ Millennium. FemaleMan_Meets_ OncoMouse™: Feminism and Technoscience*, New York: Routledge.

Haraway, D. (2003), *The Companion Species Manifesto*, Chicago: Prickly Paradigm Press.

Haraway, D. (2008), *When Species Meet*, Minneapolis: University of Minnesota Press.

Hare, B. et al. (2002), 'The Domestication of Social Cognition in Dogs', *Science*, Vol. 298, 22 November, pp. 1634–6.

Irigaray L. (1985), *Speculum of the Other Woman*, trans. G.C. Gill, Ithaca, NY: Cornell University Press.

Iveson, R. (2013), 'Deeply Ecological Deleuze and Guattari: Humanism's Becoming-animal', *Humanimalia*, Vol. 4, No. 2, pp. 34–53, at http://www.depauw.edu/humanimalia/issue%2008/index8.html (accessed 23 March 2016).

Jardine, A. (1984), 'Woman in Limbo: Deleuze and His (Br)others', *SubStance*, No. 44/45, pp. 46–60.

Kerepesi, A. et al. (2015), 'Dogs and Their Human Companions: The Effect of Familiarity on Dog–Human Interactions', *Behavioural Processes*, Vol. 110, January: *New Directions in Canine Behavior*, pp. 27–36.

Kerkhove W. van (2004), 'A Fresh Look at the Wolf-Pack Theory of Companion-Animal Dog Social Behavior', *Journal of Applied Animal Welfare Science*, Vol. 7, No. 4, pp. 279–85.

Kubinyi, E. et al. (2007), 'Comparative Social Cognition: From Wolf and Dog to Humans', *Comparative Social Cognition of Dogs*, Vol. 2, pp. 26–46.

Kuzniar, A. A. (2006), *Melancholia's Dog: Reflections on Our Animal Kinship*, Chicago: University of Chicago Press.

LeGuin, U. (2005), 'The Wife's Story', in *The Compass Rose*, New York and London: Harper Perennial.

Lindblad-Toh, K. et al. (2005), 'Genome Sequence, Comparative Analysis and Haplotype Structure of the Domestic Dog', *Nature*, Vol. 438, No. 8, December, pp. 803–19.

Lingis, A. (2003), 'Animal Body, Inhuman Face', in Cary Wolfe (ed.), *Zoontologies*, Minneapolis: University of Minnesota Press.

MacCormack, P. (2014), 'Introduction' to P. MacCormack (ed.), *The Animal Catalyst: Towards Ahuman Theory*, London and New York: Bloomsbury.

MacCormack, P. (2015), 'Art, Nature, Ethics: Nonhuman Queerings', *Somatechnics*, Vol. 5, No. 2, pp. 120–34.

Massumi B. (2014), *What Animals Teach Us About Politics*, Durham, NC: Duke University Press.

Mech D. (1999), 'Alpha Status, Dominance, and Division of Labor in Wolf Packs', *Canadian Journal of Zoology*, Vol. 77, pp. 1196–203.

Palmer C. (2006), 'Killing Animals in Animal Shelters', in The Animal Studies Group, *Killing Animals*, Urbana and Chicago: University of Illinois Press.

Range, F. et al. (2015), 'Testing the Myth: Tolerant Dogs and Aggressive Wolves', *Proceedings of the Royal Society B*, Vol. 282, p. 1807, at http://rspb.royalsociety-publishing.org/content/282/1807/20150220 (accessed 23 March 2016).

Range, F. and Z. Viranyi (2014), 'Wolves are Better Imitators of Conspecifics than Dogs', *PLoS ONE*, Vol. 9, No. 1, at http://journals.plos.org/plosone/article?id=10.1371/journal.pone.0086559 (accessed 23 March 2016).

Ryan. D. (2010), 'Dominance Meme: Out-lived Extreme?', *Veterinary* Times, Vol. 40, No. 7, 22 February.

Sands, D. (2014), '"Beyond" the Singular? Ecology, Subjectivity, Politics', in P. MacCormack (ed.), *The Animal Catalyst: Towards Ahuman Theory*, London and New York: Bloomsbury, pp. 49–65.

Shukin, N. (2000), 'Deleuze and Feminisms: Involuntary Regulators and Affective Inhibitors', in I. Buchanan and C. Colebrook (eds), *Deleuze and Feminist Theory*, Edinburgh: Edinburgh University Press.

Sillero-Zubili C. and J. Marino (2004), *Ethiopian Wolf*, at http://www.canids.org/species/Ethiopian_wolf.pdf (accessed 23 March 2016).

Smuts, B. (2006), 'Between Species: Science and Subjectivity', *Configurations*, Vol. 14, Nos 1–2, Winter–Spring, pp. 115–26.

Sternthal S. (2010), 'Moscow's Stray Dogs', *Financial Times*, 16 January.

Stivale, C. J. (2014), '*Etre aux aguets:* Deleuze, Creation, and Deterritorialization', in P. MacCormack (ed.), *The Animal Catalyst: Towards Ahuman Theory*, London and New York: Bloomsbury, pp. 69–80.

Vanderwees, C. (2009), 'Companion Species Under Fire: A Defense of Donna Haraway's *The Companion Species Manifesto*', *Nebula*, Vol. 6, No. 2, pp. 73–81.

Vitamvor, X. (2009), 'Unbecoming Animal Studies', *Minnesota Review*, Vol. 2010, No. 73–4, pp. 183–7.

Ward, C., E. B. Bauer and B. B. Smuts (2008), 'Partner Preferences and Asymmetries in Social Play Among Domestic Dog, *Canis lupus familiaris*, Littermates', *Animal Behaviour*, Vol. 76, No. 4, pp. 489–99.

Weissberg, Z. (2009), 'The Broken Promises of Monsters: Haraway, Animals and the Humanist Legacy', *Journal for Critical Animal Studies*, Vol. VII, No. 2, pp. 21–61.

Williams, L. (2009), 'Haraway Contra Deleuze and Guattari: The Question of the Animals', *Communication, Politics & Culture*, Vol. 42, No. 1, pp. 42–54.

Wolfe, C. (2003), *Animal Rites: American Culture, the Discourse of Species, and Posthumanist Theory*, Chicago: University of Chicago Press.

PART II

VECTORS OF BECOMING-IMPERCEPTIBLE: THE MULTIPLICITY OF THE PACK

Chapter 4

Louis Malle's Kleistian War Machine: Becoming-Animal, Becoming-Woman, Becoming-Imperceptible in *Black Moon* (1975)

Colin Gardner

Introduction

In *A Thousand Plateaus*, Deleuze and Guattari note that, 'If becoming-woman is the first quantum, or molecular segment, with the becomings-animal that link up with it coming next, what are they all rushing toward? Without a doubt, towards becoming-imperceptible. The imperceptible is the immanent end of becoming, its cosmic formula' (1987: 279). More importantly, this molecular assemblage is connected directly to the Kleistian war machine, that pure form of exteriority or deterritorialisation, a 'climate of infection' where one multiplicity of bodies is invaded by another, producing a series of affective encounters and lines of flight. It is in this sense that 'All of Kleist's work is traversed by a war machine invoked against the state, by a musical machine invoked against painting or the "picture"' (1987: 268). This places Kleist in direct contrast to, say, Kafka, for as Deleuze and Guattari argue, 'Kleist's question isn't "What is a minor literature and, further, a political and collective literature?" but rather, "What is a literature of war?"' (1986: 55). For Deleuze and Guattari, Kleist's *Penthesilea* is paradigmatic of this molecular strategy. Ostensibly a radical rewriting of the ancient war between the Greeks and the Amazons, Achilles and Penthesilea betray their respective States (and their associated machines), one by disobeying his commander, the other by choosing her enemy, allowing them to become lovers rather than bitter foes. Together, they form a new assemblage of *affective* war, 'Achilles in the act of becoming-woman, Penthesilea in a becoming-dog' (1987: 278). Although their revolt ends in a tragic death for both parties, as Mathieu Carrière points out, their union portends 'the utopian promise of an uncoded, intensive love, and hence of a fulfillment of "Kleist's great desire – to live as two in madness"' (Carrière 1985: 102; cited in Bogue 2003: 123).

Drawing heavily upon Lewis Carroll's *Through the Looking Glass, and What Alice Found There*, Louis Malle's coming of age surrealist fable *Black Moon* (1975) effectively starts where *Penthesilea* leaves off. The latter's battle of the sexes is now the backdrop to a form of waking dream as a teenage fugitive, Lily (Cathryn Harrison), is led through a series of depersonalised movements by a mysterious unicorn to a secluded Dordogne farm. It is here that Kleist's utopian 'mad duality' is manifested though a strange, non-Oedipal and non-hierarchical family dynamic – the animals and children are treated as equal agencies in the narrative – in which a mute brother (Warhol legend, Joe Dallesandro, as becoming-woman) and his sheep-herding, horse-riding sister (Alexandra Stewart as becoming-animal) – both, reinforcing their physical androgyny, also named Lily – live with a group of feral, naked children and their bedridden elderly mother (Brecht theatre veteran, Thérèse Giehse), whose sole 'companions' are a two-way radio transmitter and a talking rat named Humphrey. Discussing the film in a 21 September 1975 episode of the French TV programme, *Pour le cinéma*, Malle observed that, 'The house and the characters living in it represent a different world, a parallel universe where things don't happen in the usual way. It's a world, for example, where people communicate in ways other than speech. In our world, we only communicate with words. They communicate by touch, or with their eyes. This is one of the film's themes: Words are so worn out that they're almost useless. The animals almost talk more than the humans' (Malle 1975). In addition, conventional family roles are also inverted, with Sister Lily breastfeeding her own mother and both siblings reserving their most affective form of contact through Malle's own form of Kleistian 'musical machine', i.e. staged love duets from Wagner's saga of doomed lovers, *Tristan und Isolde* (whose own culminating *liebestod* significantly parallels that of Kleist in *Penthesilea*). Although by film's end Brother and Sister Lily become violent antagonists, caught up in the ravages of the ongoing gender war, Lily the teenager inherits the farm's deterritorialised 'velocity of affect' (Deleuze and Guattari 1987: 356), adopting Sister Lily's role of the breastfeeding mother by suckling both the old woman and the unicorn, all in relation to the becoming multiplicity of the pack: in short, a true war machine that envelops both protagonists and spectators alike in a transformed zone of indiscernibility.

Kleist's War Machine and Nonhuman Becoming

In their analysis of Kleist's war machine, Deleuze and Guattari draw direct associations between becoming-animal and smooth space as affective modes of becoming and the creation of the nonhuman image. Affect is of course a complex, often contested term and should be distinguished from affections, just as percept is different from perceptions, for as Deleuze and Guattari point out, 'The affect goes beyond affections no less than the percept goes beyond perceptions. The affect is not the passage from one lived state to another but man's nonhuman becoming' (1994: 173). Taking this a step further, Brian Massumi draws a clear distinction between affect and emotion. Affect is a matter of emergence, with one foot in the virtual (the autonomy of relation) and the other in the actual (functional limitation):

> What is being termed affect . . . is precisely this two-sidedness, the simul-taneous participation of the virtual in the actual and the actual in the virtual, as one arises from and returns to the other . . . Affects are *virtual synesthetic perspectives* anchored in (functionally limited by) the actually existing, particular things that embody them. The autonomy of affect is its participation in the virtual. *Its autonomy is its openness.* (2002: 35)

However, affect is also susceptible to capture and closure, which Massumi defines as the role of emotion, but he also recognises that something will always escape and that 'The escape of affect *cannot but be perceived*, alongside the perceptions that are its capture' (2002: 36).

If we apply this two-sided distinction between and the virtual and the actual to the war machine and its attempted capture by the overcoded State machine, we see a similar by-play between lines of flight and their re-appropriation, between de- and reterritorialisation and their spatial corollaries, the smooth and the striated. First of all, it's necessary to note that the so-called 'war machine' doesn't have war *per se* as its direct outcome, for as Deleuze points out, 'we define "war machine" as a linear assemblage which constructs itself on lines of flight. In this sense, the war machine does not at all have war as its object; it has as its object a very special space, *smooth space*, which it composes, occu-pies, and propagates. *Nomadism* is precisely this combination "war machine-smooth space"' (Deleuze and Parnet 1987: 33). As a result, the war machine is far more creative and artistic – because it is innately deterritorialising, muddying the difference between inside and outside, place and space (what the geographer Marcus Doel calls 'splace' – 1999: 9) – than militaristic. Because smooth space – non-linear and un-demarcated – is a space of becoming, flux and metamorphosis, the war machine constitutes a pure form of exteriority, a deterritorialisation which constructs assemblages which in turn open up creative lines of flight (i.e. new connectivities and collectivities). However, it's important to note that the two spaces are not dialectically in opposition, for just as the war machine and the State machine are always mutually implicated, so 'the two spaces in fact exist only in mixture: smooth space is constantly being translated, transversed into a striated space; striated space is constantly being reversed, returned to a smooth space. In the first case, one organizes even the desert; in the second, the desert gains and grows; and the two can happen simultaneously' (Deleuze and Guattari 1987: 474–5). The nomad/State dualism is often mediated by a third term that breaks the dialectic: the machinic phylum or subterranean flow of pure becoming (Nietzsche) or the universal aggregate of action/reaction (Bergson) that flows between them and on which they depend. As Deleuze and Guattari point out, the great phylum is what selects 'through the intermediary of assemblages' (398).

Kleist's writing is everywhere 'traversed by a war machine' because, as a 'climate of infection', war-as-becoming constitutes an affective encounter and multiplies itself through its very nature as a form of contagion. It is, in this sense, a particular kind of Spinozan ethics, or more accurately an ethico-aesthetics of the ahuman subject, an enquiry into what a body (and therefore thought) can do. In this sense, Kleistian aesthetics constitutes an account of different forms of experience and the will to experiment through a combination of intensities and their corresponding speeds and slownesses. As Deleuze puts it in a key passage in *Spinoza: Practical Philosophy*:

> Every reader of Spinoza knows that for him bodies and minds are not substances or subjects, but modes. It is not enough, however, merely to think this theoretically. For, concretely, a mode is a complex relation of speed and slowness, in the body, but also in thought, and it is a capacity for affecting and being affected, pertaining to the body or thought. Concretely, if you define bodies and thoughts as capacities for affecting and being affected, many things change. You will define an animal, or a human being, not by its form, its organs, and its functions, and not as a subject either; you will define it by the affects of which it is capable. (1988: 123–4)

Ultimately, Kleist pursued non-personal affects over specifically human sentiments, largely because affects ignore the distinction between exterior and interior and defy rational control. They also disrupt logical, linear time, constructing a more stratigraphic temporality, 'where "before" and "after" indicate only an order of superimpositions' (Deleuze and Guattari 1994: 58).

It is here that we discover a key *figure* for both Deleuze and Kleist, what Ronald Bogue calls 'The master figure of affect', namely 'that of the point of intersection of two infinite lines, "the abstract point where two comets, two chains of events cross . . . at the same time the center of immobility and the trace of most frightening speeds"' (Carrière 1985: 13; cited in Bogue 2003: 119). In Kleist's famous essay, 'On the Marionette Theater', for example, this takes the form of the immobile point of the actor/marionette's centre of gravity through which unconscious and mysterious forces may pass – mechanical but also 'divine'. Bogue rightly ties this to yet another definition of affect, for 'An affect is such an immobile point, and from a psychological perspective it is experienced as a break in continuity, a gap in consciousness, a jump or leap into a hole . . . The affective point is at once the juncture of forces colliding at maximum acceleration and a motionless, catatonic seizure.' It is also a form of time-image, for 'The affect is a break in the continuity of rational consciousness and a hiatus in the regular flow of chronological time. In such a moment of atemporal disequilibrium, no sense of self exists, no separation of inside and outside' (Bogue 2003: 120).

Firstly, one could argue that this is a perfect description of the teenage Lily's adventures at the farmhouse in Malle's *Black Moon*, where time seems to stand still in a multiplicitous dream state; but secondly (and through a stratigraphic, as opposed to causal, connection), it also evokes Kleist's 1807 play, *Penthesilea*, where the intertwining of the personal and political aspects of war create a chain reaction of affective intensities, combined with extreme physical violence, that serves to deterritorialise the body into a series of warring multiplicities. As Carrière puts it, 'Infection is the encounter of at least two enemy populations on the same territory, on the field of battle. It is a form of affective encounter' (1985: 9–10; cited in Bogue 2003: 119). In Kleist's play, the warring factions are represented by the Greeks and the Amazons and their contagious, affective representatives are Achilles and Penthesilea herself.

Kleist's *Penthesilea*: the Abnormal and the Contagion of Becoming

Penthesilia, Queen of the Amazons, doesn't appear in Homer's *Iliad*, so much of her story has been pieced together from other sources, including Pseudo-Apollodorus's *Bibliotheca* and Arctinus of Miletus's *Aethiopis*. According to these and other accounts she was the daughter of Ares and

Otrere and, following the accidental slaying of her Amazon comrade Hippolyte, led her troops into the Trojan War in support of King Priam, who had promised her purification of her blood-guilt. After the defeat of Hector, she slew many Greeks in battle but was ultimately killed by Achilles who, enraptured by her beauty and valour, promptly fell in love with her after her ceremonial burial by the Trojans. Achilles' comrade, Thersites, so reviled him for his un-Homeric sentimentality that Achilles killed him in revenge.

It's tempting to see Kleist's radically revised version of the story as a straight dialectic between two contrasting approaches to war, and indeed, as Bogue points out, the play opens on the Plains of Troy with Odysseus discussing with his troops the highly problematic presence of the Amazons, a pure, unallied force of destruction who seem to fight for no cause, 'an anarchic war machine set loose against the State machines of Greece and Troy' (2003: 121). This would seem to tally with Deleuze and Guattari's claim that 'No one has portrayed the situation of the man of war, at once eccentric and condemned, better than Kleist. In *Penthesilea*, Achilles is already separated from his power: the war machine has passed over to the Amazons, a Stateless woman-people whose justice, religion, and loves are organized uniquely in a war mode' (1987: 355). As Deleuze explained to Claire Parnet, 'The great ruptures, the great oppositions, are always negotiable; but not the little crack, the imperceptible ruptures which come from the south' (Deleuze and Parnet 1987: 131–2). By this account, the Amazons as war machine constitute such a rupture, an irresistible force of metamorphosis, destroying all stable codes and social relations, epitomising Deleuze and Guattari's description of the warrior as a form of traitor 'to the world of dominant significations, and to the established order' (1987: 41).

However, Bogue rightly argues that the Amazons are as much of a State machine as that of the Greeks and Trojans, imbued with their own inviolable codes and ethics of war. They were the descendents of Scythians who had been conquered by Vexoris, king of Ethiopia. Vexoris killed all the male Scythians and planned to rape all the women but the latter fought back by stabbing the men. Thus, as Penthesilea later recounts to Achilles, 'And in a night the murderers had their itch / Well satisfied, with knives, till they were dead' (Kleist 1998: 93). It was during this night of cathartic violence that a nation came into being:

Hence let there be a sovereign nation founded,
A State of women where the arrogant,
Imperious voice of man shall not be heard;

That gives itself its laws in dignity,
Obeys itself, provides its own protection. (94)

From these origins a set of customs and bodily characteristics were forged to solidify the Amazons' warrior identity: each cut off their right breast the better to adapt their bodies to wielding a bow and arrow; in order to procreate they waged eternal war against neighbouring tribes so that they might abduct their strongest male foes for mating purposes. These codes are in turn reinforced by two sacred rites: 1) The Feast of Flowering Virgins, which inaugurates each hunt for new men (each Amazon is declared a 'Bride of Mars' and then, 'like a fire-blazing storm', they fall upon their prey); 2) The Feast of Roses, which celebrates their victorious return from battle. Here, the male captives are adorned with roses and invited to orgiastic pleasures with their conquerors. As Bogue points out, 'Both rituals are institutions that regulate deterritorializing forces, and both are in constant danger of collapsing into an unrestricted play of violence and eros' (2003: 121–2).

Crucial to the first sacred rite is that only the Priestess may name the individual enemies to be attacked: i.e. no one is allowed to select an individual opponent. Kleist's play hinges on the violation of this prohibition when Penthesilea specifically selects Achilles as her foe, thereby allowing the playwright to focus on their tragic love/combat and the contagion of affect that it unleashes. As Deleuze reminds us:

> Choosing is the Promethean sin *par excellence*. This was the case with Kleist's Penthesilea, an Ahab-woman who, like her indiscernible double Achilles, had chosen her enemy, in defiance of the law of the Amazons forbidding the preference of one enemy over another. The priestess and the Amazons consider this a betrayal that madness sanctions in a cannibal identification. (1997: 79)

For Deleuze and Guattari, this is not uncharacteristic of the multiplicitous pack, for 'wherever there is multiplicity, you will also find an exceptional individual, and it is with that individual that an alliance must be made in order to become-animal' (1987: 243). Obviously, in alignment with their anti-Oedipal stance, there can be no lone wolf, but there is always a leader of the pack, what Deleuze and Guattari call the Anomalous (a 'supernormal' role played, as we shall see, by the old mother in *Black Moon*, a role that the teenage Lily inherits and ultimately expands).

It's important not to muddle the concept of the anomalous with that of the abnormal, for while the latter has a number of set characteristics, whether specific or generic, the anomalous is always positioned in relation to a multiplicity or a pack. More significantly,

> The anomalous is neither an individual nor a species; it has only affects, it has neither familiar or subjectified feelings, nor specific or significant characteristics. Human tenderness is as foreign to it as human classifications. Lovecraft applied the term 'Outsider' to this thing or entity, the Thing, which arrives and passes at the edge, which is linear yet multiple, 'teeming, seething, swelling, foaming, spreading like an infectious disease, this nameless horror.' (Deleuze and Guattari 1987: 244–5)

The anomalous is also a phenomenon of bordering, not in so far as it creates a delimiting margin for a multiplicity in order to rein it in through a process of reterritorialisation, but rather to spawn becomings in relation to other multiplicities, through a process of subtracting or adding new dimensions, for beyond the borderline the multiplicity will by necessity always change its nature. In short, 'no band is without this phenomenon of bordering, or the anomalous' (1987: 246).

It is this defiant, violating choice that expresses Penthesilea's bordering role as an anomalous affective force, whereby her 'demonic element leads her into a dog-becoming' (Deleuze and Parnet 1987: 42). Kleist also plants another, more personally affective reason for this choice: Penthesilea's mother – on her deathbed – has sworn Penthesilea to take Achilles as her husband. This raises a key question: does a mother's dying request override the prohibition? Kleist scholar and translator Joel Agee argues that it does:

> Her love fills the other women with incomprehension, pity and rage, but she does not, as is frequently claimed, rebel against her nation or even break a supposed Amazon law when she sets her sights 'on one head' instead of leading her armies home with their human loot. Her mother on her deathbed has given her a virtual assignment to capture Achilles, and lest there be any doubt, her friend Prothoë confirms that she has not acted in violation of custom. (Agee 1998: xxvii; Kleist 1998: 100–1)

Yet, one could also argue that the drama is less about tragic necessity in a classical (read: Oedipal) sense than about 'jumping from one affect to another' (Carrière 1985: 79; Bogue 2003: 122). Similarly, it seems to matter very little that Achilles has also violated the State machine by disobeying Odysseus and Agamemnon and throwing in his lot with the Amazons. What *is* important is the various becomings that are unleashed by their actions – that is the contagion of affective war – and the harnessing of the pack or multiplicity by destructive forces of violence.

Kleist develops these becomings through a series of affective stutterings and catastrophes on a specific plane of consistency (as opposed to organisation), jumping from one assemblage to another, for as Deleuze and Guattari note,

> Kleist multiplies 'life plan(e)s,' but his voids and failures, his leaps, earth-quakes, and plagues are always included on a single plane. The plane is not a principle of organisation but a means of transportation. No form develops, no subject forms; affects are displaced, becomings catapult forward and combine into blocks, like the becoming-woman of Achilles and the becoming-dog of Penthesilea. (1987: 268)

The latter becomings are realised through a combination of deception and a breaking of the Amazon code of the unacceptability of defeat. Equally important, as Hilda Brown (2003) rightly argues, is Penthesilea's *todesreife* or 'ripeness for death' which, far from being associated with the Freudian dyad of Eros/Thanatos, is better described as an affirmative incorporeality or becoming-imperceptible, what Deleuze calls the ultimate crack. Interestingly, as Brown notes, 'In a letter of 1807 Kleist himself refers to death as a "refrain" of life, by which, I think, he means a summation and carrying over of essential elements from the one to the other sphere' (2003: 209). Indeed, Rosi Braidotti stresses the Spinozist, affirmative nature of death as becoming: 'Death is not entropy or return to inert lifeless matter, but rather the opening up of new intensities and possibilities of the in-human or non-human kind . . . Death can be experienced as becoming; as merging with the endless generative energy of a cosmos that is supremely indifferent to humans' (2006: 151). The important thing is not to disappear but to die in your own fashion, of a piece with one's life: 'To desire actively to die our death is the same as wanting to live life as intensely as possible. My life is my own story about dying in my own fashion . . . thus expressing my desire as *potentia*' (2006: 152).

In Penthesilea's case, scene 14 provides a structural crux – a premonitory 'ripe moment' – for she believes that she has triumphed over Achilles, thus giving her the highest fulfillment in the face of death: perhaps the highest desire on earth. But, 'The sober fact is that the reverse is true: Achilles has taken her prisoner but has connived with Prothoë in a ruse whereby he feigns defeat in the hope of gaining time to persuade her to return to Greece with him for a while' (Brown 2003: 215). With the truth of the matter quickly revealed, Penthesilea is horrified at her defeat – unacceptable according to Amazon code – and the two lovers retreat to their respective camps. Not to be thwarted, Achilles devises a new plan, challenging her to combat so he can deliberately lose the fight and become her prisoner. But the emotionally unhinged queen has embraced darker, wilder forces, and sets her hunting dogs on

Achilles at the very moment that she shoots him through the throat with an arrow:

> Achilles: 'Penthesilea! My bride! What are you doing?
> Is this the rosy feast you promised me?' . . .
> She sinks – tearing the armor off his body –
> Into his ivory breast she sinks her teeth,
> She and her savage dogs in competition . . .
> The blood was dripping from her mouth and hands. (Kleist 1998: 128)

Thus, in this hybrid orgy of violence, animalism and cannibalism, Achilles's passive becoming-woman is devoured by Penthesilea's becoming-animal: 'As she merges with the multiplicity of the pack, "the assemblage of gracious war becomes the machine of fascist war; the war of love becomes the war of Mars, the destroyer god"' (Carrière 1985: 71; Bogue 2003: 123).

In *A Thousand Plateaus* Deleuze and Guattari see this outcome of reterritorialisation – in the form of destructive disintegration – as a typical Kleistian transition from an internal characteristic of affect to a pure exteriority:

> feelings become uprooted from the interiority of a 'subject,' to be projected violently outward into a milieu of pure exteriority that lends them an incredible velocity, a catapulting force: love or hate, they are no longer feelings but affects. And these affects are so many instances of the becoming-woman, the becoming-animal of the warrior (the bear, she dogs). Affects transpierce the body like arrows, they are weapons of war. The deterritorialisation velocity of affect. Even dreams (Homburg's, Penthesilea's) are externalized, by a system of relays and plug-ins, extrinsic linkages belonging to the war machine. (1987: 356)

Brown provocatively suggests that this culminating orgy is exacerbated by Penthesilea's overdetermined, ecstatic response to the earlier 'ripe moment' in scene 14, which is retroactively seen as a false ecstatic dawn with an over-theatricalised motivation, thereby questioning the legitimacy of her affirmative, affective response to 'death-in-life' from the beginning. 'These two "ripe moments" experienced by Penthesilea, and so ardently desired by her', argues Brown,

> are projected into a timeless vacuum, out of sync with the dramatic action developing around and upon her. As defined by her, such ripeness could only be validated in the postheroic, posttragic realm, where no such time constraints exist. This, to my mind, illustrates the problematic status that Kleist confers on the concept of ripeness and suggests the impossibility of its being attainable within a given time frame. (2003: 217)

With time inextricably 'out of joint' in the form of an affective dehis-
cence, all that remains is Penthesilea's self-inflicted *coup de grace*, a
combination of catatonia – this affect is too strong for me – and flash
– the power of this affect sweeps me away, 'so that the Self (*Moi*) is
now nothing more than a character whose actions and emotions are
desubjectified, perhaps even to the point of death. Such is Kleist's personal formula: a succession of flights of madness and catatonic freezes
in which no subjective interiority remains' (Deleuze and Guattari 1987:
356). Such is the danger of the line of flight that short-circuits because
of a latent danger it conceals: in this sense Penthesilea's suicide is itself
a premonition of Kleist's own *todesreife*, culminating in his suicide pact
with the terminally ill Henriette Vogel on the banks of Kleiner Wannsee
in 1811.

Black Moon: Becoming-Woman and Becoming-Animal

Louis Malle's challenge in *Black Moon* is to reinvent the classical battle
of the sexes by reinvigorating the war machine, yet at the same time
avoiding its capture by the suicide pact. As Deleuze and Guattari pose
the problem:

> All Kleist's work rests on the following observation: there is no longer a
> war-machine on a grand scale like that of the Amazons, the war-machine
> is no longer anything more than a dream which itself vanishes and gives
> way to national armies (*the Prince of Homburg*); how can one reinvent a
> new type of war machine (*Michael Kohlhaas*), how can one trace out the
> line of flight in spite of knowing that it leads us to abolition (suicide pact)?
> To wage one's own war? How otherwise is one to outmanoeuvre this final
> trap? (1987: 143)

Black Moon re-harnesses the dream (an inquisitive 'Alice' as the film's
culminating Anomalous) to reinvigorate Kleist's Utopian promise of an
uncoded, intensive love, by dismantling it onto a new line of flight, as a
new assemblage across and between multiplicities that dissolves the difference between individual and collective. The result is the creation of
new borders, new thresholds, new deterritorialisations.

Although *Penthesilea* is only obliquely referenced in *Black Moon*,
neither Kleist nor, as we shall see, becoming-animal, are strangers
to Malle's *oeuvre*. In his 1962 film, *Vie Privée*, starring Marcello
Mastroianni and Brigitte Bardot, Malle uses the opposing worlds of
popular cinema and elitist theatre to set up a stalled becoming, represented by the classic dialectic between the passive female and the active

male. As Geneviève Sellier rightly argues, the film is 'built around the opposition between a passive and alienated mass culture on the one hand, to which the character played by Bardot is for the most part reduced, and an elite culture on the other, embodied by the art editor played by her costar, Marcello Mastroianni' (2008: 201). From the start, Bardot's actress character Jill is constructed as an object to be observed, and as she is constantly badgered by paparazzi she is never presented as the active subject of her own story. This is accentuated by the ever-present male voice-over 'that comments on her deeds and gestures and gives us access to her thoughts in the manner of a Balzacian omniscient narrator' (202). In contrast, Mastroianni's Fabio is associated not only with high art – acting in a way as Malle's own alter ego – but also a specifically Kleistian narrative, as he is in the process of staging the latter's *Das Käthchen von Heilbronn oder Die Feuerprobe* (*Katie of Heilbronn or The Trial by Fire*) (1807–8) at the Spoleto Festival in Italy. It is while observing this ambitious outdoor spectacle from one of the surrounding rooftops (in an effort to avoid the prying eyes of the press) that Jill falls to her death (an accident, or suicide?). As Sellier notes, 'Her fall into the depths is filmed in slow motion, accompanied by Verdi's *Requiem*, and the film ends with this suspension of time and narrative, as though the filmmaker could only accord her a poetic dimension at the moment she dies' (203).

Interestingly, in a pair of letters from 1807–8, Kleist himself acknowledged the specifically dialectical connection between *Käthchen* and *Penthesilea*. Thus, in a missive to Marie von Kleist from late autumn, 1807, he writes: 'I am now eager to learn what you would have to say about *Käthchen*, because she is the obverse of *Penthesilea*, her opposite pole, a creature as powerful through submission as Penthesilea is through action?' (Kleist 1807). Kleist recontextualises their relationship as a mathematical formula in a subsequent letter to Heinrich J. von Collin, dated 8 December 1808: 'Because he who loves *Käthchen* cannot completely disregard *Penthesilea* because they belong together like the + and - of algebra, and they are one and the same being, only imagined out of contrary relations' (Kleist 1808). Significantly, in a discussion of stylistic commonalities between Melville and Kleist, Deleuze himself also plays up the connection, commenting in *Essays Critical and Clinical* that both writers' characters not only belong to, and inhabit, a primary nature but that they *constitute* it:

> Everything sets them in opposition, and yet they are perhaps the same
> creature – primary, original, stubborn, seized from both sides, marked

merely with a 'plus' or a 'minus' sign: Ahab or Bartleby. Or in Kleist, the terrible Penthesilea and the sweet little Catherine, the first beyond conscience, the second before conscience: she who chooses and she who does not choose, she who howls like a she-wolf and she who would prefer-not-to speak. (1997: 80)

One could argue then, that in *Black Moon* Malle redresses the balance in relation to the earlier film, setting up the '+' to counterweigh *Vie Privée*'s '−', while also reaffirming the war machine as an affirmative becoming.

With great economy, Malle establishes the main themes of the film in its opening sequence. Teenage Lily is first introduced speeding in her Honda 600 coupe through the wilds of the Dordogne at dusk when she accidentally runs over and kills a badger, sniffing inquisitively in the middle of the road. Lily, disguised in a man's hat to avoid the attentions of the male army, screeches to a halt, but at the sound of off-screen explosions she fears for her safety and drives on. We are immediately aware that we have been flung, *in medias res*, into an ongoing war (which is quickly revealed as a war between the sexes), but also that Lily, given her responsibility for the badger's demise, is not yet the agency of her own line of flight as a multiplicity, as becoming-animal. As she continues her drive through the winding country lanes, Lily auto-tunes the car radio and we hear fragments from various broadcasts, including pronouncements of Kantian judgement – 'Shall I describe to you the crime and vice that is being committed in the large cities of the world?' and '. . . I want to talk about your sin.' Suddenly we hear a duet of voices from *Tristan und Isolde*, specifically the love duet from Act 2 ('O sink hernieder, Nacht der Liebe), which Malle will later reprise during a performance by the children at the farmhouse: 'Descend, O Night of love, grant oblivion that I may live; take me up into your bosom. . .'. Lily then stops the car in the face of more explosions and gunfire. We see a dead woman soldier at the side of the road as the love duet picks up on the words '. . . release me from the world!' ('löse von der Welt mich los!'). The duet continues until Lily encounters a roadblock and is forced to witness the brutal execution of female captives by their male counterparts, perhaps a visceral reference to Nazi brutality in Malle's previous film, *Lacombe Lucien*, which was shot in the same location.

This introduction of the Wagnerian refrain serves two main purposes: firstly it sets up a premonition of Tristan and Isolde's eventual *liebestod* as a becoming-imperceptible, but it also alludes to the 'musical machine invoked against painting or the "picture"' that we touched on earlier (and which will play out with tragic consequences at the film's finale).

In this sense the duet is another facilitator of Lily's line of flight, encapsulated in the song's closing lines just as she turns off the radio at the roadblock: 'the glorious presentiment of sacred twilight extinguishes imagined terrors, world-redeeming'. This flight from the ravages of the State machine is then picked up by the first overt reference to becoming-animal as she continues to deterritorialise in search of an outside. As Lily speeds away from the roadblock, she first encounters a flock of sheep (the animal pack as multiplicity) and a snake in the grass as she attempts to clear some rocks from the roadway. However, this first contact with primary nature (eschewing any reductive attempts to read the snake psychoanalytically or symbolically) is immediately reterritorialised when she witnesses seven women soldiers, wearing gas masks, brutally kicking a captive. It is only when Lily gives herself up to the world of dreams that she harnesses her journey or 'balade' to a true becoming. Thus she 'awakens' to see a black centipede crawling up a rock, a green grasshopper lying diagonally across a stick, two May bugs skittering around in the grass, and is suddenly startled to hear the sounds of muted cries of pain. Where are they coming from? It turns out that they are emitted from a tiny flower that she's crushing with her body (our first introduction to nonhuman affects). She straightens up, lost in thought.

It's important to note that, as Deleuze points out in *Cinema 2: The Time-Image*, this episode constitutes an *implied*, as opposed to an explicit dream. The former includes instances of reverie, waking dream, strangeness and pure enchantment. Implied dream is usually accompanied by a shut-down of motor extension and human agency: 'she is prey to a vision, pursued by it or pursuing it, rather than engaged in an action ... possessed by an almost hallucinatory sensuality. She is closer to a visionary, a sleepwalker ...' (Deleuze 1989: 3). Instead of a full-fledged action-image, subjective motility gives itself up to a 'movement of world', whereby 'it is no longer the character who reacts to the optical-sound situation, it is a movement of world which supplements the faltering movement of the character' (59). Malle had already explored this phenomenon – where bodily states link up with an ahuman movement – in his earlier, 1960 feature, *Zazie dans le métro* (see Gardner 2014), and *Black Moon* constitutes its fullest manifestation:

> The frightened child faced with danger cannot run away, but the world sets about running away for [her] and takes [her] with it, as if on a conveyor belt. Characters do not move, but, as in an animated film, the camera causes the movement of the path on which they change places, 'motionless at a great pace.' The world takes responsibility for the movement that the subject can no longer or cannot make. (Deleuze 1989: 59)

It is at this exact moment that Lily first 'sees' the unicorn (who later speaks with a woman's voice), sitting by a tree accompanied by a low electronic hum on the soundtrack, as if to underline her association with the ethereal, the otherworldly and a possible deterritorialising connection to an incommensurable outside. As the unicorn takes off through the shrubbery, we see a horse and rider (Sister Lily) emerge from behind a screen of trees. Teenage Lily gives chase and the lure of the unicorn and her androgynous namesake lead her to the farmhouse, where she is immediately ensconced in the world of becoming-animal in the form of a pack of naked children, running wild through the grounds with their ever-present pig, and a noisy gaggle of geese.

The unicorn, then, has now adopted the role of facilitator of Lily's true line of flight from the State war to the war machine itself. As Deleuze notes, *Black Moon* is the apotheosis of becoming-animal in Malle,

> where the depersonalized movements take the heroine with the unicorn from one world to another and still another: it is by running away from the initial images of violence that the heroine moves from one world to the other, in the sense that Sartre says that each dream is a world, and even each phase or image of dream . . . Each is marked by animals, and is peopled by inversions (sound inversion of speech, aberrations of behaviour such as when the old woman talks to the rats and sucks the girl's breast). In Malle, it is always a movement of world which brings the character to incest, prostitution, or disgrace . . . In the whole cinema of enchantment these universalized, depersonalized and pronominalized movements, with their slow motion or rushing, with their inversions, pass just as much through nature as through artifice and the manufactured object. (1989: 60)

Which is, of course, just as pertinent to Kleist as it is to an analysis of the time-image in postwar cinema.

It is at the farmhouse that we first encounter Brother and Sister Lily, the manifestation of Kleist's desire to transcend both gender difference and the autonomy of the subject through an 'uncoded, intensive love', where the couple are re-manifested in the 'one' yet also manifested again in a twinned duality, the essence of Spinozan *conatus* as the actualisation and maximum harnessing of bodily forces as more or less *potential*, as a purely nomadic subjectivity, forever in process, forever in transformation. Malle himself admitted that 'We're not sure which is male and which is female. They're an androgynous pair. I was intrigued by our search for unity, common to us all. It's like they're one character split into two bodies' (1975). It is perhaps no accident that Malle also sets up clear resonances to Kleist's tragedy, for Brother Lily's androgyny, his predilection for occupying the role of the doomed lover Tristan by singing Wagnerian arias as he rakes leaves in the garden, and his reliance on human touch as his sole means of everyday communication, associate him directly with the haptic, becoming-woman of Kleist's Achilles. As Malle himself confirms, 'Another thing that interested me is that it's a sensual film. It's not about ideas, but about images, sounds and even scents. Characters often touch. It's a film about touch. I tried to make it as embodied as possible and to capture the physical aspect' (1975). Meanwhile, Sister Lily's association with horses and the flock of sheep – which she systematically butchers to feed the children – allow her to fill Penthesilea's role as becoming-animal, but without the savage antagonism to her lover that proved so costly in the original narrative. That both siblings are called Lily not only serves to break gender expectations but also allows Malle to extend his Kleistian utopia to include (and ultimately absorb) the new interloper, the teenage Lily, for as Braidotti pointedly argues, 'The Life in me does not bear my name, "I" inhabits it as a time-share' (2006: 154). It is thus more appropriate to describe the three 'Lilys' as a pack rather than a shared kinship or heredity, for as Deleuze and Guattari insist, 'We oppose epidemic to filiation, contagion to heredity, peopling by contagion to sexual reproduction, sexual production. Bands, human or animal, proliferate by contagion, epidemics, battlefields, and catastrophes' (1987: 241).

Given that the true war machine propagates through contagion, a key problem with *Black Moon*'s pastoral utopia is its tendency to hermetically squeeze out all association and connection with the outside. Apart from the occasional intrusion of the gender war within the farm's walled perimeter – at one point Lily stumbles across a dead female soldier and is horrified to see chickens plucking out her heart – and the ephemeral sound of distant artillery (which is in turn easily mistaken for rolling thunder), for the most part the siblings are content to live a solitary existence as part of the general multiplicity of the animal pack. This, of course, runs counter to the very mechanism of becoming, for as Deleuze and Guattari make clear, multiplicities must constantly renew themselves by adding and subtracting dimensions, in short by extending and changing their borders:

> This is our hypothesis: a multiplicity is defined not by the elements that compose it in extension, not by the characteristics that compose it in comprehension, but by the lines and dimensions it encompasses in 'intension.' If you change dimensions, if you add or subtract one, you change multiplicity. Thus there is a borderline for each multiplicity; it is in no way a center but rather the enveloping line or farthest dimension, as a function of which it is possible to count the others, all those lines or dimensions constitute the

pack at a given moment (beyond the borderline, the multiplicity changes nature). (1987: 245)

This, as we have seen, is where the Anomalous plays a key role, for 'The Anomalous is always at the frontier, on the border of a band or a multiplicity; it is part of the latter, but it is already making it pass into another multiplicity, it makes it become, it traces a line-between. This is also the "outsider"' (Deleuze and Parnet 1987: 42).

Although teenage Lily will ultimately fulfill this role by film's end, she actually inherits it from the siblings' bedridden mother, whose presence defies both a clear-cut human identity and a fixed time or place. 'In simplified terms,' observes Malle, 'her character represents a certain form of wisdom or knowledge tinged with aggression and derision. At the same time, the shadow of death hangs over this character' (1975). Apart from her intimate, supernormal relationship with Humphrey – which associates her affectively with the animal pack, with the surpassing gesture of becoming-rat in an act of what Massumi calls 'Reciprocal unframing. Double deterritorialization' (2014: 61) – she is the only figure at the farmhouse with a direct contact with the outside, facilitated by her two-way radio transmitter (significantly, Humphrey's incomprehensible prattling sounds uncannily like radio static). 'We don't know who she's speaking to, but we start to wonder if she might be somehow controlling what's going on', notes Malle (1975). More importantly, she provides us with a direct stratigraphic (i.e. non-linear) link to the Trojan War (and by extension, the context of Kleist's drama): 'What? They've taken the city? (Pause). A wooden horse? My God. Priam? Priam's dead you say. What about Helen? Hello!!' Despite her suspicion of Lily as a rival 'outsider' – 'She's being very quiet. I don't like it . . . unintelligible' – she continues confiding with her radio connection: 'Paris!' (presumably the son of Priam, not the city). Then, with a degree of paranoia: 'If she finds out about the Greeks . . .'.

During this episode Lily is preoccupied, thumbing through a photo album which features pictures of the old woman in her prime (most likely publicity shots from Thérèse Giehse's Brechtian days), culminating in a head shot of the unicorn. The continuity (and contiguity) of images suggests a direct connection between the two: has the woman become-unicorn, or vice versa, or are they interchangeable entities? That Sister Lily breast feeds her mother and teenage Lily ends up breast feeding both the old woman *and* the unicorn suggests a latent multiplicitous connectivity, reinforced by the old woman's determination to keep Lily away from the bedroom window lest she spot the unicorn (her alter ego?) grazing in the garden. Significantly, both the woman and the unicorn are equally cryptic about explaining their mutual relationship to Lily, offering by turns to disclose everything but ultimately revealing nothing:

> Lily: 'You know, the old lady upstairs. She didn't want me to see you.'
> Unicorn: 'Oh Lord, you mean that babbling biddy on the wireless upstairs. Don't pay any attention to her. She's not even real.'
> Lily: 'What do you mean she's not real? I touched her, I spoke to her, I even saw her die.'
> Unicorn: 'I mean what I mean. And my little one, I could give you some precious information concerning that old hag.'

Significantly, the unicorn's first spoken words are a direct citation from Shakespeare's *Macbeth*, Act 5, Scene 5: 'Out, out, brief candle! Life's but a walking shadow. . .' as if to indicate that neither language nor representation will suffice to express or 'explain' a multiplicity.

Moreover, the unicorn seems to exist outside of strict chronological time: 'wasn't like this before', she complains, 'old lunatic . . . drives me batty . . . I'm leaving right away . . . and I won't be back for another 154 years. . .'. In this regard she is closer to what Deleuze and Guattari call a haecceity, a set of relations of speeds and slownesses, operating in lieu of subjective emotion. Haecceities are:

> a mode of individuation very different from that of a person, subject, thing, or substance. We reserve the name *haecceity* for it. A season, a winter, a summer, an hour, a date have a perfect individuality lacking nothing, even though this individuality is different from that of a thing or a subject. They are haecceities in the sense that they consist entirely of relations of movement and rest between molecules or particles, capacities to affect and be affected. (1987: 261)

In many ways, haecceities can also be seen as another form of Nietzsche's *untimely*, 'the innocence of becoming (in other words, forgetting as opposed to memory, geography as opposed to history) . . . Creations are like mutant abstract lines that have detached themselves from the task of representing a world, precisely because they assemble a new type of reality that history can only recontain or relocate in punctual systems' (1987: 296). It is in this sense that Lily and the unicorn form a new collective assemblage that, as we shall see, multiplies and expands the affective pack towards a new outside.

Conclusion: From Becoming-Animal to Becoming-Imperceptible

According to Patricia MacCormack, 'Becomings begin as inter-kingdom, towards becoming-imperceptible, through zones of relation without imitation or hierarchical filiation and equivalence' (2012: 31); which in many ways is an excellent summation of *Black Moon*'s ontological trajectory. But first, Malle must overcome the capture of the war machine by the latent, destructive forces of the Kleistian *todesreife*. In this sense, events come to a climactic head during a staging of the aforementioned love duet from Act 2 of *Tristan und Isolde* – 'O sink hernieder, Nacht der Liebe' ('Descend O Night of Love') – which the sibling Lilys stage in their living room with two of the farm's resident children as leads (touchingly sung by future operatic stars, Anthony Roden and Sylvia Lindenstrand). As if drawn by some mysterious force to her allotted role, teenage Lily accompanies the singers at the piano, while Sister Lily applies her brother's make-up in readiness for their own roles as Tristan and Isolde. Malle's selection of this particular duet is significant because it encompasses the moment where the two lovers praise the darkness that shuts out all false appearances and accept their final security in the night's eternal embrace: 'then am I myself the world; floating in sublime bliss, life of love most sacred, the sweetly conscious undeluded wish never again to waken'.

Malle initially utilises the sequence to fully integrate the farm community in the collective experience of the musical refrain as a form of ludic play: while Lily accompanies the child leads, other children listen intently or smear their faces with make-up as random sheep wander bleating around the room, adding their affective voices to the mix. However, following the original Wagnerian libretto, the distant voice of Isolde's handmaid Brangäne warns that it will soon be daylight ('Einsam wachend in der Nacht'), but the enraptured lovers are completely oblivious to any danger, comparing the night to death, which will ultimately unite them in a passionate *liebestod*. Malle expresses this threat via a time-lapse shot of the garden through the living-room window as night rapidly turns to day amid a cacophony of Wagnerian *stürm und drang*. Not only are the lovers' best laid plans forestalled but the relationship between Brother and Sister Lily also collapses at the same moment: all because of a painting!

Before this musical apotheosis, Lily had noticed a canvas hanging in the old woman's room of a medieval warrior slicing an eagle in two while a maiden turns away in horror. At the climax of the love duet, Brother

Lily breaks character and also pulls out a sword, moving threateningly from child to child as his sister watches with increasing foreboding. At the end of the piece, Lily turns away from the piano to discover that the room is empty: did she imagine it all? She runs into the old woman's room and finds her crumpled bed deserted, an unhappy Humphrey waddling to the door, muttering. Malle then zooms into the painting and we see the eagle's wing clearly sliced off (a line of flight forestalled: an obvious denial of becoming). Suddenly, we hear the screeching cry of an actual eagle as it flies into the room and lands on the piano, just as Brother and Sister Lily burst through the doorway, brawling. The painting now literally comes to life as Brother Lily attacks the eagle, decapitating it after a long, drawn-out struggle. Sister Lily also emulates the picture by turning away in disgust (she represents becoming-animal, after all), while teenage Lily screams in horror. In effect, Brother Lily has reversed the process of the Kleistian war machine, invoking the painting against the musical machine while at the same time renouncing his own becoming-woman to return as the castrating Oedipal male – a classic reterritorialisation.

This 'return of the repressed' (as State machine) thus serves to capture and ensnare the farm's functioning multiplicity, and Sister Lily responds with utter hatred. With teenage Lily observing from the bedroom window, a savage battle of almost mythological proportions ensues between the two siblings. As a result, this experimental unity in multiplicity splits once more into two, and having failed to kill each other they end up joining the gender war on opposing sides. This is what Jean Oury calls a return to *normopathy*, for as Massumi explains, 'Normopathy magnifies the minimal difference opened by the paradox of play into a monumental difference that is taken over-seriously. The gap is erected into a structural divide, which is defended at all costs in the name of "the way things are." No mixing allowed: play or fight, but for sanity's sake don't contrive to do both at once' (2014: 70). In response to this new psychotic regime, all that is left is for Lily to inherit her allotted role as the Anomalous and restore the multiplicity by adding and subtracting new borders, new lines of flight. Firstly, she impersonates the old woman, lying on her bed, staring into her hand mirror and attempting to call out on the radio transmitter: 'Hello? Can you hear me? Hello. Is nobody there?' Secondly, a snake, from which she had earlier recoiled, slithers between her legs as she dozes off to sleep and she seems to calmly absorb it into her body (Lily becoming-serpent). The snake, of course, has little or no symbolic or metaphorical connection to an Oedipal scenario but is rather another manifestation of the pack or multiplicity, a point reinforced by Malle cutting to an establishing shot of the farmhouse, where we see (and hear) a huge gaggle/cacophony of turkeys in the foreground and a flock of sheep bleating by the front door. Suddenly, as we cut back to the bed, the animal noises are replaced by a familiar electronic hum. Lily stirs, looks up and sees the unicorn (the old woman's alter ego), sitting by the fire, chewing. She gets out of bed and approaches as the unicorn licks her lips. 'Just a minute, please', says Lily and she turns to the dresser, applies alcohol to her nipples and turns towards the camera: freeze frame!!

The freeze-frame is perfectly apt at this point because what follows – Lily's merger with the eternal flow of becomings – is innately unrepresentable because it lies outside of specific time and place. This is *Black Moon*'s moment of radical immanence, of becoming-imperceptible. Braidotti puts it best when she argues that:

> I think the becoming-imperceptible is the point of fusion between the self and his/her habitat, the cosmos as a whole. It marks the point of the evanescence of the self and its replacement by a living nexus of multiple interconnections that empower not the self, but the collective; not identity, but affirmative subjectivity; not consciousness, but affirmative interconnections. (2006: 154)

This merging with our ever-changing environment is what Guattari calls 'chaosmosis': 'It is the becoming-world of the self' (Braidotti 2006: 157), but a world always suspended between the 'no longer' and the 'not yet', in other words a time of Aion as opposed to Chronos. Lily's suckling of the unicorn is to enter a timeless immanence, where the human is reborn in and through a becoming-animal (who is in turn nurtured through a becoming-human) as pure affect. This, for Brian Massumi, is where deterritorialisation becomes absolute, 'the unframing opens an escape hatch leading away from all known arenas of activity given in nature. Becoming-animal is the never before seen, the never done or previously felt' (2014: 57).

References

Agee, J. (1998), 'Introduction' to Heinrich von Kleist, *Penthesilea: A Tragedy*, trans. J. Agee, HarperCollins.

Bogue, R. (2003), *Deleuze and Literature*, New York and London: Routledge.

Braidotti, R. (2006), 'The Ethics of Becoming-Imperceptible', in C.V. Boundas (ed.), *Deleuze and Philosophy*, Edinburgh: Edinburgh University Press, pp. 133–59.

Brown, H. M. (2003), 'Ripe Moments and False Climaxes: Thematic and Dramatic Configurations of the Theme of Death in Kleist's Works', in Bernd Fischer (ed.),

A Companion to the Works of Heinrich von Kleist, Rochester, NY: Camden House, pp. 209–26.

Carrière, M. (1985), *Pour une littérature de guerre: Kleist*, trans. M. Ziegler, Arles: Actes Sud.

Deleuze, G. (1988), *Spinoza: Practical Philosophy*, trans. R. Hurley, San Francisco: City Lights Books.

Deleuze, G. (1989), *Cinema 2: The Time-Image*, trans. H. Tomlinson and R. Galeta, Minneapolis: University of Minnesota Press.

Deleuze, G. (1995), *Negotiations*, trans. M. Joughin, New York: Columbia University Press.

Deleuze, G. (1997), *Essays Critical and Clinical*, trans. D.W. Smith and M.A. Greco, Minneapolis: University of Minnesota Press.

Deleuze, G. and F. Guattari (1986), *Kafka: Toward a Minor Literature*, trans. D. Polan, Minneapolis: University of Minnesota Press.

Deleuze, G. and F. Guattari (1987), *A Thousand Plateaus: Capitalism and Schizophrenia*, trans. B. Massumi, Minneapolis: University of Minnesota Press.

Deleuze, G. and F. Guattari (1994), *What is Philosophy?*, trans. H. Tomlinson and G. Burchell, New York: Columbia University Press.

Deleuze, G. and C. Parnet (1987), *Dialogues*, trans. H. Tomlinson and B. Habberjam, New York: Columbia University Press.

Doel, M. (1999), *Poststructuralist Geographies: The Diabolical Art of Spatial Science*, Lanham, Boulder and New York: Rowman & Littlefield.

Gardner, C. (2014), 'Out of the Labyrinth, into the Métro: Becoming-animal, the Waking Dream and Movements of World in Raymond Queneau and Louis Malle's *Zazie dans le métro*', in P. MacCormack (ed.), *The Animal Catalyst: Towards Ahuman Theory*, London and New York: Bloomsbury Publishing.

Kleist, H. von (1807), 'Letter to Marie von Kleist', Dresden, Spätherbst. Spiegel Online Kultur, Projekt Gutenberg – DE, *Heinrich von Kleist: Briefe* (No. 118), at http://gutenberg.spiegel.de/buch/briefe-7043/9 (accessed 17 December 2014).

Kleist, H. von (1808), 'Letter to Herrn Heinrich von Collin', Hochwohlgeboren zu Wien, Dresden, den 8. Dezmbr. 1808. Spiegel Online Kultur, Projekt Gutenberg – DE, *Heinrich von Kleist: Briefe* (No. 141), at http://gutenberg.spiegel.de/buch/briefe-7043/10 (accessed 17 December 2014).

Kleist, H. von (1998), *Penthesilea: A Tragedy*, trans. J. Agee, New York: HarperCollins.

MacCormack, P. (2012), *Posthuman Ethics*, Farnham: Ashgate.

Malle, L. (1975), Interview in 21 September episode of the French television program, *Pour Le cinéma*. Criterion DVD reissue of *Black Moon*.

Massumi, B. (2002), *Parables for the Virtual: Movement, Affect, Sensation*, Durham, NC: Duke University Press.

Massumi, B. (2014), *What Animals Teach Us About Politics*, Durham, NC: Duke University Press.

Sellier, G. (2008), *Masculine Singular: French New Wave Cinema*, trans. K. Ross, Durham, NC: Duke University Press.

Chapter 5

Ant and Empire: Myrmetic Writing, Simulation and the Problem of Reciprocal Becomings

Zach Horton

While Deleuze's conceptual and affective ligaments with animals are multitudinous, I wish to differentiate between two primary roles that his nonhuman creatures play within his and Guattari's thought: that of *diagram* (of a rhizome) and that of *vector* (of becoming). As diagram, the animal is a multiplicity of molecular forces, a set of intensive relationships of motion and rest, a group being, a pack of any-animal-whatever. This is the animal-function Deleuze and Guattari develop in their introduction to *A Thousand Plateaus* ('Rhizome') and '1914: One or Several Wolves?' The Deleuzian animal diagram is distinguished from the human diagram by its inherent multiplicity – its assemblage form – and its concomitant potential to spread, swarm, cluster, diffuse, etc. As vector of becoming, on the other hand, the animal is a singularity, not a destination or even a metastable state, but a direction, a line of flight from majoritarian molarity. This is a prescription for virtuality, and is the animal Deleuze and Guattari have in mind in their famous chapter '1730: Becoming-Intense, Becoming-Animal, Becoming-Imperceptible . . .'. The Deleuzian animal vector is distinguished from the human point by its distance along a line of becoming, its relative position between the metastable state of molar human identity and a diffusion of being into molecularity.

What is the relationship between these two animal functions? Does the vector point towards the diagram as a kind of destination (seemingly a contradiction)? Does the diagram offer a normative model by which to evaluate particular species for suitability as vectors of becoming? Is the relationship temporally ordered: first a contemplation, a virtual kinship on the plane of consistency, a diagrammatic melding that will later be actualised in a process (vector) of becoming? In an attempt to further excavate the conceptual assemblage pointed to by these queries, as well as to problematise it, I will subject it to an onslaught by perhaps the most voracious of all animals: the ant.

The ant appears to occupy the beguiling position of perfectly fulfilling the roles of both diagram and vector. As such, it poses a problem for the authors of *A Thousand Plateaus*. While becomings-animal are meant to be continual movements of transformation away from a centre (ultimately leading only *through* the animal towards the molecular, towards becoming-imperceptible), the ant, when figured by the human, leads curiously *back* to the human. We shall examine a number of examples of this troubling return that is more than a reterritorialisation, that is in fact a *reciprocal becoming*. As we shall see, when writers and simulation designers produce speculative vectors of human-becomings-ant, they quite often simultaneously produce reciprocal ant-becomings-human that paradoxically negate the ant as rhizomatic diagram. As such, the ant is a limit case for Deleuze and Guattari: can the animal in principle be made to serve both the role of diagram and vector? To answer this question we must turn to a form of creative speculative activity that I will refer to as *myrmetic*. I mean to suggest by this coinage (a play on the Greek for 'ant' and 'imitation') the uneasy conjunction of rhizomatic ant subjectivity with human inscriptions of it that are, as we shall see, both mimetic themselves and concerned with the potential for mimesis in ant dynamics. We will examine the myrmetic writings of Henry David Thoreau, H. G. Wells, Bernard Werber and E. O. Wilson, as well as several myrmetic simulation games, in order to excavate the labyrinthine tunnels of ant writing, with their dark forebodings of human apocalypse and oubliettes of reciprocal becomings.

Ant as Diagram

'You can never get rid of ants because they form an animal rhizome that can rebound time and again after most of it has been destroyed', note Deleuze and Guattari in their only mention of ants of which I'm aware (1987: 30). As a model multiplicity, ants are resilient to attack: they are one body or substance, but if you break it, wound it, or divide it, it easily reforms, flows into another form, according to what Deleuze and Guattari deem 'principles of connection and heterogeneity: any point of a rhizome can be connected to anything other, and must be' (1987: 7). The ant is both one and many, a network in which each node is in principle connected to every other node. 'The colony, in other words the superorganism, can be subdivided into any conceivable combination of sets of its members', enthuse Bert Hölldobler and Edward Wilson, the world's leading myrmecologists. 'It can then be manipulated experimentally and reconstituted at the end of the day, unharmed and ready for replicate treatment at a later time' (1990: 3). This mesmerising (mesmyrising?) malleability in the laboratory takes on ominous overtones in the natural habitat of ants, if ant documentaries are to be believed. 'We humans like to think that *we* run the world', begins a classic episode of *Nova* devoted to the subject, 'but in many ways it is really [the ants] who run the show. When ants march together, little can stand in their way' (*Little Creatures* 1995). A more recent Discovery Channel documentary notes ominously, accompanied by the low apocalyptic rumblings of its musical score, that 'When social behaviour is taken to the extreme, it becomes something great: a superorganism' (*Wild City* 2013). This is to say that the great multiplicities that are ant colonies possess emergent properties roughly analogous to those of individual organisms: a collective brain, digestive system, reproductive system, limbs, etc. Emergent organs. What humans think of as individual ants are better conceived of as cells in a larger being, specialised for certain tasks, but performing them only as part of a larger system. This capacity for scale-shifting communitarianism has been achieved through an evolutionary process of de-Oedipalisation: the entire colony's reproductive potential is invested in the queen organ. Male ants are only produced on rare occasions, and then only to spread the colony's genetic material outside of the nest. The males, nothing more than 'guided missile[s] loaded with sperm' (Wilson 2010: 177), mate with these exogenous queens-to-be and quickly die. All other ants in a colony, from queen to soldier to worker, are female. Without reproductive concerns, ants can accomplish astonishing feats of nest building, predation and ecological dominance. As *Wild City of Ants* makes clear, 'Their societies are hard wired for efficiency and expansion. Destined to dominate everywhere they live, from city street to rainforest to desert.'

If ants possess, according to these documentary media, a kind of manifest destiny to dominate every ecological niche on planet earth, it is due to their properties and capacities of flow. Zhongyang Liu and David Hu, physicists at the Georgia Institute of Technology, have studied the ways that fire ants 'can act like a fluid or a solid, depending on the situation'. 'To flow, they moved around, rearranging themselves in the group, acting like a thick fluid. When the aggregation struggled to keep its shape, the ants clung to each other, acting like an elastic solid – rubber for example' (Gorman 2013). The successful treatment of fire ants – whose behaviour is not unique among ant species – within the paradigm of fluid dynamics suggests that ants are the rhizomatic organism(s) *par excellence*, composed, one might say, 'not of units but of dimension, or rather direction in motion' (Deleuze and Guattari 1987: 21). Hölldobler and Wilson characterise the internal structure of ant colonies as one of 'dense heterarchy'. This is to say that ant castes are organised as distinct strata, but without a commanding caste or centre: 'the highest level of the ant colony is the totality of its membership rather than a particular set of superordinate individuals who direct the activity of members at lower levels'. Decisions are made through emergent consensus from the bottom up. Chains of communication and command are perfectly rhizomatic in a colony: 'any member is likely to communicate with any other member' (Hölldobler and Wilson 1990: 355). Communication propagates through complex chemical secretions (sometimes augmented by visual or aural expression) capable of signalling various states of alarm, the location of food, prey, or an advantageous new nesting site, as well as caste identification, the need for more members of a particular caste, the danger posed by a worker who has dared to lay eggs (the sole privilege of the queen), the death of an ant, etc. These signals propagate fluidly, reinforced or redirected by other individual ants, flowing alongside bodies that continually form new conjunctions with them. In this sense thought is fully embodied, never abstracted from concrete flows of food and other matter. Emergent structures are composed on a plane of immanence saturated by the flow of bodies.

Conceptualising ants as superorganisms emphasises that their organisational forces are not necessarily in alignment with their centre of subjectivity, but run the risk of reterritorialising molar identity at a different scale. Henry David Thoreau expresses precisely this scalar unease at the unstable site of myrmetic subjectivity in a famous example of nineteenth-century ant writing:

> One day when I went out to my wood-pile . . . I observed two large ants, the one red, the other much larger, nearly half an inch long, and black, fiercely contending with one another . . . Looking farther, I was surprised to find that the chips were covered with such combatants, that it was not a *duellum*, but a *bellum*, a war between two races of ants, the red always pitted against the black, and frequently two red ones to one black. The legions of these Myrmidons covered all the hills and vales in my woodyard, and the ground was already strewn with the dead and dying, both red and black. It was the only battle which I have ever witnessed, the only battle-field I have ever trod while the battle was raging; internecine war; the red republicans on the one hand, and the black imperialists on the other . . . I was myself excited somewhat even as if they had been men. The more you think of it, the less the difference. And certainly there is not the fight recorded in Concord history, at least, if in the history of America, that will bear a moment's comparison with this, whether for the numbers engaged in it, or for the patriotism and heroism displayed. (Thoreau 2000: 215–16)

Thoreau, emerging from his cabin in the woods – symbol of harmony and peace – discovers a raging war that he first mistakes for a duel: a rivalry, misunderstanding, or murderous animosity between two molar individuals. Apprehending the full scale of the conflict requires of the amateur naturalist a greater sensory perspicuity, a second survey. This second stage of encounter with the ants produces in the terrain of his writing a distended landscape, a transformation of his wood pile into a topography marked by hills and vales, and capable of hosting legions of soldiers bent on dominating it. Two scalar movements characterise Thoreau's prose here: one downward to resolve the very small and one outward to laterally resolve an expanded surface. Despite the excitement felt by the author as a result of this scalar expansion, the Homeric rush of large-scale martial narrativity, his next action remarkably telescopes his field of action:

> I took up the chip on which the three I have particularly described were struggling, carried it into my house, and placed it under a tumbler on my window-sill, in order to see the issue. Holding a microscope to the first-mentioned red ant, I saw that, though he was assiduously gnawing at the near foreleg of his enemy, having severed his remaining feeler, his own breast was all torn away, exposing what vitals he had there to the jaws of the black warrior, whose breastplate was apparently too thick for him to pierce; and the dark carbuncles of the sufferer's eyes shone with ferocity such as war only could excite. (217)

A remarkable scalar reterritorialisation marks this passage. Thoreau literally isolates these individual ants from the larger theatre of action he had discovered, magnifying them within an inverted tumbler, which serves simultaneously as instrument of capture and optical observation. This compulsion to isolate, to magnify, to trade topography for faciality (locking eyes with those dark carbuncles shining with ferocity), expresses the diagrammatic contours not of the ant, but of ant writing. 'I never learned which party was victorious, nor the cause of the war', admits Thoreau, unable to resolve both scales at once. The ant awes the human in its vast multiplicity, but is ultimately engaged only at the level of the individual: magnified and isolated as singular organism or re-molarised as anthropomorphic legion or individual (super)organism. 'I felt for the rest of that day as if I had had my feelings excited and harrowed by witnessing the struggle, the ferocity and carnage, of a human battle before my door' (218). The ant, in speculative encounter with the human, is scale-bifurcated, its own becomings bent backwards towards a becoming-human. And yet this becoming-human is refracted through this very bifurcation, becoming an oscillation – a struggle to map the scale-fluidity of the ant rhizome.

Ant as Vector

H. G. Wells's great myrmetic story from 1905, 'Empire of the Ants', chronicles the adventures of Captain Gerilleau, a Portuguese Creole ordered up the Amazon to a remote settlement in Brazil. His assignment is to 'assist the inhabitants against a plague of ants', which leads him to suspect 'the authorities of mockery' (Wells 1977: 1). Gerilleau complains to his friend, the English engineer of his vessel, 'What can a man do against ants? Dey come, dey go' (2). But it turns out that the ants in question are particularly vicious, and have nearly routed a small village, raiding its homes, forcing its human occupants to flee, and killing one young man. Still, Gerilleau is indignant: 'When I joined dis service I joined to fight men. Dese things, dese ants, dey come and go. It is no business for men' (6). The nomadic, fluid ant is not a proper adversary for a colonialist bent on controlling territory. Gerilleau's thoughts soon transition, however, from the coming and going of the ants to a more open-ended diagrammatic inquiry: 'Gerilleau's mind was full of ants and what they could do . . . "What can one do with ants?"' (8). These dual questions continue to haunt the Captain throughout the text: What can ants do? What can we do with ants? This two-vectored query is precisely the question of becoming for Deleuze and Guattari:

> We know nothing about a body until we know what it can do, in other words, what its affects are, how they can or cannot enter into composition with other affects, with the affects of another body, either to destroy that body or to be destroyed by it, either to exchange actions and passions with it or to join with it in composing a more powerful body . . . These affects circulate and are transformed within the assemblage: what a horse 'can do'. (1987: 257)

These are, certainly, Gerilleau's thoughts, a terrain of potentiality mapped by Wells. Ants come and go, humans stay: a colonial binary. Ants are a fluid mass, humans a set of territorialising homesteaders. When ants come to *this* village, humans flee, becoming fluid themselves, dissolving around and melting away from their solid infrastructure. When a boy makes the mistake of returning home, of crossing the threshold into enclosed domestic space, he finds that the ants that have *come* have not yet *gone*. His body enters into a composition with theirs briefly: 'Presently he comes out again – screaming and running. He runs

past them to the river. See? He get into de water and drowns de ants . . .
That night he dies, just as if he was stung by a snake' (Wells 1977: 6).
A line from house to river, traced by screams, inaugurates two flows –
water over the human body, washing away the ants, and poison through
the bloodstream. And then a strange reciprocal death that scrambles the
linguistic codes of animality: Gerilleau delivers the denouement of this
story as a snake simile, but this snake stings rather than bites. What can
ants do? The linguistic transference of this simile, the human body poisoned by ants as if from a stinging snake, furthers a line of becoming into
a potentially infinite series. If the ants can poison as a snake, the snake
can sting. For Deleuze and Guattari every becoming initiates a series: X
becomes Y, but Y then becomes Z. 'Captain Ahab is engaged in an irresistible becoming-whale with Moby-Dick; but the animal, Moby-Dick,
must simultaneously become an unbearable pure whiteness, a shimmer-
ing pure white wall, a silver thread like a rampart' (1987: 304). In this
way becoming is virtual: what it produces is radically new, plucked from
potentiality itself, not the concrete possibilities afforded by comfortable
taxonomy. 'But what *can* one do?' asks Gerilleau hopelessly, not quite
up to the task of becoming-animal (Wells 1977: 23).

Gerilleau's uncertainty about the affects of the ants, their potential
configurations and compositions, reaches its apotheosis when his boat
encounters a village that has been completely taken over by the myrmidons, its huts now mixed with complex earthworks. Having already
encountered a derelict boat filled with the voracious ants and lost two
crew members trying to board it, Gerilleau is left in a panic: 'To send
a landing party – it is impossible – impossible. They will be poisoned
. . . If we land, I must land alone, alone, in thick boots and with my
life in my hand. Perhaps I should live. Or again – I might not land. I do
not know. I do not know' (Wells 1977: 23). The choice – between not
landing, landing as an individual, or landing as a group – is one that
Gerilleau cannot make until he has answered the question, 'what can
one do?' What are the conditions of possibility for the human to act as
a collective? To remain on the boat without acting at all? At issue is not
Gerilleau's bravery or cowardice, but only his successful or unsuccessful
attempt to formulate a vector of becoming. Can the human become ant?
The problem, as Gerilleau recognises, is that when the human becomes
ant, the ant wins on its own turf by mobilising its vastly superior potentiality for articulated motion. To remain a molar, individual human
is even worse: what can one human do in relation to an ant superorganism? The remaining alternative is to stay on the boat, to suspend
encounter and affect.

For human colonialists, remaining on the boat means ceding territory, conquering nothing, atrophying the Empire. The problem facing Gerilleau, then, is this: in order to remain human, the colonialists must become something other, but their vector of becoming in this case shoots straight through the evolved ant colony that is slowly territorialising the Brazilian jungle, and thus into inevitable (and unwinnable) conflict. To Wells, no mechanism is available to effect the further becoming suggested by Deleuze and Guattari: the animal's becoming further along this vector. Instead, Wells rolls out the heavy artillery of irony. '"I have decided," said the captain . . . *I shall fire de big gun!*" . . . Heaven knows what the ants thought of it, but he did . . . there was an effect of going into action about the whole affair, and first they hit and wrecked the old sugar-mill, and then they smashed the abandoned store behind the jetty' (Wells 1977: 24–5). Having thus pointlessly destroyed their own colonial infrastructure, a non-action standing in for action, a point standing in for a line, they retreat back down the river and leave this problem of becoming to the Colonial Office.

Reciprocal Becomings

French novelist Bernard Werber picks up Wells's project, while recognising that ant becomings cannot take place within zero sum games of settler colonialism. His contemporary ant novel, *Les Fourmis* (published in English under the title *Empire of the Ants*, appropriately mimicking Wells's title), opens with an inheritance: Edmond Wells has left his basement level apartment to his (adult) nephew Jonathan. The structure contains an ancient passageway that leads deep into the bowels of the earth, from which no one seems to return. The narrative follows various humans down this tunnel, only to pull back before they reach the end, jumping to the perspective of other characters who have not yet made the journey. These broken human tales make up a bit less than half of the text. Most of the rest is devoted to the adventures of several ant protagonists: a soldier, a worker and a male. Part of the vast Federation, they experience massive battles such as the one that played out at Walden Pond in 1846, encounters with various other insects, and the development of several ant technologies, including the harnessing of beetles for warfare and rafts for river navigation. The soldier eventually discovers a great secret: the queen of the Federation is in fact in communication with the 'guardians of the end of the world', giant pinkish creatures that bring sudden death to ants who venture too far into their territory.

At the end of the novel, the human narrative comes into sharper focus, as the latest victims of Uncle Edmond's basement tunnel finally meet the small community of previous venturers, who are now living in Edmond's secret laboratory, assembled within a subterranean, seventeenth-century church built by persecuted Protestants. There Edmond built, and Jonathan has perfected, a computerised 'Rosetta stone' device that is capable of translating between spoken human language and scented ant language. The human interface consists of a computer screen and keyboard; the ant interface is a robotic ant named 'Livingstone' connected to the device via two-way tubes. Livingstone occupies a special chamber in the ant city located above the church, accessible only by Queen Belo-kiu-kiuni and her retainers. A mass spectrometer converts the queen's pheromones into electronic signals rendered as human-readable text. When humans enter text into the computer, a vast storehouse of chemicals is drawn upon to compose the approximate meaning in ant, secreted above by Livingstone. Edmond Wells, who decoded the ant language, built this apparatus, and initiated communication with the queen, is described by his nephew as 'a kind of Christopher Columbus' who 'discovered a new continent between our toes' (Werber 1999: 272). The references to English missionary David Livingstone and Spanish explorer Christopher Columbus ironically frame the colonial trope of contact. These contemporary, postcolonial Parisian humans have no imperial designs, if only because this recently discovered continent is worth very little given its relative scale. The ants, on the other hand, turn out to harbour imperial designs: the climax of the novel sees the reigning colony destroyed by rivals, its nest occupied by a new colony, led by Queen Chli-pou-ni, who seizes the means of communication with the humans.

Les Fourmis catalyses three lines of becoming as a myrmetic work: the reader's identification with ant protagonists, the reader's identification with human characters encountering ants, and the philosophical mediations of Edmond's great unfinished text, The Encyclopedia of Absolute and Relative Knowledge, which is excerpted throughout the novel. The first is marked by the thoughts and experiences of ant characters rendered in third-person limited perspective. Here we gain access to the inner lives of ants, but the effect is jarring and anthropomorphic, as if ant affects were run through an alpha version of the Rosetta stone computer: 'His antennae drooped stupidly on his forehead. He felt useless and degraded, as if he no longer lived for others but for himself alone' (Werber 1999: 37). In this experiment in ant-writing, Werber always renders the perspective of ants in this mode of bourgeois subjectivity, the purview of the novel form since its inception. While colony-wide collective action is explored in the novel, it is only described from the perspective of individuals, reterritorialising the perspective of superorganism cells into individuated subjects. When the male ant protagonist meets the female worker for the first time, the result is at least as absurd as the purple prose of the human Romance novel: 'And what a female! He took the time to look her over. She had shapely slender legs decorated with little hairs that were deliciously sticky with sexual hormones . . . He wanted to have AC with her. Yes, absolute communication' (73). Titillating stuff, and when AC actually happens two pages later, the effect of intercourse is not to meld identities but to further individuate them: 'Pheromones passed from one body to the other through the thousands of little pores and capillaries of their segments. Their thoughts married. Their ideas were no longer coded and decoded but delivered in all their original simplicity: images, music, emotions and scents' (75). This uncoded exchange, no doubt the envy of many human marriage counselling patients, produces not something new, not an emergent structure, but only the perfect, noise-free Shannonian communication channel, further reifying and differentiating the relative positions of the sender and receiver. This 'marriage of thought' remains Oedipal. Werber's admirable effort to present the life of the ant to the reader thus ends up downloading human consciousness into an ant body: every signified corresponds to a myrmidon milieu, but as readers we may as well have tapped into the sensory circuits of Livingstone, that stalwart antdroid that will never escape Deleuze and Guattari's warning that 'becoming is certainly not imitating, or identifying with something' (1987: 139).

Werber's human characters, unlike the ants of the novel's title, perform essentially the same action as a series. Other than the dead Edmond and his nephew Jonathan, these characters are interchangeable. Every one of them decides to descend into the basement tunnel, despite the many warnings that have come before. Every one of them disappears from the narrative once they have initiated this action. For the reader, the narrative point of view resides within a character only until they make this decision, start on this path. Only at the end of the novel do all of these missing persons turn up again, and when they do, something has changed. We learn that Jonathan has built a set of traps into the tunnel that render it unidirectional. Neither he nor anyone else can exit once they have entered. Thus the menagerie of curious humans who have ventured out of the narrative re-emerge as a collective, living together in the centuries-old church underground. They spend their time growing food, reading Edmond's book of wisdom, and communicating with the ant colony above them. As Jonathan explains, this experience has changed them:

> We're obliged to live together, to complement one another and think as one. We have no choice. If we don't agree, we'll die. And there's no way out. Now I don't know if it comes from my uncle's discovery or what the ants are teaching us simply by existing above our heads, but for the time being our community is getting along like a house on fire . . . You can't have personal ambitions when you're living in a little group under the ground. (Werber 1999: 286)

For Werber's human characters, there has been a narrative break in the continuum of their individual consciousnesses. They have returned as something nonhuman in the sense of non-fully-individuated. Without actually imitating the ants, they appear to be on their way to becoming simultaneously molecular and collective: the scalar oscillation that defines the ant diagram. Their conditions for survival and thus diagram of potential action are approaching that of the ants above. This is a line of becoming.

Edmond's *Encyclopedia of Absolute and Relative Knowledge* makes up the third major component of the text. An entry appears at every textual juncture between ant perspective and human perspective. This running encyclopaedia acts as a mediating machine. Many entries address the reasons ants and humans perceive the world differently: 'For ants, on the other hand, time is relative. When it is hot, the seconds are very short . . . This elastic time gives them a very different perception of the speed of things from our own. To define a movement, insects use not only space and duration but also a third dimension, temperature' (Werber 1999: 76). A later entry: 'Each neuron in our brains and each individual in the anthill holds all the information, but only their collective activity gives rise to consciousness or "three-dimensional thought"' (134). Three-dimensional thought, just like three-dimensional time, is a capacity that humans and ants share, yet experience differently. On the plane of consistency, these concepts can be aligned and conjoined, but not without careful differentiation and mediation. Ant writing works to effect this, creating a body without organs, a virtual substrate outside of the ant and human worlds in which this assemblage of human-ant thought can arise. Edmond's encyclopaedia works both positively and negatively, establishing connections and indicating false directions founded only on analogy: 'It was long thought that computers in general and artificial intelligence programs in particular would mingle human concepts and present them from a new angle ... But even when it is presented differently, the raw material remains the same: ideas produced by human imaginations. It is a dead end. The best way to renew thought is to go outside the human imagination' (253). To become ant is not to understand the ant on human terms, or to imitate its behaviour. It is to produce a new plane of thought and action oblique to the determinate series. The ant is the catalyst to divert human thought from its well-worn trajectories. 'What would happen', asks Edmond, 'if, instead of running parallel to one another, the two forms of intelligence cooperated?' (288).

This seductive dream of interspecies communication plays out at all three levels of becoming-ant in the novel: Edmond's encyclopaedia becomes devoted to the task of simply recording his interactions with the ants. It details, for instance, how he communicated to the ants the concept of the wheel, whereupon the queen immediately grasped the technological potential of such a movement machine. Meanwhile, in the present human world, the new subterranean colony emerges in all of its narrative potential. On the ant side, however, trouble is brewing. Chli-pou-ni, the new queen, communicates with the humans and asks them 'Why?' Though the humans respond with confusion, Chli-pou-ni decides that they are the principal enemy of her people: 'It was they, the human beings, who had done it [wiped out their old colony]. Mother knew them. She had always known them. She had kept it a secret' (Werber 1999: 295). After cutting off communication with the humans, she remains, at the novel's end, in deep contemplation, refusing to give an immediate order that would clarify how they are to deal with the human nest below them. The text ends, then, not with an affirmation of interspecies communication and cooperation, but with a vision of its negation. Even Edmond's final encyclopaedic entry negates his earlier optimism: Ants predate humans by a hundred million years, and are likely to postdate them by a similar span of time. 'We are just a three-million-year-long accident in their history. Moreover, if extraterrestrials ever landed on our planet, they would be in no doubt about it. They would try to talk to them. Them, the true masters of the Earth' (294).

Werber's novel thus diagnoses a problem at the same time that it engineers a potential narrative becoming. Human subjectivity sutured to an ant body, the first level of myrmeticism, collapses into itself. The reconstitution of the human according to ant-like conditions of subterranean collectivity and food production do indeed produce a vector of becoming. According to Deleuze and Guattari's formula, one becomes animal and the animal becomes-other. In this case, however, as in much ant writing, the ants' own vector of becoming is inverted with regard to that of the human. Instead of a minor becoming continuing along the initial line of the major becoming, the minor becoming doubles back and opposes the first.

Les Fourmis presents us with a perfectly formulated example of reciprocal becoming and demonstrates its reactivity: diegetically, the ants gain the technological prowess and individuated communication channels of humans, and end up expressing nothing less than Nietzschean *ressentiment*. Revenge catalyses the ants' future vector of becoming, a reactive response to the territorial appropriations of humans rather than a joyous expression of ant life lived for its own sake. Extra-diegetically, the novel places the reader in a paradoxical position: as sutured to an ant body, denied human corporeality until the final pages, forced to imagine life confined to a subterranean chamber communicating only with ants, and forced to consider the geological timespan of ant being. The novel, human textuality itself, which conspicuously fails to signify ant consciousness, exists within this 'accidental' blip in ant history, a history that extends far enough back and forward to saturate possible becomings that originate from the ant. From this perspective, the human, as textual being, can initiate exactly these sorts of becomings, but finds, when such a vector is followed far enough, only an asignifying abyss where a tiny, segmented, describable ant body seemed to be. Human-becoming-ant on the myrmetic plane of consistency triggers a reciprocal becoming simply because the ants' becoming saturates a similar plane that extends through temporal scales inaccessible to the tragically historical human reader.

Werber's novel, which directly invokes Wells's 'Empire of the Ants' through its colonial motifs and the character of Edmond Wells, merely extends its logic to the postcolonial and postecological context of a human territoriality that has become diffuse, multi-vectored and geographically saturated. Ant and Human empires are roughly co-extensive in space, but their scalar mismatch renders fluid their topological relationship: whose territory is inside whose? Werber's text points back towards Wells, who had speculatively mapped this scenario when he ended his story with an ironic inversion of Europe's vector of colonial becoming: 'By 1920 [the ants] will be halfway down the Amazon. I fix 1950 or '60 at the latest for the discovery of Europe' (Wells 1977: 28). Wells's ant-becoming Empire narrativises ant colonialism in comically human terms, on a human historical timeline. As we have seen, however, the relevant unit of ant becoming is no longer the mile or year, but rather millennia.

Homogeneity and Difference

Do any of the preceding observations present a problem for Deleuze and Guattari? Is becoming-ant paradigmatic, or a special case? The Bible suggests the former in its myrmetic injunction: 'Go to the ant, thou sluggard; consider her ways, and be wise' (Proverbs 6:6). Henri Bergson suggests the latter, making a case for ant singularity: 'It has been said of the ants that, as man is lord of the soil, they are lords of the sub-soil . . . The evolution of the arthropods reaches its culminating point in the insect, and in particular in the hymenoptera [the order of insects that includes ants], as that of the vertebrates in man' (Bergson 1998: 134). For Bergson the ant is equivalent to humans in 'success' (measured as territorial dominance and adaptive capacity), but of a qualitatively different *élan* or impulse: instinctive rather than intelligent. Synthesising E.O. Wilson's contributions to the documentary, the narrator of *Little Creatures Who Run the World* offers a similar opinion, noting that 'on almost every count – success through geologic time, geographic range, and sheer weight of numbers – ants and other social insects come out ahead', but Hölldobler and Wilson add the proviso that 'our advantage – and responsibility – lies in the fact that we can think about these matters and they cannot' (Hölldobler and Wilson 1990: 597). Both Wilson and Bergson consider the ant adaptively superior to the human, while suggesting that it occupies an analogous position atop the evolutionary ladder, but on a radically different branch or plane. Wilson's relatively recent myrmetic novel, *Anthill*, attempts to drive this home by inserting, in the middle of its central narrative arc about a boy who devotes half of his life to saving the precious Lake Nokobee tract of Alabama wilderness where he grew up, a seventy-four-page story of two ant colonies living on that land. Titled 'The Anthill Chronicles', it 'presents the story as near as possible to the way ants see such events themselves' (Wilson 2010: 170). The Chronicles chiefly concern an ant colony benefiting from a mutation that causes it to no longer attack its ant competitors, instead enrolling them into an unstoppable supercolony that destroys nearly every other life-form in the area. This homogenising advance is only halted when human 'gods' appear out of nowhere and poison the lot, allowing a significantly more humble colony nearby to recover and grow in a more ecologically sustainable manner.

The difference between ants and humans, according to Wilson, is all too clear in this myrmetic morality play: ants have built-in mechanisms (Bergson's 'instinct') that allow them to dominate their territory while maintaining internal difference that keeps their numbers in check and their impact on their environment sustainable, while humanity contains no such inbuilt constraints, and must therefore impose them through conscious design (Bergson's 'intelligence'). While Bergson privileges the human intellect for its capacity to engage in virtual becomings, Wilson suggests that the ingrained, instinctual (structural) 'wisdom' of the ants is significantly more effective at promoting the aims of life more generally on a planet facing rapid climate change and its sixth great extinction. If humans are to avoid the planetary homogenisation of life and ecosystem produced in miniature by the mutated ants of Lake Nokobee, they must follow the example of ordinary ants and remain fitted to their ecological niche. Ants, for Wilson, have already charted humanity's futures. Once again, they saturate all human vectors of becoming.

Ovid had already acknowledged as much in the *Metamorphoses*, following his harrowing description of a plague that wiped out almost the entire human population of Aegina with King Aegeus' vision of ants marching upon an oak tree:

> Here, hard at work
> My eyes fell on an endless train of ants
> Huge loads in tiny mouths, all following
> Their private path across the wrinkled bark.
> In wonder at their numbers, 'Grant', I said,
> 'Thou best of sires, so many citizens
> To me and stock again my empty walls!' (Ovid 2009: 163)

The subject-less king's addressee, Jove, grants him his wish, transforming the colony of ants into humans to repopulate his kingdom with this 'thrifty, toiling lot' that he names 'Myrmidons' in order to 'tell in truth their origin'. An entire kingdom of human subjects coaxed forth from the wellspring of ant becoming. Wilson's narrative, in describing a dangerous superfluity of ants, draws from the same well, but positions these Myrmidons in the analogical role of humans. Ironically, while Wilson wishes to uphold a distinction between the ecological wisdom of ants and the corresponding foolishness in humans, in his ecological fable writ small, the human exterminators take Jove's place as the only available *deus ex machina* to sweep away the cancerous hoards of ecological offenders. Yet even in this muddled metamorphosis, it is the seemingly limitless capacity of ants to regenerate that underwrites the return to ecological normalcy at Lake Nokobee.

Ant as human and ant as ant: Wilson's experiment in myrmetic allegory reveals the ant, once again, as a countervalent force, a becoming-human that turns the myrmetic vector against itself. In the terms with which I opened this chapter, ants serve as a saturated *diagram* of fluid multiplicity, but as a negating *vector* of (human) becoming. The reason is that the ant diagram contains within it sufficient fluidity – whether we characterise this as overdetermined articulations of movement, creative evolutionary potential, or an overwhelmingly vast spatio-temporal scale – to saturate any attempt to engage it as vector in speculative thought. The ant sounds the depth of our virtual dimensions, but the echo it returns through the chasms of time bear mocking witness to the pathetic scale, the eternal belatedness, of the human.

Simulation and Empire

E. O. Wilson and Bert Hölldobler published their monumental study of ants in 1990, the year after Will Wright released his genre-defining computer game, *SimCity*. Wright read the tome and was sufficiently inspired to base his next game on its concepts (Seabrook 2014). The result, *SimAnt*, attempts once again to suture the player to ant consciousness. Diegetically, the human is marked by otherworldly alterity, represented in the game's basic map as a pair of disembodied feet that occasionally appear out of nowhere, squashing everything in their path. The player has two essential sets of controls, each in its own window. The first determines the general production programme of the colony: the relative ratios of workers, soldiers and breeders, and their behavioural priorities (foraging, digging and nursing). The settings made by the player determine the types of flows that emanate from the queen. The second set of controls, however, require the player to choose and then control a single ant. Depending on the caste of the selected avatar, she can dig tunnels, forage for food to bring back to the nest, or lead an attack on the enemy (red) ant colonies. When the player's ant avatar dies, she is 'reborn' as a newly hatched ant in the queen's nursery. Thus, while the player lives an unlimited number of lives, and can even switch to any other member of the colony at any time, the effect is always to individuate a single cell of the colony, a point amid the general flows of the simulation.

Another map available to the player affords a large-scale view of the game's world, which turns out to be a smallish suburban back yard. At this scale, no ants can be seen, but a young boy – possessor of the deadly feet – sometimes appears, talking to himself or interacting with a dog on the other side of the fence. These human actions take on a monolithic character, large-scale events that can determine the fate of worlds, but which remain curiously detached from both individual ant movements and the strategic reconstitution of colony-wide flows. While designing this game, Wright became fascinated with simulating the house and the boy, to the point of hatching an idea for a new game (Wright 2004). This one would involve the simulation of individual humans within the immediate environs of their homes. The result would eventually become the best-selling PC game in history, *The Sims*. The rhizomatic potentials of the ant become – as a line through *SimAnt* – multi-scalar human gameplay that is ultimately reterritorialised upon the movements and rhythms of the individual human body. Human becoming ant becoming human.

Later ant simulators attempt their own lines of flight from this scale-specific obsession with the human form. *Empire of the Ants*, based upon Werber's novel, deterritorialises *SimAnt* from the back yard, and eliminates simulated humans from the gameplay. The player controls groups of ants as aggregates, directing them to carry out various nest maintenance, foraging, exploration and combat tasks in what quickly becomes a tedious, routinised struggle for survival. Moving further in this direction, *Myrmedrome*, which designers Simone Cacace and Emiliano Cristiani bill as 'a real ant colony simulator', restricts human gameplay to setting global parameters such as scent evaporation rate, maximum ant age, etc. Once the simulation starts, the player can only watch, at different scales and informatic granularity, the fate of two ant colonies unfold. Ants lay pheromone trails, engage in combat, forage for food, die of starvation, attempt to grow their nests, etc. The secret to this fascinating simulation lies in its bottom-up structure. Instead of programming an intricate world from the top down to act as a gamescape for strategising humans, *Myrmedrome* begins with a set of simple rules for ant behaviour, which are subject to the simulation's global variables. These, plus a simple terrain map with two anthills and several patches of food, serve as the starting conditions. The complex behaviour displayed during the simulation run is entirely emergent. Various tools, such as a 'scent view' that makes pheromone trails visible, can be toggled on and off, rendering the underlying mechanisms of the simulation visible to the user. In this way, the simulation itself serves as a form of becoming. Whether or not the emergent properties it produces match any actual ant species is of secondary interest.

As Manuel De Landa has argued, computer simulations are 'assemblages made out of operators and data', real but not necessarily actual (2011: 201). They depend on the actual existence of some mechanism or another, but don't depend on any *particular* material substratum. Thus the simulation is paradigmatically diagrammatic, charting the possibility space of the virtual as sets of emergent properties that cannot be reduced to particular sets of causally deterministic interactions. For De Landa, employing Deleuze's particular brand of realism, this 'implies an ontological commitment to the autonomous existence of topological singularities, or more generally, to the structure of possibility spaces' (19). In this case, the simulation can describe the virtual becomings of ants all the better for not relying upon a database of actual ant characteristics. *Myrmedrome* does not imitate or represent ants so much as it produces a real space that is diagrammatic and, potentially, vectored. As De Landa emphasises, however, the virtual understanding of simulation as assemblage requires us to incorporate scale as an irreducible element of our analysis: 'natural phenomena exhibit a recurrent part-to-whole relation, in which wholes at one scale become parts at the next larger scale, and . . . interactions between scales can be either left out of a model or added exogenously' (16). As we have seen, it is precisely the muddling of scalar considerations such as these that has mired ant writing in confusion over the site of myrmetic consciousness. Becomings exist not at the level of consciousness but *between scales*. Ants saturate many scales with multiple vectors of becoming, from the microscopic to the global, from the temperature-variable microsecond to geological epochs. Humans are multi-scalar as well, but have a long way to go to catch up with the ants. This is one reason that ant-becomings are so tempting and yet so horrifying for human readers: they decompose and recompose the molar subject. Ant writing too has a long way to go before it can chart vectors that do not bisect the human individual. The right sort of simulation, we have reason to hope, could chart a virtual vector of becoming for both humans and ants that removes any myrmetic reliance on legacy, species-specific properties of consciousness. Such a real possibility space could interact with other systems of flow, including the linguistic (ant writing) and material (flows of ant and human bodies). Such considerations hold out the possibility for a human-ant-other becoming that is not reciprocal and thus negative. This would require, however, a more robust engagement with the relationship between properties, diagrams and scalar becomings.

Even still, we are not quite out of the woods yet. I want to close by way of considering a remarkable fusion of ant writing and simulation that takes the form of a proposed game for Google's augmented reality eyewear, Glass. *Swarm!* isn't actualised, but exists as an elaborate fundraising pitch and 'Game Bible' by its designers Jon Lawhead and Daniel Estrada. They describe the game as a 'Massively Multiplayer Online Augmented Reality Simulation (MMOARS) game in which you are an ant foraging, fighting, and working tirelessly for your Colony and your life!' (Uswak 2013). *Swarm!* is meant to take advantage of Google Glass, itself envisioned as a network of wearable computers that combine wireless Internet access with real-time tracking via GPS with bidirectional optical feeds embedded in the glasses themselves. Thus a Glass wearer can be tracked as part of a massive online 'ant' simulation, leaving a digital pheromone trail behind, while simultaneously viewing the game's 'augmented reality' as a set of *other* players' trails, superimposed over the actual world she encounters: sidewalks, streets, buildings, etc. What Glass brings to this simulation, then, is the coupling of a virtual environment with the actual one that defines the player's everyday peregrinations. *Swarm!* enrolls players as ants, but does not ask them to sit in front of a screen that produces some form of ant interface. Rather, it enrolls each player's entire *umwelt* (lifeworld) along with her individual consciousness and legal-financial-psychological identity: 'Swarm! begins when you leave your home with your Glass, and will play in the background as you go about your normal activities' (Lawhead and Estrada 2013). Furthermore, 'players' feed their movements into the system even when they aren't actively 'playing': 'Since Swarm! collects data periodically whether or not you engage the app, users can decide their own level of immersion while still contributing meaningfully to the game environment' (*Swarm!* Fundraising Pitch).

Because the game converts a player's movements, rhythms and actions into a large-scale simulation and then back as blocks of sensation for other players, the line of demarcation between 'real life' and 'gameplay' or 'simulation' is deliberately elided. The game converts actual movement into virtual paths at the same time that it 'pushes' aggregate paths back to players as additional features of their *umwelten*: paths of others that can be followed as a becoming, traced as a history, intersected or avoided. 'Players' movement patterns are visualised as colourful trails on a map card, which *Swarm!* can push on request to your Glass display. These trails are designed so they cannot be used to locate or track any individual uniquely. Instead, we're interested in the broader patterns of behavior' (*Swarm!* Fundraising Pitch). Fundamental to the concept of *Swarm!*, then, is a series of scale-shifts. A single Glass wearer becomes a path, but at the level of the simulation (produced as the aggregate flow of data into Google's servers), a mass of movements emerges at an entirely different scale. This agglomeration of intersecting, reinforced paths traces the contours of a city's infrastructure, a population's rhythms.

Michel de Certeau famously theorised the authors of these paths as '*Wandermanner*, whose bodies follow the thicks and thins of an urban "text" they write without being able to read it . . . The networks of these moving, intersecting writings compose a manifold story that has neither author nor spectator, shaped out of fragments of trajectories and alterations of spaces' (de Certeau 2011: 93). For de Certeau, visibility emerges from an experience of height, from the scopic drive of verticality (obtained in his case by climbing to the 105th floor or the World Trade Center in New York City). Significantly, *Swarm!* produces these emergent patterns not in the consciousness of a vertically distant observer, but in its digital simulation. As De Landa reminds us, emergence produces an ontological commitment to a real virtuality at the same time that it severs any necessary causal link to the *particular* interactions at lower scales that ostensibly brought it about. This is the ontological equivalent of de Certeau's phenomenological distinction between the writers of and the legible text itself that emerges from urban space. The significance of *Swarm!* lies in the feedback loop that it produces between scales: its *Wandermanner* go about their everyday lives, walking in the city, while a new set of virtual interactions emerges within Google's simulation. Then, without a godlike observation point, without any radical change in perspective, the Glass system delivers the virtual potentials of this aggregate back to its individual enrollees in the form of new lines, objects and potential interactions on the surface of their everyday milieu. The emergences at one scale have been interfaced with the lower-level interactions at a much smaller scale. This will, in the designers' eyes, produce a new set of second-order emergences: 'Swarm! is more than just a game. It's a framework for engaging the crowds as they navigate shared public spaces. Swarm! is a radical experiment in self-organization' (*Swarm!* Fundraising pitch).

While the game involves many elements of ant writing, such as playing as a member of a particular caste, foraging for food, engaging in aggressive behaviour against rival 'colonies' and sharing tasks with members of one's own, its greatest potential of becoming-ant lies not in these imitative practices, but in the production of new types of movement that can only arise at larger scales, and do so regardless of the player's in-game engagement. Elements of the resulting virtual spaces are then pushed back to individual users, modifying their everyday phenomenological experience. They can begin to read the monumental text they are writing, at least in fragments, at the same time that they engage a world of movement and rest that is wholly non-individuated. This coupling of medial technics with insect diagrammatics is part of a larger set of medial becomings that Jussi Parrika describes as 'insect media' or 'natural technics': 'A primary characteristic of insects, metamorphosis, is transported to the heart of technics, and technics becomes an issue of affects, relations, and transformations, not a particular substance' (Parrika 2010: xxx). It is in this recursive process of experiencing the kind of emergent behaviour evident in *Myrmedrome* while simultaneously taking part in it, the merging of ant diagrammatics and ant becomings, that *Swarm!* approaches something akin to the Deleuzian concept of becoming-animal.

Swarm! is, however, only a virtual text. The game, if it is ever deployed at the mass scale necessary in order for it to function as a fully articulated becoming-ant machine, will subject all of its players to enrollment by market forces. Big data functions by converting the actions of individuals into patterns that can be used for prediction. Surveillance functions similarly. Players of *Swarm!* would become ant only in order for ants to become consumers and targets, the perfectly enrolled members of their control society. Of course, software protocols could be implemented to limit the data that could be harvested from the system. The larger point, however, is this: humans are already ants. To become collective, fluid and supple flows of dividuals, producers of new forms of movement and thought, mappers of new scales, is certainly a set of vectors worth pursuing. At the same time, however, these potentials have been virtually produced and captured by humanity's own emergent forces: surveillance systems, infrastructural systems, the diffuse power structures of control societies, and the multi-scalar networks and flows of globalised capital, which Michael Hardt and Antonio Negri refer to as deterritorialised Empire.

Could not the ant becomings composed by Thoreau, Wells, Werber, Wilson and Wright, intersecting the present in *Swarm!*, also be read as a genealogy of Empire? Ants are perhaps the most imperial animal on the planet; they cannot help but be humanity's foil, envy, horror and destiny. Ant becomings molecularise the individual subject, but are refracted by empire – the Empire of the Ants that exhausts all possible empires of the human – leaving the ants to come and go, writing their own colonial trajectories. What is a human subject to do? Choose a different animal, or choose a different empire? One can't escape, in any permanent way, the reterritorialising forces unleashed by all becomings. For Deleuze and Guattari 'the subject is born of each state in the series . . . consuming-consummating all these states that cause him to be born and reborn' (1983: 20). As dividual, the subject is constituted by the configurations through which it passes. If thought, which describes a further possible space independent of the subject, is to keep up, to constantly renew its own lines of flight by carving them out of the virtual, it must become and remain nomadic. Any animal becoming must be temporary, a series and not a destination, if it is to elude the forces of capture that will gleefully harness its intensities, forces that are unleashed by the becoming itself. The relationship between thought and subject, between Ant and Empire, must be parsed in terms of scale if we are to avoid reciprocal negation. They (be)come, they go . . . but they also jump scale. Can this practice be made sustainable, a leaping, trans-scalar vector? For us ants, this means we must continue to toil away, catching brief glimmers from time to time of those other scales that might be emancipatory lines of flight or might be the spider web that will finally ensnare us. Both have the smooth, shiny sheen of a body larger and smaller than ourselves, and we can't quite see, from this vantage point, whether it is ant or human, whether or not it possesses organs. What is one to *do*?

References

Bergson, H. (1998) [1911], *Creative Evolution*, unabridged edition, Mineola, NY: Dover Publications.

de Certeau, M. (2011), *The Practice of Everyday Life*, trans. S. F. Rendall, Reprint edition, Berkeley: University of California Press.

De Landa, M. (2011), *Philosophy and Simulation: The Emergence of Synthetic Reason*, London: Continuum.

Deleuze, G. (1986), *Cinema 1: The Movement-Image*, Minneapolis: University of Minnesota Press.

Deleuze, G. (1992), 'Postscript on the Societies of Control', *October*, No. 59, Winter, pp. 3–7.

Deleuze, G. and F. Guattari (1983), *Anti-Oedipus: Capitalism and Schizophrenia*, trans. R. Hurley, M. Seem and H. R. Lane, Minneapolis: University of Minnesota Press.

Deleuze, G. and F. Guattari (1987), *A Thousand Plateaus: Capitalism and Schizophrenia*, trans. B. Massumi, Minneapolis: University of Minnesota Press.

Empire of the Ants (2001), video game, designed by Julien Marty. France: Microids.

Gorman, J. (2013), 'Ants That Can Flow Like a Fluid, or Move Like a Solid', *NYTimes.com*, 17 December 2013.

Hardt, M. and A. Negri (2001), *Empire*, Cambridge, MA: Harvard University Press.

Hölldobler, B. and E. O. Wilson (1990), *The Ants*, 1st edn, Cambridge, MA: Belknap Press.

Lawhead, J. and D. Estrada (2013), 'Swarm!' at https://docs.google.com/document/d/1yeK34abm8kfuDqAma-d18rQ48a7MaonPwgmnyxgN4F4/edit (accessed 13 November 2014).

Little Creatures Who Run the World (1995), television episode, *Nova*. USA: 31 January.

Myrmedrome (2007), computer simulation, programmed by Simone Cacace and Emiliano Cristiani.

Nietzsche, F. (2009) [1887], *On the Genealogy of Morals*, trans. D. Smith, Oxford: Oxford University Press.

Ovid (2009), *Metamorphoses*, trans. A. D. Melville, Reissue edition, Oxford: Oxford University Press.

Parikka, J. (2010), *Insect Media: An Archaeology of Animals and Technology*, Minneapolis: University of Minnesota Press.

Seabrook, J. (2006), 'Game Master', *The New Yorker*, 30 October 2006.

SimAnt (1991), video game, designed by Will Wright. USA: Maxis.

Swarm! Fundraising Pitch (2013), video, by Jon Lawhead and Daniel Estrada. USA: 5 June, at https://www.youtube.com/watch?v=H5qthqBaajI& (accessed 13 November 2014).

Thoreau, H. D. (2000), *Walden and Other Writings*, ed. Brooks Atkinson, New York: Modern Library.

Uswak, I. (2013), 'Swarm! Google Glass Game – our chance to build the first MMO for Glass', 21 May, at http://glass-apps.org/swarm-google-glass-game (accessed 13 November 2014).

Wells, H. G. (1977) [1905], *The Empire of the Ants and Other Stories*, New York: Scholastic.

Werber, B. (1999), *Empire of the Ants*, trans. Margaret Rocques, New York: Bantam Books.

Wild City of Ants (2013), television special. USA: National Geographic, 27 August.

Wilson, E. O. (2010), *Anthill: A Novel*, New York: W.W. Norton & Co.

Wilson, E. O. and B. Hölldobler (1988), 'Dense Heterarchies and Mass Communication as the Basis of Organization in Ant Colonies', *Trends in Ecology & Evolution*, Vol. 3, No. 3, pp. 65–8.

Wright, W. (2004), online chat. 8 January, at https://web.archive.org/web/2006 1019071720/http://simcity.ea.com/community/events/will_wright_01_08_04.php (accessed 12 November 2014).

Chapter 6

Music-Becoming-Animal in Works by Grisey, Aperghis and Levinas

Edward Campbell

The concept of 'becoming-animal', first developed by Deleuze and Guattari in their study of Kafka and later in *A Thousand Plateaus*, is one with rich potential for the exploration of a number of recent musical artworks. It links them not only with composer Olivier Messiaen, the bird-lover par excellence, for whom so many of his compositions are birdsong become music (or music become birdsong), but also with his pupils Gérard Grisey and Michaël Levinas as well as the Paris-based Greek composer Georges Aperghis.

In the plateau '1730: Becoming-Intense, Becoming-Animal, Becoming-Imperceptible . . .', an entire section is given over to 'Becoming-Music' (Deleuze and Guattari 1988: 299–309) and it is stated there that 'musical expression is inseparable from a becoming-woman, a becoming-child, a becoming-animal that constitute its content' (299). So it is, according to Deleuze and Guattari, that 'music takes as its content a becoming-animal' (304) and is seemingly always 'caught up in an indivisible becoming-child or becoming-animal' (Deleuze and Guattari 1986: 5).

For Deleuze and Guattari, becoming 'is not a correspondence between relations'. Nor is it 'a resemblance, an imitation, or, at the limit, an identification' (1988: 237). In this way, becoming-animal 'does not consist in playing animal or imitating an animal' and 'the human being does not "really" become an animal' since 'what is real is the becoming itself' (238). Following Jacob von Uexküll, they relate all becoming, including becoming-animal, to 'the power of affect' (243), and acknowledge that animal becoming relies on counting the affects of a given animal, the tick, for example, having only three (51, 257). While each becoming-animal is distinguished from every other by its affects, this is not an isolated condition but rather one which has to be seen in a chain of ever-more-molecular becoming, alongside 'becomings-woman, becomings-child' all the way to 'becomings-elementary, -cellular, -molecular, and even becomings-imperceptible'. Indeed, 'becomings-molecular take over where becomings-animal leave off' (248).

While all of the musical works considered in this chapter are rich in becomings, we will consider them for the most part in relation to becoming-animal. The temporalities at play in certain late works by Gérard Grisey embody aspects of animality, and the three times of *Le Temps et l'écume* (1988–9) – 'normal', extremely compressed and extremely slow – are indicative of the dramatically contrasting temporal frames of humans, insects/birds and whales. In the opera/experimental music theatre piece *Avis de tempête* (2004), Georges Aperghis produces a 'fetish reading' of *Moby-Dick* in which 'Melville's universe impregnates the entire spectacle' (Houdart 2007: 66, 25), as Aperghis confronts the theme of fragmented subjectivity. Finally, Michaël Levinas identifies 'the animal dimension of the instrumental world' as key for the opera *La Métamorphose* (2011), which is based on Kafka's short story and in which the composer hybridises the sound worlds of the 'vocal, instrumental and animal' (Levinas 2012: 18).

Gérard Grisey and the Time of Humans, Birds, Insects and Whales

Becoming-animal in the work of Gérard Grisey is inextricably linked to his rethinking of musical time, a career-long preoccupation that is evident from the titles of works such as *Tempus ex machina* (1979), *Le Temps et l'écume* (1988–9) and *Vortex Temporum I-II-III* (1994–6). Grisey's earlier spectral works, *Périodes* (1974), *Partiels* (1975), *Modulations* (1976–7) and *Transitoires* (1980–1) from the cycle *Les Espaces acoustiques*, all have time that is extremely stretched to the extent that this is 'the privileged time in the spectral music of the 1970s' (Baillet 2004: 213; Grisey 2008: 267). Grisey was thinking already in *Périodes* of a 'fuzzy periodicity' in which 'periodic events . . . fluctuate slightly around a constant, analogous to the periodicity of our heartbeat, breathing or footstep' (Grisey 1987: 245). Developing this idea, he notes that 'acceleration and deceleration, just like periodicity, form part of our daily experience: cardiac and respiratory rhythms which determine the different phases of sleep subject us to those phenomena every night' (252).

Beyond periodicity and dilated time, Grisey conceives of musical structures requiring variable 'type[s] of perception' and which operate with flexible temporal structures on different scales (1987: 268). Consequently, from 1986 onwards he juxtaposes or superposes different temporalities within a composition. *Talea* (1985–6), the first work in which this is achieved, has two temporalities, a 'normal' time which corresponds to the rhythm of 'the word in daily discourse' (part 1) and a stretched time similar to that of his earlier works (part 2) (Hervé 2004: 16–17). Interest is still fixed firmly in this work on the rhythm of the human listener's life.

Beyond *Talea*, Grisey begins to present several time scales within the same work, all based on the same 'archetypal object', adding a new, rapid and contracted time to the dilated and 'normal' times of earlier pieces. In this way, the dilated and the contracted offer symmetrical times surrounding a mediant value, all of which Grisey comes to think of in naturalist terms. Grisey, like Messiaen, connects musical temporality in multiple ways with a range of non-musical times stretching from cosmology to various aspects of nature, the environment and the animal world. His focus on the time of humans and birds, in particular, is clearly redolent of his former teacher's great interest in musical ornithology, but while Messiaen spells out exactly which species of bird is performing at any given moment within his scores, Grisey is more concerned with temporal scale than with naturalistic accuracy. Just as Messiaen layers eighteen birdsongs in the *Épôde* from *Chronochromie* (1960), some of Grisey's later works layer the temporalities of humans, birds/insects and whales.

Grisey is concerned with situating the human within a larger scale of times in which the screaming sounds made by a whale, which can be rather overwhelming to a human and which may appear to be very long and to lack articulation, may be nothing more than a consonant when thought in relation to the whale, since whales operate within an entirely different time-frame. In a similar way, the momentary, fast, agitated and high-pitched sound of a birdsong may again be a more significant utterance for a bird which operates within a much more contracted time-frame (Grisey 2008: 245). The birdsong must be transposed one or two octaves lower for it to be heard at a speed and within a pitch range that is manageable for human listeners. For Grisey, the particular temporalities he identifies are only brief examples from a continuum of empirical possibilities extending from 'the birth of the stars to living organisms' (41). In this way, he rejects the 'anthropocentrism' that he detects in previous conceptions of musical time, which presume that man is 'at the center of time, a listener fixed at the very center of the work to which he is listening!' (Grisey 1987: 242–3).

Le Temps et l'écume (Time and Foam) (1988–9) for percussion, synthesizers and chamber orchestra is the first of Grisey's compositions to be based on this notion of three contrasting musical times – 'normal', extremely compressed and extremely slow – that are based on the temporal frames of humans, birds/insects and whales, and which follow one another successively and abruptly in the formal unfolding of the work (Grisey 2008: 247–8; 154). As Grisey tells us, the piece 'navigates between the music of whales, that of men and that of insects' and 'the same gesture . . . is passed through the sieve of these relative times so distanced from one another that a cell lasting a second can become a formal process covering almost the entire duration of the piece' (154). The form of the piece at the global level is nothing more than the succession of the three temporal frameworks. In the first section, in human time, an easily perceptible figure is performed thirteen times in around seven minutes; in the second, the gesture is compressed into one sequence lasting around thirty seconds, sounding in insect/bird time, and the final, extended section unfolds in much slower and dilated whale time over ten minutes, in which the gesture is enunciated only once (Baillet 2000: 185–98; 2004: 214).

Where three temporalities are juxtaposed in *Le Temps et l'écume*, four temporal processes are superposed in *L'Icône paradoxale* (1992–4), a work in which the temporal material is related not to humans, birds/insects and whales but rather to the proportions (3–5-8–12) underlying the composition of Piero della Francesca's fresco the *Madonna del Parto* (Grisey 2008: 156–7). While Grisey does not invoke the times of whales, birds or insects systematically in connection with this piece, he relates its contracted temporality to Conlon Nancarrow's *Studies* for player piano, which he suggests work with 'biological rhythms infinitely more rapid than those of language' (259). For Grisey, Nancarrow's music, which is extremely compressed in time, is 'written for and by insects or little animals' (272). Indeed, this 'insect music . . . stimulates our perception . . . to the point of irritation' (199).

In *Vortex Temporum I-II-III* (Vortex of time) (1994–6) for piano and five instruments, which constitutes the unfolding of an arpeggio in variable times, Grisey uses the same material in different times, now described as 'ordinary', 'more or less dilated' and 'more or less contracted' (158). These three times 'circulate from one movement to the other in temporal constants that are as different as that of men (the time of language and of breathing), that of whales (the spectral time of sleep rhythms), and that of birds or insects (time contracted to the extreme where its contours become blurred)' (159). In this case, the time of the first movement relates to human breathing, the second has the same material in dilated time, and the third is a 'sort of large-scale projection of the events from the first movement' (159–60).

For Grisey, it is essential to know 'where one is situated . . . in the scale of time' (Grisey 2008: 245) and, perceptual difficulties notwithstanding (271), his approach is a creative one in which he re-thinks musical time and embeds the human within a multiplicity of environments ranging from that of insects and birds to whales and beyond. For Baillet, the three times of *Le Temps et l'écume* and *Vortex Temporum* are really a development of Messiaen's rhythmic characters ('personnages rythmiques') (Baillet 2004: 211), a concept that is taken up explicitly by Deleuze and Guattari in *A Thousand Plateaus*.

In a short theoretical study of musical time, 'Tempus ex Machina', Grisey conceives of sounds not as 'defined objects' but as 'force fields given direction in time' that 'are infinitely mobile and fluctuating; they are alive like cells, with a birth, life and death, and above all tend towards a continual transformation of their own energy. There exists no sound which is static, immobile, any more than the rock strata of mountains are immobile' (Grisey 1987: 268). It is in this respect that he proposes 'an ecology of sound, like a new science placed at the disposal of musicians' (269). The link connecting sound and language entails that 'at its most violent it remains human . . . affirm[ing] the individual and the singularity of his voice'. Despite this rooting of music in the human, Grisey identifies a molecular level in which

> The composition of process springs from everyday gestures and, even by that, frightens us. It is inhuman, cosmic and provokes a fascination with the Sacred and the Unknown, reaching out to what Gilles Deleuze defined as the splendour of ON: a world of impersonal individuations and pre-individual singularities. (Grisey 1987: 269)

To this extent, he recognises that from around 1975 the principal goal of spectral composition consisted in 'the liquidation of fixed categories' in favour of 'synthesis and interaction' (Grisey 2008: 45), and music is described as 'the becoming of sounds' (48). Thinking of the characteristics of sound, namely attack, resonance and decay, as analogous to 'birth, life and death', Grisey suggests that 'sound resembles an animal; time is simultaneously its atmosphere and its territory. To treat sounds outwith time, outwith the air they breathe, would be to dissect cadavres' (52).

Aperghis, Becoming-animal and Moby-Dick

The music theatre or operatic works of Georges Aperghis form unique assemblages of components from a wide range of heterogeneous milieus, including images, actions, sounds, music, language, literary texts and technological components. Since the foundation of the *Atelier Théâtre et Musique* in 1976, Aperghis has developed and experimented with new methods and techniques for the creation of music theatre and operatic works in terms of literary construction, musical composition and stage production, each work starting without any fixed plan and in an empirical, experimental way. These works are the result of the molecularising of musical, sonic, linguistic, gestural and visual material in ways that are consonant with Deleuze and Guattari's thought.

Animality has been important to Aperghis from early in his compositional career. His third opera *Histoire de loup* (1976) is based on Freud's case of the Wolf-Man. Reflecting on this Freudian reference, Aperghis states that he could 'not see life other than under a ludic aspect, without taking human actions seriously, with the impression that one is always playing at something'. Noting further that he has a 'tendency to not separate the animal world from the human world very much' and that 'humans can be majestic as certain animals', he concludes that 'in the story of the wolf these two paths are presented' (cited in Miller 1983). The three on-stage personnages in his music theatre piece *Conversations* (1985) are 'without psychological character' and behave in ways that lie between the human and the animal (Aperghis cited in Rothstein 2003: 2). François Regnault, a collaborator on the music theatre piece *Machinations* (2000), notes Aperghis's fondness for 'combining the associations of differential phonemes ... submitting them to gestures and chemically pure behaviours'. This, he suggests, 'allows him to communicate with the listener, with the spectator, almost without the mediation of sense, beyond all communication so that the speaker and the listener generate, in the space of the representation, a kind of mineral, vegetal, acoustic and perceptible animal community' (Regnault 2004).

Avis de tempête ('Storm warning') from 2004, described by Aperghis as a 'real opera', is an assemblage that results from collaboration with a librettist, a video artist, computer technicians, a scenographer, a conductor, four performers (two men, two women) and an instrumental ensemble. It is an assemblage in a state of constant deterritorialisation, in which the heterogeneous elements leap from one milieu to another and where, as Aperghis says, 'an abstract sound becomes the voice of an actor, a phoneme becomes running water, a character may be divided up and then reconstructed elsewhere' (Aperghis 2005: 16).

The becoming-animal, here as elsewhere, is only one line of flight in a work that is complex and multiple in resonance. Aperghis's idea at the outset was the creation of a spectacle dealing with all kinds of storms, pertaining not only to meteorology but also to war, the human passions and the financial markets (Houdart 2007: 53). He proposed it to musicologist and literary collaborator Peter Szendy as 'a spectacle on tempests, meteorological tempests, amorous tempests, stock-exchange tempests, tempests under a skull, in a glass of water' (25). While Szendy was invited to write a text for the work, and he in fact produced an essay on tempests, the completed text was pieced together by Aperghis and features multiple fragments from Herman Melville's *Moby-Dick* along with less extended borrowings from Kafka, Baudelaire, Shakespeare, Victor Hugo as well as the Beaufort Wind Force Scale.

Szendy's essay, which takes Melville's *Moby-Dick* as its general starting point, and which was delivered in installments, allowed Aperghis to clarify the purpose of the piece as he set to work on the production of electronic sound material at the Institut de Recherche et de Coordination Acoustique/Musique (IRCAM), the music section of the Centre Georges Pompidou in Paris. Consequently, when he came to write the score, the electronic material had already been produced, and Szendy's essay, which became a book in its own right, was almost finished (Houdart 2007: 53–4). Aperghis describes *Avis de tempête* as a 'fetish reading' of *Moby-Dick* and he acknowledges having had the book 'in mind' during the composition of the work 'in a rather fantasmic state' (66). Szendy is nevertheless correct in noting that 'Melville's universe impregnates the entire spectacle' and, he adds,

> I think in particular to the moment of inflation – that which is small (a subject, an individual, a man) is inflated to the dimension of the universe, welcomes all, is nourished by everything, and at the same time explodes. He only remains in bits and pieces. This is what happens in *Moby-Dick*. The writer identifies himself with the whale. He describes the whale as a text. He himself becomes a sort of text. He says that he writes on his skin, even on his own body, the text of a long poem (of which we can suppose that it is the text of *Moby-Dick*), and that there is not enough space on his body. What happens in the spectacle on the visual and sound planes is a little like this. A microcosm which would wish to hold everything and which explodes it. (Houdart 2007: 25–6)

Moby-Dick is identified by Deleuze and Guattari as 'one of the greatest masterpieces of becoming; Captain Ahab has an irresistible becoming-whale, but one that bypasses the pack or the school, operating directly through a monstrous alliance with the Unique, the Leviathan, Moby-Dick' (1988: 243). They tells us that 'Ahab chooses Moby-Dick, in a choosing that exceeds him and comes from elsewhere, and in so doing breaks with the law of the whalers according to which one should first pursue the pack ... the becoming-whale of Captain Ahab' (244). The becoming-animal is always an alliance with 'the Anomalous', in the case of *Moby-Dick*, but also in Kafka's animal becomings, and the anomalous 'has only affects'.

The completed literary text for *Avis de tempête*, which cannot be summarised, was formed simultaneously with the music, Aperghis describing its gestation as 'instinctive'. There is no linear narrative and all narrative continuity or sense of cause and effect is avoided. While Melville's whale, Moby-Dick, does not appear anywhere in the text, Aperghis and Szendy invoke the biblical character of Jonah, himself the one-time guest of a whale on account of a storm. In the novel, a preacher, in the midst of a great storm, delivers a sermon on the theme of Jonah, Melville's narrator Ishmael observing that the preacher 'seemed tossed by a storm himself', an insight that appears in the first number of the opera.

Fragmented subjectivity is a prominent theme throughout, and the work opens with a quotation from the final chapter of *Moby-Dick*: 'this old skull cracks so, like a glass in which the contents turned to ice, and shiver it' (Melville 1851: 622). The phrase 'skull cracks' is a recurrent motif throughout *Avis de tempête* and skulls feature also in the fragment 'the lightning flashes through my skull; mine eyeballs ache and ache', again from *Moby-Dick* (560). Shakespeare's *King Lear* is cited: 'Blow, winds, and crack your cheeks! rage! blow!', and a passage from Kafka's *Diaries* reads: 'a segment has been cut out of the back of his head. The sun, and the whole world with it, peep in. It makes him nervous, it distracts him from his work, and moreover it irritates him that just he should be the one to be debarred from the spectacle' (Kafka 1976: 391). Faced with the disaster of a ship's hold that is leaking valuable whale oil, Melville's Captain Ahab proclaims defiantly, 'Let it leak! I'm all aleak myself' (1851: 526), which, for Aperghis, now describes the plight of the dissolving subject. It is redolent of Deleuze's comment on the motif of the 'scream' in the paintings of Francis Bacon, where 'the mouth ... is no longer a particular organ, but the hole through which the entire body escapes, and from which the flesh descends' (Deleuze 2005: 19).

From Thomas De Quincey's *Confessions of an English Opium-Eater*, Aperghis cites the text 'upon the rocking waters of the ocean the human face began to appear ... my agitation was infinite, – my mind tossed – and surged with the ocean' (De Quincey 1998: 72). There is also the solitariness of Melville's Pip cast adrift in the ocean, in the chapter 'The Castaway', as the 'ringed horizon began to expand around him' (1851: 462), and Melville writes here of 'the intense concentration of self in the middle of such a heartless immensity' (462). This theme of solitariness is continued with Ishmael's great line from the epilogue to *Moby-Dick:* 'And I only am escaped alone to tell thee' (634), onto which Aperghis appends the previously unrelated line, 'the other parts of my body' (501).

Melville, describing Captain Ahab at work in his cabin on his sea charts, says that 'it almost seemed that while he himself was marking out lines and courses on the wrinkled charts, some invisible pencil was also tracing lines and courses upon the deeply marked chart of his forehead' (227). Ishmael notes that 'I was crowded for space, and wished the other parts of my body to remain a blank page for a poem I was then composing' (501), presumably *Moby-Dick* itself, and latterly *Avis de tempête*. For Szendy, the great whale Moby-Dick is a 'document, a trace' in 'the great archive of the world' which allows 'the sketching of a line' (Szendy 2004: 43), and he writes of the reading of this text in terms of 'chains or connections', of intermittent 'links' and ultimately of 'delirium' (44, 39). This reading is 'confounded with zigzags, with the angular motions that confuse markers and expectations', and it is one 'in which linearity would break down, zigzagging among lightning bolts and resounding thunderclaps' (19).

The stage setting of *Avis de tempête* includes a number of screens which hang over the stage as fragments of a presumably shattered sphere, perhaps the cracked skull mentioned in the literary texts. They may also be the sails of a ship, perhaps the whaling ship from *Moby-Dick*. Images of either the faces of the performers or of landscapes are projected onto these screens, become distorted and vanish. For Célia Houdart (2007: 18–22), the whistling and breathing of the ensemble, which nestles within the space of the skull, suggest a beached whale, while the realistic and abstract images on the screens may be the real and imagined goings-on inside a human head. A woman spins while speaking of fear and of a storm and the orchestral conductor performs in a scat-like manner. There is a tower which may be a lighthouse, a lightning conductor or the mast of a ship, which a man climbs up onto. It may also suggest intelligence-gathering. Instrumental and electronic sounds pass imperceptibly from one to the other. There are brusque sounds 'like the cry of an animal' (19). A solemn choral piece is performed with a detail from the Sistine Chapel relayed onto a screen. The soprano circles around addressing herself to the camera while reciting a fast, rhythmic text. A moment of calm is called for before war-like sounds are heard and 'the performers metamorphose into the electronic components of a video game'. The woman is overwhelmed with a torrent of words and fragments of phrases in French and English, with two cordless cameras in her hands. 'As the words come into contact with one another, they become strange animals.' Everything on the stage seems to swirl around in the image that is projected and she becomes the sole 'fixed point'. There is the sound of a pinball machine, 'phonemes shatter', 'clusters of chords', a foghorn, 'high-pitched notes', 'thunderclaps' and 'explosions'. The conductor announces that 'the text is written on his forehead' and ultimately it 'is written . . . on the bodies of the performers and . . . the spectators', Houdart concluding that the end of the piece is 'the beginning of a living book' (18–22).

In one sequence, the image of actress Johanne Saunier 'is mixed live with a flux of video material' producing 'a purely electronic tempest, an attack of pixels', so that the decisive elements within the image are distorted with 'numerical errors and viruses' (Houdart 2007: 28). The video images are often exaggerated or blurred, subjects are not completely identifiable and images shift. For example, Houdart describes how an image of 'flat blue sky' stirs and becomes abstract until we realise that we are actually looking at a mouth. Faces and landscapes exchange properties as 'a lake becomes an eye, an eyelash a fern' (77). The performers carry mini cameras in order to film live images which are mixed with recorded images to the extent that it is unclear where the live and pre-recorded sequences begin and end. As Houdart notes, the screens are shaped in 'the form of a broken cranial box', which suggests that in viewing the work, the audience member penetrates into her or his own mental space (80).

A wide range of vocal possibilities is used in *Avis de tempête*, including speech, singing, murmuring and yelling to the point that the instrumental and the vocal are not always clearly distinguishable. Signification in the work operates precisely in non-semantic ways and it is not important whether words or phonemes are spoken or sung since they are capable of being understood, for the most part, to a minimal degree (Houdart 2007: 88–9). For Aperghis, it 'is post-Beckett. People who are on the verge of something. Even Captain Ahab, with his heroic side, is cracked. All over. He walks with a prosthesis. He takes the lightning' (cited in Houdart 2007: 57). Finally, commenting on the detailed shots of human features – for example parts of a human face – Aperghis states that he sees

> the human a little bit like an animal. I say to myself, for someone who does not know the human race, who comes from a cave for example, if he sees a face, this must be appalling, unbelievable this white thing with a hole in the middle. It is as bizarre as a dinosaur, as a fly. (64)

Levinas, Kafka and *La Métamorphose*

Like Grisey, Michaël Levinas studied composition with Messiaen and, if he does not share his former teacher's fascination with birds, animals including birds are of much more than passing interest in his music. With Levinas's sonic hybridisations in the *Ouverture pour une fête étrange* (1979) for two orchestras and electronic device, sound is amplified to the point that it becomes 'an almost animal living mob' (Levinas 2002: 71). Of the musical spectacle *La Conférence des oiseuax* (1985), he acknowledges that his treatment of the French language is modified to evoke an 'animal cry' (251), and the 'animal world' is drawn upon as a sonic filter. In the rawness of the hybrid sounds, in this and earlier works, he detects a 'physical, animal, vocal energy, of the order of the cry' (252).

Levinas identifies 'the animal dimension of the instrumental world' as key for the opera *La Métamorphose* (2011), based on Kafka's short story, although the work operates on multiple levels and cannot be reduced solely to that of the becoming-animal. Impressed by the paintings of Hieronymus Bosch, with their 'instrumental allegories that extend the animals' snouts, horns, serpents, bells, in which vocality and monstrosity are combined' (Levinas 2012: 18), he states that *La Métamorphose* 'develops a completely different set of themes from *La Conférence des oiseuax*' while authorising 'comparable hybridisations between these three sound worlds: vocal, instrumental and animal'.

Like Melville, Kafka is identified by Deleuze and Guattari as a 'great author of real becomings-animal' (Deleuze and Guattari 1988: 243) who in addition shows throughout his writings an interest in 'a pure and intense sonorous material that is always connected to *its own abolition* – a deterritorialized musical sound, a cry that escapes signification, composition, song, words' (Deleuze and Guattari 1986: 6). Deleuze and Guattari recognise that 'for Kafka, the animal essence is the way out, the line of escape' (35), in a line of becoming that is not metaphorical, symbolic or allegorical and which goes to the point of molecularity (58).

Levinas's *La Métamorphose* comprises two separate texts: a prologue 'Je, tu, il' culled by the composer from a play dedicated to him by Valère Novarina, followed by the main body of the piece, an adaptation of Kafka's *Metamorphosis* made by Emmanuel Moses, Levinas and Benoît Meudic. As with his earlier operas, *Go-gol* (1996) and *Les Nègres* (2003–4) (after Jean Genet), *La Métamorphose* questions 'the identity of the subject (who is the "I"? who is the "Other"?)'. In working with

Novarina, he was enlisting 'the creator of a language of variation, muta-tion, metamorphosis' (Levinas 2011a: 8) and, with specific reference to Kafka's story, he asks the writer whether 'the subject, the I . . . remain[s] within a human body which metamorphoses into a cockroach?' (Levinas 2011b: 13). Novarina, for his part, describes his text as a 'pronominal scene with animal temptation inside' (Novarina and Levinas 2012: 26), recognising within it 'the spectre of an animal future' and stating that 'it is in this presence of animalisation that *Je, tu, il* rhymes or counter-rhymes sometimes in secret with [Kafka's] *Metamorphosis*' (27).

As with Aperghis, the fragmentation of human subjectivity is implicit from the outset in Novarina's text in the division of voices 'je', 'tu' and 'il' who, in the first of the three fragments, strip back human activities and values to the limited functions of eating, becoming, thinking, speak-ing, sleeping and dying.

> Let us eat at crooked tables before the Metamorphosis takes place!
> Life, here you are!
> Let us eat our bodies to pass on!
> Let us put the world in order in order to think it!
> Let us eat to die, eat to sleep, eat to speak
> The *athanamorphose* ['l'athanamorphose'] of Franz's *phorphoserie* will
>   come in its own time. (Novarina 2011: 4)

In this way, the pre-human and pre-animal flux, the metamorphosis of matter, is summoned so that:

> Matter transfigures itself in time
> Oh in my entrails: the sound reached me!
> Our mother the mental case is captive to her gravitating:
> She rises and falls in the body without man and without animal. (5)

If eating is a mode of transformation or metamorphosis, 'this meal transfigures us into people who pass away in our brains'. Pursuing this metamorphosis to the natural end of all living things – death – we are told that, 'once in the earth, we will seek buried reason under our step' followed by the 'cessation of thought'; and the fragment ends with the thought that, 'one day you will see man become a celebrated bug'. Fragment 2, 'The Sacrifice of Isaac', marks a distinct change of regis-ter and features the much-interpreted story from the book of Genesis. When Isaac (now 'Je') asks, 'where is the sheep?' for the sacrifice (6), the father ('tu') replies, 'there is no sheep my son', but in a Kafka-like metamorphosis of the biblical tale, 'Il' enquires, 'Sir! am I going to trans-form myself into a cockroach ['cafard']? into a sheep? into a cockroach

['blatte']? into a cockchafer ['hanneton']? . . . No! . . . You will save me'
(7). The fragment ends with the lines:

> 'Man reproduces the animal trait for trait' and nowhere: 'the geometer
>   love' ['L'amour géomètre']
> And now?
> We are singing the ode to Darwin!
> Ah but man says!
> I'm not descended from the animal, that's where I'm going! (7)

In the third and final fragment, *Il* has the text, 'we will rule these animals
on earth', to which *Je*, *Tu*, *Il* and 'the other' recite a list of 105 amphib-
ians, reptiles and insects, actual and mythical in a vocal *tour de force* (8).
It begins with the four acoustic voices which are soon multiplied electronically and at speed, suggesting a fast-forward replay of the stupefy-
ing proliferation of historical evolutionary forms, species and genera.
The fragment ends with the proclamation, 'Hail the metamorphosis!'

After Novarina's prologue, Kafka's story is told in five madrigals.
From the opening section of Madrigal 1, 'Gregor awakening', the sound
of Gregor's voice indicates beyond doubt that we are no longer dealing
with human subjectivity. Treatment of the voice is particularly important in *La Métamorphose* and the role of Gregor is given to a singer with
extremely idiosyncratic vocal qualities, equally comfortable in the divergent registers of countertenor and baritone. Levinas notes in the score
that 'Gregor's voice "*suggests and does not suggest*" a form of animality.
The countertenor who can also become a baritone expresses AN ambiguity between the child, man and animality OF THIS HARROWING
METAMORPHOSIS OF GREGOR SAMSA.' For Levinas, 'it is not a
question of imitating animal cries but of using the principles of [instru-
mental] hybrids' that he had developed in his previous operas (Levinas
2011b: 14), and he writes of 'a slow metamorphosis of the voice' (13).

In bars 1–15 of Madrigal 1, Gregor's voice is divided into two musical
lines, both with the same rhythms and pitches, a repeated, intoned G
natural, drooping sighs at the end of phrases and fragmented echoes. By
bar 16, his vocal line has proliferated to six simultaneous voices, notated
on five staves, with a very simple harmony consisting mostly of open
fifths and octaves. As Levinas notes of the electronic treatment of the
voice, this is 'less a doubling or a hybridisation than a reduction of the
voice: one chord per note, each chord being arpeggiated, and each note
of the arpeggio sculpted according to its own curve. Shadows and delays,
inner life of the voice as polyphony' (2012: 19–20). The section finishes
with a highly distorted, intoned G# in bars 18–29 where the voice

is much more denatured electronically, the conflict of the opening G natural and the concluding G# highlighting the dissonant and alienated situation in which Gregor finds himself. The falling modal figure in bar 16 – the centre of the section – not only conveys something of Gregor's predicament and mood but also this new descent of 'man' and the multiple voices suggest a molecularising of unified, human subjectivity. The sluggishly intoned vocal line with its layering, staggering, drooping final notes and fragmented echoes embodies a consciousness that has become strange to itself, to alter slightly a phrase from Melville's *Moby-Dick* and Aperghis's *Avis de tempête*.

The next section of the madrigal, 'Période 4' (bb. 30–73), opens with Gregor's voice, but it is the voice of the mother that is most prominent, along with Gregor's increasingly indistinct soundings, and the listener seems to experience the world from inside Gregor's befuddled head. While his mother informs him that it is quarter to seven in the morning, time to get up, reflecting that 'he is a boy who has nothing in his head other than his profession', Gregor muses ironically not on his beastly condition but on the stupidity of the career he finds himself in, with its early rises, anxieties about missing train connections and the lack of friendly or durable relationships. His voice is distorted electronically from the outset, and where the sense of the text is not clearly perceptible, its variously presented, descending motif continuously reinforces the affect. The text sung by his mother and father becomes progressively indistinct as we share something of Gregor's becoming-animal with its attendant loss of understanding at the level of the human. The sonic ensemble becomes a sluggish, drunken soup of mostly asignifying sound, though some phrases still emerge distinctly enough, primarily Gregor's name, which is repeated over and over by his parents. Madrigal 1 is the becoming-animal of Gregor in consciousness, as he awakens to his new form and to the perceptions of an insect, and, as the scene progresses, linguistic sense is increasingly less evident and rhythms become more irrational.

In the second madrigal Levinas produces the kinds of rough sounds he had used previously in *Les rires du Gilles* (1981), and there are little fanfares, exotic sounding arpeggios and animalesque snorts and roars, amongst which the remaining human characters sing their lines. The Chief Clerk enters with a crude portamento figure that is repeated several times and which Levinas identifies in the score as 'the cry' ['le cri']. He continues with a rambunctious, arpeggiated Bb minor figure which resolves onto a triad of F major, again repeated several times, at once a tonal relic and a somewhat crude reminiscence of mid-nineteenth-century French opera. It is followed by the timbrally richer, more refined and rather exotic arpeggios that herald 'Gregor's lament and supplication', this time sung in countertenor voice and with complete audibility (bars 58 ff.). Levinas states that it was necessary to produce 'tears in the sound', even a 'long sob'. The lament is 'neither totally human nor perfectly animal' and Gregor's voice is divided, sub-divided and multiplied (Levinas 2012: 19). Where the arpeggiated figure sung by the Chief Clerk 'must have an authoritarian and coarse accent' and is a clearly molar entity, the vocal part given to Gregor is much more shifting and molecular in character. After the return of the distorted, polyphonic voice of the first madrigal, the Chief Clerk recognises that Gregor's is 'the voice of a beast'. Following further snorts and roars, the father's 'sinister psalmody', where he reveals the family's dependence on Gregor's earnings, is accompanied by the sound of the thousand feet of a millipede. The madrigal ends with Gregor's voice, a vocal multiplicity, as he recognises that what is happening to him is not a dream and that he is increasingly separated from the human.

Conclusion

In each of the works considered in this chapter, multiple becomings are involved simultaneously. This is clear in the macroscopic temporal frames of Grisey's works with the times of insects/birds, humans and whales, but also in the multiplicity of the sound spectrum now molecu-larised and reconstituted. As we have seen, Grisey's earlier work focuses on variable types of human perception and on perspectives masked by daily life, as envisaged through human heartbeat, breathing, footsteps, the rhythms of the phases of sleep and of spoken language. This human-centred phenomenology gives way in his works of the 1980s to a much more expansive ecology of sound where the processes of the human are now placed next to the temporal characters of insects, birds and whales in a spectrum of possibility that stretches from the cosmic to the pre-indi-vidual singularities of impersonal individuations and the liquidation of fixed categories. It is striking that in doing so, Grisey draws very close to Deleuze and Guattari, who note 'the Bergsonian idea of a coexistence of very different "durations", superior or inferior to "ours", all of them in communication' (1988: 238). In this respect, Grisey is close to his teacher Messiaen who 'presents multiple chromatic durations in coalescence, "alternating between the longest and the shortest, in order to suggest the idea of the relations between the infinitely long durations of the stars and mountains and the infinitely short ones of the insects and atoms"' (309).

Avis de tempête is an exploded reflection on fragmented subjectivity and possibly the realignment of shards of subjectivity on the anomalous figure of Moby-Dick. Aperghis does not separate human and animal worlds, which ultimately are molecularised to the degree that he operates in an environment that is equally 'mineral, vegetal, acoustic, [and] perceptible'. *Avis de tempête*, among other things, is Captain Ahab's becoming-whale, and Aperghis, for whom the human and the animal are not so distant, represents the strangeness of the human-become-animal.

Novarina's text 'Je, tu, il', the prologue to Levinas' *La Métamorphose*, is a rich reflection on becoming-animal in which the memory of Kafka's story is melded together with Darwinian science and Old Testament theology. Levinas's opera, like that of Aperghis, is a daring, idiosyncratic work that is only possible because of the wide range of techniques and expressive means developed in the composer's earlier works. His sonic hybridisations embody becoming-other in the realm of sound and music and are ideally placed to form the material through which Gregor's tale of becoming-animal is reconfigured with its multiplicities, animal cries and laments. While the earlier reflections of Deleuze and Guattari on Kafka, music and becoming-animal are not the subject of explicit comment from Levinas, *La Métamorphose* is a rich re-envisioning of Kafka's story that goes well beyond simple representation. The human and the animal exist on a continuum of possibility which this time is simultaneously biological and theological, as the form of the biblical genealogy is given new Darwinian content and then reversed so that the animal, no longer the precursor of the human, is now its destination.

The observation that 'all becomings begin with and pass through becoming-woman' and that this 'is the key to all other becomings' (Deleuze and Guattari 1988: 277) is borne out by aspects of *Avis de tempête* and *La Métamorphose*. In *Avis de tempête*, the role of the female dancer/vocalist is important in the molecularising of sound (fragments of French and English language and fragments of texts), and the molecularising of visual images, resulting from her dervish-like swirling, are projected in real time onto the multiple screens which form the cranium/whale-like structure within which the piece is performed. In *La Métamorphose*, the role of Gregor is given to a countertenor with a five octave vocal range, a vocalist Levinas had previously used in his opera based on Genet's *Les Nègres*.

Consonant with Deleuze and Guattari, imitation of the animal or resemblance to its sounds is not what is accomplished in any of these works, though there can also be 'moments of imitation' (Deleuze and Guattari 1988: 275). The temporal frames of Grisey's works produce new temporal relations in which aspects of birdness, insectness and whaleness emerge without resort to the musical transcription or aping of animal sounds. Beyond the representational or imitative qualities of earlier musics, in each of these works a Deleuzo-Guattarian diagram is drawn in which music no longer evokes animality but rather itself becomes animal, and each composer envisages the animal in terms of particular sonic affects. Becoming-animal in all three works is primarily a question of sound. In Grisey, the temporality of each becoming-animal is equally decisive. In Aperghis and Levinas, the fragmentation and multiplicity of the animal is apparent, in the former through the shattering of words and phonemes and the juxtaposing of partial identities, in the latter in the hybridising of sound and the molecular multiplication of the voice. In this way, the becoming-animal in each case is determined by a certain number of clearly indicated affects, which ultimately for Deleuze and Guattari are the markers of the anomalous.

References

Aperghis G. (2004), *Avis de tempête*, score, realised by Luc Brewaeys, at http://www.aperghis.com/selfservice.html (accessed 16 December 2008).

Aperghis, G. and P. Szendy (2004), *Avis de tempête*, libretto, final version as published in the programme for the Festival Agora de l'IRCAM.

Aperghis, G. et al. (2005), 'Storms', in CD booklet, trans. Jeremy Drake, Cypres: CYP5621, pp. 15–18, Brussels.

Baillet, J. (2000), *Gérard Grisey: Fondements d'une écriture*, Paris: L'Harmattan.

Baillet, J. (2004), 'La relation entre processus et forme dans l'évolution de Gérard Grisey', in *Le Temps de l'écoute: Gérard Grisey ou la beauté des ombres sonores*, ed. Danielle Cohen-Levinas, Paris: L'Harmattan, pp. 193–220.

Deleuze, G. (2005), *Francis Bacon: The Logic of Sensation*, London: Continuum.

Deleuze, G. and F. Guattari (1986), *Kafka: Toward a Minor Literature*, trans. D. Polan, Minneapolis: University of Minnesota Press.

Deleuze, G. and F. Guattari (1988), *A Thousand Plateaus: Capitalism and Schizophrenia*, trans. B. Massumi, London: Athlone.

De Quincey, T. (1998), *Confessions of an English Opium-Eater*, Oxford: Oxford University Press.

Grisey, G. (1987), 'Tempus ex Machina: A Composer's Reflections on Musical Time', *Contemporary Music Review*, Vol. 2, No. 1, pp. 239–75.

Grisey, G. (2008), *Écrits ou l'invention de la musique spectrale*, ed. Guy Lelong with the collaboration of Anne-Marie Réby, Paris: Musica Falsa.

Guattari, F., G. Aperghis and A. Gindt (2000), 'L'hétérogenèse dans la création musicale', in *Chimères*, Vol. 38, pp. 9–12, at http://www.revue-chimeres.fr/drupal_chimeres/files/38chi02.pdf (accessed 30 September 2014).

Hervé, J.-L. (2004), 'Formes et temporalités dans les dernières oeuvres de Gérard Grisey', in *Le Temps de l'écoute: Gérard Grisey ou la beauté des ombres sonores*. Textes réunis et présentés par Danielle Cohen-Levinas, Paris: L'Harmattan, pp. 15–21.

Houdart, C. (2007), *Avis de tempête: Georges Aperghis: Journal d'une œuvre*, Paris: Editions Intervalles.

Kafka, F. (1976), *Diaries, 1910–1923*, New York: Schocken.

Kafka, F. (2007), *Metamorphosis and Other Stories*, London: Penguin.

Levinas, M. (2002), *Le Compositeur trouvère: écrits et entretiens (1982–2002)*, ed. Pierre Albert Castanet et Danielle Cohen-Levinas, Paris: L'Harmattan.

Levinas, M. (2011a), 'Note d'intention du compositeur', in Dossier pédagogique La Métamorphose, p. 8, at http://www.opera-lille.fr/en/season-10–11/bdd/cat/opera/sid/99230_la-metamorphose (accessed 5 August 2013).

Levinas, M. (2011b), 'Lettre de Michaël Levinas à Valère Novarina', in Dossier pédagogique La Métamorphose, pp. 13–14, at http://www.opera-lille.fr/en/season-10–11/bdd/cat/opera/sid/99230_la-metamorphose (last accessed 5 August 2013).

Levinas, M. (2012), '. . . Things like that happen – rarely, but they do happen'. Interview with Michaël Levinas, carried out by Jean-Luc Plouvier, in CD booklet, AECD 1220, pp. 18–25, Brussels.

Melville, H. (1851), *Moby-Dick or, The Whale*, at http://www.feedbooks.com/book/54/moby-dick (accessed 20 April 2012).

Miller, J. (1983), Extract from 'L'Ane, le magazine Freudien' (mai–juin). Propos recueillis par Judith Miller, at http://www.aperghis.com/notices/loups.html (accessed 30 September 2014).

Moses, E., M. Levinas and B. Meudic (2011), libretto for *La Métamorphose*, pp. 9–18, at http://www.opera-lille.fr/fichier/o_media/9132/media_fichier_fr_encart.meta.pdf (accessed 5 August 2014).

Novarina, V. (2011), 'Je, tu, il, prologue à La Métamorphose', pp. 4–8, at http://www.opera-lille.fr/fichier/o_media/9132/media_fichier_fr_encart.meta.pdf (accessed 5 August 2014).

Novarina, V. and M. Levinas (2012), '"Take whatever you wish": Interview with Valère Novarina and Michaël Levinas', Remarks collected by Danielle Cohen-Levinas, in CD booklet, AECD 1220, pp. 26–8, Brussels.

Regnault, F. (2004), 'Aperghis littéral', at http://www.aperghis.com/lire/litteral.html (accessed 30 September 2014).

Rothstein, E. J. (2003), 'Le théâtre musical d'Aperghis: un sommaire provisoire', at http://www.aperghis.com/txt.html (accessed 10 November 2010).

Szendy, P. (2004), *Les Prophéties du Texte-Léviathan. Lire selon Melville*, Paris: Minuit.

Szendy, P. (2007), 'Sources', in Célia Houdart (ed.), *Avis de tempête: Georges Aperghis: Journal d'une oeuvre*, Paris: Editions Intervalles, pp. 25–6.

Chapter 7

Un/Becoming Claude Cahun: Zigzagging in a Pack

renée c. hoogland

> Experience is that mass of affects, projects and memories that must perish and be born for a subject to arrive at the expression of what it is. (Lyotard 1991: 122)

> Becoming can and should be qualified as becoming-animal even in the absence of an endpoint that would be the animal become. (Deleuze and Guattari 1987: 238)

Considered odd, obscene, a genius nonetheless, at the time she created her best-known works, French photographer and writer Claude Cahun (1894–1954) cuts an unruly figure in literary criticism and art history. Her recalcitrant *faux* autobiography, *Aveux non avenus* (*Disavowals, or, Cancelled Confessions*) (1930) has encouraged the artist's association with high modernism and Surrealism. Since the recovery of her photographic self-portraits in the late 1980s, Cahun has similarly been claimed, often in association with artists such as Cindy Sherman and Ana Mendieta, for an affirmative (feminist) gender and/or queer politics, and thus reined into an equally 'serious' cultural-political undertaking. Neither the subsumption by the larger framework of a (predominantly male) avant-garde movement, nor her 'domestication' within a project of identity politics, can contain the playful yet defiant ethico-aesthetic unreason that her work so singularly, and, occasionally, quite violently, enacts and obtains. I hence propose a different approach.

Cahun's disavowed confessions as much as her theatrical self-stagings, a proliferation of so many masked selves/others, expose and inscribe the mobility, the proliferous and mercurial nature of a self that is never one, and never once and for all, but, instead, a continuously shifting configuration of fragments and collages: assemblages of singularities that are always in a multiplicity, in a pack. Laying no claim to legitimacy or authenticity, these inscriptions or traces of un/becoming otherwise escape dominant modes of expression, be they Surrealist or queer. Cahun's work has nothing to do with recognition or imitation, nor does it constitute a relation of representation; it therefore makes little sense to ask after its underlying meanings, politics or morals. My argument in this chapter is that Cahun presents us, both in her writing and in her photographic work, with the sometimes successful, sometimes 'botched' experience of becoming in the absence of any final term or form. By, first, exploring the artist's defiant view of the un/becoming self with the help of Alfred North Whitehead, I want to indicate the ways in which her works do not so much represent 'anything' at all but rather effect an alternative mode of relating (to self, to the world, to art) that is essentially aesthetic in nature, a question of feeling. Second, I will reflect upon her myriad self-presentations in light of Gilles Deleuze's notion of becoming to suggest the traces of a becoming-animal in Cahun that moves beyond destruction into the zone of indiscernibility, where a work, or, perhaps, an *oeuvre*, comes into view – an *oeuvre* that nonetheless remains decidedly outlandish, anomalous.

Claude Cahun was born as Lucie Renée Mathilde Schwob. Under her adopted (gender-ambivalent) *nom de plume*, she started out as a writer and poet. Today, she is best known as a photographer: in the 1920s and early 1930s, she produced a remarkable number of photographic self-portraits, only one of which was published in her lifetime. Her published writings include *Heroines* (1925), a series of monologues based upon female fairy-tale characters intertwined with witty comparisons to contemporary images of women; the already mentioned *Aveux non avenus*, a collection of essays-poems illustrated with photomontages; and several essays in magazines and journals. Cahun's photographs, mostly small prints that were never collected or exhibited, only came to critical attention when they were found, stuffed in a couple of boxes, after the death of her life partner, Suzanne Malherbe, better known as Cahun's artistic collaborator Marcel Moore, in 1972. A multi-talented artist, whose work has resisted classification in traditional critical terms, Cahun was one of the few women to be associated with Surrealism during its most vibrant years, even if she never presented herself as such. She was referred to by André Breton as 'one of the most curious spirits of our time'.

Breton made this comment shortly after the publication of *Aveux non avenus* in 1930. His use of the adjective 'curious', meaning anything ranging from strange, odd, peculiar, unusual, bizarre, weird, eccentric, queer, unexpected, unfamiliar, extraordinary, abnormal, to anomalous, surprising, incongruous and unconventional, would appear to place

Cahun in the margins, or, indeed, in an anomalous position in relation to a Surrealist aesthetic agenda, as Breton's peculiar choice of words unmistakably suggests. With its author already positioned on the fringe or the borderline of leading artistic and literary movements, the fact that the book was published in an edition of only 500 copies did not do much to increase Cahun's fame – or notoriety – outside a small circle of performers and writers in Paris. Indeed, it did not have much of an impact at all and, as Jennifer Mundy writes in her introduction to the English translation, 'was soon forgotten' (Mundy 2007: xvi). Cahun's response to this lack of 'success' underlines her minoritarian position in the Parisian art world of the times, with which she did not feel much affinity in any case: '"In vain, in *Disavowals* I tried – through black humour, provocation, defiance – to shake my contemporaries out of their blissful conformism, their complacency . . . Ostracism was more or less the general response. Aside from the silence [the book was met with] the basest insults"' (Cahun, cited in Mundy 2007: xvi).

Despite the fact that she appears to have suffered from the rebuffs she received from both reputable Paris publishers and from the city's vanguard literary society (Latimer 2006: 66–7), Cahun stuck with her choice to write an anti-autobiography, to stay true to the 'very essence of [her] temperament' (cited in Latimer 2006: 67). If the word 'temperament' can be associated with embodied and embedded being – with mood, intensity, sensitivity, feeling – rather than with conscious and unconscious thought, then Cahun's work (both written and visual) urges us to foreground or prioritise the question of aesthetics. Aesthetics, that is, not as a particular style, and not only, or, perhaps, not even, as the critical reflection on art and beauty, but in its more foundational sense, as *aesthesis*, as perception and sensation, as the fully animated yet pre-personal experience of affect.

Disavowals is generically all over the place – the text, loosely divided into nine chapters, contains letters, snippets of conversations, philosophical reflections, fables, maxims and recorded dreams. The untranslatability of its title (and it would take seventy-seven years for an English translation to appear at all), ambiguous and indecipherable as it is, further suggests the futility of 'reading' these disavowed confessions as the inscription of a rational, stable, unitary, molar self. The indeterminateness of Cahun's *faux* autobiography is carried over into the visual aspects of the book, a crossing of perceptual boundaries, which is apparent from the original cover, where words and letters literally double up as ambivalent figures. 'Aveux' can be understood as either 'avowals' or 'confessions'. Usually loosely translated as 'disavowed', the phrase 'non avenus', however, meaning 'invalid' or 'void', renders the title opaque. The play on words may thus, as Tirza True Latimer writes, well 'capture the spirit of the title, which references, with the word "confessions", an entire autobiographical tradition while canceling it out in the next breath'. Latimer sees in this 'cancelation' the book's critical thrust, which is visually reflected in the cover graphic, 'creating out of the self-contradicting title a canceling "X" – with the palindrome "NON" reiterated at its crux' (2006: 66). Yet, most French-speaking readers would at once recognise the phrase in its legal resonance, where the word 'confessions' has less to do with the inscription of a self in the form of an auto-biography or memoir than with an admission of guilt or responsibility within a (legal/discursive) system relying on truth, meaning, validity and credibility. In this context, the book's title evokes a sentence such as 'Les aveux extorqués sous la contrainte physique et mentale sont nuls et non avenus', which translates as 'A confession extracted from a person under physical or mental duress is null and void', and which is probably as familiar as the notion 'statute of limitations' is to speakers of American English. The phrase 'confessions null and void', in its intrinsic connection with verbs like extort, extract, wring, wrench, thus simultaneously points up the operation and the defiance of systems of representation, as systems of meaning and being, and the violence they effect in the mandatory production of a responsible, accountable, reliable and definable self. No such self can be found in or extracted from *Disavowals*.

All but one of the chapter titles in the book consist of a set of (mock) initials, for example, R.C.S., X.Y.Z., I.O.U, which appear in the table of contents followed by, in parentheses, the word for a feeling or disposition (fear, self-love, sex, vanity, lying, greed, self-pride), some of which reoccur several times (fear: 3x; sex 3x). Chapter II is called 'Myself (self-love)'. As a series of void confessions, then, *Disavowals* inscribes energies, thoughts and feelings that do not converge into a recognisable personality, but rather result in, work towards, a discontinuous becoming in order to affirm life:

> I discovered within my vanity the philosopher's stone of love. With it I can perform the transmutation of joys: from signs I'll make sounds; from sounds I'll make scents; from scents I'll make kisses; from kisses I'll obtain caresses . . . It's obvious that I have this power – but do carry on as though it were nothing! (Cahun and Malherbe 2007: 61)

The opening sentence or, rather, non-sentence underlines the centrality of perception and sensation – over and above either conscious reflection or the unconscious functioning of thought beyond the control of reason that the Surrealists were so interested in. It reads: 'The invisible adventure.' Some critics have taken this phrase as a starting-point to argue against Cahun's co-optation into and by a Surrealist aesthetic. Jennifer Mundy, for instance, writes that while her work, especially the collages, to some extent shares the visual aesthetic of Surrealism, Cahun did not share their interest in the 'plumbing of the unconscious, the concept of which she seems to have doubted'. Indeed, Mundy continues, 'for her, the expression of the conscious mind, with all its contradictory impulses and equivocal emotions, was a complex enough task'. She goes on to suggest that such complexity is reflected in the notes, vignettes and longer 'sections of coded and disguised fantasy' that make up the bulk of these cancelled confessions (Mundy 2007: xvii). True, as suggested, the text lacks overall structure, and is punctured on the micro-level by a variety of paragraph markers – that we would nowadays probably call special characters, symbols or icons: stars, hearts, eyes, mouths – which, almost like playing cards, suggest connections, a family resemblance even, but which ultimately remain elusive.

Both its structural incoherence and the illegibility of the visual aspects of the text nonetheless encourage me to reject Mundy's claims; after all, conscious thoughts, complex and contradictory as they may be, *do* allow for articulation, for being brought under the reign of the signifier, for being captured in the chains of signification. What ultimately remains invisible, however, are feelings. Feelings are not only by definition invisible, they are also inherently fleeting, elusive and ever-changing. Feelings pass and are never the same: we cannot feel anything twice. This, I submit, is why representation always fails to capture the 'invisible adventure' of becoming – an insight that is borne out by the paragraphs following Cahun's opening gambit:

The invisible adventure.

The lens tracks the eyes, the mouth, the wrinkles skin deep . . .
the expression on the face is fierce, sometimes tragic. And then calm – a knowing calm, worked on, flashy. A professional smile – and voilà!
   The handheld mirror reappears and the rouge and eye shadow. A beat. Full stop. New paragraph.
   I'll start again. (Cahun and Malherbe 2007: 1)

In this passage, the autobiographer is first 'looking' at herself through a lens, then in a mirror, and then through the veil of words. Neither recording device, nor reflective surface, nor words produce anything stable or consistent or true: there is no underlying truth to this self. Rather, tracking, tracing, inscribing the 'I' produces a myriad self that is as ephemeral, and as null and void, as the moment it tries to capture as soon as it assumes representational form; or, perhaps better, is forced into representational form. In this respect, there is no distinction between the conscious and the unconscious self. As we see a few lines below:

> No point in making myself comfortable. The abstraction, the dream, are as limited for me as the concrete and the real. What to do? Show a part of it only, in a narrow mirror, as if it were the whole? Mix up a halo with spatters? Refusing to bump into walls, bump into windows instead? In the black of night.
>
> Until I see everything clearly, I want to hunt myself down, struggle with myself. Who, feeling armed against her own self, be that with the vainest of words, would not do her very best if only to hit the void bang in the middle.
>
> It's false, it's very little. But it trains the eye. (Cahun and Malherbe 2007: 1)

The focus in this passage on seeing, on vision, on perception, to some extent explains Cahun's obsessive practice of self-staging, both in a variety of roles (gender, class, age), in the endless range of photographs with mirrors, in the doublings, the masks, and in her self-presentations in relation to the outside world – for instance, material objects big and small, some of which engulf her body, others merely half-covering parts of it them – in historical and theatrical costumes, natural or garden scenes, the ocean, the beach and buildings. It also points to the 'void bang in the middle', the absence, rather than the mere constructedness of the (molar, stable) self. This is not a 'void' in the sense of non-existence, however; it rather indicates that selves, our own and others', are not so much assemblages of conscious or unconscious thoughts, but first and foremost an affective affair, the product of perception and sensation: invisible, fleeting, never to be repeated, never the same; it is in *aesthesis*, in perception and sensation, prior to both conscious and unconscious thought, that selves are continuously produced and perish.

In approaching Cahun's work from a perspective that neither seeks to establish her position in an art historical or a literary critical framework, nor one that asks questions about the political – feminist, queer – significance of her work, I am not denying that such questions cannot or should not be meaningfully asked (I will come back to his below). I am, however, trying to connect the aesthetic effects of Cahun's sometimes quite disturbing verbal and visual self-trackings and -tracings to recent work in affect theory and, especially, to Alfred North Whitehead's (1861–1931) theory of pure feeling. According to Whitehead (who wrote around the same time as Cahun), the basis of experience is emotional.

He thereby places aesthetics, rather than ontology or ethics, at the centre of both philosophy and being.

Whitehead's theory of feeling issues in an affect-laden notion of subjectivity in which *aesthesis*, or sensual perception, plays a constitutive role within a non-phenomenological model of becoming. Becoming in this context, as Steven Shaviro points out, is 'not continuous, because each occasion, each act of becoming, is unique', and any appearance of duration, of endurance, or continuity, needs to be actively produced, over and over again (2009: 19). Whitehead posits a notion of the self that is not so much a pre-existing entity that 'phenomenologically "intends" the world', but rather something that emerges from its encounters with the world: each subjective, embodied and perceptual encounter – whether with actual, physical objects, or with ideas or 'mental acts' – produces the subject 'anew', as so many new selves, as 'fresh event[s]'. Accordingly, neither the world nor the self is ever finalised, let alone finalisable, for the latter comes into being in the 'very course of its encounter with the world' (Shaviro 2009: 21), which is, in its turn, in flux, and multiply informed by such encounters.

Since experience generally is the occasion, the 'moment', at which the subject is born, and at which it is born anew, in its singularity, over and over again, as so many fresh events in an ongoing process of discontinuous transformation, aesthetic experiences not only change from one person to another, as much as they change cross-culturally and historically, but they also bring forth, in a Heideggerian sense, the subject itself as a threshold occasion that will never be the same from one encounter to the next. Hence, the world is not only a messy place, but also an open space in which anything, any object, material or mental, may provide the occasion for becoming anew. Since such occasions are essentially perceptive or sensual in nature, they are prior to language, prior to thought. What I subsequently make of a certain experience, that is to say, in reflective contemplation after the event, enchaining it in discourse or representation, is an effect of conscious or critical thought, subject to the law of reason, rather than the effects of the activity of experience itself.

On Whitehead's view, actual entities or occasions are thus produced and produce themselves in their actualisation, as discrete finite units of becoming. Rather than substances or essences, actual entities are what is given in experience, processes in their actual givenness, that are issued forth by being delimited from the total multiplicity of the universe. Objects are not given as such, but acquire a limited givenness in each actual entity: the 'determinate definiteness of each actuality is an expression of a selection' from the multiplicity of these objects (or forms). But the critical point is the 'insistent particularity of things experienced and of the act of experiencing', an act which has no sooner 'happened' or it is gone, to be 'superseded' by other actual occasions of experience (Whitehead 1978: 43).

Within such an aesthetics of sensation, the subject does not pre-exist, but is born anew in each fresh encounter with an object (whether physical or mental). As Whitehead succinctly puts it, 'The word "object" . . . means an entity which is a potentiality for being a component in feeling; and the word "subject" means the entity constituted by the process of feeling, and including this process. The feeler is the unity emergent from its own feelings' (1978: 88). For Whitehead, there is thus neither a subject, as there is for Kant, who 'projects' the world, from which the world 'emerges', nor is there a subject, as there is for phenomenologists, who 'intends' the world. With Whitehead, I reject the presupposition of the existence of a consciousness that intends the identity of an object, or of a perception, and I follow him in recognising the constitutive or *poietic* function of the aesthetic event, as creative activity, as a process of becoming that critically hinges on the non-personal, or presubjective nature of affect.

Since the final unity of subjective form is, in Whitehead's words, the 'individual immediacy of an occasion', its 'moment of sheer individuality', the occasion must be seen as an 'absolute reality', which enjoys its decisive moment of 'absolute self-attainment as emotional unity', only to 'perish into the status of an object for other occasions' (Whitehead 1967: 177). This entails that every occasion is sensitive to the existence of others, that actual entities take account of, or 'perceive', one another, and, therewith, that the subject emerges from the total multiplicity of forms (or chaos) as a multi-componential process.

In all of Claude Cahun's work – her photos, collages, as much as in her 'confessions null and void' – similar forces of de- and reterritorialisation are at play. The very multiplicity of selves that she appears to project into language, onto images, onto a graspable visuality, testifies to a dynamics of dissolving identities, of becoming and unbecoming, of emergent selves that perish as soon as they are actualised (in discourse, in representation). The surplus of visuality, the excessive discursive inscriptions (*Disavowals* runs on for more than 200 pages), thus at once point to the lure of representation, to its inevitable failure in capturing identity once and for all, and to these various stagings' operation as themselves aesthetic events, the occasions for the production of precisely that which remains, and must remain, invisible, the 'absolute self-attainment as emotional unity' of the self as event, in a discontinuous process of transformation.

Let me illustrate this messy process with a slightly longer quote from *Disavowals*:

> Express oneself: humiliate oneself? – Yes, but for the right reason.
>
> Trample on this, this flesh of my flesh. Draw on remorse, weigh on my memory, on my obese statue, the only springboard that doesn't give way under me.
>
> Is that shapeless, enormous, distressing, horribly voluptuous thing lying across my path? Opportunist soul: running over the body.
>
> 'Soul'. I misused the word. Superstition, obsession with the unknowable. What I cannot chew is precisely what I like to bite off. 'Love', 'Conscience', 'God', 'selflessness'! . . . I, Jewish to the point of using my sins for my salvation, of putting my by-products to work, of always surprising myself, my eye hooked over the edge of my own waste-paper bin. (Cahun and Malherbe 2007: 26–7)

Mundy characterises 'Cahun's parodic view of the self as a rather poorly assembled patchwork of thoughts . . . that had no real claim to substance or longevity' (Cahun and Malherbe 2007: xvii). I agree. But rather than seeing this parodic view of the self as something merely borne out in terms of gender and sexuality, as some feminist art historians have claimed with regard to Cahun's highly stylised and emphatically staged androgynous self-portraits, I propose that hers is a perverse aesthetic that marks its dynamic force through the production of threshold becomings, defying the need for a ground. As so many occasions of becoming, the proliferation of masks, or doubles, or mirrored selves, signifies the embrace of a dissolved self that becomes no more and no less than the expression of its many, multiplying actualisations, and, therewith, the proliferation of equally unusual, bizarre, unexpected and unfamiliar selves that obtain only to dissolve, to be voided or annulled. To recall the quote from Lyotard with which I began: 'Experience is that mass of affects, projects and memories that must perish and be born for a subject to arrive at the expression of what it is' (1988: 12). In Cahun's own words: 'Beneath this mask, another mask. I will never be finished lifting off all these faces' (2007: 183).

The dynamic force of affect in Cahun opens up a space for the proliferation of changing assemblages, for the forging of new connections. Such affirmation need not be altogether pleasant, positive or 'beautiful'. Inevitably, there is a certain kind of violence at play as well, or rather, a violation of the rules of certainty, of meaning, of being. But by insisting that there is no meaning underlying any of the masks that she dons, Cahun emphatically celebrates the sites where the self remains invisible yet irrepressibly emergent in its 'absolute reality' as a threshold occasion, at play in the spaces between. It is this process of becoming-other, of becoming-imperceptible, which brings me to Deleuze's becoming-animal.

Cahun's lack of interest in the hidden secrets of the unconscious, in the phantasmatic, links her self-stagings to Deleuze's and Guattari's concept of becoming in a direct and obvious way. 'Becomings-animal', they write, are 'neither dreams nor fantasies. They are perfectly real' (1987: 238). Such realness is manifest in the photographic surface in which the artist's infinitely mutable body appears. Let me take a moment to explain this point. Cahun's project, I have suggested, is neither an epistemological nor a psychological one, but rather an aesthetic, or, perhaps, an ethico-aesthetic one. This may explain her early and consistent use of the modern medium of photography. The paradox of surface and depth that characterises aesthetics generally acquires particular salience and a specific complexity in the context of photography. The creation and perception of photography forces the theoretical questions of meaning and being almost inevitably into the realm of a complex aesthetics: the immediacy of the perception of the pictorial surface takes precedence over the depth of meaning and context, yet the critical distance required for aesthetic judgement would appear to have taken the upper hand in most if not all forms of traditional art historical approaches to the medium. Cahun, in contrast, uses the (at the time quite primitive) technology of the hand-held camera to explore possibilities for a complex aesthetics that keeps the paradox of surface and depth, the inherent doubleness of the image, especially the photographic image with its long history of ostensible indexicality, in suspense.

Just as she rejects the stability of the writing of the self, the possibility of capturing 'life' in the reductive format of an 'autobiography' in *Disavowals*, so does Cahun insist on the opacity and mutability of the embodied and embedded self in her visual self-stagings. Some feminist art critics have, as mentioned, framed their discussions of Cahun's work, especially the photomontages, in the context of Surrealism (Chadwick and Ades 1998; Holm 2012), and/or highlighted the disruption of traditional gender roles in her self-portraits (Rice and Gumpert 1999), thus casting her gender as, in Carolyn J. Dean's words, a 'site of mobility' (1996: 73). Dean argues against such an approach because it tends to 'immobilise' and/or render irrelevant what she herself posits as the most radically disruptive site of the artist's practice, that is, her lesbianism, which, when placed in the historical context of a thoroughly bourgeois and normatively heterosexual Surrealism, not merely questions the 'dichotomy between homosexuality and bourgeois culture', but also, and more importantly, challenges 'any immobile, transcendental concept of "Art"' (81, 71). Dean introduces the term the 'trope of the body double' to characterise Cahun's disruptive aesthetic practice, a trope she deems 'especially pertinent' in view of the fact that the artist's texts and photomontages 'invoke theatricality and cinematic illusion as the privileged vehicle of subject formation' (81). Dean uses the trope of the 'body double' quite effectively to foreground lesbianism in Cahun as that which 'represents the loss of referentiality in the guise of an identity category embodied either metaphorically (the stand-in) or metonymically (the fetish)'. Lesbian desire (though never mentioned or articulated) is thus argued to represent the '*undoing* rather than the fashioning or production of identity' (86).

While I consider Dean's foregrounding of lesbian desire as a force of undoing, of de-subjectivation, in Cahun's work compelling (and personally reassuring), I ultimately find it unsatisfactory as well. First, as I have indicated, the artist's self-stagings are by no means limited to the androgynous, gender-bending and theatrical instantiations that have gained her a (limited) fame and notoriety, and that stand at the centre of Dean's analysis. As much and as often as Cahun appears in 'masculine' or excessively (hence theatrically) 'feminine' attire, in wigs and with a shaved head, in masks, in front of mirrors, naked, covered in drapes, in stage costumes, and so on, she always emphatically stages her 'selves' in and against prominent material backgrounds: against a doorway, near a granite wall, reclining on sand, against a blanket, on a sheet, in leaves, in a rock pool, on a sun dial, in snow, on grass, in a cupboard, among flowers, at a dining table, against a pebble dash wall, in an archway. In the majority of the self-portraits, her clothing (or lack thereof) is as 'expressive' of a mood or energetic force as are the various objects (skulls, flowers, frames, mirrors, walking sticks, dumbbells, and so on) and, indeed, the various animals (cats) that appear either with her or alone in a series of portraits. Since these 'props' (a misnomer in this context, but for lack of a better term) appear as charged with affective force as the human body/shape/face with which they are visually assembled, I submit that Cahun's photographic work does not so much 'represent' a loss of referentiality in metaphorical or metonymic terms, but instead *presents* – on the pictorial surface of the photographic image, which appears to us, first and foremost, in its perceptual immediacy, and prior to its conventional/indexical depth – multi-componential assemblages, which, in their singularity, as compounds of affects, are real and material, and thus neither illusions nor vehicles for something else.

'Becoming', Deleuze and Guattari, write, 'produces nothing other than itself' (1987: 238). Becoming, as I put it earlier, is a creation, a work. Dean sees Cahun's representation of lesbian desire – in its simultaneous tangibility and indecipherability – as 'no giddy repudiation of epistemological certainties, no celebration of unknowability', but instead, as an 'ironic, cynical, and never-complacent insistence that responsible knowledge, like art, can only ever refuse its own stability even when it appears continuous with a stable canon' (1996: 91). Approaching Cahun's work, I have suggested, as, in the first instance, a site of aesthetic activity, makes clear that its project is not an epistemological one. Nor do her self-stagings strike me as either cynical or even primarily critical. This is not so much because of the historical fact that the more than 300 pictures she took during her lifetime never reached an audience, spent the largest part of their lives stuffed in a box, clandestinely, out of the public view, invisible. More importantly, especially within the context of the (Whiteheadian) aesthetics of sensation briefly outlined above, the photographic work, just as I have tried to show in relation to *Disavowals*, shifts the traditional subject-object relation to a post- or nonhuman moment, a moment where the object is no more and no less than, to recall Whitehead's own words, an 'entity which is a potentiality for being a component in feeling', whereas the subject is the 'entity constituted by the process of feeling . . . the unity emergent from its own feelings' (Whitehead 1978: 88).

To the aspects of love and feeling (or affect) that are central to Cahun's work, I would finally like to add the question of ageing, a phenomenon that only comes into view if we do not restrict our focus to the early, most startlingly spectacular 'gender-bending' self-portraits that (feminist and art) critics of her work have largely restricted themselves to. Like Whitehead, Deleuze and Guattari point out that becoming is always a becoming anew: it is not an ongoing process of beginning *again*, but a discontinuous event following the unmaking, the undoing, of that which (in Whitehead: feelings) has been momentarily sustaining the self. The condition for a successful becoming is an unbecoming, a desubjectivation or deterritorialisation. Cahun's self-portraits, even the ones that appear identical, never really are: almost all of her staged selves appear in several, different prints, cropped in various formats, including or excluding the objects and parts of the backgrounds that determine their pictorial reality, that (de-)form the assemblage. Sometimes the 'same' self differs from one print to the next by a slight shift of the body, a turn of the face, a redirection of the look. In one, showing a young Cahun, in profile, sitting down in what appears to be a monk-like position – cross-legged, arms folded, ascetic – the break between the two existing prints is quite startling: at first they appear to be merely differently cropped, one more narrowly focused on the sitting body than the other. But a closer look brings a quite dramatic difference to light: between the two shots, the artist has shaved her head. Becomings do not run in a circle: they require a rupture, a break, a destruction of the molar form. Such destructions may be subtle (as in the shaving off of a half inch of hair), and they may be big breaks. But there are also breaks that are largely imperceptible, the 'micro-cracks, as in a dish' (Deleuze and Guattari 1987: 198).

Leonard Lawlor takes this type of 'micrological cracking' in Deleuze and Guattari, which he primarily associates with the 'cracks of aging', to be the actual agent of becoming, i.e. 'these experiences in which one is finally aware that one has lost something of oneself' (Lawlor 2008: 172, 173). In *A Thousand Plateaus*, these micro-cracks are the answer to the question, 'what has happened?': 'In truth, nothing assignable or perceptible: molecular changes, a redistribution of desire such that when something occurs, the self that awaited it is already dead, or the one that would await it has not yet arrived' (1987: 198–9). It is this process of imperceptible change, a becoming that involves love, a 'love that I shall choose, and that shall choose me, blindly, my double, just as selfless as I' (1987: 199) that I ultimately encounter in Cahun's creation, her *oeuvre*, the radicalness of which I think is missed by critics who restrict their focus to the early 'androgynous' or theatrical portraits. For what such limited critical accounts suggest is that the artist stopped staging her (changing) selves after her younger, boyish figure and features had given way to the micrological cracks of her advancing age. The opposite is true. In fact, as far as I can tell on the basis of existing archives, she continued to take pictures of herself almost until the moment of her death. Significantly, these later self-stagings – especially the ones taken after she and Marcel Moore had left Paris, and therewith the high-ceilinged apartments that had thus far framed their artistic collaborations, to settle on Jersey, the largest of the Channel Islands (in 1937) – become increasingly elaborate, moving out into the world of things, of nature, into a posthuman zone. The micrological cracks of aging, the discontinuity of the un/becoming self are starkly visible in the later works, perceptible only in the reality of the photographic moment, while at the same time inscribing ever more forces in a multiplicity, becomings-animal involving a 'pack, a band, a population, a peopling' (Deleuze and Guattari 1987: 239).

Un/becoming Claude Cahun results in a work, an outlandish *oeuvre* that inscribes an opening up to the world – a line of flight – in a process of non-reciprocal becoming-animal, a becoming-minor, a becoming-imperceptible. No irony, really, then, in the fact that the artist was marginalised in and by the leading avant-garde of her times, an anomaly; or that even her published work remained unrecognised both then and in the years to come; or that her photographs remained hidden until the death of her lifelong companion and collaborator in 1972. Cahun does not so much offer us a critique (of gender, of sexuality, of bourgeois heteronormativity). Her project is neither a question of imagination nor of understanding. A complex aesthetics, enfolding affect, love and destruction, the work does not stand in for something else, does not constitute a representational relation with a referent. A creation within a zigzagging structure of becoming, the work comes into view, as something perfectly real, becoming-imperceptible, and invites us to become with it, to join the pack, to enter into the compound of the forces that it generates.

References

Cahun, C. and S. Malherbe (2007), *Disavowals*, trans. S. DeMuth, Cambridge, MA: MIT Press.

Chadwick, W. and A. Dawn (1998), *Mirror Images*, Cambridge, MA: MIT Press.

Dean, C. J. (1996), 'Claude Cahun's Double', *Yale French Studies*, Vol. 90, pp. 71–92.

Deleuze, G. and F. Guattari (1987), *A Thousand Plateaus: Capitalism and Schizophrenia*, trans. B. Massumi, Minneapolis: University of Minnesota Press.

Holm, M. J. (2012), *Women of the Avant-garde, 1920–1940*, Louisiana, Denmark: Louisiana Museum of Modern Art.

Latimer, T. T. (2006), 'Acting Out: Claude Cahun and Marcel Moore', in Louise Downie (ed.), *Don't Kiss Me: The Art of Claude Cahun and Marcel Moore*, New York: Aperture, pp. 56–71.

Lawlor, L. (2008), 'Following the Rats: Becoming-Animal in Deleuze and Guattari', *SubStance*, Vol. 37, No. 3, pp. 169–87.

Lyotard, J-F. (1991), *The Inhuman*, trans. G. Bennington and R. Bowlby, Cambridge: Polity Press.

Mundy, J. (2007), 'Introduction', in C. Cahun and S. Malherbe, *Disavowals*, Cambridge, MA: MIT Press, pp. vii–xvii.

Rice, S. and L. Gumpert (1999), *Inverted Odysseys*, Cambridge, MA: MIT Press.

Shaviro, S. (2009), *Without Criteria*, Cambridge, MA: MIT Press.

Whitehead, A. N. (1967), *Adventures of Ideas*, New York: Free Press.

Whitehead, A. N. (1978), *Process and Reality*, ed. D. R. Griffin and D. W. Sherburne, New York: Free Press.

PART III

ANIMAL POLITICS, ANIMAL DEATHS: TRANSVERSAL CONNECTIVITIES AND THE CREATION OF AN ETHICO-AESTHETIC PARADIGM

Bridging Bateson, Deleuze and Guattari Through Metamodelisation: What Brian Massumi Can Teach Us About Animal Politics

Colin Gardner

Introduction: 'The Included Middle'

The idea of 'the included middle' as a transversal movement of becoming, a zone where intensities 'pick up speed', is a key characteristic in Deleuze and Guattari's definition of both the rhizome and the plateau as unlocalisable relations, a matter of coming and going rather than starting and finishing. Thus, 'A rhizome has no beginning or end; it is always in the middle, between things, interbeing, *intermezzo*. The tree is filiation, but the rhizome is alliance, uniquely alliance' (Deleuze and Guattari 1987: 25). Similarly, 'A plateau is always in the middle, not at the beginning or the end. A rhizome is made of plateaus' (21). Significantly, Deleuze and Guattari appropriate the term 'plateau' from the English anthropologist/cyberneticist, Gregory Bateson (1904–80), specifically his seminal 1972 collection of lectures and essays, *Steps to an Ecology of Mind*. As they point out:

> Gregory Bateson uses the word 'plateau' to designate something very special: a continuous, self-vibrating region of intensities whose development avoids any orientation toward a culmination point or external end. Bateson cites Balinese culture as an example: mother-child sexual games, and even quarrels among men, undergo this bizarre intensive stabilization. (1987: 21–2)

In the latter context, Bateson's analysis indicates how potentially damaging and long-lasting Oedipal scenarios – including 'the curious confusions between fighting and lovemaking, the symbolic identifications of orgasm with death' (Bateson 2000: 112) – are circumvented through deliberately contrived uses of sexual play and the breaking of cumulative tension, methods that could also be applied to quarrels and, in extreme cases, combat and warfare. Thus a boy's mother might titillate the child towards the brink of a mild sexual climax but hold back at the last instance, forcing the child to engage in an alternative form of interaction, most likely culminating in a temper tantrum. The mother responds by showing complete indifference or by playing the role of an amused spectator, as if to show that 'it's all a game' and not to be taken seriously. The upshot is that the child learns to deeply distrust such involvement and avoid similar scenarios on subsequent occasions. As Bateson explains:

> The perhaps basically human tendency towards cumulative personal interaction is thus muted. It is possible that some sort of continuing plateau of intensity is substituted for climax as the child becomes more fully adjusted to Balinese life. This cannot at present be clearly documented for sexual relations, but there are indications that a plateau type of sequence is characteristic for trance and for quarrels. (2000: 113)

This 'anti-Oedipal' form of metacommunicative play has clear ramifications for Deleuze and Guattari's subsequent formulation of the 'included middle' in relation to various forms of becoming (particularly becoming-animal) because continuing regions of intensity tend to preclude the likelihood of stable localisation, interruption or delineation by external frames. This is of obvious value in any attempt to bypass binary or dialectical thinking which is intrinsically based on a system of transcendent origins and teleologies whereby the processual 'middle' is always excluded as a matter of course. Instead, Deleuze and Guattari take a Spinozist step by arguing that 'A plateau is a piece of immanence. Every BwO is made up of plateaus. Every BwO is itself a plateau in communication with other plateaus on the plane of consistency. The BwO is a component of passage' (1987: 158).

Bateson's plateau also forms an important connective 'bridge' to Guattari's notion of mental ecosophy which, like Freud's 'primary process', is both pre-objectal and pre-personal. Significantly, Guattari also calls this

> the logic of the 'included middle', in which black and white are indistinct, where the beautiful coexists with the ugly, the inside with the outside, the 'good' object with the 'bad' ... There is no overall hierarchy for locating and localizing the components of enunciation at a given level. They are composed of heterogeneous elements that take on a mutual consistency and persistence as they cross the thresholds that constitute one world at the expense of another. (2008: 36)

Following Bateson, in *The Three Ecologies* Guattari also redefines ecology as a non-hierarchical interplay of three different areas: the material (ecology, biophysical); the social (cultural and human); and the perceptual (which treats the mind as an interactive system characterised by an exchange of information). 'In fact', explains Bateson, 'what we mean by information – the elementary unit of information – is a difference which makes a difference, and it is able to make a difference because the neural pathways along which it travels and is continually transformed are themselves provided with energy. The pathways are ready to be triggered. We may even say that the question is already implicit in them' (2000: 459). Batesonian difference is always part of a total cybernetic circuit where it constantly connects rhizomatically to other systems and plateaus. In other words, Bateson argues for the innate interconnection and interpenetration of the three ecologies to the point of deterritorialising them towards an infinite outside that guarantees their difference and infinite becoming.

More importantly, this is also a de-hierarchised system, where humans are given no more preference than nonhumans or material objects, and neither is raised above the 'worlding' capabilities of nature. In this sense, geomorphism, anthropomorphism and biomorphism are equally embedded, with the aesthetic acting as a vital catalyst. 'The unit of survival is organism plus environment', states Bateson. 'We are learning by bitter experience that the organism which destroys its environment destroys itself' (2000: 491). Guattari develops many of these notions in his later work on ecosophical aesthetics, most specifically in *Chaosmosis* and *What is Ecosophy?*, where he developed a processual philosophy of the ecological through the use of asignifying components that think beyond the conventional split between subject and object, human and nonhuman, subjectivities and world. In this way the ecological is transformed into a machinic, decentred ethico-aesthetic paradigm, a subjectivity-without-a-subject.

Towards an Affirmative Animal Politics Through Metacommunicative Play

So how do we move from a theory of 'the included middle' to the possibility of an affirmative animal politics that can privilege the supernormal tendency in animal life? This is the primary task of Brian Massumi's *What Animals Teach Us About Politics*, which draws heavily on Bateson's essay, 'A Theory of Play and Fantasy', first published by the American Psychiatric Association in 1955 (2000: 177–93). Massumi structures his book as a kind of practical user's manual geared towards a greater creative vitalism of life, in Nietzsche's sense of 'that dark, driving power that insatiably thirsts for itself' (Nietzsche 1983: 60). The book's title essay is a relatively short reflection on animal play as the staging of a metacommunicative paradox, an expression of difference and singularity on one hand and, through vitality affect, mutual inclusion and transindividuality on the other.

These open-ended, fluid ludic gestures are followed by a series of fourteen propositions that act as a preliminary sketch for a practical philosophy (in Spinoza's sense) 'to be Filled in according to Appetite' (Massumi 2014: 38). Massumi devotes the second half of the book to three supplementary essays that apply Bateson's ludic principles to three main areas: 1) writing, where, according to Deleuze and Guattari, the human 'becomes-animal' most intently (specifically through the role of the 'anomalous' in Kafka's *Metamorphosis* and Melville's *Moby-Dick*); 2) the Zoo-ological reduction of the animal to an object of spectatorship (via a constructed zone of indifference), and the concomitant need for a mutual inclusion of the animal and the human via an enactive, sympathetic gesture of double deterritorialisation (producing a zone of *indiscernibility* of difference); and 3), lest one fall into abhorrent species-ism and anthropomorphism, 'Six Theses on the Animal to be Avoided' (91). Massumi's main objective in the supplements is to open a gap between Bateson's original theory of animal play and the affirmative politics that might flow from it, whereby 'Only an enactive *ecology* of a diversity of animal practices, in a creative tension of differential mutual inclusion, can begin to do the trick' (89).

So what does Bateson's theory of play demonstrate and how does it force us to rethink the very nature of instinct and, by extension, politics? Firstly, as Massumi points out, we must rethink the human as immanent to animality, for 'Expressing the singular belonging of the human to the animal continuum has political implications, as do all questions of belonging' (2014: 3). This entails moving beyond anthropomorphism, in relation not just to animals but also to ourselves as standing apart from other animals, 'our inveterate vanity regarding our assumed species identity, based on the specious grounds of our sole proprietorship of language, thought, and creativity' (3). In this sense, Massumi's project has obvious Spinozist roots, attempting to construct an animal politics and carry it to the limit of what it can do by forging new rhizomatic connections/plateaus with other bodies through a combination of sympathy and creativity. In this respect, the project begins and ends in play.

For Bateson, animal play revolves around the reciprocal imbrication of 'differencings' through mutual inclusion in a process of continual variation. Massumi develops this notion through an analysis of a play fight between wolf cubs, which is similar (through abstraction) to its analogue, actual combat, whereby 'Each ludic gesture envelops a difference in a display of similarity' (2014: 4). Similar to, *but not the Same*. In short, the ludic gesture stages a paradox, whereby a wolf cub bites and at the same time says 'This is not a bite, this is not a fight, this is a game', standing in for the suspended analogue: real combat. 'In a single gesture,' argues Massumi, 'two individuals are swept up together and move in tandem to a register of existence where what matters is no longer what one does, but what one does stands-for' (5).

This level of abstraction is what Massumi calls game's '-esqueness', its metacommunicative level which self-reflexively mobilises the possible, a situation (or in Deleuze and Guattari's terminology, a people) to come as vital gesture. At this point Massumi makes a useful contrast between vitality affect and categorical affect: 'Vitality affect corresponds to the -esqueness of the act: its manner. Categorical affect is what the act manneristically confirms itself to be about. It is what is commonly called "emotion"' (2014: 26). The former is essentially a power of the false. It generates a simultaneity of incompatible presents that enact a to-ing and fro-ing between the now and the future, what *is* and what *could be*. In this regard play is a fundamentally relational and trans-situational process that moves across and between intersecting existential territories. The latter – categorical affect – adds a dimension of order and sameness, a 'truth' to counter vitality affect's falseness, thereby providing the 'what' that the lived abstraction deterritorialises. However, it's important to note that there is rarely a clear-cut demarcation between the two affects, between play and non-play. They always exist in a dynamic relation of mutual inclusion.

Massumi also makes an important distinction between embodiment or incarnation – the body as an empty receptacle waiting for some form of content to fill it – and corporeality. The latter is always dynamic, produced in, by and for the event – incorporated into the event as pure becoming. Corporeality is thus inseparable from the action and its dynamic form of expression as vitality affect (although categorical affect always serves to anchor it to a specific situation). In short:

> Corporeality is *lived importance*. Vitality affect . . . corresponds to *lived abstraction* and the deterritorialization associated with its playing out. Corporeality as lived importance is a necessary accompaniment to the vital play of abstraction that gives the situation what degrees of freedom may be -esqued out of it. (2014: 29)

In this sense, metacommunication (as -esqueness) precedes its denotative communication, for the latter needs the pre-human level as a precondition for language: 'Animal play creates the conditions for language. Its metacommunicative action builds the evolutionary foundation for the metalinguistic functions that will be the hallmark of human language, and which distinguish it from a simple code' (2014: 8). As Bateson himself ludically puts it, 'These actions in which we now engage do not denote what those actions *for which they stand* would denote' (2000: 180). Another way of putting this is that 'The playful nip denotes the bite, but it does not denote what would be denoted by the bite' (180), which suggests that the word 'denote' is being used in two differing degrees of abstraction and that we must be careful not to see them as synonymous.

One can argue then that the ludic gesture metacommunicates by its very nature: it comments on what it's doing as it does it – 'I'm not biting, I'm nipping' – thereby opening the analogical gap, but at the same time the gesture's abstraction puts into play a conditional difference: combat is also present but held in suspense by the *stylism* of the play and its ludic logic (not unlike the pre-rehearsed moves in professional wrestling). The result is a zone of indiscernibility without differences being erased: game and combat are performatively fused without being confused, their differences actively coming together. This is another way of saying that ludic gestures produce transindividual transformation via a performative act while at the same time retaining their affective force across the ludic divide. Thus the power of affect in the abstraction is no less profound than that in its analogue: the play bite can induce just as much fear as its combat equivalent in the same way that a projectile coming out of a movie screen can still induce terror in the spectator as if it were real. What is particularly important here is Massumi's creative variation on 'the included middle'. When play and combat come together, their union creates a third dimension – the included middle of their mutual influence. However, animals and humans react differently to this mutual interface. While humans experience paradox as a breakdown of the capacity to think – which causes agitation and in extreme cases, paranoia – animals are activated by it: in play the animal actively and effectively affirms paradox, raising its actions to a metacommunicative level where it prepares itself for the rigours of combat by having rehearsed the moves in advance.

Blurring the Map–Territory Relation

Bateson is fully aware of how the paradoxical nature of the ludic gesture detrimentally affects human thought's conceptual striving for a logical ideal. Deleuze and Guattari are, of course, no fans of the latter, for 'Logic is reductionist not accidentally but essentially and necessarily: following the route marked out by [Gottlob] Frege and [Bertrand] Russell, it wants to turn the concept into a function' (1994: 135). Bateson illustrates the playful slippage between denotation and its ostensible referent by turning to Alfred Korzybski's 1941 book, *Science and Sanity*. Here, Korzybski (1879–1950), the Polish-American scholar notable for developing a theory of General Semantics, outlines a theory of map–territory differentiation to show that 'a message, of whatever kind, does not consist of those objects which it denotes ("The word 'cat' cannot scratch us")' (Bateson 2000: 180). This kind of denotative relationship is similar to that of a map to a territory where there is an implicit understanding that the one is not the same as the other. As Bateson argues:

> Denotative communication as it occurs at the human level is only possible after the evolution of a complex set of metalinguistic (but not verbalized) rules which govern how words and sentences shall be related to objects and events. It is therefore appropriate to look for the evolution of such meta-linguistic and/or metacommunicative rules at a prehuman and preverbal level. (180)

This metalinguistic separation allows us, at least in theory, to show that the actions of 'play' are related to (or denote) other actions of 'not play'. Of course, in practice, the differences often become blurred. Threat, for example, resembles play, in so far as actions denote, but are different from, other actions. A clenched fist is different from an actual punch but at the same time alludes to a possible future punch. This might be extended to histrionic behaviour and deceit, which is common among birds. 'A jackdaw may imitate her own mood signs,' notes Bateson, 'and deceit has been observed among howler monkeys' (2000: 181). Indeed, threat, play, bluff and histrionics usually occur in combination (especially with children) and in the human world are often seen in situations of gambling and risk. 'It is probable that not only histrionics but also spectatorship should be included within this field', adds Bateson. 'It is also appropriate to mention self-pity' (182). He also notes a strong ludic component to social ritual, where there has to be a clear-cut discrimination between denotative action and that which is to be denoted, for example in peace-making ceremonies. He cites the example of the Andaman Islanders in the Bay of Bengal, where peace is cemented after each opposing side is given the ceremonial freedom to strike the other without fear of further reprisals. However, there is always a strong risk that the dividing line between map and territory might break down so that ritual (ludic) blows will slip over into the real blows of warfare.

As the map-territory relationship starts to blur, the ludic often takes on the characteristics of the aesthetic, particularly writing, which Deleuze and Guattari associate directly with a form sorcery, of becoming-animal. 'If the writer is a sorcerer', they note, 'it is because writing is a becoming, writing is traversed by strange becomings that are not becomings-writer, but becomings-rat, becomings-insect, becomings-wolf, etc.' (1987: 240). Borges is perhaps the most notable example in this regard, specifically his 1946 one paragraph 'miniature', 'On Exactitude in Science', which is metacommunicatively ludic on multiple levels. Credited (fictionally) as a quotation from 'Suárez Miranda, *Viajes de varones prudentes*, Libro IV, Cap. XLV, Lérida, 1658', the text imagines an empire where the science of cartography 'attained such Perfection that the map of a single Province occupied the entirety of a City, and the map of the Empire, the entirety of a Province. In time, those Unconscionable Maps no longer satisfied, and the Cartographers Guilds struck a Map of the Empire whose size was that of the Empire, and which coincided point for point with it' (Borges 1998: 325). Needless to say, with the map and the territory at the exact same scale, the map was functionally useless and subsequent generations gave it up to the ravages of the elements. 'In the Deserts of the West, still today, there are Tattered Ruins of that Map, inhabited by Animals and Beggars; in all the Land there is no other Relic of the Disciplines of Geography' (325). Although Bateson doesn't cite this specific story, his general comments are more than apt: 'Here we can recognize an attempt to deny the difference between map and territory, and to get back to the absolute innocence of communication by means of pure mood-signs' (2000: 183). Clearly, for play to be constructive and collaborative, both parties must be able to discriminate between mood signs and messages that simulate them (threat, histrionics, and so on). In a key passage, Bateson stresses that:

> If we speculate about the evolution of communication it is evident that a very important stage in this evolution occurs when the organism gradually ceases to respond quite 'automatically' to the mood-signs of another and becomes able to recognize the sign as a signal: that is, to recognize that the other individual's and its own signals are only signals, which can be trusted, distrusted, falsified, denied, amplified, corrected, and so forth. (2000: 178)

So how might this be a lesson in politics? Because the ludic – recognising that signals are only signals – presupposes *collaboration*. Or, as Massumi argues, 'The ludic gesture is impotent unless it captures the other's attention' (2014: 35). By anticipating the partner's countermoves, point and counterpoint generate a mutual inclusion which might be dubbed 'sympathy' or, alternatively, 'primary consciousness'. 'Sympathy is the transindividual becoming brought into being by intuition's acting out', notes Massumi. And again, crucially for our purposes, 'Sympathy is *the mode of existence of the included middle*' (35). As the thinking-doing of life, sympathy thus plays out (and at) the in-between, but immanently from the inside, not from an outside overview (like cognition). In other words, this is not a dialectical move but rather a genealogical one, in Nietzsche's sense of unearthing the origins of bodily forces and their vitalist becomings.

Case Study 1: The Excluded Middle in *Dr. Cyclops*

We might usefully expand our discussion so far by applying the sympathetic principle of 'the included middle' to a pair of filmic examples that also take the form of overt political allegories. Both *Dr. Cyclops* (Ernest B. Schoedsack, 1940) and *The Incredible Shrinking Man* (Jack Arnold, 1957) feature combative situations with strong ludic potential whereby humans are shrunk to miniature size and subsequently threatened by now monstrous house cats and spiders. Both films stress the dangers of technology out of control, *Dr. Cyclops* in the form of a mad scientist who is allegorically associated with the megalomaniacal dictatorships of the Axis powers at the outbreak of the Second World War, while *The Incredible Shrinking Man* is a classic Cold War feature concerned with the dangers of atomic power and nuclear radiation during the height of the arms race between NATO and the Soviet bloc. However, while *Dr. Cyclops* is a conventional Homeric-style narrative built on predictable binary oppositions between 'good' and 'bad' science (thereby necessitating an 'excluded middle' to enable the direct combat between the film's collective of Odysseus-like heroes and its dictatorial, short-sighted 'Polyphemus'), the later film undertakes a radical metamodelisation of the science fiction genre as a whole to not only celebrate 'the included middle' but push it to an extreme immanence that celebrates Spinoza's third level of knowledge – *scientia intuitiva* (intuitive knowledge) – as pure Life, pure bliss, where all binaries dissolve into a molecular becoming.

Dr. Cyclops establishes its clear-cut (and reductive) political binarism from the opening scene. Dr Alexander Thorkel (Albert Dekker), who is widely recognised as the greatest living authority on organic molecular structure, has just made a major scientific breakthrough in cell biology in his remote laboratory in the heart of the Peruvian jungle. He shows his findings to his former pupil and colleague, Dr Mendoza (Paul Fix), proudly proclaiming that 'I used sufficient radium to tear it to shreds, yet I have been able to keep it alive.' The idealistic Mendoza – who had envisaged joining his mentor in the creation of The Thorkel Institute, 'a palace of healing' – is horrified that the maniacal scientist might use the radium mine for nefarious purposes and orders him to stop at once and burn all his research notes. 'Are we then country doctors?' responds Thorkel. 'You do not realise what we have here. In our very hands, we have the cosmic force of creation itself. In our very hands, we can shape life, take it apart, put it together again, mould it like putty.' 'But what you are doing is mad', insists Mendoza. 'It is diabolic! You are tampering with powers reserved to God.' Thorkel: 'That is good. That is very good. That is just what I am doing.' Having established the 'mad scientist playing God' trope (much like Baron Frankenstein), Thorkel is now free to murder Mendoza and continue his work undisturbed.

However, there is an apparent glitch, because we immediately cut to the 'North American Research Foundation' in New York City where we learn that Dr Rupert Bullfinch (Charles Halton), an expert in the molecular structure of organic tissue, has been summoned by Thorkel, who is in need of urgent assistance. Flattered at the prospect of aiding a fellow scientist of such repute, Bullfinch immediately recruits Dr Mary Robinson (Janice Logan), an expert in microscopic work, and together they engage an extremely reluctant mineralogist, the highly droll and lethargic Dr Bill Stockton (Thomas Coley), a last-minute substitute for another scientist who has fallen ill. On arrival in the jungle, they rent some mules from Steve Baker (Victor Kilian), a miner who thinks that Thorkel may have discovered a rich mineral deposit. He invites himself along under the pretext of caring for his animals: 'If the mules go, I go.'

On arrival at Thorkel's encampment, the biologist asks each of the scientists to examine a specimen through his microscope. It turns out that his eyesight is too poor for him to make an accurate diagnosis by himself. Stockton immediately identifies iron crystal contamination, which causes disintegration of structure. Far from being disappointed, Thorkel is delighted: his sole methodological error has been confirmed and the last obstacle to the success of his research has been overcome. Then, to the group's utter amazement, he thanks them for their services and asks them to leave. Bullfinch is outraged: 'you summoned me, Dr Rupert Bullfinch, 10,000 miles just for this?' Instead of leaving as ordered, Bullfinch insists that the group remain in camp so that they might pressure Thorkel to reveal more about his research. They are joined by Thorkel's assistant, Pedro (Frank Yaconelli) who is concerned about the 'disappearance' of his horse, Pinto. Matters come to a head when the ever-curious Steve discovers that the entire area is rich with pitchblende, a source of uranium and radium. When confronted, Thorkel reveals that he has been using the radium from a deep shaft in his encampment to shrink living creatures, including Pinto, whose off-screen neighs have sparked the curiosity of Pedro, who believes that his horse has finally returned.

At this early stage, the film misses a golden opportunity to explore 'the included middle' between animal and human by failing to exploit Pinto's change in size to a mere miniature, 'confined' to a small crate. Reduced to a mere two feet (six hands) at best, Pinto has lost his entire function as a horse. He can no longer be ridden and in many ways would be better suited as a lap dog. In Massumi's terms, he takes on a potential '-esqueness', whereby vitality affect might override categorical affect to create a creative, trans-situational process where Pinto and Pedro would be forced to renegotiate their earlier horse-rider relationship in terms of mutual inclusion, as a becoming-other. However, this is never pursued further, for Pinto conveniently disappears from the narrative. In any case the issue becomes moot when Thorkel locks the entire group, including Pedro, inside his radiation chamber. Using Bill's information about iron contamination, he corrects the flaw that has killed his prior specimens and the group awakens the following day to discover that they have been shrunk to a height of twelve inches.

Again, the film plays it safe by simply reversing, rather than transforming, the human-animal relationship, whereby the latter are now bigger than the former and once benign pets and chickens constitute a serious threat to survival. Constructive play is eschewed in favour of combat, so that the captives are not only forced to flee from Thorkel, but also his cat Satanus, who viciously attacks them like an oversized black panther. Ironically, they are saved by Pedro's dog, Tipo, who chases off the cat (as if to restore the natural order, at least in the animal world). A proud Pedro approaches his beloved pooch only to find that Tipo is stand-offish, completely confused by the fact that his master is now smaller than he is. Significantly, instead of ludically attempting to bridge the gap, Pedro automatically reads Tipo's reaction as a mood-sign, not as a signal 'which can be trusted, distrusted, falsified, denied, amplified, corrected, and so forth' (Bateson 2000: 178). In other words, there is no 'sympathy' between them, only Pedro's resort to an explanatory logic. As he says to the group: 'He is my dog. But who is Pedro?'

In order to conform to the conventions of the Classic Hollywood Model, *Dr. Cyclops* needs to play out its narrative trajectory according to what Noel Burch calls 'The Large Form', or S-A-S[1] (situation-action-situation[1]), which Deleuze dubs the action-image. Its defining characteristics are active modes of behaviour taking place within determined milieus where we move from an initial situation (in this case a jungle community terrorised by Thorkel's experiments and omnipotent control over his laboratory) to a transformed situation (the liberation of the group) via the intermediary of an action (the killing or demise of Thorkel). This usually includes the formation and eventual consummation of a love interest (in this case between Bill and Mary) which helps to cement the stability of the new situation and move it towards a progressive future (marriage, children, and so on). For this to happen, our group of heroes must be returned to their original size. After snaring Dr. Bullfinch using a butterfly net, Thorkel brushes aside his threats of revealing his crimes to the scientific world and instead carefully measures and weighs him. He quickly discovers that Bullfinch is growing, realising that the effect of his experiment is only temporary. 'What will you do?' demands Bullfinch. Thorkel: 'As you and your fellows develop toward normal size, you will interfere with my work, and that is something I cannot permit.' As the others look on in horror, Thorkel murders Bullfinch and strives to hunt the others down before they can reach normal size and turn him into the authorities.

The film then degenerates into a conventional action adventure with the added twist of the miniaturisation of its action-heroes. The four survivors escape the jungle compound and attempt to launch Pedro's small boat (now cumbersomely huge) while they are attacked by a caiman crocodile. Once again, Tipo is a potential saviour but the tables are turned when Thorkel uses him to track down his master. Realising that his presence is a liability due to Tipo's loyalty – in other words the dog–master relationship, constructed on an 'excluded middle', is intact despite the change in scale – Pedro lures Thorkel away from the group and is shot dead for his pains. Instead of trying to escape (after all, the enemy must be vanquished) the remaining three fugitives hide in one of Thorkel's specimen cases and he unknowingly carries them back to his laboratory. While Thorkel works on his apparatus in the compound, Bill, Steve and Mary align his shotgun towards his bed so that they can shoot him when he turns in for the night. Unfortunately, he falls asleep at his desk, well out of the line of fire. However, this setback allows the film to create a more Homeric denouement, whereby Thorkel's Polyphemus-like 'blindness' might be exploited for more epic ends. The group proceeds to hide his spare glasses and before he awakens manage to smash one of the lenses of the pair on his desk. 'Now you can call me "Cyclops", because I have one good eye', proclaims the scientist as he stumbles around blindly trying to catch the trio. Ultimately, he ends up at the mineshaft, hanging precariously by a rope before Steve cuts him down and he plunges to his death into the source of his precious radium. The film ends with an expected coda: it is months later, the three survivors have returned to civilisation and they are back to their original size. Surprise, surprise: Bill and Mary are in love.

So what does *Dr. Cyclops* teach us about politics? Unfortunately, little more than we knew already. Any creative potentiality in terms of human-animal relations and ludic metacommunication through '-esqueness' are necessarily eschewed in favour of underlining Thorkel's megalomania, specifically his obvious association with the Axis threat in both Europe and the Pacific. Power relations are kept firmly in their place throughout, and the natural order of things is restored by film's end. The Homeric heroes, acting collectively, have conquered the singular enemy, by exploiting the one chink in his armour – his poor eyesight. Film historian John Brosnan perceptively notes the topicality of the film's political stance, particularly its warning about the prospect of a nuclear apocalypse (five years before the first A-Bomb test), but also how Thorkel, 'with his shaven head and thick, round glasses . . . resembles the wartime caricature of the "beastly Jap"' (Brosnan 1991: 30), particularly propaganda posters depicting General (and future prime minister) Hideki Tojo. In this respect, the film reinforces its inherent binarism with an added layer of racism, so that Thorkel is 'othered' on much the same level as his nonhuman specimens within the diegesis itself. As Massumi argues:

> Reinforcing the separating line between structured differences in order to brace the framing against the slippage and blurring that comes with paradox corresponds to neurotic normativity, which invests itself body and soul in the compulsion to repeat the same, to the extent humanly possible. (2014: 70)

The result is a 'normopathy' where the differential divide is not simply unbridgeable but monumental.

Case Study 2: The Included Middle in *The Incredible Shrinking Man*

For the bulk of its relatively short eighty-minute running time, *The Incredible Shrinking Man* seems to fall into many of the same nor-mopathic traps as *Dr. Cyclops*. Told exclusively in flashback with an accompanying voice-over by its protagonist, the film opens as Scott Carey (Grant Wilson) and his wife Louise (Randy Stuart) are sunbath-ing on his brother's cabin cruiser as they drift aimlessly on a calm ocean. However, as Louise slips below deck to grab a can of beer from the freezer, a passing mist envelops Scott, inexplicably covering him in glittery particles. Louise rejoins him and helps him towel down but the damage has already been done. In combination with an accidental expo-sure to an insecticide while driving, the mist causes a chemical reversal of the growth process: Scott has begun to shrink. At first, the change is barely perceptible: his clothes seem slightly too large, he is losing weight. Indeed, Louise finds the new, slimmer Scott to be even more attractive. But then, he is an inch shorter, then two. Within weeks he is three feet tall, and a media sensation. Crowds are camped outside his front door and the press never stop calling. 'I felt puny and absurd, a ludicrous midget' bemoans Scott. 'Easy enough to talk of soul and spirit and exis-tential worth, but not when you're three feet tall. I loathed myself, our home, the caricature my life with Lou had become. I had to get out. I had to get away.'

He forms a brief liaison with Clarice (April Kent), a sideshow attrac-tion who is also abnormally short (shorter even than Scott), but when Scott notices that he is no longer taller than her he breaks it off and returns to his domestic nightmare. He continues to shrink and at a mere six inches lives in a doll's house at the foot of the stairs. One day, Louise inadvertently lets the cat in as she pops out to the store and Scott is attacked by the giant 'beast'. He bolts to the cellar, using the door to shield himself against his former pet, but the door shuts against him and he plummets several feet into a box, his fall fortunately cushioned by a combination of rags and clothes. Returning home and seeing no sign of her husband (the cellar door has slammed shut), Louise is convinced that the cat has eaten him. Full of remorse, she is persuaded by Scott's brother Charlie (Paul Langton) to leave the house and start life anew.

Although Scott's 'death' makes national headlines, he is actually very much alive, his main concern now being the ability to find food and sustenance. Moreover, he has a rival: a giant spider that is not only foraging for the same food source but also has alimentary designs on

Scott himself. After an initial skirmish, Scott opines: 'In my hunt for food I had become the hunted. This time I survived, but I was no longer alone in my universe. I had an enemy, the most terrifying ever beheld by human eyes.' What makes matters worse is that unlike the captives in *Dr. Cyclops*, who are at least starting to grow back to normal size, Scott is continuing to shrink. It's now a race against time: he must defeat his rival before he loses the necessary strength.

It must be admitted that Scott's confrontations with his cat are little different from the combat scenes in *Dr. Cyclops*. Early in the film, when Scott is almost full-size, we see him pick up the cat and toss him playfully to the floor. The cat's subsequent attack on the doll's house simply reverses the animal-human hierarchy, with a six-inch Scott now in fear for his life. There is nothing 'combat-esque' about the conflict that might create a qualitative difference between a ludic gesture and the analogue gesture it invokes and which inhabits it. As we already noted, in Massumi's ideal world, 'Combat and play come together – and their coming together makes three. There is one, and the other – and the *included middle* of their mutual influence' (2014: 6). The exclusion of the middle becomes all the more apparent when Louise returns home and the cat is immediately restored to its 'normal' scale in relation to the house as a whole. Similarly, the battle with the spider is predicated on Scott's need to adapt to his new 'world' but still apply the same principles of combat that he would invoke had he been normal size: 'The cellar stretched before me like some vast primeval plain, empty of life, littered with the relics of a vanished race. No desert island castaway ever faced so bleak a prospect . . . My prison, almost as far as I could see, a gray friendless area of space and time, and I resolved that as man had dominated the world of the sun, so I would dominate my world.'

Scott's subsequent tactics in luring the spider away from his web and food involves no mutual inclusion through abstraction. To declare that 'this is not a fight, this is a game' relies on the participants agreeing that 'I'm on a different register standing in for the suspended analogue.' However, there is no suspension in this case: Scott impales the spider on a nail and finally attains his reward: a crumbling piece of stale cake. 'This was the prize I had won. I approached it, in an ecstasy of elation. I had conquered. I lived.' Under conventional narrative circumstances this might have been an ideal place to conclude the story, leaving Scott to enjoy his moment of glory knowing full well that he will continue to shrink after the film has ended. However, the screenplay was adapted by Richard Matheson, the creator of the classic television series *The Twilight Zone*, from his own novel. We would thus come to expect something far more complex than a mere celebration of transcendent Being.

Indeed, even in the fresh flush of victory, Scott immediately feels incomplete. He breaks off a piece of cake, but cannot bring himself to eat it: 'even as I touched the dry, flaking crumbs of nourishment, it was as if my body had ceased to exist. There was no hunger. No longer the terrible fear of shrinking. Again I had the sensation of instinct. Of each movement, each thought, tuned to some great, directing force.' He collapses face down in the dirt. We then dissolve to the night sky followed by an angle down on Scott as he slowly staggers to his feet: 'I was continuing to shrink, to become . . . what? The infinitesimal? What was I? Still a human being? Or was I the man of the future?' Clearly something remarkable is happening which brings us more fully into alignment with Massumi's ideal of a lived abstraction, where the human is inherently immanent to animality (and vice-versa). Instead of playing out the ludic at the expected level of animal-human play, the film suddenly transforms it into an entire ontology, whereby 'the included middle' supersedes the narrative's entire teleology, turning the ostensible 'denouement' into a pure becoming, a plateau of pure Batesonian '-esqueness'.

Thus as a microscopic Scott approaches the camera and steps through the (now enlarged) holes of a wire mesh, he muses on the possibility of an entirely immanent new creation: 'If there were other bursts of radiation, other clouds drifting across seas and continents, would other beings follow me into this vast new world? So close – the infinitesimal and the infinite. But suddenly, I knew they were really the two ends of the same concept. The unbelievably small and the unbelievably vast eventually meet – like the closing of a gigantic circle.' Deleuze associates this form of immanent reality with what he calls 'a transcendental field': 'What is a transcendental field? It can be distinguished from experience in that it doesn't refer to an object or belong to a subject (empirical representation). It appears therefore as a pure stream of a-subjective consciousness, a pre-reflexive impersonal consciousness, a qualitative duration of consciousness without a self' (Deleuze 2001: 25).

It is at this point that Scott finally realises the answer to the riddle of the infinite: 'I had thought in terms of man's own limited dimension. I had presumed upon nature.' He looks up to the heavens: 'That existence begins and ends is [tight on Scott] man's conception, not nature's.' At this point the camera cuts back and forth between Scott's subjectivity and the infinite night sky, but then the two start to dissolve into each other: 'And I felt my body dwindling [we zoom out to show an infinitesimal Scott indistinguishable from the leaves on the ground], melting, becoming nothing. My fears melted away. And in their place came acceptance.' Then, we dissolve to the stars, galaxies: 'All this vast majesty of creation, it had to mean something. And then I meant something, too. [A spiral galaxy]. Yes, smaller than the smallest, I meant something, too. To God, there is no zero. I still exist!' The music reaches a crescendo, fade out.

Conclusion: From Metacommunication to Metamodelisation

In many ways, the film has followed Deleuze and Guattari's progression from becoming-animal (a metacommunication of the included middle) to their ultimate goal of becoming-imperceptible: the immanent end of becoming, its *cosmic* formula:

> To be present at the end of the world. Such is the link between imperceptibility, indiscernibility, and impersonality – the three virtues. To reduce oneself to an abstract line, a trait, in order to find one's zone of indiscernibility with other traits, and in this way enter the haecceity and impersonality of the creator. One is then like grass: one has made the world, everybody/everything, into a becoming, because one has made a necessarily communicating world, because one has suppressed in oneself everything that prevents us from slipping between things and growing in the midst of things. One has combined 'everything' (*le 'tout'*): the indefinite article, the infinitive-becoming, and the proper name to which one is reduced. Saturate, eliminate, put everything in. (Deleuze and Guattari 1987: 280)

Scott has embraced this condition of saturation where immanence is its own container, where the two ends of a spectrum extend to infinity, where everything is middle. In short, he has redefined the model of what it means 'to live', just as the film has redefined the model of the action-image, whereby the ostensible hero no longer needs to act, in the traditional sense, in order to transform an initial situation (Deleuze's S-A-S[1] formula), but simply to *become*, so that subject and determined milieu are mutually enveloped by the vitality affect of play's aesthetic yield as a surplus value of life.

This eschewal of human agency is all the more progressive given the film's Cold War context. Instead of giving us the usual warnings about the dangers of an unregulated arms race and the catastrophic ecological ramifications of nuclear radiation, the film actually affirms a radical new becoming beyond the ideological binarisms of East and West, communism and democracy, man and nature. As Scott puts it, given other bursts of radiation, 'Would other beings follow me into this vast new world?' More importantly, his ecstatic proclamation that 'I still exist' is the ultimate affirmation of a non-subjective life, an affirmation of Bateson's ecological dictum, 'organism plus environment', for 'We will say of pure immanence that it is A LIFE, and nothing else. It is not immanence to life, but the immanent that is in nothing is itself a life. A life is the immanence of immanence, absolute immanence: it is complete power, complete bliss' (Deleuze 2001: 27).

Ultimately, and this is perhaps Massumi's key point and what brings him most clearly into alignment with Bateson's ecology and Guattari's ecosophy, is that what animals teach us about politics is the philosophical equivalent of play's metacommunication, namely metamodelisation. According to Guattari, metamodelisation reorients theoretical activity by taking into account the diversity and interconnectedness of modelling systems themselves. It is by its very nature transindividual: 'I have proposed the concept of ontological intensity. It implies an ethico-aesthetic engagement with the enunciative assemblage, both in actual and virtual registers. But another element of the metamodelisation proposed here resides in the collective character of machinic multiplicities' (1995: 29). In short, metamodelisation privileges the primacy of the supernormal tendency in animal life, so that, as Massumi concludes, 'What we learn from animals is the possibility of constructing what Guattari calls an *ethico-aesthetic paradigm* of natural politics (as opposed to a politics of nature). The idea of natural politics has been well and truly debunked by critical thinking over the last century. Now it is time to relaunch it, well and -esquely – marshaling all the powers that the false nature provides' (2014: 38).

References

Bateson, G. (2000), 'A Theory of Play and Fantasy', in *Steps to an Ecology of Mind*, Chicago: Chicago University Press, pp. 177–93.

Borges, J. L. (1998), 'On Exactitude in Science', in *Collected Fictions*, trans. A. Hurley, Harmondsworth: Viking Penguin, p. 325.

Brosnan, J. (1991), *The Primal Screen: A History of Science Fiction Film*, London: Orbit Books.

Deleuze, G. (2001), 'Immanence: A Life', trans. A. Boyman, in *Pure Immanence*, New York: Zone Books, pp. 25–31.

Deleuze, G. and F. Guattari (1987), *A Thousand Plateaus: Capitalism and Schizophrenia*, trans. B. Massumi, Minneapolis: University of Minnesota Press.

Deleuze, G. and F. Guattari (1994), *What is Philosophy?*, trans. H. Tomlinson and G. Burchell, New York: Columbia University Press.

Guattari, F. (1995), *Chaosmosis: An Ethico-Aesthetic Paradigm*, trans. P. Bains and J. Pefanis, Bloomington and Indianapolis: Indiana University Press.

Guattari, F. (2008), *The Three Ecologies*, trans. I. Pindar and P. Sutton, London: Continuum.

Massumi, B. (2014), *What Animals Teach Us About Politics*, Durham, NC: Duke University Press.
Nietzsche, F. (1983), 'On the Uses and Disadvantages of History for Life', in *Untimely Meditations*, trans. R. J. Hollingdale, Cambridge: Cambridge University Press.

Chapter 9

Becoming-shewolf and the Ethics of Solidarity in *Once Upon a Time*: Feminist and Posthumanist Re-assembling of Little Red Riding Hood

Nur Ozgenalp

Yellow Eyes of a Wolf

> Who has not known the violence of these animal sequences, which uproot one from humanity, if only for an instant, . . . giving one the yellow eyes of a feline? A fearsome involution calling us toward unheard-of becomings. (Deleuze and Guattari 1987: 240)

As the full moon still shines at the greyness of dawn, a burning arrow crosses the sky and lands on the snow-covered field. A man shouts 'Red, look out', and saves a girl from the targeted arrow. The arrow sizzles when it enters the snow and the fire on it dies off. Legionnaires on horses approach them from the forest and the man and the girl in the red cloak discuss moving away. The girl tells the man to leave and that she will take care of the soldiers. She looks at the full moon and says, 'I am giving you a head start.' As she takes her red cloak off, the camera moves towards her, composing what Deleuze calls an affection-image. Her eyes turn into the *yellow eyes* of a wolf as she starts the process of becoming-shewolf. She turns and starts running towards the approaching soldiers and within seconds she is jumping on them in the guise of her shewolf body, metamorphosing in-between the action of her jump. Then, a howl rises in the woods.

The television series *Once Upon a Time*'s first season, sixth episode ('Heart of Darkness'), starts with this scene. *Once Upon a Time* is a fairy-tale drama that brings Fairyland (that of Snow White and other fairy-tale characters) and the present world into spatio-temporally parallel universes. The Evil Queen in Fairyland casts a curse and as a result, all the fairy-tale characters end up living in the present-day fictional town of Storybrooke, losing all memory of their original Fairyland personae. *Once Upon a Time* practises different ways of transgressing and challenging fixed definitions of the body. The show presents narratives of continuously inter-transforming characters and engages in a discussion on the limits of the body and soul, and those of females and animals in particular. Red, the girl in the red cloak, appears as two variations of the same character: Red (Riding Hood) in Fairyland and Ruby in Storybrooke. In the episodes 'Red Handed' and 'Child of the Moon', the show focuses on the story of Red/Ruby and proposes a micropolitics of 'becoming', particularly of becoming-woman and becoming-animal.

This chapter studies *Once Upon a Time*'s subversive and transgressive formation of the Red Riding Hood story in relation to feminist theory and posthumanist studies. In one version of the traditional telling of the story, through the act of cutting her way out of the wolf's stomach, there is an element of resistance in the character. *Once Upon a Time* takes this resistance a step further by putting the wolf inside the girl. The episode 'Red Handed' shows that Red Riding Hood is actually the wolf. Subsequently, the series speculates on Red/Ruby's becoming-woman and becoming-animal. This brings out a question that will serve as the focus of this chapter: what happens when the wolf is the girl? And, additionally: what kinds of affects are born from this particular serial and televisual version of Red Riding Hood? Since *Once Upon a Time*'s character goes through the process of both becoming-woman and becoming-animal, her transformation becomes the screen embodiment and embrainment of twenty-first-century feminist and posthumanist debates.

Previously on Feminist and Posthumanist Theories

Read historically, the story of Red Riding Hood evolves in alignment with feminist and posthumanist theories. The early versions are more open to psychoanalysis with their binary oppositional construction and family originated definitions. The socialising of the characters was limited to their family members. However, some of the older versions and newer interpretations of the story are more open to Deleuze and Guattari's schizoanalysis, especially in their explicit interaction with the concept and affect of becoming. Furthermore, feminist and posthumanist philosophers and theoreticians, such as Donna Haraway, Judith Butler, Rosi Braidotti, Patricia Pisters, Luce Irigaray, Hélèn Cixous, Patricia MacCormack and Claire Colebrook, have been working through the concepts of becoming-woman, becoming-animal and becoming-molecular within the framework of their own disciplines in an attempt to understand and push their potentials.

For example, Rosi Braidotti writes about the transformations occurring through the history of feminist theory: 'What was once subversive is now mainstream . . . Feminist philosophers have invented a new brand of materialism, of the embodied and embedded kind' (2005: 177). Feminist theories and their subversive tactics are welcomed by popular culture, which is involved with the social and political in a more transgressive way than before. Patricia MacCormack suggests that 'bodies, politics, dominance and oppression transform and alter through time (history) and space (geography) . . . Feminist politics is . . . a form of molecular politics – it makes extended connections and forges alliances like a multi-armed chain of molecules' (2012a: 2). With this molecular politics of multiplicity, the body, soul and brain are freeing themselves from dualistic definitions and becoming conjoined in cooperative contexts. Patricia Pisters argues that 'A "Deleuzian feminism" seems to be gaining territory, going beyond the often-heard feminist critiques on the concept of becoming-woman that are due to an implicit traditional concept of the body (including the mind-body split)' (2003: 109–10). Claire Colebrook adds: 'We are post-capitalist, post-linguistic, post-political, post-racial and yet not fully post-feminist. We have gone through the performative turn, the affective turn, the nonhuman turn, the theological turn and the ethical turn, and yet we seem to keep turning back to woman' (2013: 429). She concludes with a suggestion of post-gender feminism:

> We are now in a post-feminist era. We have achieved whatever could be achieved via gender politics . . . Becoming-woman would be a post-feminist concept, a way of thinking the transition from molar women's movements to a micro-politics in which both man and woman would be abandoned as basic political units. (436)

As the debates on the Deleuzo-Guattarian concept of becoming-woman continue in the feminist arena, posthumanist theoreticians have refreshed the discussion with the latest studies in animal philosophy. Braidotti, for one, welcomes the unfolding of posthumanist practices in feminist theory: 'Post-humanism is a fast-growing new intersectional feminist alliance. It gathers the remains of post-structuralist anti-humanism and joins them with feminist reappraisals of contemporary genetics and molecular biology in a non-deterministic frame' (2005: 178). Likewise, on the televisual screen, Once Upon a Time gets intensively involved with posthuman ethics, which is a legacy of Spinozan ethics. MacCormack introduces the concept:

> Ethics is a practice of activist, adaptive and creative interaction which avoids claims to overarching moral structures . . . Posthuman Ethics exam-

ines certain kinds of bodies to think new relations that offer liberty and a contemplation of the practices of power which have been exerted upon bodies. (2012b: 1)

Motivated by these shifts, this chapter studies Little Red Riding Hood's story in *Once Upon a Time* in relation to an ethics of solidarity, which is a correlation of twenty-first-century feminist and posthumanist practices.

Morals of Red Riding Hood

For a better understanding of how Red/Ruby's transformation acts as the screen avatar of current feminist and posthumanist studies, it is convenient to start from the origins of the story and its suggestions. In a short schematic view: the Red Riding Hood fairy-tale tells the story of a little girl who goes to her grandmother's house, passing through the forest, with a basket on her arm. In the forest, she encounters a wolf that wants to eat the food in the basket. Red Riding Hood tells him that she is going to visit her grandmother and they depart. When Red Riding Hood reaches the house, her grandmother seems different to her. Soon she finds out that it is actually the wolf lying in her grandmother's bed. The wolf attempts to eat her and the ending varies depending on the specific version of the story.

'Little Red Riding Hood' has its origins in tenth-century French folk-lore and has changed significantly throughout history (Berlioz 2005: 63). In the first written version (Perrault 1697), the tale finishes when Red Riding Hood climbs into the bed with the wolf. This dark finale – with its implication of 'getting into bed with atavistic forces' – suggests the moral implications of not being a well-bred girl. The Brothers Grimm also wrote two serial versions in a similar moralising manner (Grimm 1812). The first account reformulates the original ending by having the girl and her grandmother saved by a huntsman.[1] The second establishes solidarity between the women. The girl and the grandmother, learning from their experience with the previous scenario, trap the new wolf in the chimney and drown him in a pot over the fire.[2] Still, their solidarity does not liberate the characters due to the constricting Oedipal and dualistic norms of the stories. These early versions mostly consider moral values as the main drive of the fairy-tale and act as a great attraction centre to psychoanalysis due their approach to familial kinship and sexuality.[3]

The early forms of the tale concentrate on three main themes. The first is a warning to little girls about the dangers of the outside world.

Mothers and grandmothers act as agents of the moral and molar system by advising the female protagonist, who is at the phase of passing from girlhood to womanhood, to behave appropriately. 'Stay on the path, do not talk to strangers, and obey your mother.' The girl cannot freely live her childhood and is forced into a framed adulthood. The patriarchal system imposes its values on her growth and blocks her becoming. Deleuze and Guattari, in their chapter on becoming, stress that such normative binary thinking is imposed on the body: 'The question is fundamentally that of the body – the body they steal from us in order to fabricate opposable organisms. This body is stolen first from a girl: stop behaving like that, you're not a girl anymore, you're not a tomboy, etc.' (1987: 276).[4] Red Riding Hood cannot go through the process of becoming-girl and becoming-woman. Instead, she falls into the system of binary oppositions of culture-nature, man-woman and human-animal. The little girl stays strictly on the path and grows up into a molar and dichotomic system.

Secondly, the red cloak acts as a common item in these moral versions. It saves the girl from the dangers of the forest, night and wolf, in short from the outside world. Additionally, the cloak's colour connotes the puberty of the girl (Dundes 1991: 27–8).[5] From the perspective of Spinozan ethics, the issue is neither the cloak nor its redness, but the moral and molar values that are charged on it. It disconnects the girl from external encounters. With its over-protectiveness, it does not let her experience life. In the origins of the story, puberty starts when the girl leaves home and learns to make her own decisions. In one version, the girl escapes with the help of laundresses.[6] Although this version has connotations of solidarity, again it cannot critique the moral setting and stays inside the borders of strictly molar lines. This time, the elderly women (laundresses) represent 'cleanness', as opposed to the girl's redness (puberty). Moreover, the girl is 'saved' only when she accepts being 'clean' according to conventional norms. Her rescue does not come out of her actions and choices, but is imposed on her from the outside.

The narrative's third main theme is sexuality. Depending on the stories' approach to the latter, their content changes accordingly. Most of the early versions stay within molar and moral lines. Perrault finishes the first written version with the words:

> I say Wolf, for all wolves
> Are not of the same sort;
> There is one kind with an amenable disposition

Neither noisy, nor hateful, nor angry,
But tame, obliging and gentle,
Following the young maids
In the streets, even into their homes.
Alas! Who does not know that these gentle wolves
Are of all such creatures the most dangerous! (Dundes 1989: 73)

Perrault explicitly portrays young men, the girls' potential sexual partners, as dangerous wolves. Starting with his version, sexuality becomes moralised and turns into an experience that Red Riding Hood must resist to stay clean and pure. The wolf, as the sexual seducer, becomes the gentle but sexually hazardous man-animal; in short, the embodiment of otherness.

However, there are also transgressive and subversive versions of the story. These varieties practise becomings in accordance with Deleuze and Guattari's insistence 'that subjection was not the sole logic' and that 'other forms of language, perception and embodiment would be possible, beyond the current logic of Oedipal individualism' (Colebrook 2013: 430). In this view, these Red Riding Hoods and their stories are the genealogical precursors of Red/Ruby from *Once Upon a Time*.

The Genealogy of Red/Ruby

There are various fruitfully transgressive versions of the story.[7] Here we will consider four characters from different films as siblings of Ruby, due to their approach to ethics and sexuality:[8] Rosaline in Neil Jordan's film, *The Company of Wolves* (1984), Will and Laura in Mike Nichols's *Wolf* (1994), and Red Riding Hood in David Kaplan's short film *Little Red Riding Hood* (1997). *Once Upon a Time*'s creators, Edward Kitsis and Adam Horowitz, emphasise that they prefer to write strong female characters instead of 'passive princesses or damsels in distress' (Campbell 2011). Therefore, their Red Riding Hood is not passive, fearful and moral in her proximal encounters. All three of these films construct their characters similarly to Red/Ruby regarding ethics. Additionally, they use the tools of the cinematic medium artfully in narrating becoming. The interactive formation of mythology, fairy-tales and the cinematic medium turns into a joyful collective assemblage in *Once Upon a Time* and its ancestor films.

Kaplan's short film, *Little Red Riding Hood*, extends the borders of filmic narration by telling the original story with a pinch of playfulness. Kaplan transforms the girl into a seductive young woman and the wolf into a gentle man. Red gets into bed with the wolf; she realises that the wolf is not her grandmother. She tells the wolf she must go to the toilet; however, the clever wolf ties a string around her finger to stop her from fleeing. The girl responds to the wolf's cleverness with intelligence. She ties the string to a branch, looks at the wolf and slowly goes away. Her departure does not happen as a panic escape, but as a decision based on her sexual desires. She does not want to share an imposed sexuality with the wolf, so she leaves to make new external connections. Additionally, Kaplan's Red tricks the wolf and rescues herself without any need for other saviours.

The Company of Wolves is a transformed version of the Red Riding Hood story based on Angela Carter's three short stories (Carter 1990). Carter re-writes myths and fairy-tales and re-assembles them with transgressive elements. Director Neil Jordan, co-writing the film's script with Carter, carries her intercorrelating style onto the screen by interweaving different spaces, temporalities and dreams within each other. *Once Upon a Time*, due to its serial and mosaic storytelling, appropriates the interlacing and serialising style of *The Company of Wolves* and composes a similar multidimensional and ongoing heterogeneous universe. In *The Company of Wolves*, four mini-films – narrating werewolf becomings – accompany the main story in a 'Chinese-box structure'. It is significant that a mental shift occurs from the first story to the last one. The first two portray werewolves as dangerous and aggressive creatures while the third provides room for alternative interpretations with its story placed in between revenge and justice. Finally, Rosaleen relates the fourth one, which tells of the unjust treatment meted out to a werewolf. In this case, a shewolf comes to town without any harmful intentions, but gets shot by a villager. She turns into her human form and a priest helps her recover. Afterwards, she returns home safely. The last story discloses a new way of thinking by narrating the interaction and transformation on both sides: human becoming-werewolf (of the priest) and werewolf becoming-human (of the shewolf). Rosaleen tells this story to a wounded wolf, while gently petting him. Jordan's Rosaleen turns out to be as equally seductive as the wolf. She likes the wolf and wants to go with him. As she follows her desires without the interruption and entrapment of moral and molar lines, her transformation starts by choosing the wolf as her partner; she also starts becoming-wolf.

Mike Nichols's *Wolf* narrates Will and his companion Laura's story of becoming-werewolves. As Deleuze and Guattari put it: 'you can't be one wolf, you're always eight or nine, six or seven' (1987: 29). There must be at least two to start the pack and its concomitant interaction and inter-transformation. The more, the merrier. Laura discovers her beasty side when she encounters Will. Both, together, liberate their bodies from humanity-restricted thinking, flow into post-anthropocentric zones, and start becoming posthuman. Will and Laura embrace an ethics of interaction and start the process of becoming-wolf. *Once Upon a Time*'s Red/Ruby and her sisters and brother(s), Kaplan's Red Riding Hood, Jordan's Rosaleen and Nichols's Will and Laura, all practise the potentials of their bodies by interacting with others, experiencing sexuality without moral and Oedipal restrictions. They enter into multiplicities and start becoming-animal.

In *The Company of Wolves* and *Wolf*, the female characters transform into werewolves. And in Jordan's film and *Once Upon a Time*, Red Riding Hoods specifically become werewolves. What happens when the wolf is inside the girl? How does the story of Red/Ruby become the screen embodiment and embrainment of a twenty-first-century (post) feminist theory and posthuman ethics of solidarity? How does a television series, *Once Upon a Time*, apply cinematic aesthetics to practise transgression and transformation on screen? This chapter poses these questions by following Red/Ruby's trajectory. *Once Upon a Time*, in particular, practises a very Deleuzian – de-centred, non-linear and indefinite – storytelling style that directly interacts with a (post)feminist, posthuman ethics of solidarity.

Becoming-girl

Once Upon a Time introduces Ruby as a young woman, just passing through adolescence. She works at her grandmother's diner in Storybrooke as a waitress. She seems to be bored with her life, which in her opinion has no purpose or direction. At the beginning of the episode 'Red Handed', she talks in a flirtatious manner with a customer, who tells his adventures of travelling around the world. When her grandmother orders her to stop flirting and do the diner's bookkeeping, they argue and Ruby leaves her job and home to explore the external world. In parallel, her Fairyland persona Red disobeys her grandmother's rules as well. She secretly kisses her childhood friend Peter from her bedroom window. Becoming-girl is the first step to Red/Ruby's transformation, for as Deleuze and Guattari stress, 'Children are Spinozists' (1987: 256). Becoming-girl is the starting point for Red/Ruby to practise and experiment with 'new relations that offer liberty and a contemplation of the practices of power which have been exerted upon bodies' (MacCormack 2012b: 1). Both Red and Ruby opt out from the daily routines and morals imposed on their bodies by beginning from the middle point between girlhood and womanhood. Like her sisters in Kaplan's and Jordan's films, she is at the age of puberty, neither child nor woman; exactly '. . . between a child and a woman, no longer a little girl, not yet a woman . . . [which] makes [her] the perfect figure to reveal the possibilities of becoming' (Pisters 2003: 112). Ruby/Red's stories begin with disobedience and resistance to moral oppressions and restrictions. She leaves the segmental molar categories imposed on her, strips off the dualism of man-woman, child-adult, and enters into inbetweenness, which is full of potentials.

In relation to sexuality, all Reds are free of the moral entrapments of society. Sexuality is new to them, but they decide on their own actions. They do not strictly obey their mothers or grandmothers, 'they slip in everywhere, between orders, acts, ages, sexes; they produce n molecular sexes on the line of flight in relation to the dualism machines they cross right through' (Deleuze and Guattari 1987: 277). Jordan's Rosaleen chooses her desires over moral values just as Kaplan's Red enjoys playing with the concept. In *Once Upon a Time*, Red just starts experiencing kissing. Her friend Peter accompanies her in this passage to adulthood desires. Moreover, sexual repressions are not even an issue for *Once Upon a Time*'s Red/Ruby. In Storybrooke, Emma and Mary Margaret encounter Ruby talking to Dr Whale, who seems to be seductively inviting Ruby to his place. They worry, thinking that Ruby is all alone, defenceless and vulnerable, so they ask her if she is fine and if the doctor was bothering her. Ruby's answer shows how competent she is at making her decisions in relation to desires and that she has no problem managing these issues: 'The day I can't handle a lech is the day I leave town.' She is well capable of living ethically, concerning her desires in relation to others. Because she has nowhere to go, Mary Margaret offers her help and invites Ruby to her place to figure things out. In Fairyland, Red mirrors Mary Margaret's act of solidarity by helping Snow White (Mary Margaret's Fairyland persona). She offers Snow White, who is running away from the Evil Queen, a place to stay.

Becoming-woman

In *Once Upon a Time*, becoming-woman starts between the interactions of the two women. They learn to become-woman in relationality and solidarity. Red helps Snow, Snow helps Red. Red's solidarity is not only reserved for female companions, she also assists male characters and the village community as a whole. In other words, her support for others is not gender selective, which conforms to the current posthumanist stress on the ethics of solidarity as well as recent feminist theory's focus on collective and interactive movements between men and women instead of aligning feminism only with women's rights. Thus, for example, the United Nations Women's branch started a solidarity campaign called HeForShe, inviting the participation of men working for gender equality. The campaign was introduced by Emma Watson[9] and in a single day it gathered positive reactions, especially on social media (Monde 2014). In her speech, Watson invited everybody to discuss this shift in feminist theory and proposed collective and interactive solidarity actions. Red/Ruby is the fictional screen avatar of this concept: she does not distinguish between men and women. She cares for and tries to help everyone.

In Fairyland, Red and Snow track the wolf's paw prints to Red's window and assume that Peter is the wolf without his knowing it. Red decides to help him by spending the night by his side and tying him up before he shapeshifts again. To trick Red's grandmother, Snow wears Red's cloak and stays in Red's bed instead of her. The wise grandmother realises that Red is out without her cloak but, unfortunately, it's too late. Snow learns from her that Peter is not the wolf: Red is. Red's cloak was a magical item, preventing her transformation. In *Once Upon a Time*, both the red cloak and grandmother figures perform different functions than in the early moral and molar versions of the tale. The cloak acts as a magic vest to stop Red turning into a wolf. It is not a sign of puberty or a protection from sexuality. Additionally, its preventive status alters when Red/Ruby learns to control her transformation. *Wolf*'s Will has a similar magic item, a silver amulet, which stops him turning into a wolf. Both Red/Ruby and Will use their magical items in their ethical decisions and actions. The items do not rule them, but the wolflings control their own actions by using these magical items within an ethics of solidarity.

The elder female figure in Red/Ruby's story initially appears as morally oppressive and excessively protective. However, the episode 'Red Handed' reveals that the grandmother was also a werewolf. And her behaviour in Storybrooke was actually geared towards helping Ruby practise her own way of becoming-woman. She was not forcing Ruby into a limited life, but essentially giving her the opportunity to develop her own responsibilities by taking charge of Granny's café. *Once Upon a Time* narrates Red/Ruby's story within the rubric of Spinozan ethics: 'not only destroy[ing] good sense as the only direction; also destroy[ing] common sense as the assignation of fixed identities' (Pisters 2003: 109–10). Red/Ruby questions her identity through her becoming processes: the series shows her shifts in-between Red and Ruby, childhood and adulthood, girlhood and womanhood, human and animal because she does 'not belong to an age, group, sex, order, or kingdom: [she] slip[s] in everywhere, between orders, acts, ages, sexes' (114). Red/Ruby escapes the molar system by staying outside dualism and entering in-between. She continuously composes herself in multi-directional transformations and interactive relations. By experimenting on her Spinozan body, she explores its (un)limits and becomes elastic in her individuations. Deleuze comments on this elasticity of the body, brain and soul: 'we can hardly recognize the same individual. And is it really indeed the same individual?' (Deleuze 1992: 222). Red/Ruby constantly transforms into new subjectivities and explores her potentials through becomings. At the end of 'Red Handed', Ruby apologises to her grandmother for misunderstanding her intentions and adds that it is hard to be like her grandmother. Becoming like her grandmother is not a moral transformation, but an ethical one. The latter is not a figure of oppression but an elder, a wise woman, who pushes Ruby to her limits so that she can explore her potentials and extend them through interactions. Red/Ruby's grandmother teaches her to act within an ethics of solidarity and be responsible for her actions. Moreover, embodying both becoming-woman and becoming-animal, she shows an ethical way of becoming-werewolf to Red/Ruby.

Becoming-animal

'Red Handed' does not show Red's transformation into a wolf via a literal focus on her body, but instead shows it through its affect on Peter's face. Moreover, because Red is unconscious of her bestiality at the beginning, she hurts her companions and is ultimately caught red-handed.[10] In this respect, *Once Upon a Time* shows how she learns to accept and control her bestiality. Deleuze proposes that 'the man who suffers is a beast, the beast that suffers is a man' (2004: 25). Red/Ruby's becoming-animal thus starts with her realisation of her bestiality and suffering from it, notably when she learns that her beast side has killed someone. She transforms through her suffering. Becoming-animal 'constitutes a single process, a unique method that replaces subjectivity' (Deleuze and Guattari 1986: 35–6). Red/Ruby was already a were-wolf being inside but was not experiencing the process of becoming-werewolf. She starts becoming-woman and becoming-animal together, when she recognises her werewolf side in relation to externality. For her, the only way left was to become impersonal, to replace subjectivity with otherness in relation to external forces. Red/Ruby is therefore beyond animal-human duality, she is posthuman in her werewolf becoming, neither a wolf nor a human, caught in a continuous transformation of becoming-werewolf. Her material becomings are beyond Oedipal and molar descriptions. She passes from human to wolf, wolf to human, girl to woman, woman to girl, Red to Ruby, and Ruby to Red continuously. Similarly, *Once Upon a Time*, as mentioned earlier, does not follow a linear storytelling of her becomings; it embodies and embrains a style of becoming similar to the continuous transformations of its character(s). Red/Ruby is a posthuman character in a posthuman narrative.

Donna Haraway, in her book *When Species Meet* (2008), disagrees with Deleuze and Guattari's approach to wolf-human becomings and their favouring over dog-human becomings.[11] It is important to note that Red/Ruby has to be a werewolf in this narrative due to the monstrosity of werewolves. Braidotti quotes Borges's classification of animal types: 'those we watch television with, those we eat and those we are scared of' (2013b: 68). She proposes these categorisations of animals as Oedipalised, instrumental, and/or fantasmatic. It is important to note that Red/Ruby is not a friendly or consumed animal-human becoming. Her terror and monstrosity are significant. The otherness is monstrous and unacceptable on molar lines, for as Brian Massumi stresses, 'Becoming-other goes from the general to the singular, returning thought to the body grasped from the point of view of its transformational potential – monstrosity' (1992: 107). Red/Ruby learns to cope with molar lines through her becoming-monstrous on molecular lines. Bradiotti states: 'Contemporary horror and science-fiction ... show an exacerbated version of anxiety in the form of the "otherness within"' (2000: 163). Pisters adds, 'monstrosity ... is seen as something terrifying and threating to human identity. [However,] Deleuze provides the tools to construct more flexible forms of identity and subjectivity, grounded in "matter" and "memory" but never fixed' (2003: 141). *Once Upon a Time* uses these tools to unfold Red/Ruby's story and shows the potentials of becoming-werewolf. More importantly, Red/Ruby's monstrosity as a werewolf is also linked to her becoming-woman. Her monstrosity not only addresses her becoming-other by turning into a dangerous, fearful animal, but also includes her femaleness. Braidotti points 'to the century-old connection between the feminine and the monstrous' (2000: 157) and suggests that in the male-dominated society and especially in 'Western thought ... "she" is forever associated to unholy, disorderly, subhuman, and unsightly phenomena' (2013a: 80). Red/Ruby, as a shewolf, is an enemy to mankind, an outsider in her civilisation, an 'other' in her co-operating becomings.

In 'Red Handed', living in a molar system, Red/Ruby obeys moral orders. Towards the end, she learns about her werewolf potential and experiences the outcomes of repressing them: she blacks out every time she transforms. In 'Child of the Moon', Red/Ruby discovers and remembers how to use and control her potential. In Fairyland, she encounters a man called Quinn, who is also a werewolf. He tells her that she can control her transformations and takes Red to the secret lair of a werewolf pack. There, she meets her mother Anita and learns from her to accept her wolf side; and this process leads her to controlling her becoming-werewolf potential.

'Child of the Moon', for the first time in the series, shows the transformation of Red/Ruby through her own eyes. Previously, her becoming-wolf had appeared on Peter's terrified face in 'Red Handed' and with a close-up (affection-image) of Red's determined expression in 'Heart of Darkness'. In this episode, the screen experiences Red/Ruby's transformation with her. Intensive and proximal point-of-view shots slide through the forest as if the images are coming from a wolf's eyes. Red's blackouts fade away as her wolf-becoming covers the screen with an in-between image of dream and actuality. She runs through the woods, experiences multisensations of pores, moments, particles and molecules. Running through forces, intensities and vibrations, Red embraces her becoming. Deleuze and Guattari state, 'you become animal only molecularly' (1987: 275) and suggest haecceities as zones of becoming (261). As Red transforms into a body without organs, the televisual screen itself becomes a haecceity. 'Child of the Moon', in alignment with Deleuze and Guattari's words, visualises and sonorises the becoming-molecular process by (de)composing the image towards pure-perception. These perception-images are so near-sighted that, instead of creating 'a grand godlike position that subsumes all viewpoints, . . . [they link] a multiplication of smaller and smaller perceptions, decreasing the distance and elevation of the authorial voice' (Colebrook 2013: 431). The televisual image becomes *haecceity*, 'a possible lens that opens a new world' (433), a new potential of relating with earth, 'where zones of being shift toward non-molar alliances' (MacCormack 2012a: 1). This pure perception-image does not serve the story in any way, but expresses the pure affect and percept of becoming-werewolf.

Colebrook calls '"becoming-woman" . . . a process of saturation, in which the force of the world composes the writer (or perceiver) as a canvas or zone of perception, nothing more than a refraction of a shower of atoms' (2013: 438). In *Once Upon a Time*, a narration of becoming surfaces. Like Deleuze and Guattari's 'Continuum inhabited by unnameable waves and indefinable particles', with Red, the televisual screen 'become[s] progressively more molecular in a kind of cosmic overlapping' (1987: 248). It is a condition of becoming-molecular, becoming-imperceptible and becoming the BwO. Pisters equates *Wolf*'s narration of Will's transformation as the effects of drugs.[12] Deleuze and Guattari suggest that with drugs, '(1) the imperceptible is perceived; (2) perception is molecular; (3) desire directly invests the perception and the perceived ... perception becomes molecular at the same time as the imperceptible is perceived' (282). Pisters suggests that Will experiences drug affect with his wolf-becoming. With 'Child of the Moon', the televisual screen becomes a drug in the Deleuzo-Guattarian context, for the screen 'appear[s] as the agent of becoming ... The unconscious as such is given in microperceptions' (Pisters 2003: 168–9). Red learns from Anita how to become a werewolf; however, her transformation does not end here. She continues her metamorphosis in relation to others, forces, intensities, and delves into the ethics of solidarity.

Becoming-shewolf

Snow, following Red, finds the werewolf pack in their secret place. The Evil Queen's soldiers, chasing her, enter the lair and kill some of the werewolves. Anita blames Snow for their deaths and orders Red to kill her friend to become a true wolf of the pack. When Red refuses, Anita attacks Snow. Red gets in-between and Anita falls on a pike and dies. *Once Upon a Time*, with its subverted and radical narrative, thereby opens a discussion on the mother's death. How can the mother's death be approached? Is it Irigaray's Electra complex[13] or a different practice of ethics? And how does this event assist to further propagate Red's becoming?

Firstly, the relationship between Red and Anita is not constructed through familial connections. They are mother-daughter, but Red meets Anita in old age. Anita never takes the position of the mother of the family in Red's life. If there must be a mother figure in Red's life, her grandmother fits this category more appropriately as she was responsible for her upbringing. Yet, the narrative either strictly tries to stay away from familial kinship ties or challenges them. Additionally, there is no father figure; Red's father is never introduced. Therefore, there is no traditional mommy-daddy-me origination relationship, Oedipal or Electral. Both Anita and the werewolf pack serve as a multiplicity of mentors in Red's transformation. Red's becoming-werewolf 'has its own reality, which is not based on resemblance or affiliation but on alliance, symbiosis, affection, and infection' (Pisters 2003: 144). Even Anita underlines the importance of solidarity between sisters and brothers when she teaches Red how to become a werewolf. Still, Deleuze and Guattari ask:

> But what exactly does that mean, the animal as band or pack? Does a band not imply a filiation, bringing us back to the reproduction of given characteristics? How can we conceive of a peopling, a propagation, a becoming that is without filiation or hereditary production? A multiplicity without the unity of an ancestor? (1987: 241)

Red/Ruby is a hybrid born out of multiplicities and her relation to other multiplicities. She is not born from a mother as a shewolf. Becoming-shewolf is like becoming-woman in werewolf terms. In her becoming-shewolf, Red is a peopling without filiation. She discovers rhizomatic fields when she encounters Anita and her pack. The latter act as catalysts in Red's transformation, but they are not the reason for it. Red learns becoming-werewolf from Anita and the pack, but starts becoming-shewolf when Anita and the werewolves try to kill her friend. In this collective transformation, Red's proximal encounter is Snow in her becoming-shewolf. With her, Red practises 'Affinity: related not by blood but by choice' (Haraway 2004: 13). She makes a choice and chooses solidarity.

Secondly, in Anita's case, becoming-werewolf, with its drug-like effect, reminds us of the dangerous zones of the BwO. Anita loses herself in her wolfness. She discriminates between humans and animals and moreover orders Red to do the same. She becomes fascistic and falls into a black hole by composing a wolf identity. Colebrook sees such identity as fatal and suggests activating 'anti-self-consciousness' (2013: 430). Anita fails at performing anti-self-consciousness and traps herself back in molar lines. Additionally, Red does not kill Anita. Anita causes her own destruction by 'wildly destratifying' (Deleuze and Guattari 1987: 160). When she orders the murdering of Snow, deciding on the life of another, she becomes a fascistic body. Red learns from her mother not to be like her. In her interaction with Anita and the pack, Red practises creative ways of becoming 'on the verge of discovering a rhizome' (21), but never harming others by crossing the thresholds of solidarity ethics.

Thirdly, Deleuze, in his reading of Spinoza's text on Orestes' and Nero's killings of their mothers, shows that there are different acts of killing, depending on the compositions and decompositions of relationships. He states:

> Orestes kills his mother because she killed . . . Orestes' father . . . According to Spinoza, Orestes associates his act, not with the image of Clytemnestra whose relation will be decomposed by this act, but rather he associates it

with the relation of Agamemnon which was decomposed by Clytemnestra. In killing his mother, Orestes recomposes his relation with the relation of his father. (Deleuze 1981)

Similarly, Red acts within the ethics of solidarity when she blocks her mother's attack. Her action is not aimed at 'killing her mother', but at 'saving a companion'. She rescues a friend, a sister, from the attack of her mother. She frees herself from hereditary kinship and enters into heterogeneous crowds. 'Being free, according to Spinoza, is being able to accept all the changes that occur during one's lifetime, seeing that they are necessary according to an internal logic (but not strictly according to a fixed identity)' (Pisters 2003: 127). *Once Upon a Time* shows that Red has no problem with her mother as her kin; she simply reacts to Anita's damaging action. In the internal logic of the series, Anita causes her own destruction. When Anita dies, Red and Snow bury her. *Once Upon a Time* reminds us that Anita's death was not intentional when Red and Snow stand in solidarity together at a female fellow's burial. Pisters writes '["power of acting"] is a matter of our conatus being determined by adequate ideas from which active affects follow. It is having a desire that relates to what we know to be most important in life' (127–8). For Red, helping others and saving the continuity of life are the most important things in her life.

In 'Child of the Moon', while Red learns to become-shewolf in Fairyland, Ruby (her Storybrooke persona) struggles with her metamorphosis on a different level.[14] After the curse breaks in Storybrooke, the approaching first full moon worries Ruby. She questions her ability to control her transformation. Her friends David and Belle believe in her and help her. Spencer, who wants to remove David from his Sheriff position, labels Ruby as a criminal and tries to frame her. With David and Belle's help, Ruby remembers how to control her becoming again. In both stories, Red/Ruby's becoming-shewolf occurs in solidarity. She helps others with her werewolf super-senses (extraordinary hearing, smelling, and seeing abilities) and protects them from attacks (Prince Charming from Evil Queen's soldiers and Snow White from werewolves in Fairyland, Emma and David in Storybrooke). She enters into heterogeneous intensities and forces by practising an ethics of solidarity with her friends.

Ethics of Solidarity

In the internal logic of the series, David becomes shewolf as well, since becoming is not resembling or imitating, but transforming in relation to others. David, Belle and Ruby all start becoming-shewolf by practising the ethics of solidarity. Becoming-shewolf should not be framed as a 'she' becoming. It is not reserved for females, just as becoming-woman is not confined only to women. It is, like becoming-woman, beyond 'racial, gendered, sexual, ethnic or historically embedded bias . . . [it is] a pure becoming' (Colebrook 2013: 432). Shewolf's 'she' comes from the ongoing collective movement of feminist and posthumanist theory which also invites male companions to actions of gender equality. It is a shift of perception. Colebrook summarises:

> Becoming-woman might possess some privilege or legitimacy, not just because it was not the perception of man, and not because it would be perception from another point of view, but because it would shift the problem of point of view. Becoming-woman would not be perceiving as a woman, but perceiving in such a way that perception would be a form of becoming. (2013: 433)

Becoming-shewolf in *Once Upon a Time* is a transformation beyond dualistic definitions. It is not a molar struggle like old-school feminism; it is a becoming in solidarity. As Deleuze and Guattari suggest, 'the woman as a molar entity *has to become-woman* in order that the man also becomes- or can become-woman' (1987: 276). Colebrook adds, 'one must be woman-manly or man-womanly . . . Some collaboration has to take place in the mind between the woman and the man before the art of creation can be accomplished' (2013: 429). In *Once Upon a Time* becoming-shewolf is a metamorphosis beyond orders, acts, ages, sexes; it is post-anthropocentric and post-gender solidarity in practice. Red/Ruby becomes shewolf, not animal, not woman, but both and many more; as Deleuze states, 'in order to "become," . . . [she] create[s] something new' (1995: 171). Red/Ruby's becoming-shewolf, her creation of something new, is certainly the screen image of the collaboration between feminism and posthumanism: it is the televisual-image of solidarity ethics.

A new Deleuzian (post)feminism is forming in relation to a posthumanist ethics of solidarity. Bradiotti's call for 'the feminist nomadic thinkers of the world to connect and negotiate' (2013a: 94) is actualised in campaigns like HeForShe, composing collective becomings in solidarity. Likewise, television series, interacting with political and cultural arenas, embrace the affirmation of differences, by creating narratives and narration of 'and. . .and. . .and. . .' instead of 'or. . .or. . .or. . .'. MacCormack proposes that 'Watching [television series] . . . is a certain becoming, a launching of the self into new modes of thinking, feeling the parameters and meanings of one's own body' (2012a: 14), and she emphasises popular culture's transformational effect on political theory. Joining the (post)feminist and posthumanist mental shift, *Once Upon a Time* experiments 'by taking certain image types into new territories (by "deterritorialising")' (Pisters 2003: 137). Watching television series can be a new way of deterritorialising; entering into becomings; making rhizomatic connections between a multiplicity of bodies, brains and souls; and practising an ethics of solidarity.

Notes

1. There are also other versions of the story with different male saviours, such as a woodcutter from the forest.
2. In other variations, the grandmother hides in the closet and saves Red Riding Hood, or they both save themselves by cutting their way out of the wolf's belly.
3. For Bettelheim's Freudian analysis, see Bettelheim 2010. See also Clark 1987 for a study of Angela Carter's Red Riding Hood stories within the framework of binary oppositions, such as 'feral domineering mate and gentle submissive female'.
4. Patricia Pisters also works on the stolen body of the girl in her analysis of *Alice in Wonderland* (2003: 112).
5. Alan Dundes, in his psychoanalytical work, finds the red cloak to be a tool of the passage to womanhood. See Dundes 1989.
6. In this version, the laundresses spread sheets over a river, creating a bridge. After the girl runs over them, they release the sheet bridge and the wolf, following her, falls into the river and drowns. See Beckett 2008.
7. Additional alternative versions can be found online. The animations Betty Boop's *Dizzy Red Riding Hood* (1931) and Tex Avery's *Red Hot Riding Hood* (1943) play with the sexuality concept intensively. Little Red Riding Hood is also one of the central characters in the 1987 Broadway musical *Into the Woods* by Stephen Sondheim and James Lapine. The latter includes the song, 'I Know Things Now', where Red Riding Hood sings about the affects she has from the encounter with the wolf as 'excited, well, excited *and* scared'. The animated films *Hoodwinked!* (2005) and *Hoodwinked Too! Hood vs. Evil* (2011) depict Red Riding Hood as a girl rebelling and becoming-woman. Orenstein's *Little Red Riding Hood Uncloaked* (2008) covers alternative readings of a variety of Red Riding Hoods.
8. These protagonists engage in sexuality in Deleuzo-Guattarian ways. The latter's approach to sexuality is different from that of psychoanalysis. In *Anti-Oedipus* (1983: 108) they state that 'everything is sexual', and open sexuality to the social and political. Sexuality is a becoming, a joining of two or many forces, a case of experiencing with desires through intensities. See Deleuze and Guattari 1983 and 1987, for example, p. 39. For more on Deleuze and sexuality, see Beckman 2011.

9. Emma Watson is a popular young actor, who started her career with the role of Hermione in the *Harry Potter* films (2001–11).
10. Understood as being caught in the act of a crime, especially murder, which also gives a visual image of having hands reddened with blood.
11. Haraway's critique has provoked much debate in feminist and posthumanist studies. Her approach to animal-human relationships and proposition of affirmative companionship are important; however, posthuman ethics studies human-animal relationships on a different assemblage. Rosi Braidotti writes that the 'posthuman approach moves beyond "high" cyber studies [Haraway, Hayles] into post-cyber materialism and posthuman theory. A nomadic zoe-centred approach connects human to non-human life so as to develop a comprehensive eco-philosophy of becoming' (2013b: 104). More discussion on the subject can be found in Braidotti 2006 and in MacCormack 2012b.
12. A thorough Deleuzian analysis of the films *The Company of Wolves* and *Wolf* can be found in Pisters's 'Logic of Sensations in Becoming-Animal' in Pisters 2003. She proposes a 'depersonalising' of the affection-image to narrate the transformation of the characters. *Once Upon a Time* carries the legacy of *Wolf* and transforms it into a mixture of the affection-image and perception-image.
13. Luce Irigaray proposes an Electra Complex for girls as an equivalent to the Oedipal Complex of boys. She examines the concept of matricide within the framework of psychoanalysis. See Irigaray's 'Body Against Body: In Relation to the Mother' in Irigaray 1993. For more on Irigaray's analysis, see Green 2012 and Jacobs 2007.
14. It is significant that there is no mother figure in Ruby's story in Storybrooke. Spencer, who tries to frame Ruby as a criminal, is the mirror image of Anita in the parallel story.

References

Beckett, S. L. (2008), 'Little Red Riding Hood', in *The Greenwood Encyclopedia of Folktales and Fairytales*, ed. Donald Haase, Westport, CT: Greenwood Press, pp. 583–8.

Beckman, F. (ed.) (2011), *Deleuze and Sex*, Edinburgh: Edinburgh University Press.

Berlioz, J. (2005), *Il faut sauver Le petit chaperon rouge*, Paris: Les Collections de L'Histoires n. 36.

Bettelheim, B. (2010), *The Uses of Enchantment: The Meaning and Importance of Fairy-tales*, New York: Knopf Doubleday Publishing Group.

Braidotti, R. (2000), 'Teratologies', in C. Colebrook and I. Buchanan (eds), *Deleuze and Feminist Theory*, Edinburgh: Edinburgh University Press.

Braidotti, R. (2005), 'A Critical Cartography of Feminist Post-postmodernism', *Australian Feminist Studies*, Vol. 20, No. 47, pp. 169–80.

Braidotti, R. (2006), *Transpositions: On Nomadic Ethics*, Cambridge: Polity Press.

Braidotti, R. (2013a), *Nomadic Subjects: Embodiment and Sexual Difference in Contemporary Feminist Theory*, New York: Columbia University Press.

Braidotti, R. (2013b), *The Posthuman*, Oxford: John Wiley and Sons.

Campbell, J. (2011), 'Lost's Kitsis, Horowitz Start at the Beginning with Once Upon a Time', *Comic Book Resources*, 25 August 2011, at http://spinoff.comicbookresources.com/2011/08/25/losts-kitsis-and-horowitz-start-at-the-beginning-with-once-upon-a-time (accessed 25 October 2014).

Carter, A. (1990), 'The Company of Wolves', 'The Werewolf' and 'Wolf-Alice', in *The Bloody Chamber and Other Stories*, Harmondsworth: Penguin Books.

'Child of the Moon' (2012), *Once Upon a Time*, Season 2, Episode 7, directed by Anthony Hemingway. USA: ABC, 11 November.

Clark, R. (1987), 'Angela Carter's Desire Machine', *Women's Studies*, Vol. 14.

Colebrook, C. (2013), 'Modernism without Women: The Refusal of Becoming-Woman (and Post-Feminism)', *Deleuze Studies*, Vol. 7, No. 4, pp. 427–55.

The Company of Wolves (1984), UK: ITC.

Deleuze, G. (1981), 'Spinoza', *Le Course du Gilles Deleuze. Cours Vincennes*, trans. T. S. Murphy, at http://www.webdeleuze.com/php/texte.php?cle=34&groupe=Spinoza&langue=2 (accessed 5 November 2014).

Deleuze, G. (1986), *Cinema 1: The Movement-Image*, trans. H. Tomlinson and B. Habberjam, Minneapolis: University of Minnesota Press.

Deleuze, G. (1992), *Expressionism in Philosophy: Spinoza*, trans. M. Joughin, Cambridge, MA: Zone Books.

Deleuze, G. (1995), *Negotiations, 1972–1990*, trans. M. Joughin, New York: Columbia University Press.

Deleuze, G. (2004), *Francis Bacon: The Logic of Sensation*, trans. D. W. Smith, London: Continuum.

Deleuze, G. and F. Guattari (1983), *Anti-Oedipus: Capitalism and Schizophrenia*, trans. R. Hurley, M. Seem and H. Lane, Minnesota: University of Minneapolis Press.

Deleuze, G. and F. Guattari (1986), *Kafka: Toward a Minor Literature*, trans. D. Polan, Minneapolis: University of Minnesota Press.

Deleuze, G. and F. Guattari (1987), *A Thousand Plateaus: Capitalism and Schizophrenia*, trans. B. Massumi, Minneapolis: University of Minnesota Press.

Dundes, A. (1989), *Little Red Riding Hood: A Casebook*, Madison: University of Wisconsin Press.

Dundes, A. (1991), 'Interpreting Little Red Riding Hood Psychoanalytically', in James M. McGlathery (ed.), *The Brothers Grimm and Folktale*, Urbana: University of Illinois Press, pp. 16–51.

Green, L. (2012), 'Myths, Matricide and Maternal Subjectivity in Irigaray', *Studies in the Maternal Journal*, Vol. 4, No. 1.

Grimm, J. and W. (1812), 'Rotkäppchen', *Kinder- und Hausmärchen*, Berlin: Realschulbuchhandlung.

Haraway, D. (2004), *The Haraway Reader*, New York: Psychology Press.

Haraway, D. (2008), *When Species Meet*, Minneapolis: University of Minnesota Press.

'Heart of Darkness' (2012), *Once Upon a Time*, Season 1, Episode 16, directed by Dean White. USA: ABC, 18 March.

Irigaray, L. (1993), *Sexes and Genealogies*, trans. G. C. Gill, New York: Columbia University Press.

Jacobs, A. (2007), *On Matricide: Myth, Psychoanalysis, and the Law of the Mother*, New York: Columbia University Press.

Little Red Riding Hood (1997), directed by David Kaplan. USA: Little Red Movie Productions.

MacCormack, P. (2012a), 'Becoming Hu-Man: Deleuze and Guattari, Gender and *3rd Rock From the Sun*', *Intensities: Journal of Cult Media*, at https://intensitiescultmedia.files.wordpress.com/2012/12/maccormack.pdf (accessed 20 February 2014).

MacCormack, P. (2012b), *Posthuman Ethics: Embodiment and Cultural Theory*, Farnham: Ashgate.

Massumi, B. (1992), *A User's Guide to Capitalism and Schizophrenia: Deviations from Deleuze and Guattari*, Cambridge, MA: MIT Press.

Monde, C. (2014), 'Emma Watson Embraces Feminism, Introduces "HeForShe" Campaign in Speech at UN Meeting', *New York Daily News*, 22 September.

Once Upon a Time (2011–), television series, created by Edward Kitsis and Adam Horowitz. USA: ABC.

Orenstein, C. (2008), *Little Red Riding Hood Uncloaked: Sex, Morality, and the Evolution of a Fairy Tale*, New York: Basic Books.

Perrault, C. (1697), *Histoires ou contes du temps passé or Les Contes de ma Mère l'Oye*, Paris.

Pisters, P. (2003), *The Matrix of Visual Culture: Working with Deleuze in Film Theory*, Stanford: Stanford University Press.

'Red Handed' (2012), *Once Upon a Time*, Season 1, Episode 15, directed by Ron Underwood. USA: ABC, 11 March.

Wolf (1994), directed by Mike Nichols. USA: Columbia Pictures.

Chapter 10

Hannibal *aux aguets*: On the Lookout for New *Rencontres*

Charles J. Stivale

Literature begins with a porcupine's death, according to Lawrence, or with the death of a mole, in Kafka: 'our poor little red feet outstretched for tender sympathy.' As Moritz said, one writes for the dying calves. (Deleuze 1997a: 2)

Introduction

In *L'Abécédaire de Gilles Deleuze*, a significant video interview produced in 1988–9 but not transmitted until 1994–5, Gilles Deleuze discusses with Claire Parnet the crucial link between creativity, the very possibility of thinking, and animality, through the practice of 'être aux aguets' (being on the lookout) for *rencontres* (encounters). In key segments of *L'Abécédaire*, Deleuze makes both implicit and explicit links between the cluster of concepts to which he associates 'être aux aguets'. In Deleuze's view, creativity is precisely a concept of new perspectives that enable the creation of new worlds, new time-spaces and (to use a concept he develops with Félix Guattari) new 'refrains'. Just as animals live constantly *aux aguets* and thereby must define their territory and assure their very existence in specifically delimited ways at every second, so too do artists and philosophers open themselves to possibilities of innovation and thought through the violence that they risk in having an idea through a genuine *rencontre* – a potentially threatening, frightening encounter that might open them to an entirely new mode of perception and sensation, a completely new 'refrain'.

Having previously considered 'être aux aguets' in terms of creation and deterritorialisation (see Stivale 2014), I will deploy this concept here in a perhaps unorthodox domain by considering how 'being on the lookout' for new *rencontres* constitutes the essential practice of the character Hannibal Lecter, created by Thomas Harris in several novels (*Red*

Dragon, *Silence of the Lambs*, *Hannibal*, *Hannibal Rising*), and depicted by different actors (Brian Cox, Anthony Hopkins and Gaspard Ulliel) in film adaptations of these four books,[1] and, most recently, portrayed by the Danish actor Mads Mikkelsen in the commercial television series *Hannibal* (produced by Bryan Fuller). What I would like to consider is how an array of Deleuzo-Guattarian concepts – among which are the animal, 'être aux aguets', becomings and involution – create a creative assemblage when linked to this fictional print, cinematic and televisual production, in order to open these productions and the Deleuzian concepts to an alternate and creative reading.

To start, I need first to discuss briefly the available corpus. In each of Harris's novels, the author develops this character in ways that allow us to understand Hannibal as a highly refined individual who can not only sense physically the presence of any threat through extraordinary perceptual powers (most notably, olfactory), but can also categorise, store and then recall any such scents/essences through access to a Memory Palace, a personal inner database. Of particular interest is the temporal disjunction of the presentation of this Palace: whereas it appears 'in action' as it were in the 1999 novel *Hannibal* (the sequel to 1988's *The Silence of the Lambs*), the Palace is formally introduced in the opening pages of the 2006 novel, *Hannibal Rising*, a prequel to the series that traces the origins of the young Lecter.[2] The films necessarily provide edited versions of the fuller textual treatments, and yet they offer a visual complement to the books, thereby enhancing the reader's understanding of the character's remarkable power.

As for the television series, the viewer there finds a hybrid Hannibal: he has yet to be 'discovered' for the skilled and voracious criminal that he is, and hence remains deceptively unrevealed, and thus akin to (although much more mature than) his youthful incarnation in the origin tale, *Hannibal Rising*. As an adult observer and consultant to FBI investigations and to their participants, he is thus able to cleverly manipulate those around him (as he still does from captivity both in *Red Dragon* and *Silence of the Lambs*) for creative slaying by proxy. Yet, he also develops his own murderous and cannibalistic agenda, emphasised – indeed enhanced visually (for the viewer) and in gustative display and consumption (for the episodes' characters) – through the highly skilled culinary art that he exhibits to his numerous invited guests (some of whom later become the meal!). Furthermore, not only are the strategically selected guests usually uninformed (or misinformed) about the courses on the menu, the producers of the series take great pains to have the meals correspond thematically to successive facets of the ongoing investigations.[3] In this way, these different texts (a term under-stood quite broadly) combine the results of the title character being ever 'on the lookout' with increasingly developed tastes in all things sensual, especially scents and fine dining, and a complementary refinement in the manners and ritual with which such sensual pursuits ought to be enjoyed.

For the purposes of this analysis, I choose to focus primarily on season 1 of the NBC series, not only because the thirteen episodes show Hannibal at his most creative – neither incarcerated (as in *Red Dragon* and *The Silence of the Lambs*), nor hunted (as in *Hannibal*) – but also because the multi-faceted deployment of his skills unfolds in relation to the writers' extremely creative expansion of the Lecter narrative. For the reader of *Red Dragon*, and the subsequent viewer of both versions, the actual Lecter–Will Graham encounter that resulted in Lecter's imprisonment occurred previously, outside the current narra-tive, as is true of Graham's even earlier violent and traumatic encounter with Garrett Jacob Hobbs. This back story, touched on briefly in *Red Dragon*, is mined by Brian Fuller, producer of the *Hannibal* TV series, as the series's starting point – how Graham apprehended the serial killer (Hobbs) known as 'the Minnesota Shrike', resulting in Hobbs's death at Graham's hands. However, what is most important for understanding the Hannibal becomings is that Graham's first big case (apprehending Hobbs) *precedes* the discovery of Lecter's crimes and true character.

Rather than undertake a strictly narrative analysis,[4] I will consider how specific concepts proposed by Deleuze and Deleuze-Guattari emerge within this narrative and find renewed creative potential, especially as regards the concept of the animal. I will conclude by reflecting on how the NBC series reveals Hannibal Lecter as deploying his very own socio-pathic *critique et clinique*, the critical as well as the clinical skills neces-sary for the comprehension, manipulation and execution of the most subtle practices *aux aguets*.

Becoming (Blocks of Becoming)

> Does it not seem that alongside the two models, sacrifice and series, totem institution and structure, there is still room for something else, something more secret, more subterranean: *the sorcerer* and becomings (expressed in tales instead of myths and rites)? (Deleuze and Guattari 1987: 237)

Let us first consider what is arguably the *raison d'être* for Hannibal's endeavours, his ongoing becomings. A hindrance to understanding his becomings, for readers/viewers of *Red Dragon* and *Silence of the Lambs*

at least, is that imprisonment would seem to impede severely any becomings. But as any reader/viewer knows, Hannibal's will is not to be
denied, due to his skill at manipulation and uncanny intuition about
what buttons to press on his interlocutor to achieve his own ends.
Moreover, even in confinement, we can witness the becomings that
he inspires, most notably in the fan letter written to Lecter by Francis
Dolarhyde (a killer in *Red Dragon* nicknamed 'the Tooth Fairy'), part
of which includes: 'The important thing is what I am *Becoming*. I know
that you alone can understand this . . . [signed] Avid Fan' (Harris 1981:
101, original emphasis). In light of Lecter's notoriety, Dolarhyde recognises a kindred spirit, someone who, he suspects, is as fully engaged
as he is in self-transformation, in becoming. Dolarhyde also notes that
FBI special investigator (and profiler) Will Graham interests him, and
lightly scolds Lecter, 'You should have taught him not to meddle' (102).
However, as I mentioned above, in seasons 1 and 2 of the *Hannibal*
series, we witness Graham's meeting with Lecter while he is still at
liberty well *before* the Dolarhyde episode, having abandoned his career
as surgeon (under circumstances yet to be explained and explored) and
working as a practising psychiatrist. In this capacity, he is truly free to
explore a broad range of becomings, unwittingly abetted by the entire
justice apparatus of the FBI.

To complete this *ouverture*, let us recall Deleuze and Guattari's insistence that 'becomings-animal . . . are perfectly real', but most crucially, 'a
becoming lacks a subject distinct from itself; but also . . . it has no term,
since its term in turn exists only as taken up in another becoming of
which it is the subject, and which coexists, forms a block, with the first'
(1987: 238). Hannibal Lecter instinctively realises this important first
principle of becoming, that it *is* in itself, that it is ongoing without term,
and thereby encompasses yet other becomings, into which it is sub-
sumed. This facet of becomings explains, in my view, why Will Graham
is so remarkable a find for Hannibal since Graham's profiler gift of
pre-vision – his pure, empathic openness to becomings-other – offers
to Lecter the truly rare raw material not only for manipulation, but for
perversely creative exploration of unimagined becomings. And given
the focus of Graham's, and subsequently Lecter's, ruminations – the
victims of the Shrike followed by the strategic copycat murders staged
(by Lecter) for Graham's benefit – these becomings encompass a vast
domain of becomings-animal.

Involution and the Sorcerer

> Who has not known the violence of these animal sequences, which uproot one from humanity, if only for an instant, making one scrape at one's bread like a rodent or giving one the yellow eyes of a feline? (Deleuze and Guattari 1987: 240)

We slowly approach the animal and 'being on the lookout'. For a second principle of becomings is that of becomings as alliance (and not filiation). Deleuze and Guattari point to the 'block of becoming' formed by the wasp and the orchid, 'from which no orchid-wasp can ever descend' (1987: 238). The rejection of filiation leads them to propose the term 'involution' 'for this form of evolution between heterogeneous terms ... Involution is creative ... To involve is to form a block that runs its own line "between" the terms in play and beneath assignable relations' (238–9). And unbeknownst to those with whom Hannibal enters into alliance, a particular becoming is in progress, a creative involution such that what the skilled members of the Behavioral Sciences Unit (BSU) believe they are examining, from victim to victim, is entirely different from what Lecter has in mind. Put another way, thanks to his own ability to pre-sense (in contrast to Graham's ability to pre-view, to create pre-visions), Hannibal *aux aguets* moves the investigations along paths that best serve his own ends and, in fact, needs. It is only to Will Graham, with his raw talent of pre-vision, that the gradual truth behind this process of involution occurs.

But how this comes about necessarily complicates the Deleuzo-Guattarian perspectives, because in their view, 'becoming-animal always involves a pack, a band, a population, a peopling, in short, a multiplicity' (1987: 239). However, the most evident packs in season 1 of *Hannibal* – Will and his particularly homey becoming-animal with his own personal pack of rescue animals *chez* Graham in (wait for it) Wolf Trap; the BSU team and their constant (and required) search for evidence – are at odds with the involution initiated by Hannibal *aux aguets*. 'Animal characteristics', insist Deleuze and Guattari, 'can be mythic or scientific. But we are not interested in characteristics; what interests us are modes of expansion, propagation, occupation, contagion, peopling. *I am legion*' (239, my emphasis). Although Lecter does not necessarily reveal any inherent multiplicity in the form of multiple personality disorder, what emerges from his practice is an uncanny ability to attract – and eventually, once a captive, serve as a role model for – a legion of serial killers. As Deleuze and Guattari continue, 'the Wolf-Man [is] fascinated by several wolves watching him. What would a lone wolf be? . . . What we are saying is that every animal is fundamentally a band, a pack. That is has pack modes, rather than characteristics . . . It is at this point that the human being encounters the animal' (239). Hannibal Lecter is no different, but whereas he appears to affiliate himself with the BSU-pack and, through this, to the Graham-pack, he does so all the better to camouflage his true pack alliance, to the band of brothers whose practice is intent on robbing others (usually women, but in Lecter's practice, not exclusively so) of their existence, some in the form of creative tableaux.

One may well ask: What does it say about Deleuze and Guattari's perspectives that they lend themselves so readily to a Hannibalian reading? Yet, any reader of *A Thousand Plateaus* knows quite well that these authors seek their references from whatever sources they deem useful. After all, they begin the plateau on 'becomings' with reference to the film *Willard*, and as they develop becomings-animal, they find their reference points in a Lovecraft text and von Hofmannsthal's 'The Letter of Lord Chandos' (1987: 240).[5] What they derive from these sources is the importance of 'unnatural participations', relations of 'unnatural nuptials' into which writers frequently enter:

> Writers are sorcerers because they experience the animal as the only population before which they are responsible in principle. The German pre-Romantic Karl Philipp Moritz feels responsible not for the calves that die but before the calves that die and give him the incredible feeling of an unknown Nature – *affect*. For the affect is not a personal feeling, nor is it a characteristic; it is effectuation of a power of the pack that throws the self into upheaval and makes it reel . . . A fearsome involution calling us toward unheard-of becomings. (240)

For Hannibal *aux aguets*, however, there really seems to be no clear distinction between 'natural' and 'unnatural' in terms of his 'participations'. A memorable image of this kind of affect, the self reeling and thrown into upheaval (which is not necessarily loss of control), occurs in *The Silence of the Lambs*, with Lecter (Anthony Hopkins) smeared with blood, the solitary-unit prison guards maimed and dead around him, while their killer veritably floats in a euphoric bliss, deeply enraptured by the 'Goldberg Variations'.[6] Whether in the novels, the films or the television series, Hannibal responds very efficiently as a veritable 'sorcerer', but in his own way, 'in the mode of the pack or swarm' (Deleuze and Guattari 1987: 241).

Given the back story provided in *Hannibal Rising* of Lecter's initial survival from horrific brutality during the Second World War and subsequent instruction in samurai weaponry and tactics, we find becoming-animal's link to the war machine, since 'the man of war has an entire becoming that implies multiplicity, celerity, ubiquity, metamorphosis and treason, the power of affect' (Deleuze and Guattari 1987: 243).[7] One could hardly find a better sequence of descriptors for the becomings of Hannibal *aux aguets*, but given the arc of becomings in the Graham-Lecter involution, we find this linkage within the very imagery of season 1 of *Hannibal*: 'Wolf-men, bear-men, wildcat-men, men of every animality, secret brotherhoods, animate the battlefields . . . There is a complex aggregate: the becoming-animal of men, packs of animals, elephants and rats, winds and tempests, bacteria sowing contagion. A single *Furor*' (243). In light of Lecter's manipulation of Graham specifically, and of the FBI BSU team more generally, we can see what Deleuze and Guattari mean in discussing the war machine versus the State apparatus in terms of game theory, notably chess versus Go: the coded, qualitative chess pieces versus the anonymous, collective, third-person functions of the Go discs. The FBI versus Lecter: 'Chess is indeed a war, but an institutionalized, regulated, coded war, with a front, a rear, battles. But what is proper to Go is war without battle lines, with neither confrontation nor retreat, without battles even: pure strategy, whereas chess is a semiology' (353).

While this analogy may appear to collapse at the end of season 2 with successive, bloody confrontations between Hannibal and his FBI counterparts, it is important to recall that Hannibal *chooses* to reveal himself as part of the two-fold becoming with Will Graham. Careful viewing of the season 1 episodes shows how inspired Hannibal *aux aguets* truly is in his moves, apparently on the BSU chess board, but really as a consummate Go master, a game into which he seeks to draw Graham. However, he succeeds in employing Graham's very real ailment (encephalitis) in order to exacerbate an already acutely engaged pre-visionary sensitivity into what are truly for Graham 'unnatural participations'. So Deleuze and Guattari helpfully sum things up so far: with their 'first principle' of 'pack and contagion, contagion of the pack', and a second principle, 'wherever there is multiplicity, you will also find an exceptional individual, and it is with that individual that an alliance must be made in order to become-animal . . . Every animal swept up in its pack or multiplicity has its anomalous' (1987: 243). And here we arrive at the tale.

Aux aguets: Hannibal as Anomalous

> If the anomalous is neither an individual nor a species, then what is it?
> It is a phenomenon, but a phenomenon of bordering ... The elements of
> the pack are only imaginary 'dummies', the characteristics of the pack are
> only symbolic entities; all that counts is the borderline – the anomalous.
> (Deleuze and Guattari 1987: 244–5)

In order to consider this phenomenon of bordering as a manifestation
of 'being on the lookout' through Hannibal *aux aguets*, I provide a
synthesis of the first season's episodes as a way to follow the gradual
emergence and sequential unfolding of Hannibal's particular involution
as regards the pack (Graham-BSU-Lecter) into which he enters. This
involution creates offshoots and movements to which Hannibal must
react and adapt, all ancillary developments to the central focal plot.
Given that the entire season's narrative impetus, as well as Hannibal's
involution, stem from the pilot episode, I begin with a detailed review
of its key points.[8]

Apéritif (episode 101)

Inserting himself carefully into the pack (recommended as a resource to
BSU chief Jack Crawford by psychiatrist mentee, Alana Bloom), Lecter
assists Will Graham with the stress he incurs as an empathic forensic
profiler. Truly *dans le milieu* at this point – entering *in medias res* (of
investigations) as well as within a particular milieu of law enforcement
– Hannibal knows well that his own ongoing series of murders is one
object of their investigations. Thus, Hannibal is *aux aguets*, first, to move
the pieces of the Go board by gleaning information about the investiga-
tory progress, and second, through his own art as killer, replenishing his
stock of human body parts to facilitate another art, his *gourmandise*.
Yet, other opportunities immediately emerge: not only can Hannibal
slowly push the highly vulnerable Graham towards unforeseen becomings, he can also skew the outcome of other investigations in progress.

Aux aguets, the animal is everywhere: the wounds of one victim
reveal antler velvet as a healing agent; another victim (Cassie Boyle) is
found in a Minnesota field, carefully posed, impaled on elk antlers. And
accompanying Graham who discovers the killer's identity, Garrett Jacob
Hobbs, Hannibal manoeuvres to phone Hobbs: speaking first to his
daughter, Abigail. This 'courtesy call' to Hobbs is brief: 'They know.'
Hannibal is curious: how will Hobbs *and* Graham react? The former
slices his wife's throat; the latter shoots Hobbs as he attempts the same

on his daughter. Having observed Graham in action without intervening, Hannibal goes to stabilise the bleeding girl after Graham receives Hobbs's final message, 'See? See?' Hannibal and Graham bond over their shared responsibility for the comatose Abigail, a strategic bond that will slowly grow, but not without inherent problems.

Amuse-bouche (episode 102), Potage (episode 103) and Oeuf (not aired)

These three episodes develop in different ways the repercussions of Graham's killing of Hobbs, and Abigail's rescue by Lecter and Graham. The strategy of each episode is to exacerbate Graham's delicate empathic nature with new murders, and also to complicate their investigations with the growing possibility that a copycat murderer is at work. As Graham's therapist, Hannibal is superbly placed to continue his involution, and ever *aux aguets*, he carefully creates tensions between Graham and his supervisor, Crawford, telling Graham, 'What you need is a way back out of dark places when Jack Crawford sends you there.' Influenced by the animal remnants – the antler attic – at Hobbs's Minnesota cabin ('a permanent installation in your Evil Minds Museum'), Graham's disturbing symptoms emerge with recurring visions of Hobbs. Hannibal also expands his domain of prey by inviting Crawford to dine ('pork' loin), probing him about the supervisor's 'delicate' treatment of Graham. At episode 102's end, while counselling Graham, Hannibal makes progress *aux aguets*, getting Graham to admit that killing Hobbs felt good.

Hannibal stirs the *potage* of different sources of tension through his continued involution in episode 103. With Abigail Hobbs recovered, Hannibal approves her return to Minnesota, and at the scene of her parents' death (the family kitchen), he keenly observes her as she cannot recall the voice on the phone (tagged by Graham as the copycat) before her father's death. Then, during a friend Marissa's visit, Abigail is confronted near her house by the brother of the stag-mounted victim (episode 101), Nick Boyle, who blames her father, and her by association. Graham's disturbed dream state heightens during the trip: a stag, Hobbs cutting Abigail's throat, the stag dropping, Graham waking up panting. What better moment, then, to push forward the collective involution: returned to the antler attic, Abigail realises the extent of her father's cannibalism ('No animal parts went to waste . . . He was feeding them to us!'), then finds Marissa impaled and displayed on antlers, another copycat victim, Graham argues. Before Abigail leaves Minnesota, Hannibal seizes the moment anew when, at the Hobbs house, startled by the hostile Nick

Boyle, Abigail reflexively guts him, as taught by her father to treat deer. Hannibal calmly knocks out Bloom, then explains to Abigail that this murder might raise suspicions of her collusion with her father, so they seal an alliance by disposing of the body. Convincing the BSU pack that the missing Nick Boyle attacked Abigail after knocking out Bloom *and* Lecter, Hannibal's final discussion with Abigail unfolds back in Lecter's library: she identifies Hannibal as the voice on the phone, and asks if he too is a serial killer like her dad. 'Not like your dad . . .', he responds. The protective Hannibal, curious about Abigail's propensity for murder, tightens the alliance by convincing her to keep their mutual secrets.[9]

In the unaired *Oeuf* episode, the BSU pack's focal crime requires that they travel to the site of the episode's focal crime (unrelated to Lecter), so with Graham absent from Wolf Trap, Lecter is entrusted with feeding his pack and mysteriously adds to Graham's set of homemade fishing lures (for reasons revealed in the season finale). In therapy, Hannibal coaxes Graham to admit that he felt like it was he, Graham, who killed Marissa: 'You felt like you were becoming [Hobbs]?' Hannibal asks; '*Not* Garrett Jacob Hobbs, Dr Lecter' . . . meaning that Graham is getting an empathic feel for the copycat (i.e. Hannibal). Connecting to the episode's overarching theme of family (hence, *oeuf*, egg), Hannibal is ever *aux aguets* with other characters: as Crawford again dines solo on 'rabbit' with Lecter, a sudden visual shows one of Hannibal's victims happily hopping away from him somewhere in the woods. Pretending to accept Alana Bloom's treatment for Abigail, Lecter betrays her trust by inviting Abigail to his home. Their alliance seems to shift to filiation as his paternal feelings emerge (a topic discussed earlier with Graham), but of course, *à la Hannibal*: he serves Abigail psilocybin tea to supervise her 'positive associations'. A justifiably irate Bloom interrupts them, chiding her colleague for being 'rude', and he dutifully apologises, then invites her to dine with him and the 'sedated' Abigail – who 'sees' the table set for her with her (dead) mom and her dad! Successive scenes of 'family' provide the episode's closure: Crawford's bedtime with his weary wife, who rejects any suggestion of their having children ('It's [too late] for me', she says), and Graham huddling alone with his rescue dog pack.

Coquilles (episode 104)

From the perspective of Hannibal *aux aguets* and his involutions, this episode requires separate commentary: Graham's psychic trauma manifests as he finds himself sleepwalking, wandering dazed on a road, followed by rescue dog Winston but also by the increasingly symbolic (snorting and nudging) antlered vision-stag. Lecter's guidance sows discord by suggesting anew that the fault lies with Crawford's relentless use of Graham's pre-visionary talents. Later Lecter piques Graham's suspicions of his deliberately seeking to alienate him from Crawford, when Hannibal accuses Crawford of abandoning Graham. However, Graham's talents are fully on display at a motel crime scene where bodies, partially skinned, are staged as angels and strung up kneeling beside the bed. Graham gradually feels less 'useful', realising that 'this [his empathic profiling] is bad for [him]', which Crawford refuses to accept. Still, Graham helps the BSU pack to conclude that the Angelmaker suffers from a cancerous tumour, and his ultimate suicide is a means to become his own angel maker. And in a hallucination, the dead Angelmaker appears to Graham to announce, 'I can give you the majesty of your becoming.'

Meanwhile, in this episode, the vast scope of Hannibal's impulses *aux aguets* is fully revealed: at dinner ('foie gras au torchon') with Crawford and his wife Bella (Phyllis), she chides Lecter for the goose dish's animal cruelty. Lecter demurs: while he admits that cruelty to animals is 'the first and worst sign of sociopathic behavior', he claims to have no taste for animal cruelty, 'which is why I employ an ethical butcher ... Be kind to animals and then eat them ... Human emotion is a gift from our animal ancestors. Cruelty is a gift humanity has given itself.' Thinking on his feet, he stuns the couple (especially Bella), first, by sniffing and precisely naming her perfume, then explaining that his 'keen sense of smell' is so acute that he once smelled stomach cancer on a former teacher. This is a strategic admission – since Bella has hidden her cancer diagnosis from Crawford, but reveals it to Lecter in a subsequent con-sultation, and later, Crawford extrapolates Bella's true condition from an interview with the Angelmaker's wife.[10] Moreover, learning details of the Angelmaker, Lecter repeats his sniffing, this time with Graham, as they both stand in Lecter's office gazing at an antlered elk sculpture. Graham finds being sniffed disconcerting, but Lecter merely advises he change his aftershave 'that smells like something with a ship on the bottle'! Yet, given the particular purpose of Hannibal's earlier sniffing, and with the proximity of all manner of hidden illness in the episode's human *coquilles*, Hannibal has surely understood something new about Graham, for which viewers must wait (episode 109).

Entrée (episode 105), Sorbet (106), Fromage (107)

These three episodes develop a particular *entrée*, the confusing identity of the Chesapeake Ripper. Assumed by some to be Dr Abel Gideon, incarcerated (as will be Lecter) at the Baltimore Hospital for the Criminally Insane (run by Dr Frederick Chilton), the Ripper's identity divides the BSU pack, and thus Hannibal is implicitly present, as well as quite active in counselling Crawford about Bella's condition. In a flashback, we understand that Crawford equates Bella's loss with the disappearance of Miriam Lass (an FBI trainee resembling Clarice Starling, Jodie Foster's character in *The Silence of the Lambs*) during the Ripper investigation two years earlier. Crawford then awakens to Miriam's phone call, hence more confusion as the BSU pack cannot agree if she could still be alive, and again if Gideon could be the Ripper. To trap the Ripper, the team (against Graham's counsel) has tabloid reporter Freddie Lounds plant a false report confirming Gideon's identity as the Ripper, which Lecter reads with evident interest. His involution is aimed squarely at Crawford through another call from Miriam originating from . . . Crawford's bedroom, where the BSU pack also discovers Miriam's prints, presumably visited by the Ripper as well! Dinner conversation at Lecter's with Drs Chilton and Bloom, over tongue and mushrooms, veers towards ethics, with Bloom wondering if Chilton might have employed 'psychic driving' by discussing the Ripper's crimes with Gideon, which Chilton denies. But after Bloom departs, Hannibal lets Chilton know that he is 'more forgiving of the unorthodox than Dr Bloom'. Another Miriam call draws Crawford to the observatory where he finds . . . a severed arm, the phone that called him, and a note: 'What do you see?' In a final chat with Crawford, Mikkelsen repeats Lecter's line about Clarice from *The Silence of the Lambs*: Hannibal tells him not to give up hope and, referring here seemingly to Bella, says, 'I believe the world's a better place with her in it.' But a final flashback reveals Miriam Lass's visit to Lecter two years earlier: as she finds drawings pointing to Hannibal as the Chesapeake Ripper, he takes her, choking her . . . but to death? A final close-up is on Crawford and Lecter sipping quietly.

Another man is brutally murdered as 106 begins, a body strangely staged – again, the Ripper or not? Hannibal keeps the BSU pack confused, and with the discovered arm identified as that of Miriam Lass, Crawford is confused 'by hope'. But this episode should more accurately be entitled *crudités*, since the major discovery is that *whoever* is doing these murders, the purpose seems to be that of careful organ harvesting – and not for recipients! Lecter's public life in the Baltimore arts community is on display, notably his plan to have the artsy hoi polloi to his home for an exquisite dinner – hence the need to stock up on meat! One patient, Franklyn Froidevaux, is so obsessed with the good doctor that, seeking friendship, he stalks him to a concert, introducing him to a friend, Tobias (setting up episode 107). And the very private Lecter meets with his own analyst, Bedelia Du Maurier, who sees through at least some of Lecter's 'meticulous construction . . . wearing a well-tailored person suit'. While the BSU pack succeeds in finding the current killer *du jour* (bodies stolen at accident sites, organs harvested in an ambulance – not the Ripper's m.o.), the episode's true focus is on Hannibal *aux aguets* for his turn in the kitchen, whereby scenes of the BSU discovery of the organ harvest are juxtaposed to Lecter happily preparing meat (aka organs). Even Graham grasps that 'the mutilations hide the true nature of his crimes'. As the Hannibal *dans la cuisine* scenes reveal, it's all about fine dining! In contrast to both Graham and Crawford, each visibly and separately alone at episode's end, the grand finale is the successful dinner party, with applause from Baltimore's *beau monde* gathered for the host, who proclaims, 'All be warned: nothing here is vegetarian! Bon appétit!'

Set up in 106 – Lecter meeting Tobias, Franklyn mentioning his (and Lecter's) taste for gourmet cheese – an unforeseen challenge emerges from Tobias whose music shop reveals, besides customary instruments, the unique creation of strings not from cat gut, but (who knew?) human intestines. Simultaneously, Graham's physical disturbances manifest with hearing strange animal cries, yet assisted by Bloom, he finds no animal traces. After Franklyn reveals in therapy his concern about Tobias's possible psychopathic tendencies, Hannibal understands that there is no coincidence when a musician (a trombone player with the Baltimore Symphony) is found on stage, with a cello neck rammed down his throat, ready to be bowed. While Graham 'sees' this murder as a unique performance killing, Lecter suggests it might be 'a serenade for another killer', sensing that, through Franklyn, Tobias is sending a message. While Graham's aural disturbances continue, Hannibal is fully *aux aguets* when he takes his harpsichord to Tobias's store for new strings, and then at dinner *chez* Lecter, Tobias frankly admits killing the trombonist, his intention to kill Franklyn, and even Lecter ('Of course,' says Hannibal, 'I'm lean. Lean animals yield the toughest gut'), that is, until Tobias had followed Lecter when he disposed of a body. The doorbell rings before Hannibal can address the reckless Tobias, who escapes. Graham appears, increasingly disturbed, but a cool Hannibal tips him off to Franklyn's confidences about Tobias. As Hannibal no doubt suspected, Graham's visit to Tobias ends in confrontation, two police officers killed, both Tobias and Graham wounded, and Tobias on the run . . . to Lecter's office where he is meeting Franklyn. The patient advises Tobias to turn himself in, but Hannibal literally takes matters in hand, snapping Franklyn's neck, thus irritating Tobias (who wanted the pleasure) – and the pair turn on each other, in viewers' first sight of Hannibal in combat. Although wounded, Hannibal kills Tobias with, yes, the elk statue! The FBI analyse the carefully rearranged crime scene (Hannibal explains, 'He came to kill Franklyn'), and in a session with Bedelia, she says he should not feel responsible for Franklyn's death, just as she did not feel responsible for the death of the patient who once tried to kill her. 'Nor should you', replies Hannibal quietly.

Trou Normand (episode 108), Buffet Froid (episode 109)

A new symptom of Graham's disorientation, a hole (*trou*) in his day, occurs at the latest murder site (a totem pole of bodies and parts), with Graham suddenly finding himself in Lecter's office. Hannibal suggests that Graham suffers from 'empathy disorder', i.e. his need to disregard his feelings about the victims and crimes is affecting him negatively. Another possible hole emerges, Abigail's remorse for her father's victims and her plan to write a tell-all story, with reporter Freddie Lounds. Both Lecter and Graham object, but when Nick Boyle's body is discovered, Crawford brings in Abigail to identify it and sharply questions her, despite protests from Graham, Lecter and Bloom. After Abigail denies any involvement, Bloom reproaches Crawford, saying '[Hannibal] has no reason to lie about any of this.' And in talking to Lecter, when Abigail admits that *she* uncovered the hidden body, Hannibal realises the growing hole in their pact: she betrayed his trust, and he needs to trust her. 'What if I can't?' he asks. (Ouch!) Despite growing instability, Graham's wacky dreams yield remarkable clarity when he dream-visions Abigail gutting Boyle. So under Graham's questions, Hannibal, calmly on high alert, explains that he lied about Abigail defending herself in order to protect her from Crawford. Graham reluctantly accepts his role to share Abigail with Lecter as one of her 'fathers', but the Lecter-Abigail filiation (in contrast to alliance) now reveals its inherent weakness. At a dinner with Abigail and Freddie Lounds, the 'fathers' express their concern about the tell-all. But alone with Abigail in his kitchen, Hannibal gets her to admit she helped her father as bait for luring his victims, and holding her close, Hannibal says she is not a monster: 'I know what monsters are; you're a victim.'

How cold Hannibal *aux aguets* can be becomes clear in episode 109: after Graham freaks out at a crime scene (a young woman, Beth LeBeau, murdered in her home, her face partially removed), he reveals his spatial dissociation to Lecter who already suspects something more is wrong when Graham is unable to draw a simple clock face (a symptom that Hannibal, of course, does not reveal). So, he consults a neurologist friend, Dr Sutcliffe, and before the MRI reveals encephalitis, Hannibal provides Sutcliffe with a detailed account of having sniffed it out earlier (episode 104), then easily convinces Sutcliffe that, by lying to Graham about his condition in order to 'study' him, 'there are great discoveries to be made'. Then, Hannibal ironically accuses Crawford of allowing Graham to deteriorate in order to fight crime, revealing his problems as possible mental illness, due to 'absorbing' the effects of crime scenes. Hannibal cagily unites the capture of the killer (identified as Georgia Madchen) to Graham's time holes. First, Lecter identifies the killer's disorder as Cotard's Syndrome – someone who believes him/herself to be dead, unable to see anyone's face. Then, dining with Lecter (*jamon iberico*), Sutcliffe's queries about Lecter's 'pig' Graham, rarified because of his pure empathy (says Lecter) like the *jamon*, reveal more fully Hannibal's method. To Sutcliffe's suggestion, 'So you set his mind on fire . . .', Lecter replies, 'Imagination is an interesting accelerant for fever . . .'. But, at Graham's next MRI, he finds himself alone, only to discover Sutcliffe dead, *as if* murdered by Georgia Madchen! To Crawford's puzzled query why Madchen would follow Graham, 'I have a habit of collecting strays' is his weak answer; and back in Wolf Trap, Graham's own pack is upset by something – Madchen herself under his bed! Captured and placed under sedation in a burn unit, Madchen's recall is important for Crawford, while Hannibal says (with prophetic irony), 'I hope, for her sake, she doesn't remember much.' For Georgia Madchen's flashback recollection reveals someone (Hannibal), faceless to her due to her condition, defacing Sutcliffe, after which he calmly hands her the scissors that were just used to de-face.

Body without Organs (pun intended)

What does it mean to disarticulate, to cease to be an organism? How can we convey how easy it is, and the extent to which we do it every day? And how necessary caution is, the art of dosages, since overdose is a danger. You don't do it with a sledgehammer, you use a very fine file. (Deleuze and Guattari 1987: 159–60)

The final three episodes that wrap up the different threads of *Hannibal* season 1 take a grim and, for Graham, disastrous turn (as if anything more grim is imaginable than what preceded). While it was implicit all along, Hannibal's interest in making himself (and others), in his own way, a body without organs is revealed fully as another facet of becomings and *rencontres*. Clearly, as carnivore, cannibal and master chef, Lecter is skilled in actually separating murdered bodies from their organs, but the sense given to the BwO by Deleuze and Guattari seems part of Hannibal's mode of becoming as well. Not only has his innate curiosity led him towards ever 'creative' destructions, Hannibal has physically abetted Graham's own becoming, that is, his gradual deteriorating drift into different altered states. Both men are thus 'occupied, populated only by intensities' (Deleuze and Guattari 1987: 153), and it is ironic, of course, that Lecter purports to practise psychiatry since it is precisely the psychiatrist as contemporary 'priest' that Deleuze and Guattari denounce as 'cast[ing] the triple curse on desire' (154). Oddly enough, Hannibal could well be cast as the somewhat stereotyped proponent of intense deterritorialisation supposedly extolled in *Anti-Oedipus*, whereas his own therapist, Bedalia Du Maurier, would be the proponent of 'Not wisdom, caution. In doses . . . injections of caution' (150), from *A Thousand Plateaus*.[11] This observation about Hannibal *aux aguets* brings me to episode 110.

Rôti (episode 110)

The episode's title begs the question: just *who* will be roasted, actually or virtually? The answer was obvious in Lecter's dinner conversation with Sutcliffe, and this exercise in involution is reinforced in another dinner conversation, with Dr Chilton. Accused by Abel Gideon of using 'psychic driving' as therapy, and thus being responsible for Gideon killing a hospital nurse, Chilton finds an apparent ally as Hannibal explains that psychic driving works only when 'the subject [is not] aware of any influence'. Driving Will Graham, left to burn, has been Hannibal's strategy, and the effects are evident in Graham's recurring nightmares, flashing back on different crime scenes' images and watching a tsunami headed his way. Still, Graham 'visions' the manner of Gideon's escape from the prison van (en route to testify against Chilton), leaving behind the guards' organs neatly tied on tree branches. Agreeing with Graham that the Ripper would not leave organs behind, Crawford says, 'Then he's trying to get the Chesapeake Ripper's attention.' Yet, Graham's breakdown accelerates during the Gideon manhunt, with hallucinations of being trapped in an antler room with Crawford yelling 'You will kill again!' Confiding his identity confusion to Hannibal, the doctor is ever helpful: 'Will, you have me as your gauge.' Back with the BSU pack, Graham points out that if Gideon is out for vengeance against his therapists, Alana Bloom is on the list – so the Graham-Bloom dance continues: she touches his face, 'You're really warm', to which he replies, 'I tend to run hot.' Hot and cool, working with the BSU pack, then lost in his downward spiral, Graham and Hannibal are linked as they mutually explore the edges of the body without organs.

Graham is in synch with the Ripper (hence with the copycat) as he concludes that the Ripper will kill Gideon for his rudeness in taking credit for the Ripper's work. The theory is confirmed when the BSU pack finds, first, Carruthers (a supposed Ripper expert) wearing a 'Columbian necktie' (Carruthers's tongue adorning his neck), his blood packed in ice (and a note, 'Please deliver to the Red Cross'): '[Gideon]'s peacocking for the Ripper', says Crawford; 'like flowers and chocolate before a first date', says Graham. Then, as they discover the Carruthers murder story *already* on *Tattle.com*, they know Freddie Lounds is captive and that her story is meant as an 'invitation' to the Ripper. But where? Back at BSU, Graham's synch continues, observing Carruthers's missing arm, signalling his location where the last severed arm was found, at the observatory. With Freddie forced to assist surgery, Dr Gideon prepares his own mode of making a body without organs, by 'reorganising' the lump-of-meat Chilton. Then, as the agents enter the observatory, Graham 'sees' a stag that he follows away into the woods, and there, taken by Gideon (who observes that Graham appears 'a little peaky'), he has Graham drive at gunpoint, of course, to Lecter's home. Graham's disoriention in his becoming prevents him from determining what is real: he 'sees' not Gideon, but Garrett Jacob Hobbs. Hannibal *aux aguets* seizes the moment: 'no one is there . . . you came alone', as Gideon looks on. When Graham goes under with a seizure, Hannibal faces Gideon and concludes their brief discussion about the Ripper with the helpful offer, 'I can tell you where to find [Alana Bloom].' To the revived Graham, Hannibal orients his fevered brain towards the need to kill Hobbs again while helping Alana Bloom. So outside her house, Graham finds Gideon/Hobbs staring in her window, and their conversation about identity confusion – Gideon talking to Graham, Graham talking to 'Hobbs' – results in Graham again 'killing' Hobbs, in fact, Gideon. The penultimate conversation, at Quantico between Lecter and Crawford, is about Graham who, despite a 105-degree temperature, still 'brought down' Gideon. Hannibal's advice that Graham lose his permission to carry a firearm is not welcomed by Crawford, and Graham is in hospital, Bloom by his side.

In a final orientation towards Hannibal's pursuit of the body without organs, the episode's conversation between Hannibal and Bedelia extends his earlier comments to Sutcliffe. For Hannibal expresses concern for Graham's madness, spreading 'like an oil spill', but Bedelia then wonders what the value of Graham's madness might be. Hannibal openly admits that Graham sees things differently, even that Hannibal sees himself in Graham. Then he adds: 'Madness can be a medicine for the modern world. You take it in moderation and it's beneficial.' Arguing for caution, Bedelia replies: 'You overdose and it can have unfortunate side-effects.' But these, argues Hannibal, 'can be temporary; they can be a boost to our psychological immune systems to help fight the existential crisis of normal life.' Like anyone who knows this story, Bedelia observes: 'Will Graham does not present problems of normal life'; but what does he present? Hannibal seems to retreat in his earlier forthright stance, for he replies somewhat meekly, 'the opportunity for friendship', whereas Bedelia cautions again that as Graham is Lecter's patient, he might need to take a step back. 'And watch him lose his mind?' asks Hannibal (perhaps hopefully); Bedelia replies: 'Sometimes all we can do is watch.' As Christi Gravett (2013) comments on this exchange: 'Being that he obviously considers himself a kind of artist, his crime scenes [being] over-the-top and often reminiscent of great works brought to life, Hannibal knows better than anyone the importance of art and literature, not only in confronting the existential predicament, but also in "restoring" the imagination.' Gravett implicitly evokes the Deleuzian sense of 'being on the lookout' and its import for making bodies without organs, with reference to British artist and theorist, Roy Ascott: 'Stop thinking about art works as objects, and start thinking about them as triggers for experiences.' Hannibal's continuous 'art work' as performance pieces – the ones we viewers know of – have been multiple, as the Chesapeake Ripper; as the copycat *of* the Ripper, Hobbs and Madchen; through careful manipulation (involution) with Graham and Abigail; and through possible surrogates in the ongoing construction of assemblages and bodies without organs. Yet, Hannibal *aux aguets* cannily knows that loose ends lead to complications, and however intriguing their becomings may be, Madchen, Abigail and Graham all require his full attention.

Relevés (episode 111)

In hospital, after Graham visits Georgia Madchen – who shares that the doctors will never know, deep down, what is wrong with him – Hannibal helpfully suggests that, deep down, Will might be suffering from dementia. Yet, Graham's casual mention of chatting with Georgia seems to correspond too closely to her finding a comb in her incubator, and as she combs her hair, the static electricity incinerates her. One down, but this coincidence sets off Graham's own instincts *aux aguets*, and when he tries to argue she was not suicidal, Crawford severely warns him off. Meanwhile, Freddie Lounds continues to collaborate with Abigail, but the reporter's theory – that Crawford and Graham killed Nick Boyle, an innocent man – forces Abigail to remain suffering and silent.

Graham's dreams become clearer: he 'sees' Georgia's death, staked in his front yard on antlers, muttering 'See? See?', and from the flames, what emerges is . . . the stag! While the animal has accompanied Graham from the start, it seems to shift now away *from* Graham towards the murderer. The vision forces him to leave the hospital and to argue to Crawford a) that Georgia was killed by the Sutcliffe killer; b) then, when the comb remains are discovered, that the Sutcliffe killer *copied* Georgia, just as in previous *copied* murders (Marissa Schurr, Cassie Boyle); and c) flashing on the antlers, that the copycat is behind *these* murders. Despite Graham making what we can judge as startlingly accurate links, Crawford cannot do so and seeks Lecter's advice about Graham, suggesting that perhaps he is protecting Abigail Hobbs. Alarm bells and battle stations for Hannibal *aux aguets*! But, when he calmly supports Graham to counter Crawford's 'confusion', Crawford visits Bedelia 'unofficially' to ask if *Lecter* might be withholding information. Faced with Bedelia's refusal to share, Crawford asks: 'How far would Hannibal Lecter go to protect a friend, specifically Will Graham?' Since Lecter has referred to Will as a friend, not a patient, Bedelia responds: 'He'd be loyal', adding erroneously, 'It seems to me that Will Graham would do well to have more friends like Dr Lecter.'

Back with the BSU pack, and heeding Graham, Crawford sets them back on the Garrett Jacob Hobbs case, while Graham approaches Abigail for help to pursue the copycat. Meanwhile, Bedelia speaks to Lecter of Crawford's visit, showing scepticism about his claims of friendship with Graham and, as his colleague, she orders, 'Whatever you're doing with Will Graham, stop.' However, in mentioning Crawford's questions about the attack on her by one of Lecter's former patients, she must reassure Hannibal, fully *aux aguets*, that she offered 'half-truths' about

the circumstances of the attacker's death by swallowing his own tongue
– especially as she is protecting her own patient, implying that Hannibal
was responsible. Then, Graham explains to Lecter his belief that since
the copycat tried to frame him, Graham, for Madchen's murder, it
must be someone with access to the investigations. Hannibal *aux aguets*
balks when Graham says he plans to return to Minnesota with Abigail
– he could omit Madchen in further confidences to Graham, but now
their filiation with Abigail may prove dangerous. Simultaneously, on
the Hobbs trail, the BSU discovers that Abigail accompanied her father
to different murder sites, but they also learn that Abigail is gone. When
Crawford confronts Lecter about Abigail and Graham, Hannibal covers
himself: claiming not to know where they are, and also confiding that
Graham has a dissociative personality state, Hannibal plays an interview recording (from episode *Oeuf*) in which Graham says it felt like
he killed Marissa Schurr. Hannibal admits that Graham was not in his
motel room the night she died, so Crawford now links Graham to three
murders, with Hannibal suggesting that Graham's dissociation has made
him 'become' Hobbs and now 'has his daughter'. 'I'm so sorry, Jack',
says Hannibal truthfully, but for his own reasons – so many opportunities for making bodies without organs now gone awry.

Back to Minnesota we go! At first cozy together on the plane, Graham
and Abigail visit the antler attic (where Marissa died). A comment by
Abigail about fishing and hunting triggers Graham *aux aguets:* 'Did you
fish or did you hunt, Abigail?' 'I was the lure. Did Hannibal tell you?'
she confesses. The fact that Hannibal *knew* visibly unhinges Graham,
and as accusations fly with Abigail, Graham's agitation leads to a seizure
and then . . . poof! Another time/space hole: he next finds himself on a
plane . . . at Dulles Airport, somehow having left Abigail back home,
alone . . . but not quite. Hannibal meets her in the kitchen, hugs her –
and they share that Graham and Crawford 'know everything'. Hannibal
speaks to her in a heartfelt manner, and their conversation is the sole
honest, forthright one in the entire series. Not only is Hannibal's disappointment evident (in the loss of likely becomings), the final line contains words that he may well have thought often about his sister, Mischa
(see *Red Dragon*):

> Abigail pauses: 'Will always said whoever called the house that morning
> was the serial killer. Why did you really call?'
> Hannibal: 'To warn your father that Will Graham was coming for him.'
> Abigail: 'Why?'
> Hannibal: 'I was curious what would happen. I was curious what would
> happen when I killed Marissa. I was curious what you would do.'

Abigail: 'You *wanted* me to kill Nick Boyle.'

Hannibal: 'I was hoping. I wanted to see how much like your father you were ... Nicholas Boyle is more important for you gutting him. He changed you, Abigail. That's more important than the life he clamoured after.'

Abigail: 'How many people have you killed?'

Hannibal, taking her hand, stroking her cheek with his thumb: 'Many more than your father.'

Abigail: 'Are you going to kill me?'

Hannibal: 'I'm sorry, Abigail. I'm sorry I couldn't protect you in this life.'

As with most of Hannibal's statements, the apology about 'this life' is not at all what it seems, given the dénouement of season 2.

Savoureux (episode 112)

Just as the penultimate episode was full of *relevés*, spicy bits, the final episode is downright *savoureux*, tasty! Two loose ends have been addressed, and with 'lost' Graham again confiding in Hannibal, they both return to find Abigail in the Hobbs home in Minnesota, but instead find an ear in the kitchen sink, vomited by Graham. Hannibal feigns reluctance as he gives Graham up to Crawford, and once processed at the BSU, Graham accepts Bloom's offer to transfer 'the pack' from Wolf Trap to her place – a shift that implies an important becoming for Graham from pack to anomalous status. However, his passing mention of 'clock drawings' alerts Bloom to have him repeat the exercise, and she realises the severity of his condition. At Bedelia's, Hannibal seemingly weeps genuine tears at the loss of Abigail, but Bedelia advises that given his links to Abigail, he should have no contact again with Graham. Yet, Hannibal has truly been *aux aguets*: the BSU pack has discovered among Graham's fishing lures four made from human remains: Cassie Boyle, Marissa Schur, Dr Sutcliffe, Georgia Madchen, hence a serial killer taking trophies. Back in the interview room, Graham now 'visions' a new image in the mirror, a brief flash of the stag's next manifestation, a man-stag, or wendigo (a half-man/half-beast figure associated with cannibalism). As Graham can only offer Crawford apparently paranoid conspiracy theories – Graham *aux aguets* is on fire, the right way! – Crawford must arrest Graham. But in the transfer van, Graham uses the Gideon escape strategy (that he previously 'saw'), breaks a finger, slides off cuffs, escapes the guard, without killing.

At a meeting with Crawford and Lecter, Bloom must admit the possibility that Graham could fake the 'clock test', after Hannibal produces his own (doctored) version, indicating Graham as normal. In a deleted scene, Graham bids farewell to his pack at Bloom's, and although conflicted, she gives him her car. At Lecter's, Hannibal explains to Graham how he *could* possibly have killed the four victims and Abigail, while Graham 'visions' images of each murder and then spies the wendigo, standing behind Hannibal. So Graham requests that they return to the Hobbs kitchen in Minnesota, while at Bedelia's, Bloom and Crawford conclude that Graham is with Hannibal, Bedelia suggesting he may still be trying to help Graham.

In the Hobbs kitchen, we have a collision of two becomings between Graham and Hannibal, two bodies without organs in construction and on the edge of obliteration. In this space of both Hobbs's and Abigail's deaths, Graham must cope with pre-visions, and Hannibal *aux aguets* attempts to sway him, revealing himself: 'If you had followed the urges you kept down for so long, cultivated them as the inspirations they are, you'd have become someone other than yourself.' These deepest hopes for Graham have, in fact, been realised, but not at all as Hannibal wished. For Graham responds, 'I know who I am. I'm not so sure I know who you are anymore. But I am certain one of us killed Abigail.' Hannibal's admission, 'Whoever that was, killed the others', causes Graham to aim his gun at Hannibal, Graham saying (rather naively), 'I am who I've always been. The scales have just fallen from my eyes.' As Crawford enters the house, Hannibal asks Graham what reason there would be for him to have acted as Graham suggests, and Graham *aux aguets* shows his full understanding of Hannibal *aux aguets*: 'You'd just be curious what I'd do, someone who thinks how I think, wind him up and watch him go.' As Graham moves to kill Hannibal, Crawford shoots him down, splattering Hannibal with Graham's blood. Looking up at them, Graham *aux aguets*, now truly alone, says 'See? See?' (like Hobbs), and 'visions' standing beside Crawford . . . the wendigo/stag-man.

With Graham in hospital in induced sleep, Crawford and Lecter bemoan how broken Graham has become. Then, Lecter brings Bedelia a complete dinner (*tête de veau en sauce verte*), and tells her he will visit Graham the next day. Bedelia responds that she thought Graham would be the patient that cost him his life, to which Lecter dissembles, 'He didn't cost me my life. He cost Abigail hers.' Bedelia is having none of it: over the 'controversial [veal] dish' (according to her), she again cautions, 'You have to be careful, Hannibal. They're starting to see your pattern . . . You develop relationships with patients. You are prone to violence. That pattern. Under scrutiny, Jack Crawford's beliefs about you might start to unravel.' Lecter then asks, 'Have your beliefs about me begun to unravel?' Bedelia, apparently also *aux aguets*, can only stare.[12]

So loose ends are managed momentarily, and although Hannibal has not achieved becoming-other with his projected making-bodies-without-organs, *not* getting there was clearly more than half the fun. The final scene, Hannibal's visit to Graham, is overdetermined in its homage value, with Graham's cell and posture staged as deliberate reminders of *The Silence of the Lambs*, and the music, 'Vide Cor Meum', the same as the opera scene from the film *Hannibal*. Despite his possible disappointment that Graham did not 'become' into his fully willing, murderous potential, Hannibal perhaps does realise that Graham has indeed become-other: he has shed his packs – the rescue dogs *and* the BSU – and has an altogether new 'person-suit', to employ Bedelia's term for Lecter. In the DVD commentary, Bryan Fuller mentions that while Crawford will soon become the new, troubled Will Graham, now Graham has become the new Abigail, suspected by the FBI, yet also an object of concern for Hannibal. The final words of season 1 are a simple exchange that, in its minimalism, appears like a challenge and a promise of so much more: 'Hello, Will.' 'Hello, Dr Lecter.'

Conclusion: Critique and Clinique

> It is all there: there is a becoming-animal not content to proceed by resemblance ... the proliferation of ... the pack, brings a becoming-molecular that undermines the great molar powers of family, career and conjugality; there is a sinister choice since there is a 'favorite' in the pack with which a kind of contract of alliance, a hideous pact, is made; there is the institution of an assemblage, a war machine or criminal machine, which can reach the point of self-destruction; there is a circulation of impersonal affects, an alternate current that disrupts signifying projects as well as subjective feelings, and constitutes a nonhuman sexuality; and there is an irresistible deterritorialization that forestalls attempts at professional, conjugal, or Oedipal reterritorialization. (Deleuze and Guattari 1987: 233)

Although the epigraph here summarises Deleuze and Guattari's understanding of *Willard*, it stands (slightly edited) in this context as a quite remarkable review of *Hannibal* season 1: the becoming-animal occurs doubly, in Graham's dissociation from the companion stag as well as from his own pack, and Hannibal's gradual mutation into the fevered image of the wendigo, or cannibal man-stag, appearing to Graham in the final episodes. The pack proliferation seems linked precisely to *molar* powers of hierarchy, especially the FBI, but gradually the very *raison d'être* of

Hannibal *aux aguets* appears, to undo the power of the pack through his anomalous position, and in fact, to draw Graham himself into a separate anomalous stance in relation to the pack. Hence, the hideous pact that is made, unbeknownst to Graham: not just the insidious 'therapy' and intervention into scientific 'discovery' via Sutcliffe, but especially the alliance/filiation with Hannibal through Abigail Hobbs. Hence too, we discover the assemblages, both war machine of the State apparatus and the criminal machine, through which the unwitting Graham and the *very* witting Hannibal dance along the edge of mutual destruction. As for impersonal affects, Hannibal feigns human feelings strategically, a pretense consistently noted by the increasingly wary Bedelia, whereas Graham's affect seems to correspond precisely to an 'alternate current', a nonhuman sexuality that precludes the awkwardness of a relationship with Bloom. Finally, under the auspices of Hannibal *aux aguets*, these numerous *rencontres* constitute so many modes of deterritorialisation, assemblages (or attempts, at least) of bodies without organs all meant to satisfy the curiosity that spurs on Hannibal's involution.

Moving into season 2, Hannibal maintains an even more strategic position to extend involutions, in fact, taking on Graham's role as FBI consultant, described by Graham as 'letting the fox into the hen house'. While the viewer knows the season's arc from the opening scene of episode 201 (Crawford confronting Lecter in his kitchen, mortal combat ensuing), the animal assumes even more significance in the second season. With Graham imprisoned (accused of being the Chesapeake Ripper) in the first seven episodes and seeking ways to entrap and then kill Hannibal, his becomings are expressed through visions of his sporadic mutation into the antlered elk, that is, indicating willing acceptance of his propensity towards murder, thus the fulfillment of Hannibal's dearest wishes for him. Then, in the second part of the season (episodes 8–13), with Graham exonerated and freed, and voluntarily resuming his therapy sessions with Hannibal, he pursues a different strategy: realising that only the most subtle approach has a chance to work if Hannibal is to be snared, Graham the dedicated angler offers himself as the bait (with the tacit approval of Crawford), playing a double game (double at the very least!) in order to convince Hannibal that his metamorphosis is moving closer to their kinship as soul mates in death-dealing.

The episode 208, *Su-zakana* (a palette-cleansing dish, to mark the shift between the first and seconds parts of the season, according to Bryan Fuller[13]), reveals Hannibal's propensity to link the animal to philosophy in one of the opening scenes. Serving to Graham and Crawford wild trout caught by Graham, Hannibal provides implicit reminders that he 'consumed all those who came before, ate their lives and works whole; and what's more, he fed their flesh to Will and Jack' (Elucipher 2014b). Then, Hannibal mentions, 'I find the trout to be a very *Nietzschean* fish. Trials of his wild existence find their way into the flavour of the flesh. We will absorb this experience, it will change us . . . Well, we are all Nietzschean fish in that regard.' To which Graham jokes: 'It makes us tastier.' Elucipher comments quite insightfully that

> Hannibal takes the Nietzschean philosophy of consuming life to its logical extreme: he eats the lives he claims, absorbs them and grows stronger. Will's joke, hinging on that instability that always haunts Hannibal's dinner table ['*everything is people*', even when it isn't], shows Will's intimate understanding of how formidable Hannibal is – after all, he's 'eaten' almost every enemy that stood in his way, and he might yet eat Will & Jack. (Elucipher 2014b)

Furthermore, it is through Graham's empathy for an unfortunate 'proto-Will' (VanDerWerff 2014), Peter Bernadone, and *his* compassion for all animals great and small, that the episode arrives at a remarkable sequence, at once of horror (first a woman sewn dead inside a horse, then Peter's social worker sewn alive inside a horse) and of wonder and intimacy, between Hannibal and Graham. Hannibal notes that the m.o. of the woman's murder signifies the horse as chrysalis, 'a cocoon, meant to hold a young woman until her death can be transformed', with Hannibal continuing: 'I agree with the pagans: the horse is divine. All beasts of burden are sacred animals.' Yet, the parallel is also evident with the process through which Graham has gone in both seasons, and one that Graham chooses to pursue, indeed to accelerate, in his strategy as lure, notably in his therapy session.

But it is in the showdown with Clark Ingram – Peter Bernadone's tormenter and the murderer of horses and sixteen women – that Graham reveals himself both in transformation and as a masterful tactician. After Ingram emerges from the dead horse's belly (put there alive by Bernadone to show him what the experience is like), Graham draws his gun on Ingram and moves towards him, threatening to fire at point blank range, with Hannibal *aux aguets* standing close at hand. Graham's motive is to avenge the cruelty against Bernadone, but Hannibal urges prudence, arguing that killing Ingram is not the 'reckoning' that Graham had promised, that is, a reckoning with Lecter. So, by pulling the trigger and letting the swift Hannibal stop the firing mechanism with his thumb, Graham reveals himself to be fully aligned with the becomings to which Hannibal has inspired him, or at least to appear so. And Hannibal is visibly aquiver with this involution, moving close to Graham and whispering: 'With all my knowledge and intrusion, I could never entirely predict you. I could feed the caterpillar, I could whisper through the chrysalis, but what hatches follows its own nature, and is beyond me.'[14] As Fuller points out (in the season 2 DVD), this is a true moment when '[their] whole bromance ... really takes new flight because this final scene is so intimate, so close and so brotherly', and for my purposes here, we can see the convergence of their shared involution.

The next four episodes reveal additional steps in Graham's attempt to con Hannibal towards a trap, including Graham moving (in episode 210) decidedly outside any pack (even his own at home), and towards Hannibal's involution by killing (presumably in self-defense) a museum restorationist and killer, Randall Tier (note: German word for animal), then mounting Tier's head onto one of his prehistoric animal restorations (*not* in self-defense). Yet, for all Graham's becomings towards Hannibal's mode of involution, his underestimation of his adversary's skill *aux aguets* leads to a small but crucial slip: as part of the lure, Graham, Crawford and the FBI have misled Lecter to think that Graham murdered Freddie Lounds – who has, instead, been held incommunicado and whom Graham visits briefly, in the final episode 213. Then, helping Lecter burn his patients' files, Graham is unaware as Hannibal sniffs the scent of Lounds's red hair on him, thereby exposing Graham's double game and treachery, and thus allowing Hannibal to be entirely prepared for successive threatening visits by Crawford, Bloom and finally Graham. As Graham lies bleeding on Lecter's kitchen floor, Hannibal first chides him for the betrayal – 'I let you know me, see me. I gave you a rare gift, but you didn't want it' – but then asks about their mutual becomings: 'Do you believe you could change me the way I've changed you?', to which Graham replies insightfully, but perhaps desperately as well: 'I already did.' Finally, taking Abigail Hobbs in his arms (surprisingly revealed as still alive), Hannibal says tenderly, 'I forgive you, Will. Will you forgive me?' as he slices Abigail's throat and drops her on the floor besides the bleeding Graham.[15] Leaving all behind wounded, possibly dying (Crawford, Bloom, Graham, Abigail), Lecter makes his way out into the rain (a new baptism, according to Bryan Fuller). For Will Graham especially, the animal vision from the kitchen floor could hardly be more ominous, as he 'sees' the wounded stag collapsed, and possibly dying before his eyes. As for Hannibal, it's up, up, and away! In the final scene, running *after* the credits, Hannibal sits happily sipping bubbly in a first-class section, flying off with his new companion in becomings, Bedelia Du Maurier.

In this way, *Hannibal* offers an alternative mode of *critique et clinique*, understood, on one hand, as 'visions' and 'auditions' by 'delirium that invents them, as a *process* driving words from one end of the universe to the other', as 'events at the edge of language', and on the other hand, as 'delirium fall[ing] back into the *clinical state*, [where] words no longer open out onto anything . . . [revealing nothing] except a night whose history, colours, and songs have been lost. Literature is a health' (Deleuze 1997a: lv). Deleuze speaks in this final work of the stammering of language, not merely as some stylistic device, but as 'a creative process that runs through all great works' (Deleuze 1997a: 55). No doubt, the Harris novels may well pale in relation to the works of Masoch, Kafka and Quignard (some authors considered in Deleuze's 'Re-presentation of Masoch' in Deleuze 1997a), but the adaptation, re-imagination and extension by Bryan Fuller's team of Harris's literary world into the televisual domain – into thirteen forty-three-minute segments in each of seasons 1 and 2[16] – allow for numerous Deleuzian effects: the creative assemblage of forms of delirium, of stammering and crying, not just the becomings of humans, but also the animal cries that poke through Will Graham's fevered auditions; the packs that accompany his multiple visions; and the newly found becomings-animal into which he mutates in season 2. In contrast, through Hannibal's exploration of curiosity through involution, his critical process unfolds as perverse artist and clinician, opening himself to the risk of *rencontres*, and walking the fine line of experimentation and disaster that constitutes any artistic creation.

Acknowledgements

Sincere thanks to Alina Cherry and her work on becoming-animal in Claude Simon, to Nala and Oliver Kozak for feline secrets, to Ann Larabee for timely encouragement, and to Colin Gardner and Patricia MacCormack for patience and inspiration.

Notes

1. Respectively, in *Manhunter* (1986); *The Silence of the Lambs* (1991), *Hannibal* (2001), and *Red Dragon* (2002); and *Hannibal Rising* (2007).
2. See the novels *Hannibal* (Harris 1999: 287), *Hannibal Rising* (Harris 2006: 1–2). On the Memory Palace, see Macknick and Martinez-Conde 2012, and on its place in season 3 of the NBC series, see Goodwin 2014. See also the DVD of *Hannibal*, season 3, disc 2, for a production short video, 'Beyond the Memory Palace', especially interesting for the explanation of how the

producers recreated the Norman Palace of Palermo (the site of Hannibal's personal palace). See also a website devoted solely to Hannibal's Memory Palace (mainly providing different props and collectibles related to the films) at http://hannibalmemorypalace.e-monsite.com (accessed 22 June 2016).

3. See the NBC *Hannibal*, season 1, disc 2 for the 'A Taste for Killing' featurette.

4. For reviews/analyses of the Hannibal series, see Peters 2014, Sepinwall 2013, Greenwald 2014 and Paskin 2013. More generally, see the essays collected in Szumskyj 2008. Elucipher (2014a) provides a menu of blog posts on an array of facets of season 1.

5. H.P. Lovecraft's *The Dream-Quest of Unknown Kadath* and Hugo von Hofmannsthal's 'The Letter of Lord Chandos'.

6. On the 'Goldberg Variations' in the Hannibal films, see Cenciarelli 2012.

7. For an intriguing analysis of Lecter's story as a result of PTSD, see BlueSorceress 2010.

8. For each episode, I refer the reader to the corresponding narrative summary on the NBC season 1 site at http://www.nbc.com/hannibal/episodes?field_season_target_id=21896 (accessed 22 June 2016). Note that the season 1 DVD package includes an entire, extra episode (which would have been 104), entitled *Oeuf*. According to Eric Goldman (2013), the episode, with a story involving violence against children, was pulled from the NBC schedule by producer Bryan Fuller due to the Newton CT shootings that followed after the episode was completed. I include comment on it to the extent that it furthers Hannibal's involution. Given the continued involution of Hannibal *aux aguets*, it is a shame this episode was generally available only in edited clips until the DVD appeared.

9. Gravett (2013) reports Fuller's understanding of this relationship with Abigail: 'Bryan Fuller admitted recently that Lecter's sister, Mischa (referenced in both the novels and films), is "at the root of Hannibal's affection for Abigail." At the end of Thomas Harris' *Hannibal*, we witness Lecter's attempt, and eventual failure, to "remake" Clarice Starling into a version of his sister. In Relevés (episode 111), we see a similar attempt with Abigail Hobbs, although in this case, Lecter's failure to "protect" Abigail ends with her death.'

10. The episode summary previously posted on http://www.nbc.com/hannibal/episodes/season-1 (no longer available) stated that Bella admits having an affair, not cancer. However, not only does the producer's cut on the DVD omit any mention of an affair, the direct look that Lecter gives Bella when he recounts his youthful cancer sniffing, as well as the arc of the entire episode, support the revelation of illness rather than infidelity. And of course, in the second counselling session, Lecter mentions, then rejects infidelity as an option for Bella, and she replies, 'I don't feel betrayed by Jack. And there is no point in being mad at cancer for being cancer', while in the couple's conversation in Lecter's office, they discuss how they will manage together as she fights her illness.

11. My somewhat oblique allusion is to the debates that occupied Deleuze-Guattarians in the 1980s when some argued that the message of caution in *A Thousand Plateaus* seemed to clash with the impression given (or, in fact, misunderstood) in *Anti-Oedipus* of the need for unbridled deterriorialisations of desire. As Deleuze says in *L'Abécédaire* when queried on the very point by Parnet of 'what is desire?' in *Anti-Oedipus*, 'it was not what they thought it was, . . . it was a little misunderstanding . . . Some people thought that desire was a form of spontaneity, so there were all sorts of movements of "spontaneity"; and others thought desire was an occasion for partying (*la fête*). For us, it was neither one nor the other, . . . whereas the so-called philosophy of desire consisted only in telling people: don't go get psychoanalyzed, never interpret,

go experience/experiment with assemblages, search out the assemblages that suit you' (Deleuze 1997b, 'D as in Desire'). Experimenting with assemblages certainly is a programme that Hannibal can endorse!

12. It is worth noting that in *Hannibal* episode 202, after paying several farewell visits (including one to Will Graham in prison, to whisper 'I believe you'), Bedelia closes up her home and escapes before Hannibal's visit, clad in his clear plastic kill suit. Her fate – to become Lecter's consort in Florence – is depicted in season 3, as is her inevitable demise. In some ways, her circumstances mirror those that Clarice Starling experiences in Harris's *Hannibal*, but without the demise.

13. Fuller's remarks are located in the episode's commentary (with Hugh Dancy) on the second season DVD. See also VanDerWerff 2014.

14. In the DVD commentary, Bryan Fuller points to this statement as an example of paying homage and attention to Thomas Harris's works, since Hannibal's statement appears, in fact, as a rumination about the captured Clarice Starling, with only minor variations, 'It occurred to Dr. Lecter in the moment that with all his knowledge and intrusion, he could never entirely predict her, or own her at all. He could feed the caterpillar, he could whisper through the chrysalis; what hatched out followed its own nature and was beyond him' (Harris 1999: 523).

15. Yet another homage to the Harris novels and their film adaptations is the music that accompanies the bloody final sequence of episode 213 'Mizumono'. Brian Reitzell's 'Bloodfest' is an adaptation of Bach's Aria of the 'Goldberg Variations'.

16. Season 3 (which aired on NBC from 4 June to 29 August 2015) employed Italian food courses, plates and reference words for episode titles, the latter notably in 302, 'Primavera', where the continued importance of the stag image is evident for the recuperated and ever visionary Graham in his renewed pursuit across Europe of Hannibal Lecter. Unfortunately, due to poor ratings in the first two seasons, NBC cancelled the show early in season 3. According to VanDerWerff (2015), the production company Gaumont could not find another production partner, so the cast was forced to disperse, with vague hopes maintained for a possible continuation.

References

BlueSorceress (2010), *Hannibal: A Method Behind his Madness?* HannibalVisionArchive, 12 March, at http://hannibalvisionsarchive.wordpress. com/2010/03/12/hannibal-a-method-behind-his-madness (accessed 22 June 2016).

Cenciarelli, C. (2012), 'Dr Lecter's Taste for "Goldberg", or: the Horror of Bach in the Hannibal Franchise', *Journal of the Royal Musical Association*, Vol. 137, No. 1, pp. 107–34.

Deleuze, G. (1997a), *Essays Critical and Clinical*, trans. D. W. Smith and M. A. Greco, Minneapolis: University of Minnesota Press.

Deleuze, G. (1997b), *L'Abécédaire de Gilles Deleuze*, dir. Pierre-André Boutang, Paris: Editions Montparnasse; Zone 1 DVD, *Gilles Deleuze from A to Z*, trans. C. J. Stivale, Cambridge, MA: The MIT Press/Semiotext(e), 2012.

Deleuze, G. and F. Guattari (1987), *A Thousand Plateaus: Capitalism and Schizophrenia*, trans. B. Massumi, Minneapolis: University of Minnesota Press.

Elucipher (2014a), *HannibalMeta*, at http://hannibalmeta.tumblr.com/archive (accessed 22 June 2016).

Elucipher (2014b), 'Meta: Hannibal 2.08, "Su-zakana" 20 April, 2014', *We Live In The Dark*, at http://elucipher.tumblr.com/post/83245376784/meta-hannibal-2–08-su-zakana (accessed 4 December 2014).

Goldman, E. (2013), 'Hannibal: "Ceuf" [sic] Review', *IGN.US*, 8 May, at http://www.ign.com/articles/2013/05/09/hannibal-ceuf-review (accessed 22 June 2016).

Goodwin, J. (2014), 'Hannibal Season 3 News Spoilers', *Fashion and Style*, 14 October, at http://www.fashionnstyle.com/articles/27836/20141014/hannibal-season-3-news-spoilers-bryan-fuller-teases-lecters-memory-palace-on-twitter-photo.htm (accessed 22 June 2016).

Gravett, C. (2013), 'The Seduction of Violence in Hannibal Lecter's Funhouse', *HannibalMeta*, 22 June, at http://hannibalmeta.tumblr.com/post/53602393916/the-seduction-of-violence-in-hannibal-lecters (accessed 22 June 2016).

Greenwald, A. (2014), 'Night of the Manhunter', *Grantland*, 12 March, at http://grantland.com/features/hannibal-nbc-hugh-dancy-mads-mikkelsen (accessed 22 June 2016).

Hannibal (2013–15), DVD, seasons 1–3, produced by Bryan Fuller. USA: Lionsgate.

Hannibal (2001), directed by Ridley Scott. USA: Universal Pictures.

Hannibal Rising (2007), directed by Peter Webber. USA: The Weinstein Company.

Harris, T. (1981), *Red Dragon*, New York: Yazoo.

Harris, T. (1988), *Silence of the Lambs*, New York: Yazoo.

Harris, T. (1999), *Hannibal*, New York: Yazoo.

Harris, T. (2006), *Hannibal Rising*, New York: Yazoo/Delacorte.

Lovecraft, H. P. (1970), *The Dream-Quest of Unknown Kadath*, New York: Ballantine Books.

Macknick, S., and S. Martinez-Conde (2012), 'NeuroSCIience in FIction: Hannibal Lecter's memory palace', *Sleights of Mind*, 7 September, at http://blogs.scientificamerican.com/illusion-chasers/hannibal-lecter (accessed 22 June 2016).

Manhunter (1986), directed by Michael Mann. USA: De Laurentiis Entertainment.

Paskin, W. (2013), 'NBC's Hannibal and Getting Full On TV Violence', *Salon*, 4 April, at http://www.salon.com/2013/04/04/nbcs_hannibal_and_getting_full_on_tv_violence (accessed 22 June 2016).

Peters, M. (2014), 'Better than Silence', *Slate*, 26 February, at http://www.slate.com/articles/arts/television/2014/02/hannibal_on_nbc_is_the_best_thomas_harris_adaptation_to_date_better_than.html (accessed 22 June 2016).

Red Dragon (2002), directed by Brett Ratner. USA: Universal Pictures.

Sepinwall, A. (2013), 'Review: NBC's Hannibal', *HitFix*, 3 April, at http://www.hitfix.com/whats-alan-watching/review-nbcs-hannibal-a-riveting-silence-of-the-lambs-prequel (accessed 22 June 2016).

The Silence of the Lambs (1991), film, directed by Jonathan Demme. USA: Orion Pictures.

Stivale, C. J. (2014), '*Etre aux aguets*: Deleuze, Creation and Territorialization', in P. MacCormack (ed.), *The Animal Catalyst: Towards Ahuman Theory*, London: Bloomsbury, pp. 69–80.

Szumskyj, B. (ed.) (2008), *Dissecting Hannibal Lecter: Essays on the Novels of Thomas Harris*, Jefferson, NC: McFarland.

VanDerWerff, T. (2014), '*Hannibal*'s Bryan Fuller on rebooting season two halfway Through', *A.V.Club*, 19 April, at http://www.avclub.com/article/hannibals-bryan-fuller-rebooting-season-two-halfwa-203515 (accessed 22 June 2016).

VanDerWerff, T. (2015), 'Hannibal season 3 finale: Creator Bryan Fuller looks back at his show's last season', *Vox*, 30 August, at http://www.vox.com/2015/8/30/9224313/hannibal-finale-recap-bryan-fuller (accessed 22 June 2016).

von Hofmannsthal, Hugo (1902) 'The Letter of Lord Chandos', at <http://depts. washington.edu/vienna/documents/Hofmannsthal/Hofmannsthal_Chandos.htm (accessed 22 June 2016); *The Lord Chandos Letter*, New York: NYRB Classics, 2005.

Chapter 11

Mister V and the Unmournable Animal Death

Laurence A. Rickels

What you risk reveals what you value, or as Heidegger would have it, the grounds of your being. By 'the grounds of being' I don't mean anything terribly abstruse – in my case, for example, horses and dogs form an important part of the grounds of my being, which can be seen by anyone who takes a ride though the countryside with me. My eyes tend to fix on any horses, dogs, ponies and so on in the landscape – they are the means by which I know the landscape. Someone else would read and know the landscape differently, by the buildings in it, say, if s/he were a historian of architecture. (Hearne 1987: 143)

When Zarathustra's loneliness speaks, it is his animals who are speaking. (Heidegger 1984: 2:45)

Setting the Missing Place of Animals

In 'Building Dwelling Thinking', Heidegger (2001) drops a date mark, the exceptional concession in fantasy, according to Freud, to the otherwise-repressed present and its ongoing extension into the recent past.[1] Heidegger's mark is a postwar readymade. The housing shortage – *Wohnungsnot* – isn't the problem, Heidegger proclaims in summing up, nor is supplying this lack the solution. *Wohnungsnot*, a word with recognition value specific to postwar Germany, identifies, as we must appreciate without Heidegger's assistance, not only the need for dwelling, but also, literally, even psychotically, the painful neediness, even anguish, of dwelling. Consider Carl Jung's (1974) famous exploration of a schizophrenic patient's *Bank-Noten* in terms of their economy and currency of anguish. I have tried to reconstruct the immediate reception of Heidegger's philosophy by a German psychotherapy installed inside psychiatry for the treatment of psychosis. The *Zolikoner Seminare* were a late arrival of this relationship, which would prove mutual once

Ludwig Binswanger introduced *Daseinanalyse*, which he conjoined out of equal parts Freud and Heidegger shortly after the appearance of *Sein und Zeit*. To call Heidegger on his contributions to the ideology of successful mourning is to meet his words on the turf and terms of this long-standing meeting in psychotherapy:

> On all sides we hear talk about the housing shortage, and with good reason. Nor is there just talk; there is action too. We try to fill the need by providing houses, by promoting the building of houses, planning the whole architectural enterprise. However hard and bitter, however hampering and threatening the lack of houses remains, the *real plight of dwelling* does not lie merely in a lack of houses. The real plight of dwelling is indeed older than the world wars with their destruction, older also than the increase of the earth's population and the condition of the industrial workers. (Heidegger 2001: 158–9)

Instead, we must ever learn to dwell, which also means to give thought to our homelessness, our uncanniness. Because we would control and secure our address, we are separated from our home, much as for Freud we are separated from the mother's body, the model home. Through the essential off-limitedness of this home or body we encounter our own bodies as limit. Thus commences for Kafka the allegory of 'Der Bau' ('The Burrow'), the multiple occupancy or cathexis of the building or body as site of symptoms at close quarters, unfolding under the aegis of security, but in addition as corpus, which Kafka's *Schriftstellersein*, his sense of being writing, scans or reformulates relentlessly.

For Heidegger the bridge becomes the architectural placeholder for the call of dwelling/building, the summons to gather together, in passing, the fourfold of being. This fourfold illuminates the modes of mortals dwelling: saving the earth, receiving the sky, awaiting the divinities, and finally initiating their own nature, 'their being capable of death *as* death' (2001: 148). For Heidegger it's either his way across old town bridges or it's the highway: 'The highway bridge is tied into the network of long-distance traffic, paced as calculated for maximum yield. Always and ever differently the bridge escorts the lingering and hastening ways of men to and fro, so that they may get to other banks and in the end, as mortals, to the other side' (150).

All the while withdrawing his introject as model, Heidegger nevertheless exposes to viewing a recognisable home, one that is well-situated in Heidegger's Black Forest neighborhood. A continuity shot with the etymologically excavated beginnings of *bauen* and *wohnen*, which are immersed in agriculture, the 200-year-old farmhouse includes niches and markings for the Before and After of living passage. In other words, the house is far removed from memorial architecture, which still models reality testing in mourning according to Freud's 'Mourning and Melancholia'. The columbarium of remembrance is instead streamlined for life's transmission. After itemising the identifiable home's proper placement in the natural setting as well as the angle of its roof for optimal winter shelter, Heidegger lets the house remember:

> It did not forget the altar corner behind the community table; it made room in its chamber for the hallowed places of childbed and the 'tree of the dead' – for that is what they call a coffin there: the *Totenbaum* – and in this way it designed for the different generations under one roof the character of their journey through time. (2001: 158)

In the original, Heidegger lets the reader stumble over the *Totenbaum*, whereupon he interrupts the tour to deliver the translation. It is, at first contact, the double of *Wohnungsnot*, or rather the inoculation against the postwar readymade Heidegger next throws up. It is the topical blind spot and thus the other stumbling block, the one he doesn't mitigate.

The farmhouse remembers that 'mortals dwell in that they initiate their own nature – their being capable of death as death – into the use and practice of this capacity, so that there may be a good death' (2001: 148). Like Freud, who adopts the position of Devil's advocate while contemplating the scenarios of meaningfulness of the death drive he is introducing (in *Beyond the Pleasure Principle*), Heidegger doesn't want the good death, at least not as 'empty Nothing', to be 'the goal'. 'Nor does it mean to darken dwelling by blindly staring toward the end' (149). It is the distress, the *Not* that must be stayed. The farmhouse doesn't correspond to an inner world of representations. Instead, what we call memory is akin to live transmission. Thinking of a specific old-town bridge is by its nature, in itself, that which 'gets through, persists through, the distance to that location. From this spot right here, we are there at the bridge – we are by no means at some representational content in our consciousness' (154). Heidegger's argument with academic psychology is not one (hands down) with or against Melanie Klein's notion of the inner world. What is being set aside by this proxy argument is the basic separateness of psychotic states of depression.

> Even when mortals turn 'inward', taking stock of themselves, they do not leave behind their belonging to the fourfold. When, as we say, we come to our senses and reflect on ourselves, we come back to ourselves from things *without ever abandoning* our stay among things. Indeed, the loss of rapport with things that occurs in states of depression would be wholly impossible

if even such a state were not still what it is as a human state: that is, a staying *with* things. (2001: 155)

All the while residing in the agricultural setting of the onset of build-ing and dwelling, Heidegger's essay doesn't even take stock of animals, let alone stay with them. And yet it is inevitably over and against animals that humans award themselves philosophical distinction in death as in life. But the relationship to animals, masterfully bypassed in the elucida-tion of things in terms of bridgework, is nonetheless encrypted within the etymological time trip that revisits the original settlement of the meanings of building and dwelling. Heidegger is training us to heed certain commands:

> Let us listen once more to what language says to us. The Old Saxon *wuon*, the Gothic *wunian*, like the old word *bauen*, mean to remain, to stay in a place. But the Gothic *wunian* says more distinctly how this remaining is experienced. *Wunian* means: to be at peace, to be brought to peace, to remain in peace. The word for peace, *Friede*, means the free, *das Freye*, and *fry* means: preserved from harm and danger, preserved from something, safeguarded. To free really means to spare. The sparing itself consists not only in the fact that we do not harm the one whom we spare. Real sparing is something *positive* and takes place when we leave something beforehand in its own nature, when we return it specifically to its being, when we 'free' it in the real sense of the word into a preserve of peace. (2001: 146–7)

The denial that sparing doesn't only mean we don't harm or kill the 'one whom we spare' is the denial to animals of a place in the staging area of essential building, dwelling, or thinking. '*The fundamental char-acter of dwelling is this sparing and preserving*', where 'this' refers to the scenario of sparing that 'also' prevails and which exceeds what has been denied. This sparing is a setting free – born free – but within the preserve, the safeguarding of 'each thing in its nature' (147).

Totem Meals

The hunter must defend against the evil eye, the dying animal's parting shot of retribution. In early cave paintings not only do we see the chase and kill of the hunt but we also recognise what follows: dancers wearing animal masks enacting mournful identification with the hunted animals. In *Totem and Taboo* (1958d), Freud argued that once we commenced keeping animals (which, deeply emotionally, meant sparing their lives, whereby we were exposed to their bare and brief life spans) their deaths came under the totemic administration of sacrifice.[2] The animal destroyed was in some sense restored inside us. While the totemic system proper disappeared with the advent of livestock, its internal reach, now more than ever, mediated our intake of what Ella Freeman Sharpe (1950) called 'the problems of food (life) and death'.[3]

Freud's retelling of Darwin's notion of a primal horde that was in the beginning of human socialisation or civilisation adds mourning to the survival of the fittest, which changes everything. Our missing link was forged into a link with the missing via the animals that initiated first interspecial contact. By mutation, the fast track of evolution, this contact high leapt out of the slow-motion evolution that put a chimp on our shoulder. Recent research has suggested that it was a sudden change in the genetic material of a couple of wolves that produced the dog, an animal given to read and follow the non-verbal communication of the human relation. Since the dogs that opened the exchange were inevitably not recognised as teachers but were mistaken to be voluntary quarry, Freud's primal father legend can be seen to emerge interspecially out of the consumption of the wrong object, guided not by revenge but by mixed messages. That the custom of eating dogs is still practised (alongside the cute dog's adoration) in East Asia, the site of this origin story according to the research, fits the primal relationship.

Civilisation commenced, Freud argues in *Totem and Taboo*, with the totemic administration of the lifetimes of domestic animals. Only on special occasions in which the entire clan participated was the totem animal slaughtered and served up in the mode of sacrifice. Because the first animals to be sacrificed and eaten were also mourned, Freud recognised in this relationship an ambivalence that could only refer to our earliest human relations of dependence. Thus the animals coming to us to be spared, cared for and eaten were inevitably identified by us as the souvenirs, ghosts or internal objects of these earliest relations. The animal that in coming close to us lays bare its lifetime also comes back to us out of the transference.

The allegorical significance of the sacrifice of the totem animal to the god of the clan diverts our attention, according to Freud, from the historical layering of the successive identifications with the father. The scene of the father's gravest humiliation – his murder and consumption – provides material for the representation of his highest triumph. One thus made amends to the father by the very act that maintained memory of the transgression against him, until one day the god was placed so high that only priestly mediation was acceptable, while the animal that was sacred or sacrificial fell out of the equation. Myths of the god killing the animal sacred to him, the animal he himself is, date from this change.

The allegorical interpretation of this replacement of the earlier father substitute by the higher god in terms of the god's overcoming of his animal nature overlaps significantly, Freud allows, with the psychoanalytic understanding of the interspecial relationship of mourning basic to sacrifice (1958d: 433–4).

By introducing the father's primal incarnation of mortality into the theory of evolution Freud already administers the injection of the paternal antibody. The animal is joined to the father's death. But what is left over and remains nonsuperimposable in this transfer – unmournable loss – is also a stowaway in the paternal relation. The totem animal occupies the cozy corner of mediation of and substitution for primal relational demands. But the animal medium, as big as lifetime, never drops close contact with finitude. We cut meat with the father's death to mix mourning into the unmournable status of the animal kept or spared, most precariously and recently as totemic pet. In other words, we eat animals to submit the brief lifetime each animal brings to us and lays bare for us to a larger economy of substitution, sacrifice or mourning. We can face the other who goes first, with the animal at the front of this line, because we eat animals.

Unmournability is hitched to the abbreviation of the time spent together. When we lose mother, child or sibling we return to the start position of losing the race against not enough time: too late too soon. It is our training as meat eaters, our initiation at and group bonding over the sacrificial meal, that protects us against the unmournable brevity of life together – which the animal kept close embodies without exception. The ancient Egyptians maintained sacred or totem animals in large groups in preserves where, entirely on their own, they grew old and died, but were then individualised in mourning as mummies that humans could now adopt. We, in contrast, keep the individual animal close to us until death opens wide a mass unmarked grave. Everyone likes your pet and spends quality time giving the animal an interspecial context for life. But when the loved one goes: shut up and get a replacement.

In *Totem and Taboo* Freud borrowed from the modern archive of anthropology the notion of two deaths to set up the parameters of haunting in mourning. The first death is at once the onset of the turbulent phase of mourning that other cultures frame as the living on of the departed in their midst. But then, after two years, the first dead are disinterred, the evidence of bones put on display, and the second dead can be granted another burial, one that books no more returns. But from within the perspective of unmourning that Freud opens up here, one out of two deaths is also the threshold that need never be crossed. If there's a first death, then the second one is murder.

Immersed in brief spans of lifetime and transferentially charged with primal losses, the spared and kept animal is already the ghostly denizen between deaths. The first death marks the onset of remembrance or haunting. Then there's the second death, and that's final. When your animal dies, there's no suffer zone of mournful metabolisation from point A to point B. You are left alone with the second death, the lost loss. But that also means that we include the animals close to us in our ongoing relations with the unmournable dead, for which the operations of proper mourning serve as booster shots building our endurance.

What looks like resistance to psychoanalysis (and thus to the transferential setting in both cases) can be identified as blind spots in the reception of Freud that obscure the continuity shots that are in fact there and allow the followers to make contributions of their own. 'The law of distribution', Elias Canetti writes in *Crowds and Power*, 'is the oldest law' (1984: 98). It underlies the totemic economy of transformation. Canetti assigns the structuring of the primal socius to the packs of prehistory. All the packs are on a dis-continuum of transformation from one into the other. In the primeval hunting pack (itself modelled on wolves) primal man no doubt 'incorporated into himself, *by transformations*, all the animals he knew' (108). Without transformation into animals man would never have learned how to feed himself. The presentiments whereby 'primitive peoples' can recognise the approach of an animal are initial signs or residues of transformations (340). Imitation (or identification) 'is nothing but a first step in the direction of transformation, a movement which immediately stops short' (370). Only the pack of lamenting or mourning offers a stay to murderous transformation – but only until the next transformation jettisons it into another formation entirely. Before transformation reabsorbs it the lamenting pack rushes towards the dying man and gathers around him 'midway between life and death' (107). This is where Freud stops short.

In *A Thousand Plateaus*,[4] Deleuze and Guattari (1987) see in 'becoming-animal' the exemplary transformation, which for them aims at 'becoming multiple' or 'becoming minoritarian'. And yet 'becoming-animal' is how the overriding investment in multiplicity is first flexed. Only through the animal pack can we become multiple. Thus the plan of becoming begins with the animal relation. Since 'becoming multiple' means 'becoming minoritarian', man as majority figure is not an option for becoming. Man must be divested of his majority share before he can become other. If 'becoming multiple' isn't the bottom line, then it requires the missing link of 'becoming-animal' and observes the double prohibition that one cannot 'become' the man in the position of majority norm and that such a man cannot enter the field of becoming. Loss is the initiation rite that precedes and constitutes the substitutive order of becoming. Thus the two trajectories of Freud's thought, featuring on one track totemic identification and, on the other, castration (whereby we are initiated into the management of loss or lack), which separate out as those of unmourning and 'successful mourning', of first and second deaths, respectively, are in fact covered by the anti-Oedipal momentum of Deleuze and Guattari's schizoanalysis.

Just as Ludwig Binswanger's analysis of *Dasein* adds to the psychotic materials to be explored details of the enfolded relationship to the future and thus opens up the surface of legibility to ever more folds, without, however, necessarily contradicting basic Freud, so Deleuze and Guattari's philosophy of becoming supplies many metabolic features in the breach or break of psychosis that might otherwise not be available in the Freudian reading. However, it doesn't, contrary to their desire to up the anti-, truly counter that reading. The argument of 'becoming-animal' does not contradict Freud but is rather immersed in a contradiction internal to Freud's thought on mourning.

Upon survival of first contact with humankind, which we have been extrapolating from *Totem and Taboo*, the dog, in the wake of his mistaken consumption, became our prosthesis in hunting and led us to gather and keep other animal species. The other animal to step outside the gathering of livestock and prove a prosthesis of human relationality and power was the horse. We follow the primal or ambivalent fit between the East-Asian provenance of the first dogs, according to the research, into the setting of a horse story in France, where they eat horses, don't they?

Mister V

Émilie Deleuze directed a horse movie named, after the horse of course, *Mister V* (2003). Released within eight years of her father's jump out the window, the movie tracks changes in relationality that commence when Mister V, otherwise an untrainable or psycho horse, flexes immense potential by clearing the wall of his pen in one impossible jump. At this point the film identifies with its own medium nature, its own trainability, and gives us a couple of staggered replays of this jump.

Luigi, who contracted with Lemoigne, a Belgian gangster, to buy Mister V to cash in on the insurance value upon the animal's fatal accident, becomes determined instead to train the talented horse to be a prize winner. During this change of heart, as his wife Cécile remembers, he was thrilled like a kid over this horse of his dreams. But then Luigi is found dead in Mister V's stall. His brother Lucas and widow Cécile decide not to treat the horse's violence against Luigi as intentional. From this point onward Mister V carries forward Luigi's loss but also exceeds it. The anxieties that accrue to the disposability of this horse crowd out any room at all for Luigi's absence. When they spared Mister V Cécile and Lucas reclaimed unmournability and raised it to totemic power. Cécile to Mister V: 'What am I to do with you? Why did you kill him? He loved you. Not a word. You don't care.' Simply but subtly, she identifies with the horse: 'You want to save your skin? Me too.' When on occasion the camera sees double, Cécile and Mister V (and the film) alternate in the fetishistic formation of the prospect of substitution. Cécile's closing contract with the horse confirms that her identification lies outside the teenage thrill of becoming-animal that Luigi and Lucas shared, and which Lucas realises in the end by letting be, the full implication of sparing. At the same time he thus enters a separate peace in the puzzling relationship to Cécile.

Lemoigne declares that he knew the father of Luigi and Lucas. The death contract put out on the horse, insured for the purchase price inflated at auction, is, however, between this figure from the underworld and Luigi alone. When Lucas stumbles across the contractual relationship, Lemoigne tries to implicate him by asking for advice on the most efficient and scientific way of disposing of the horse. That he cites DNA testing to indicate the scientific frame of reference he has in mind brings up infernal associations whereby, again in the filiation Lemoigne administers, the son can be dead sure, Dad certain, and mourning free. In the end Lucas applies his scientific savvy and gets out of his dead brother's infernal contract by switching blood samples and faking Mister V's death. The blood proof of identity was taken from another horse, Tiberius, already on schedule to go to sleep, whose dead body identifies Mister V as the casualty in the barn burning.

Batistella, the saving foreign purchaser at the end of the film, who gives shelter to Mister V, recognises in Lucas his mother's lookalike. At this point of identification – of a loss in his face – all the parties to the film's happy end begin to arrive via a reclamation that at the same time exceeds the doubling logic of insurance scam, of the underworld filiation. While the first figure, Lemoigne, belongs to the murderous underworld of substitution with benefits, the second, Batistella, re-crosses the path of the film story as contained, as container. But when he first appears at the opening horse auction he tries to get Lucas's attention, tries to say 'hi', but is overlooked and passed by. A stray connection left unidentified, without follow up, Batistella first counted as continuity error, one that could be restored, however, by the end of the film. In the medium of every film story, the continuity error is the otherwise inadvertent performance of the uncommemorated loss that appears only to disappear or hide out.

The splitting off that organises Lucas's relationship to his own body (which he has projected into the technoscience of measurement of horses in motion, his profession, and into the art of tap dancing, his hobby or fetish) is reflected and re-collected in the relationship to Mister V. In a series of scenes, eye-to-eye coordination is established between Lucas and Mister V, which stabilises the horse in the stable, while movement extends the bond unto a fantastic correspondence. In one scene Lucas's modified dance steps are given (or edited) in exchange with Mister V's matching steps. But is this identification the imitative kind that Deleuze and Guattari for some reason allow in scenarios of neurotic or perverse domestication of pets but throw out of the animal relationship they raise to the power of transformational identification on the way to becoming multiple? Stanley Cavell (2009) argues succinctly that it's not that everything the animal can do we can do better – or vice versa – but that anything the animal does that appears to be the same as what we do is allegory. It's not accidental or historical that we first opened the study of human anatomy over animal cadavers. The animal goes first – and that's our allegory.

Vicki Hearne (1987) approached the animal relation via the ennobling and letting be that training secures. What Hearne's reading strongly suggests is that trainability (or answerability) is the bottom line of all relationality.[5] She's not talking behaviour modification or adaptation. We meet the horse not through sweetness but in beauty, which, says Rilke, marks the onset of terror, or, according to Shakespeare, harbours as its vulnerability, already inside it, the cancer of grief. Hearne uses these quotes as the bookends for setting aside the sections of her study of animal training and philosophy dedicated to horses. Her central case study relates the story of Drummer Girl's retraining.

> For a few steps, then, she achieved under saddle what horsemen call 'self-carriage', and those moments of congruence and contact with her own splendor accomplished more than years of people babbling about her sweetness and prettiness had. She was in any event neither sweet nor pretty. She was, however, beautiful. (1987: 135)

In the parenthetical introject that follows, Hearne interprets Rilke's line to indicate that knowledge of beauty leads to knowledge of loss of beauty, which is knowledge of death. Horses lack the time scheme that keeps us on schedule with mortality. 'Their concept of time might be expressed by saying that the names of their tenses are "not yet, here and gone." You can't make appointments with such tenses, but you can remember, and you can anticipate the future with no little anxiety' (1987: 164–5). While horses thus have 'some sensitivity to the knowledge of death', they and their riders are relieved of this knowledge 'in the tremendous concentration of horsemanship' (165). What we learn from horses (and dogs) is the connection that comes from being answered. In Kleinian terms we renew with these animals our vows with the internal good objects. Vulnerability is something 'horses can learn from us – not the grammar of mortality, not a knowledge of their own, but rather a participation in ours' (164). There is a knowledge that lies in answering and waiting, which extends through mourning.

The best example Hearne can give of this crossing over in the meeting between horse and horse trainer brings us back to Drummer Girl. After citing Steinkraus on the rogue horse, the limit concept of training, like the psychopath on the human scale of treatment, Hearne counsels that the point is not the prospect of inborn fateful traits but that the rogue concept, given the declared rarity of actual rogue horses, tests at the limit the quality of the trainer.

> But the moral to take from this passage is the one about putting your heart into a rogue . . . rather than take the far greater risk of being a bad horseman. That is the risk I was unwilling to take in training Drummer Girl . . . It is also, I think, the risk Drummer Girl herself was unwilling to take – there is an equine equivalent of mediocrity, and there are horses who refuse that possibility at all costs. (1987: 146)

Following a stint of his everyday life in town suspended between lab research and tap dancing, Lucas is called back to the country by messages left on his answering machine in earshot of responsibility. Lemoigne's messages remind him of his dead brother's debt to the underworld; Cécile's messages ask him to mind that he promised not to leave her alone. That she hates being alone, her pathological state, he then and now rephrases in terms of her grief. But why should she believe him: she says she's afraid.

The psychopathy which a rogue horse like Mister V borders on or fully cathects and occupies, according to Steinkraus according to Hearne, is interpreted by D. W. Winnicott, in regard to the delinquent acts of its budding phase in antisocial children, as a harbinger of hope, which illuminates the importance of the environment in the otherwise stricken world of deprivation.[6] In its original sense, conveyed to this day in the German 'language of hunters' as *verhoffen*, 'hope' signifies an animal's startled hesitation that stops one approach and starts a new one along the lines of reality testing. The mad refusal of a horse to adapt to murderous conditions also gives traction to the humans who must re-start, double back, and pursue another trajectory.

When Lucas returns, his niece Clara announces that mummy is expecting him and directs him to the site of Cécile's partially towel-wrapped otherwise nude sunbathing. When she signals to him to sit down, the camera takes over, as earlier with Mister V's jump, and replays the gesture, which hovers in the medium. On a couple of occasions, the camera, which regularly follows the muscular back view of the horse's parts, gives close ups of the muscular back of Cécile's neck, which she then starts to rub. Another time the trans-species identification seems even stronger because denied: Cécile, angry and frustrated, shies and bolts when Lucas tries to rub the spot. In the tanning scene a slip of the towel made public her pubic part. But Lucas or the camera seems most affected when a butterfly alights on Cécile's buttocks. Cécile declares her double purpose: she's tanning herself and mourning in *plein air* and sight. 'I mourn and I tan, *c'est tout*.' Modelling the other norm specific to the turbulent phase between first and second deaths, she mourns and unmourns.

Lucas's assistance is needed now during foaling season. But when the time comes he sleeps through his morning watch, which results in the mare dying of a collapsed uterus, which need not have been fatal if stitched in time. Now he is entrusted with the milk bottle feeding of the foal. He must also secure a clean stall, which means clearing away the corpse of the mother by tractor and forklift.

Cécile dismisses the gravity of a mishap that could have happened to her: at least the foal was saved. She and Lucas cover up the circumstances of the mare's passing, though the stable hand, Jean-François, isn't fooled. It's a matter of measuring the time in which to save, the time allowed to elapse and collapse. When Jean-François asks about the timing, Lucas answers that he doesn't know. Jean-François earlier resisted the decision by Cécile and Lucas to continue with the horse farm and even to sustain the investment in Mister V rather than shoot the killer. He warns that she will be swindled, which she translates into his view that all women are sluts. To which he supplies the matching non sequitur: 'Nobody can replace him.' Shortly after Luigi's funeral, when

Lucas gazed at the stall wall that he and Luigi earlier watched Mister V clear, the jump to remember, Jean-François, the guardian of piety, spits out the bitterness he can't swallow: 'Master of all you survey?'

Following the nerdish mishap that cost the mare's life, Lucas's clumsiness and carelessness while trying to bind Mister V make it easy for the horse to corner him in the stall. But this time the horse doesn't kill his human. He bites him instead, whereupon Lucas passes out. Isn't this a scene of identification with the departed, over which Mister V watches? Lucas blames the incident on his own lack of experience. When Cécile points out that the horse could have killed him, Lucas counters: 'But he didn't. I saw him.' The doctor who treats Lucas's wounds expresses shock that Cécile didn't put the horse down after her husband's death. He refers to the rumour mill set spinning on account of this sparing: 'If you knew what they say.' Lucas urges Cécile to stick to her resolve not to kill Mister V: 'If we kill him we'll never know.' Know? 'If Luigi was right.' The vet and doctor bills will make the maintenance of the farm that much more difficult. Lucas declares that he will take a longer leave from work, not a vacation but now a sabbatical. They embrace, kiss, and the rest is substitution. But it is a success (and succession) story that wrecks Lucas, who must start over.

Mister V leads Lucas to separate out this incestuous union into individuals who can in time restart as a couple. On the morning after, Clara brings Lucas a present from Lemoigne: it's a needle for injecting the horse. The one-night understanding of substitution and successful mourning is no match for (or with) the relationship to Mister V. Lucas moves into the barn to improve his watch over the other mare on schedule to foal. What becomes of this mare is left suspended in continuity error, which is in this instance a preserving suspension of animation. One mother horse is forever spared in this medium abyss. In effect, however, Lucas moves in with Mister V, thereby drawing as his line in the 'and' the centrality of this horse's mortality.

While Mister V's mortality leaves no room for Luigi's absence, Lucas becomes through the relationship to Mister V his dead brother. Is the relationship between the brothers carried forward? It's certainly not incorporated as it stood. Mister V and Luigi (and the medium of motion pictures) help Lucas overcome an impasse. In the background of the opening movie titles is a shot of embodied motion, presumably that of a horse walking, but so closely cropped that it is hard to identify, even whether fore or hind parts. The enigmatic citation or summons places Lucas's relationship to embodiment in our faces. The opening scene at the auction house shows Lucas on the sidelines of the main action in charge of an information booth advertising techniques for measuring equine movement. Two bumpkins stop by to make fun of his enterprise: 'Don't mess with nature. She'll take revenge.'

When Lucas confronts his brother following the high-rolling purchase of high-strung Mister V, Luigi pleads that this insurance scam is just one last turn in the underworld to free him of the residual indebtedness that still keeps him enrolled there. Lucas next asks about Cécile, who is in recovery from a bout of depression. 'Et Cécile?' Lucas asked his brother, thus placing the short hand over the heart of his long-standing love affair with his brother's family. Luigi promptly reports to Lucas that daughter Clara is excelling at school. That his brother's family as ready-made is only one murderous substitution away from his understanding and grasp is what the film and horse must circumvent for Lucas via the staggered prospect of survival in mourning.

Lucas flees to the safety zone of his information booth when Luigi asks for help with Mister V, kicking up a storm in the trailer. Isn't this again the uncontaining unidentified horse walking towards or away from us in the film's trailer? When Lucas pitches his research to a grant committee, the Chair asks Lucas if he rides. 'I'm talking about a miracle of creation and you ask if I ride!' Lucas wants to harness to the art and science of measurement or distinction the stride length of horses and, at a jump, the time between the forelegs coming down and the hind legs pushing off. An internal simulacrum of one of the film medium's primal scenes, Lucas's scientific project recapitulates E. J. Muybridge's proto-cinematographic photo documentation of the stride of horsepower and the time between takeoff and landing.[7] Following Mister V's jump, Luigi dismisses Lucas's second thoughts: 'For you everything's a problem.' But Lucas stands up for his job description: 'I test, I analyse.' The split-off motility with which Lucas tries to catch up in his tap dancing while it runs along unattended awaits integration via the reality testing, the work of mourning, that the inner world, upon the impact of his brother's death, holds in store.

Jean-François recognises immediately that last night was the night: 'You fuck her? When I think of poor Luigi. The horse did you a favour.' Now that he's fired, this was his parting shot. But it is the shot that gets Lucas to, and out of, the restarting gate. Traversing and reversing the citation of the onset of Nietzsche's madness of becoming, Lucas enters Mister V's stall and beats the horse. He beats into him the measure of the miracle of creation. Now when Mister V moves nervously back and forth in the stall Lucas syncs the movement up to his own, which doubles and contains the horse's nervous momentum. And now the horse can see better. Trainability, the hallmark of relationality, means that something like animal testing is enfolded, preserved and reversed inside reality testing itself, the basis, according to Freud, for ego motility and, thus, for thinking.

Clara, the only member of the inner circle of survivors who seems plainly affected by Luigi's death, wants to know why Lucas wants to live like a horse. She runs a stick along the bars of Mister V's stable until Lucas makes her stop. 'You love him more than me or mummy or daddy.' When he points to her own close relationship to her pets, she declares it's not the same. Then he picks her up and takes her into Mister V's stall to mediate their reparation, but Mister V and Clara freak out. The child runs away calling for mother. While Lucas continues with his chores about the farm, Cécile walks over to Mister V's stall with a rifle. They are eye to eye: she aims the gun and then shoots into the ceiling. The horse is always available for shooting but at the same time it proves impossible, even for jealous Cécile, to kill Mister V. On his way back from the fields Lucas encounters Cécile burning his barn stuff. That's over. She's decided to sell. 'You said you wouldn't change anything!' 'Everything has changed.' One change is that she can't go near Mister V. 'It's not his fault.' 'Then how did it come to this?'

After a visit to his brother's grave, Lucas informs Lemoigne that the horse will die: 'I'll call when it's done.' The underworld insurance scam can now be extended to fund new beginnings. The horse farm can go up in smoke, and yield its insurance value, while the senior horse Tiberius can be put to sleep right before the fire and, passing for Mister V, earn the premium insurance coverage. When Cécile returns to the site of the barn burning she says: 'It's sinister. I thought there'd be nothing left.' The horse corpse of Tiberius is still recognisable. 'Did he suffer?' No. 'Poor Tiberius. It's as if he knew.' While visiting the aging Tiberius in his stable earlier in the film she could identify the grief they shared: 'I know you miss him too.' And yet she acquiesced in the deployment of Tiberius's mortality to obtain money for Mister V twice over.

That Luigi's reputation delivers grounds for the insurers to delay settlement gives cause and pause for Lucas and Cécile to smile together. Just the same, the investigation has already concluded that the fire started by spontaneous combustion. When Lucas starts to inform Cécile what happened to Mister V, she stops him. 'For me he's dead. I don't care.' They embrace. Dead or alive Mister V counts for Cécile as dead twice over. Lucas, for his part, will see that Mister V is good and gone. We watch, with Lucas, as Cécile, moving away, strokes the back of her neck turned towards us. When we see her doing it again, it is not camera replay or medium flashback; instead we are again seeing her rubbing the spot we're in with Mister V. But it is from this spot – or out of it – that Lucas can now make plans to travel to the location of possible reunions with Cécile and Clara.

The positions in the circle of survivors are in a sense prescribed. Cécile, the wife and thus the father's delegate and guardian of the couple, is open to the prospect of substitutions passing through her. Lucas, the maternal keepsake, is guided by the unmournable Mister V to inject delay and new beginnings into the momentum of easy substitution on death drive. That Cécile can identify and be identified with Mister V delivers Lucas from being head off at an internal impasse.

At the end the extra purchase of the real Mister V by Batistella, the man returning from continuity error to recognise the missing mother in her son's face, yields the surplus cash whereby the underworld boss can be bought off. All the players on the stage of Oedipus are free to reunite at the sea, which in French is always also the mother. The film gives Lucas's face and eyes the screen. Then it closes with the landscape into which Mister V has escaped, though we also see, following in cars, the men who, Batistella calmly assures Lucas, will catch him. Watching the letting be we catch up with the blank deployment of sparing in Heidegger's thought. The blank denial of the animal relation also denies the dead a place in the setting of his thought.

Klein, Lacan and the Ghostly Inner World

The animals we keep close to our relationality at home, in the backyard, on the farm are, according to Deleuze and Guattari, perverse retrenchments of the animal relation, neurotic props of the relation's domestication and administration. But isn't 'becoming-animal' just one more way to avoid and void the responsibility to the other so specific to mourning: choose to be some exotic wild animal rather than acknowledge the wild afterlife of grief following at your heels. In *Mister V*, Clara keeps two guinea pigs. Are the little girl's pets perverse miniaturisations of domesticated family life and thus the very measure of what the psycho horse breaches? Clara's pets are related to the belittling animal identification that Lemoigne flings at Lucas for declaring Mister V's new independence of the insured death contract: 'You're a laboratory rat trying to give your life meaning.' His tirade ends: 'The horse must die!'

Upon returning home from her father's funeral Clara shows Lucas how she likes her guinea pigs to join in matrimony or kiss. In exchange she asks him to demonstrate a few tap dance steps for the couple:

they don't believe her. Freud identified small animals in dreams, for example, as representing children and siblings. These animal children, for example in the case study of Rat-Man, can bear their association in folklore with the souls of the dead all the way to the point of mourning's encryptment.[8] According to Melanie Klein, critters represent and convey the good object inner world that mourning shatters and rebuilds. They also count, on the dark side of identification, as the unborn or undead children and siblings lost and found among the inside properties of the mother's body.

Before reopening her theory of the inner world in terms of mourning and reality testing in 'Mourning and Its Relation to Manic-Depressive States', Klein (1984b) laid the foundation with her reading of the animated critters guiding a bad boy to reconciliation with his mother, inside and out. Klein's first study of a work of art as a forum for her innovations in analytic theory showcased the premise of her notion of reparation. In her 1929 article 'Infantile Anxiety Situations Reflected in a Work of Art and in the Creative Impulse', Klein considers a boy faced with homework in Ravel's opera *L'Enfant et les Sortilèges* (or in Collette's libretto). He feels an upsurge of rebelliousness against the stupid lessons: 'Want to go for a walk in the park! I'd like best of all to eat up all the cake in the world, or pull the cat's tail or pull out all the parrot's feathers! I'd like to scold every one! Most of all I'd like to put mama in the corner!' (1984a: 210). In the interior scene on which the boy's tantrum is set, the caged squirrel he attacks, like the pendulum he wrenches out of the clock, represents the father's penis inside the mother. The attack upon the mother also targets the father and thus the primal scene inside her. 'A special intensity is imparted to this danger-situation by the fact that a union of the two parents is in question' (210). Via the notion of reparation Klein consolidates her rereading of the primal scene as that of the combined parents, whose fateful combo on the inside must be separated out as individuals who can then be re-paired in sync with one's own pleasure, in which the benign internal parents participate.

When the boy goes outside, he is greeted by trees that react not to the most recent tantrum but to a whole phase of his scientific research, which already led him to knick wounds in their bark with his knife. Now he feels remorse: doubly so when the dragonfly demands back the companion the boy netted and then stuck against the wall with a pin. When the animals unite to fight the boy, they end up fighting each other. They wound one of their own, the squirrel that escaped the child's research cage, but not before the boy in his fit jabbed it with his pen. Now the boy binds the squirrel's double wound and falls back unconscious, embodying the wound or identifying with the dead his attack upon the clock released.

The attack upon the united parents at close quarters – deploying ink, ashes, steam – was excremental and sadistic (Klein 1984a: 212). The shift outside from sadism to object-love via pity and sympathy (which accompanies the advance to the genital level of development) is marked when the boy cares for the wounded squirrel (214). The hostile world becomes the friendly host. The animals praise the good child. He whispered 'Mama' which the animals repeat: it is the magic word promised by the opera's title.

We saw that the positioning of 'becoming-animal' within the medium of becoming is in conformity with the totemic relations Freud illuminates in terms of mourning between first and second deaths, while the stricture Deleuze and Guattari place on majority man evokes castration. By foregrounding castration, which renders further contact with loss beside this point, Jacques Lacan circumvented problems of unmourning, indeed championed the second death, now the sublime of the symbolic order, now the termination that follows even upon faulty thinking. When you look at the overview on poststructuralism that Deleuze contributed to a 1973 'History of Philosophy',[9] for example, it becomes evident that he was willing and able to speak the second language of Lacanian psychoanalysis. Inside this portmanteau heritage there is familiarity with Klein's work, certainly the direct source for psychotic splitting images, like the body without organs. In his introduction to the French translation of Ludwig Binswanger's *Dreams and Existence* (Binswanger's premier study in the mode he introduced of forced marriage between Freud and Heidegger), Michel Foucault summarises the French psychoanalytic setting: either Klein or Lacan.[10] For philosophers, then, at least before Derrida, there was only Lacan and the Klein inside that transmission. Don't Lacan's reflections on *Hamlet* amount to a reabsorption of Klein's 'Mourning and Its Relation to Manic-Depressive States' inside his onetime-only mourning address?

Lacan raised his bar by lifting Klein's 1940 essay up inside the symbolic grid alongside *Hamlet*.[11] Lacan, the analyst who avoided mourning and melancholia like a pest, finds that he alone recognises that in *Hamlet* 'all anyone talks about is mourning' (1982: 39). Phantoms arise because mourning rites have been curtailed or otherwise improperly carried out. The ritual value of mourning refers to and summons a 'total mass intervention, from the heights of heaven to the depths of hell, of the entire play of the symbolic register' (38). But for the Elizabethan frame it would only be wishful thinking to view the symbolic register in its entirety as still home on the range of Christianity. However Lacan does admit that while only the totality of the signifier can fill or fulfill the hole in the Real, we are faced in mourning with the 'inadequacy of signifying elements to cope with the hole'. Just as mourning must mediate a strike of loss that threatens the inner world in Klein's essay, so in Lacan's reading of mourning in *Hamlet*, 'the system of signifiers in their totality . . . is impeached by the least instance of mourning' (38). That's why the rites of mourning realign the gap opened up by a direct hit of mourning with the greater gap that is always also there, 'the symbolic lack'. What does it mean that every encounter with the loss of a loved one is the renewal of vows of substitution with the separations and sacrifices already given at the office of Oedipus by following the complex into its decline? If he rids his reading of loss of all singularity, then Lacan overshoots Klein's mark, the inner world.

Freud's and Klein's attributions of reality testing to the work of mourning press towards the encounter with the phantom. According to Freud, the mourner is compelled to submit the continuity shots of the departed to reality checks. Lacan translates this into his symbolic grid as the psychosis-like profusion of images rushing to fill the gap in the real. The consequence of Freud's decision to fill out a missing person report in consideration of mourning – both Klein and Lacan note that Freud was the first to assign an object to mourning – is in turn lost if we view Freud's introduction of reality testing in his 1917 essay 'Mourning and Melancholia' as exclusively in the disposal service of successful mourning. Klein opens her mourning essay with three citations from Freud's essay pertaining to reality testing. The third time it's the harm apparently done by Freud's passage on reality's verdict decreeing the object's non-existence that alerts us to the closeness of Klein's reading derived from Freud's collected work. Freud states that he does not know if this is in fact so but that 'possibly' the survivor lets the lost object go, satisfied with the prospect of living on. But the letting go of the goner is possibly only because, over the time of mourning, the requisite expenditure of energy has dissipated and the task is more easily done than said. As Klein shows in the essay that follows, Freud's closing words could also signify that the time of mourning undoes the initial period at the end of the death sentence handed down to the survivor according to which he must choose either to let the lost object go or to join the deceased.

What Freud did for mourning or unmourning, namely fix the focus on the object relationship, Klein did for the inner world of identifications, which are similarly embodied and personified as object relations. Already the infant builds the internal world through friendly canni-

balism of the parents. Even though altered by the infant's own phan-
tasms and impulses, the opening installation of the inner world still
corresponds to actual experiences and impressions gained from people
and the external world. Unpleasant experiences out there cause reality
testing to turn inward. In the face of dangers the child senses that he can
retain or re-attain his objects as well as their love for him and his love for
them, and thus preserve or re-establish the internal good life. Enjoyable
experiences are equally necessary though differently applied: they are
the proofs that loved objects inside as well as outside are not injured,
are safe, are not turning vengeful. If the living is easy and love and trust
increase, then the baby is able 'to test his inner reality by means of outer
reality' (Klein 1984b: 347).

Freud argues that the mourner reinstates the lost object inside the
ego. Klein adds: 'In my view, however, he not only takes into himself
(reincorporates) the person whom he has just lost, but also reinstates his
internalised good objects' (1984b: 353). Mourning thus means for Klein
in the first place to 'rebuild with anguish the inner world, which is felt
to be in danger of deteriorating and collapsing' (354). Only if life inside
and outside can be secured as going on after all, can the mourner preserve the loved object, admit him within the haunted corpus. Mourning
is just one more unhappy experience that can deepen the relationship
to inner objects and thus allow one to dig in with one's ghosts. There is
even a happiness involved in regaining them after you felt they were long
gone upon impact of the new identifiable loss. Mourning is not about
contact with loss, except as developmentally first and, over time, repeat-
able. The contact person however joins the other identifiable ghosts in
the inner sanctum, which is what the next new loss will also ultimately
threaten.

Émilie Deleuze builds her film out of the momentum of catching up
with the breach of continuity error and folds out from this movement the
double take of Lucas's unmourning, which first eclipsed his inner world
in the guise of a sinister underworld returning from the repressed, but
then, via the relationship to Mister V, also began to shore up the inner
world at its foundations and re-secure his internal good objects. After a
day of training in the field, which we followed through a series of wild
and beautiful jumps, Luigi declared that he was 'doing something right
for a change'. This time Lucas acquiesced without protest (for a change).
On the eve of Luigi's fatal accident, then, the brothers saw eye to eye on
the change that Mister V introduced. The horse was already restoring
the underworld to its inner world status, which, bigger than the two of
them, continued to stand before one brother when the other went.

According to Klein, the resecuring of primal objects that opens up the receiving line for reunion with one's departed must ultimately fail to integrate the unmournable lost object, whose group-psychological mascot remains the critter. 'Integration', which entered the psychoanalytic lexicon via Klein's 'Mourning and Its Relation to Manic-Depressive States', is the process that helps shore up the foundations of the inner world, which must bear up anew under the brunt of yet another occasion for mourning work. In time, integration became Klein's watchword for the work fundamental to successful psychoanalytic treatment.

But in her posthumously published essay 'On the Sense of Loneliness', Klein (1984c) recognised in loneliness the inevitable breakup of the therapeutic aim of integrated development. Klein presents a patient's field-mouse trip. While out in the country her patient caught a mouse for his young child back home to keep as a pet, carefully packed it in a box inside the boot of his car, and then forgot about it for a day. In the meantime it had eaten its way out of the box and crawled off to die. The story sparks association in session with 'dead people for whose death he felt to some extent responsible though not for rational reasons' (1984c: 309). According to Klein, the mouse stands for a split-off part of his self, which is lonely and deprived. By identifying with his child he too felt deprived of the mouse, his good object inside his auto, his self. By taking the object in he felt guilty and feared that it might turn retaliatory. The mouse also stands for a neglected woman: during the vacation break that had just concluded not only had he been left alone by the analyst but the analyst, too, had been 'neglected and lonely' (309).

The patient was claustrophobic via projective identification into the mother and re-introjection of these tight quarters as a crowd of resentful internal objects hemming him in. Thus he tended to feel lonely in town and free of loneliness in nature. Although in childhood he indulged in the usual scientific-destructive explorations of nature, like robbing nests, he felt that, unlike his mother, for whose frailty he felt terribly responsible, nature repaired herself. He thus transferred idealisation from his mother to nature (1984c: 308).

At first Klein introduces her client as the unlikely patient: 'a man who was not unhappy or ill, and who was successful in his work and in his relationships' (1984c: 307). And yet there was this sense of loneliness lingering and malingering from childhood which he still experienced while in town but which he felt he had overcome in relation to the countryside. Through his inner-outer relationship to nature, Klein's 'successful' patient comments, he had 'taken in an integrated object' (308). This self portrait of the patient as analyst's pet signals the kind of success that awaits wreckage.

Klein begins again with the internalised dead mouse, and then raises the ideal twin, unborn or undead. The plight of the only or youngest child, according to Klein, is the burden of death wishes directed against the unborn siblings thus barred from conception or birth. But in the end everyone is the lonely child who must summon imaginary twinships to bide the long time of the prolonged falling short of integration. Klein's patient had throughout childhood longed for a playmate his own age, a longing that was 'the result of feeling that split-off parts of his self could not be regained' (1984c: 309). Finally Klein, the neglected woman, brings it all home in the transference.

> The link with similar feelings toward his mother became clear in the material, as did the conclusion that he contained a dead or lonely object, which increased his loneliness. This patient's material supports my contention that there is a link between loneliness and the incapacity sufficiently to integrate the good object as well as parts of the self which are felt to be inaccessible. (1984c: 309)

While we are left in suspense regarding the outcome of Klein's work with this patient, the main text conveys the irreversibility of unmourning, which must be carried forward. Klein's reading of the destinal failure of integration to overcome its defence contact with disintegration brings us before the inevitable 'feeling of irretrievable loss' (1984c: 301). Klein's revalorisation of reality testing and integration in mourning attended her theorisation of the inner world, whereby she sought to contain the recent past and render it accessible. Following each direct contact with the other's death the inner world must be reinstalled – this is the essential work of mourning – between inside and outside. It is the final frontier of the reality for which we ultimately test, the reality of loss. In 'On the Sense of Loneliness', the plain text of Klein's melancholia, there is just the same an affirmation of a greater relationality basic to endless mourning. Loneliness tests the rule of relationality that the field mouse brought home to Klein's patient in denial. 'The lost parts too, are felt to be lonely' (302). The constituent parts kept apart by the inevitable shortcoming of mournful integration are parties to a parting that connects them, but as lonely together. The animal relation is the rehearsal and repetition of this integration in loneliness.

Notes

1. I also consulted the original version, 'Bauen Wohnen Denken', in *Vorträge und Aufsätze*, Pfullingen: Verlag Günther Neske, 1954, pp. 139–56. Freud's notion of the date mark was introduced in 'Creative Writers and Daydreaming' (1958a).
2. I also consulted the original, 'Totem und Tabu', in *Studienausgabe*, vol. 9, Frankfurt a/M: S. Fischer Verlag, 1974.
3. Her statement of 'the problems' can be found on p. 126.
4. The focus of my reconstruction of the compatibility of the Deleuze and Guattari reading of the animal relation and Freud's in *Totem and Taboo* is based on the tenth plateau.
5. I pursue this at greater length in my *I Think I Am: Philip K. Dick* (2011). Diana Thater invited me to compose a first formulation of my notion of the unmournable animal death in 'Pet Grief' (2009), my contribution to the catalogue for her show in Graz.
6. See, for example, Winnicott 1992. I follow out a Winnicottian allegory of 'hope' in my genealogy of postwar worlds, *Germany: A Science Fiction* (2014). A more American-centric approach to this era via slasher and splatter films can be found in my book *The Psycho Records* (2016).
7. The actor Mathieu Demy, who plays Lucas, is the son of the legendary director, while the other protagonist, Mister V, was edited together by Deleuze and Mathilde Muyard out of footage shot of seven different horses.
8. 'Group Psychology and the Analysis of the Ego' (Freud 1958b) and 'Notes upon a Case of Obsessional Neurosis' (1958c), respectively.
9. I read the German translation (Deleuze 1992).
10. Binswanger 1992. For this edition Walter Seitter translated Foucault's introduction to the 1954 French translation of Binswanger's study.
11. Around both Lacan on Hamlet and Klein on the inner world I illuminated in my study *SPECTRE* (2013) the significance of the third-party underworld organisation in the Cold War world of James Bond, which Ian Fleming introduced in anticipation of the crossover into the film medium.

References

Binswanger, L. (1992), *Traum und Existenz*, Bern/Berlin: Verlag Gachnang & Springer.

Canetti, E. (1984), *Crowds and Power*, trans. Carol Stewart, New York: Farrar Straus Giroux.

Cavell, S., C. Diamond, J. McDowell, I. Hacking and C. Wolfe (2009), *Philosophy and Animal Life*, New York: Columbia University Press.

Deleuze, G. (1992), *Woran erkennt man den Strukturalismus?*, trans. Eva Brückner-Pfaffenberger and Donald Watts Tuckwiller, Berlin: Merve Verlag.

Deleuze, G. and F. Guattari (1987), *A Thousand Plateaus: Capitalism and Schizophrenia*, trans. B. Massumi, Minneapolis: University of Minnesota Press.

Freud, S. (1958a), 'Creative Writers and Daydreaming', *The Standard Edition of the Complete Psychological Works*, trans. and ed. James Strachey, vol. 9, London: The Hogarth Press, pp. 141–54.

Freud, S. (1958b), 'Group Psychology and the Analysis of the Ego', *The Standard Edition of the Complete Psychological Works*, trans. and ed. James Strachey, vol. 18, London: The Hogarth Press, pp. 65–144.

Freud, S. (1958c), 'Notes upon a Case of Obsessional Neurosis', *The Standard Edition of the Complete Psychological Works*, trans. and ed. James Strachey, vol. 10, London: The Hogarth Press, pp. 155–249.

Freud, S. (1958d), 'Totem and Taboo', *The Standard Edition of the Complete Psychological Works*, trans. and ed. James Strachey, vol. 13, London: The Hogarth Press, pp. 1–161.

Hearne, V. (1987), *Adam's Task: Calling Animals by* Name, London: Heinemann.

Heidegger, M. (1984), 'Zarathustra's Animals', in *Nietzsche: The Eternal Recurrence of the Same*, trans. and ed. David Farrell Krell, San Francisco: Harper and Row, pp. 45–8.

Heidegger, M. (2001), 'Building Dwelling Thinking', in *Poetry, Language, Thought*, trans. Albert Hofstadter, New York: Harper, Perennial Classics, pp. 143–59.

Jung, C. J. (1974), 'The Psychology of Dementia Praecox', in *The Psychology of Dementia Praecox*, trans. R. F. C. Hull, Princeton: Princeton University Press, pp. 3–151.

Klein, M. (1984a), 'Infantile Anxiety Situations Reflected in a Work of Art and in the Creative Impulse', in *Love, Guilt and Reparation and Other Works 1921– 1945*, New York: The Free Press, pp. 210–18.

Klein, M. (1984b), 'Mourning and Its Relation to Manic-Depressive States', in *Love, Guilt and Reparation and Other Works 1921–1945*, New York: The Free Press, pp. 344–69.

Klein, M. (1984c), 'On the Sense of Loneliness', in *Envy and Gratitude and Other Works 1946–1963*, New York: The Free Press, pp. 300–13.

Lacan, J. (1982), 'Desire and the Interpretation of Desire in *Hamlet*', ed. Jacques-Alain Miller, trans. James Hulbert, in *Literature and Psychoanalysis. The Question of Reading: Otherwise*, ed. Shoshana Felman, Baltimore: The Johns Hopkins University Press, pp. 11–52.

Rickels, L. A. (2014), *Germany: A Science Fiction*, Fort Wayne: Anti-Oedipus Press.

Rickels, L. A. (2010), *I Think I Am: Philip K. Dick*, Minneapolis: University of Minnesota Press.

Rickels, L. A. (2009), 'Pet Grief', in *Diana Thater: gorillagorillagorilla*, Cologne: Walther König, pp. 64–73.

Rickels, L. A. (2016), *The Psycho Records*, London and New York: Wallflower Press.

Rickels, L. A. (2013), *SPECTRE*, Fort Wayne: Anti-Oedipus Press.

Sharpe, E. F. (1950), 'Certain Aspects of Sublimation and Delusion', in *Collected Papers on Psycho-Analysis*, ed. Marjorie Brierley, London: Hogarth Press, pp. 125–36.

Winnicott, D. W. (1992), 'The Antisocial Tendency', in *Through Paediatrics to Psychoanalysis: Collected Papers*, New York and London: Brunner-Routledge, pp. 306–15.

PART IV

ANIMAL RE-TERRITORIALISATIONS IN ART AND CINEMA

Chapter 12

Meditation on the Animal and the Work of Art

Gregg Lambert

> To constitute a territory is for me very near to the origin of the work of art.
> (Deleuze 1996: 'A is for Animal')

In the first of the series of interviews conducted by Claire Parnet, entitled *Abécédaire*, 'A for Animal', Deleuze makes some very interesting and telling statements concerning the relation between a territory and art that often bears a relation to the animal, or to the notion of 'becoming-animal', which is frequently described as a process of 'creating a relation to territory' in reference to the artist and the writer. For Deleuze, the animal has a privileged and very specific relation to the notions of territory and world, one that is based on a relative number of affects and on a process of selection (i.e. the extraction of singularities from a milieu or environment [*Umwelt*]). Very simply put, the animal entertains a relation to its world that is produced in terms of a relation to a distinctive territory, whereas the human is found to have a relation to its world, but no relation to a distinctive territory (i.e. the human being has no proper territory of its own). However, in Deleuze, the writer and the artist are often described as beings who enter into a process of becoming in which the subject loses its own proper identity as an individual or a human being and enters into a process that closely approximates, to employ Heidegger's term, the animal's 'captivation' or 'absorbtion' (*Benommenheit*) by its environment – even though the artist or the writer produces a specific world by extracting lines, fragments, colours, visions or scenes from their immediate environment (*Umwelt*) to compose a territory.

For the moment, I will leave the distinction between the concepts of territory and world undefined, since we could just as easily say that in the process of landscape painting, for example, the painter extracts these different components from his or her surrounding environment (*Umwelt*) in order to compose with them a specific world that is expressed by the work of art. Nevertheless, from the distinctive vantage point produced by this composition the form of territory neither belongs to the external environment, nor is it simply a representation of the external environment as such. Indeed, in extracting lines or colours, it is more accurate to say that something has been subtracted from the environment and reproduced in such a way that it now expresses a point of view that cannot find its cause in an external object of perception. At the same time, this new viewpoint cannot be reduced to a subjective point of view neither, but rather exists as an impersonal and yet distinct vision that is now added back to the former world in the manner of a new territory that could never be apprehended by perception or imagination alone. To describe this process in the terms employed by Deleuze and Guattari themselves: by extracting lines, scenes, fragments, even words and images, the artist or writer deterritorialises the given world, which at the same time, is reterritorialised in the specific territory of the artwork. Thus, as Deleuze suggests in 'A for animal', the three primary affects that are located in the animal world – colour, line and song – can also be found at the origin of the work of art. This, in turn, leads directly to the statement given in the above epigraph, namely, that the constitution of a territory is very proximate to the origin of the artwork.

In understanding this comparison, however, we must first determine the meaning of 'extraction' or 'selection' by a process that defines the nature of what is called, in a psychological sense, 'perception' – yet one that cannot be applied, or can only be applied, in a metaphorical sense when referring to, for example, how cells perceive other cells or how plants and animals 'perceive' their environments through signals, or 'trigger signs' (*signes déclencheurs, Merkmalträger*). Consequently, what Deleuze calls extraction is the biological selection of a constellation of affective possibilities that determine the animal's relation to the environment only in terms of active and passive affects that determine the body. Drawing on the comparative psychology of ethology, and especially von Uexküll's semiotic theory, which is then combined with Spinoza's theory of parallelism, the 'body' is not defined in terms of genus and species, but rather in terms of the number of affects that defines its affective capacity (*conatus*). As Deleuze and Guattari write:

> In the same way that we avoided defining a body by its organs and functions, we will avoid defining it by Species or Genus characteristics; instead we will seek to count its affects. This kind of study is called ethology, and this is the sense in which Spinoza wrote a true Ethics. A racehorse is more different from a workhorse than a workhorse is from an ox. Von Uexküll,

in defining animal worlds, looks for the active and passive affects of which the animal is capable in the individuated assemblage of which it is a part. (1987: 257)

For example, we can turn to the animal world to demonstrate how certain animals create a territory by the emission of signals. Birds, for example, produce specific territories through their songs and other birds will not enter, as do dogs with their barking or howling, while theirs produce a specific territory by means of lines that are drawn from their bodies. For example, spiders produce a territory as a web derived from the filament of their abdomen, wolves employ their urine to draw a territory as a sign to other wolves, and grizzly bears use their claws to scratch the bark from trees as a warning to other members of their species. Except in those special cases when a territory is constructed as 'an apparatus of capture', as in the case of spiders, or the mating songs of birds, in many of these examples the territory is made as warning: 'do not enter!' Here, we can see from these examples that a territory is very useful in that it defines an ecosphere that is capable of supporting the life of the organism (the avoidance of overpopulation, for example), and it is in this sense we can demonstrate a lack of such an economical relation of territory and population in the human species, which overflows all other zoological territories in occupying a world. Yet how might we compare the ecological and biological sense of the usefulness of territory to the work of art, and further to this ask: do artists and writers employ lines to constitute a territory for the same reason?

Passing over this question for a moment, let us first examine more closely the example of a tick given in *A Thousand Plateaus*. How does a tick 'perceive' in its own particular environment, that is, how does a tick express the relation between its body and the territory it inhabits? Here I draw two examples from *A Thousand Plateaus* that define the tick's world in terms of both the process of extraction of four basic affects (*climbing* onto a branch, *smelling* the blood of an animal, *dropping* from the branch, and *burrowing* under the animal's hide to gorge itself on its blood), and in terms of two limits or durations (the short duration of feeding after which the tick dies, and the longer duration of waiting whilst fasting, which can sometimes last for many years). In any case, what Deleuze seems to emphasise in both discussions is the incredible economy of the world of a tick – one constituted by a minimum of these four affects. It is through these four affects that a tick is capable of expressing a relation to the world that is comprised only of these affects, a sense of 'world' that has no reference to a larger world. There is only the world that is constituted by these four affects: the branch, the tree, the passing animal, the smell of blood wafting in the air, the hairy back, the thickness of the hide, the sweet taste of the meal; but also affects of duration that are both internal and external to the tick – the period of waiting, and then the sudden plunge onto the back of the passing animal, followed immediately by death. These minimal affects define a tick's world and their paucity could be called, following Heidegger, a 'poor' (*Arm*) and impoverished sense of world, even though the world of the tick is also incredibly rich with intensities in comparison with the human world.

Deleuze constantly betrays his fascination for certain animals on the basis of their so-called 'poverty', that is, by the fact that they can create a world from only a few singularities (a tick, louse, a flea, spiders *à la Spinoza*, etc.). If his choice of animals to admire appears somewhat bizarre – as it does to Claire Parnet in the interview, who calls Deleuze's choice of animals 'disgusting' – it is not at all bizarre if we consider the tick from the viewpoint of 'life itself'. That is, how amazing it is that a form of life like this could evolve from the 'specifically articulated' (Heidegger 1995: 168) or the immanence that the tick has to its environment; however, this articulation must already exist as a condition in order to extract from this environment an individuated world that expresses the area or manner of being. In other words, there must be branches and trees and an innate ability of the tick to know how to climb. There must also be a healthy supply of herbivores, omnivores and carnivores who just happen to loiter underneath branches with enough frequency to support this particular life form. Finally, there must be the scent of blood that is carried on the wind, and the development of the sense of smell to a most sensitive degree, much more sensitive than the human sense of smell, which, if we remember Freud's theory of the evolution of the five senses, was sacrificed at the expense of elevation when the human evolved from quadruped to biped. This loss is further characterised by the shift from the instinctual environment of the animal to the civilised world of the human being, which demanded, as the price of entry, a significant degree of olfactory repression. Yet here, on the basis of Freud's hypothesis, we also see an area in which the animal expresses a much more intensive (i.e. 'wealthy') relation to the environment, one in which it is the human who appears rather 'poor' in comparison. Furthermore, when compared not to the animal, but to 'life in general', the human is by contrast not simply poor, but absolutely impoverished. As Heidegger writes, 'on the contrary, life is a domain that possesses a wealth of openness with which the human world may have nothing to compare' (1995: 255). Here we find no basis for comparing human life and life itself, which is to say, 'life as a whole' – the manifold totality of living beings in both a zoological and ontological sense (as either the diversity of genus and species, or the total ensemble of living beings).

In the 1929 seminar where we find the infamous statement that the animal is 'poor (*weltarm*) in world', it is true that Heidegger restricts the openness of the animal life by a captivation of its own organs, which *absorb* the animal into the circle of its surrounding environment (*Umwelt*, literally meaning 'around world'), thus denying the animal any access to 'manifestness of beings *as such*' (1995: 236 ff.). It is the character of captivation (i.e. complete absorption by its environment) that Heidegger determines as the essential property of the animal *qua* animal, which allows this sense of captivation to stand out and become a defining characteristic in the distinction between 'an environment' and 'a world'. In other words, according to Heidegger, 'captivation' (being completely absorbed into an environment) is the peculiar property that defines the animal *qua* animal – it is what is proper to the relation between the animal and the environment that defines its proper being, and defines its manner of living its own peculiar relation to its surrounding world (231 ff.). (For example, the tick expresses a peculiar relation of a long duration followed by the relative short duration of activity and death that defines the peculiar manner of 'living' that is the peculiar property of a tick). Here, we should recall that the translation of the term 'peculiar' is related to the German *Eigenlich*, and is derived from the noun *Eigentum* (property). In their translation of *Zein und Zeit*, Macquarrie and Robinson often employ the term 'authentic', which has had some unfortunate consequences if we remember Adorno's scathing critique of what he called Heidegger's 'jargon of authenticity', which might be more properly phrased as Heidegger's 'jargon of peculiarity' (233n). However, what Heidegger was referring to as *Eigentümlichkeit* (normally, 'peculiarity') was not what we normally associate with authenticity (being proper to oneself), but instead refers to a property that is peculiar to this being, concerning the appearance of a specific trait that stands out as remarkable, in the sense of not finding this property in other beings, thus constituting the being's own peculiarity, or in other terms, its singularity.

Much has been said and written on Heidegger's statement that the 'animal is poor in world', but not much attention has been paid, first of all, to his peculiar choice of terms to describe the relationship between animal and world. We must remember, to begin with, that at this point of his analytic of finitude the definition of 'a world' is not yet given, and so Heidegger must choose the customary path of presupposing a 'human world' that is somehow different from the animal world. Therefore, according to this method of 'transposition' into the animal world (which Heidegger remarks as a peculiar capacity that belongs to human *Dasein*, one which is already demonstrated in the knowledge of biology and zoology), he also acknowledges that this 'transposedness' will not allow him simply to 'go along with the animal', and will not any gain any access to the animal's world *as such* (1995: 210). 'Transposedness into the animal world [via the knowledge of biology and zoology] can belong to the essence of man without this necessarily meaning that we can transpose ourselves directly into an animal's world or even that the *animal in general* has "a world"' (210, emphasis mine). Note that this definition of a capacity or possibility of transposedness is, at the same time, accompanied by a refusal or limitation which, at this point, primarily describes man's access to the animal world. Nevertheless, it is this peculiar possibility of *having* and *not-having*, which originally belongs to man, that is transposed onto the animal's relation to world.

Why? And, more importantly, why does Heidegger choose the term 'poverty' to define the animal's relation to world? As he asks, '*what is this poverty in world* of the animal?' (1995: 211). Of course, in the recent scholarship on the animal, many humans have been offended by this statement on behalf of animals and other nonhuman forms of life (e.g. plants, cells, machines, etc). And yet, we must recall that Heidegger is pursuing the difference between these forms of life and a traditional (i.e. metaphysical) concept of 'animality', beginning with Aristotle, according to which the animal is usually defined as lacking something essential (i.e. speech, language, reason, etc.) that, at the same time, is immediately assumed as *proper* to man – that is to say, as something given, immediately present to hand, as naturally belonging to human nature as a distinctive 'property'. Is Heidegger saying this also? Is he merely repeating a dominant statement that he draws from this tradition to define the relation between man and animal in terms of the lack of a certain capacity, or of a particular attribute? No. He is saying something different, but precisely by repeating this dominant statement in the form of a fundamental question concerning the relation between a human understanding of 'poverty' and the traditional (i.e. metaphysical) concept of animality, that is, 'to approach the essence of poverty in world by clarifying animality itself' (211):

> Even after carefully determining what it means to be deprived of something, we still do not possess an adequate answer. Why not? Because we

cannot simply conjure up the essence of poverty in world from out of a formal concept of deprivation. We can grasp this poverty only if we first know what world is. Only then are we in a position to say *what* it is that the animal is deprived of, and thus to say what this poverty in world implies. First of all we must pursue the concept of world by examining the essence of man and the world-forming character we have claimed for him: we must first examine the positive moment, then the negative moment and finally the lack. (211)

Note that in the above statement Heidegger never says that the animal is deprived of something definite like speech or language. He only says that the animal is, in a certain sense, deprived of 'world' – but again, we must ask, which world? I ask because, at this point, it is precisely the concept of world that has not yet been positively defined, nor can it be assumed as something already given! Consequently, the dominant statement that 'the animal is poor in world' could only be understood from the perspective of a previous metaphysical determination of animality, which causes the animal to appear more or less like a poor human being, except that in this case, the animal is found to be poorer than even the poorest of human beings, since it is also lacking something essential that belongs to the human being; as a result, the animal appears as a being who is both *relatively* poor and, at the same time, *absolutely* deprived.

Here we find a general definition of animality in Heidegger's analysis referring to a peculiar being that exists on a scale beween mere possibility and absolute deprivation. And yet, it is worth noting that the human is not defined as 'wealthy' in world, but rather as 'world-forming', which is not the same thing as being wealthy in all cases as a species being (and especially, if we remember, in comparison with 'life itself', in which the human appears absolutely impoverished). Moreover, let us recall that poverty, deprivation, is defined by a form of having in the mode of not having: the poor are poor because their mode of access to capital in order to acquire private property is defined in terms of deprivation – i.e. in not having access to capital, they are deprived of wealth defined in terms of private property. Do the rich not also have 'more world' than the poor if we employ the same analogy? Therefore, are animals poor or deprived of world in this sense of deprivation as well, and not by any so-called 'natural determination' of their species, but rather by an effect of a technological possibility that can be expressed as 'world-forming'? If so, then Heidegger's use of the terms of 'poverty' and 'wealth' might lead us to a more Marxist understanding of the concept of animality, which can also be found at the basis for a materialist determination of the division of labour, and especially to what Marx and Engels often referred to as the 'bestialisation' of labour-power. However, what would function as the equivalent of the access to the means of production if we were to follow this Marxian analogy? In other words, what would the animal become if it were suddenly given the possibility of being 'world-forming' like the human being? And yet, Heidegger's own definition of the animal already gives to the animal this possibility, or, in Aristotelian terms, this potentiality of becoming *weltbildend*. According to Heidegger's term, animals are animals only because they have this potentiality in the form of deprivation. They are merely deprived human beings. Therefore, we might conclude that what appear as animals are merely an extreme determination of the same principle of 'deprivation' according to which the poor are also compared to animals. But, then, the animal *qua* animal disappears. I think this is Heidegger's entire question concerning the animal: that the determination of animality that appears in the form of a species distinction may, in fact, not exist naturally. To put this differently: that what can be shown to exist in biological and zoological terms does not necessarily lead to the metaphysical determination of the species distinction between human and animal, nor even to the multifarious distinction of 'life in general', but will only lead us to a particular environment that is peculiar to human beings, which we will also find to be inhabited by other living beings such as animals and plants, and even non-living things such as machines, tables and all manner of objects as well.

At this point, I will skip to the conclusion of a very long exposition of Heidegger's seminar and simply ask the following question: what is this environment that is peculiar to man? Heidegger chooses to call it 'a world', but this is only defined negatively in contrast to the environment occupied by the animal, which is formed by what Heidegger calls (following von Uexküll) the expression of an 'eliminative character' (*Enthemmung*) of openness that is particular to an animal's complete absorption into its environment. In fact, it is through the process of eliminative behaviour that the environment is first produced in the form of an encirclement (*Umringen*) that is brought about (*errungen*) in relation to 'a continual production of an emptiness' where the particular animal lives. We can understand this production of emptiness, for example, as the air where the bird flies, or the ocean where the fish swims. In order for this particular form of life to occur and become proper to itself, there must be the eliminative character that defines its relation to an environment that is proper to it, and this is why we find so many birds in the air, and so many fish in the ocean. (Of course, there are exceptions in each species as if there is an essential indecision of life itself concerning the proper environment for each species, and the evolutionary process seems to always find ways to create new species to populate every kind of environment that exists, in which living is possible.) Is there such an environment, like water for fish or air for birds, that basically defines the nature of the emptiness in which the human dwells? Of course, we would not have to consider this question for very long before determining that there is no proper environment for the human, no particular form of emptiness that determines its own proper element, no place where we would normally expect to find the human species, unless we say that the earth itself is our particular ring, our encirclement, our species' environment. And yet, this would not be correct either, or at least not for long, as humans travel through a new emptiness, outer space, and visit other planets in order to colonise them and extract new sources of life for our species. Perhaps it is in this sense that the human is world-forming, meaning producing new environments, wider and wider circles of being, and even greater and more infinite spaces of emptiness in the totality of beings, in order to populate these vast spaces of emptiness and fill them with our species' life. Consequently, it now appears that there is no space, no environment, that is ultimately proper to man, since we find him in every environment: in the air, on the ocean, or underneath; beneath the earth, or in outer space. *Oh, how great is man! How wide his circle of life, how large a compass to measure his own peculiar form of emptiness!*

At the same time, we must also recognise that the more our species widens its circle, producing new manners of populating the emptiness that we dwell in, the more the human species 'encircles' other species and incorporates them into its own circle of life, which means that these other beings and species become incorporated into the emptiness we produce in our expansion. Consequently, animals (and indeed plants, material, or any object that can be identified with a particular area of being) become part of the empty space produced and in which the human species dwells. For example, it is precisely because of this emptiness that now determines the animal to live within our encirclement, that the animal can be slaughtered and eaten, because its being is reduced to emptiness and the human needs this emptiness in order to live and to produce its own existence. It becomes a justification for eating animals and soon the very condition of the existence for certain animals that are produced as the empty space in which the human dwells. I think we have now arrived at a point of understanding the 'peculiarity that is proper' to our species, which is that we have no proper environment. The human, as world producing, defines a particular form of life that 'encircles' every other living thing, thereby reducing them to the emptiness in which our own life is brought about and even increases its power over Life itself. Even our increasing knowledge of cellular biology is part of this process, which in the last analysis is a purely aggressive and dominating struggle (*Ringen*) to maintain this encircling ring or sphere (*Welt*) within which a specifically articulated form of life can appear. It is this struggle for the total encirclement of 'life in its generality' that Heidegger defines as our proper peculiarity as a species, and it is the fate of all other forms of life to become incorporated into the expanded circle and our struggle against the opposing power of life itself.

It might appear that I have simply become sidetracked by speaking of territory in terms of Heidegger's reading of the animal, but I do not think this is the case. And yet, we must also avoid making the territory that specifically pertains to art or writing simply a metaphor of the animal territory – which is why I raised the question of its 'usefulness' in a biological sense, which is not easily apparent and may in fact be impossible. Thus the territory that pertains to art is 'useless' in a biological or zoological sense, and does not correspond to a need on the level of the species or the organism. Therefore, the question must be phrased in the following manner: *If* the artwork produces a territory, then what is the form of territory that is specific to the work of art? In fact, though by an indirect route, we might able to formulate a response to the earlier question of what use is the artwork. It is precisely because the human as a species has no relation to a territory or an environment, that the artwork becomes useful in producing a territory, or that there is a specific sense of territory that is produced by the artwork, and this has proved useful to the human. If there is no way of proving this usefulness in a biological determination, still there must be a manner of explaining the prevalence of this activity that belongs to our species; otherwise, how would you explain the sheer number of artworks produced by our species if it did not satisfy some fundamental need on the part of our species being? To put it more simply, because the human lacks a proper territory, she becomes that peculiar being who *produces* her own proper territory through the work of art.

Thus, in this manner art maps a territory or produces a new territory on the world that represents the body without organs. As Deleuze often recounts, according to the vision of Proust, 'the world becomes fragmented and fragmentary', but at the same time 'a whole that is produced alongside all of its parts' (1997: 131). This is the function of the territory created by art. For example, Virginia Woolf understood exactly how to make a territory in this manner, which is why Deleuze and Guattari always refer to her in their definition of the territory created by the novel or the artwork, as well as in their description of a world composed of pure haecceities, or writing as a rhizome:

> The becoming-evening, becoming-night of an animal, blood nuptials. Five o'clock is this animal! This animal is this place! 'The thin dog is running in the road, this dog is the road', cries Virginia Woolf. That is how we need to feel. Spatiotemporal relations, determinations, are not predicates of the thing but dimensions of multiplicities. The street is as much a part of the omnibus-horse assemblage as the Hans assemblage the becoming-horse of which it initiates. We are all five o'clock in the evening, or another hour, or rather two hours simultaneously, the optimal and the pessimal, noon-midnight, but distributed in a variable fashion. The plane of consistency contains only haecceities, along intersecting lines. Forms and subjects are not of that world. Virginia Woolf's walk through the crowd, among the taxis. Taking a walk is a haecceity; never again will Mrs. Dalloway say to herself, 'I am this, I am that, he is this, he is that.' And 'She felt very young; at the same time unspeakably aged. She sliced like a knife through everything; at the same time was outside, looking on ... She always had the feeling that it was very, very dangerous to live even one day.' Haecceity, fog, glare. A haecceity has neither beginning nor end, origin nor destination; it is always in the middle. It is not made of points, only of lines. It is a rhizome. (Deleuze and Guattari 1987: 263)

References

Deleuze, G. (1996), *L'Abécédaire de Gilles Deleuze*, dir. Pierre-André Boutang, Paris: Editions Montparnasse.

Deleuze, G. (1997), *Essays Critical and Clinical*, trans. D.W. Smith and M. Greco, Minneapolis: University of Minnesota Press.

Deleuze, G. and F. Guattari (1987), *A Thousand Plateaus: Capitalism and Schizophrenia*, trans. B. Massumi, Minneapolis: University of Minnesota Press.

Heidegger, M. (1995), *The Fundamental Concepts of Metaphysics: World, Finitude, Solitude*, trans. W. McNeill and N. Walker, Bloomington: Indiana University Press.

Chapter 13

Becoming-Animal Cinema Narrative

Dennis Rothermel

A passage in *A Thousand Plateaus* discusses the Hollywood horror film, *Willard* (1972, dir. Daniel Mann). It's 'a "B" movie perhaps, but a fine unpopular film ... because the heroes are rats' (Deleuze and Guattari 1987: 233). The account is in the first-person singular, excusing a possibly inaccurate account of the film; it consists of plot summary, without treatment of the filmmaker's style and philosophical voice. In his cinema books, Deleuze would not bother to mention whether a film was a B movie, or its popularity, or spend very much time on plot summary, or write in the first person, or mention any film or filmmaker devoid of elements of signature style and philosophically nuanced cinematic voice. Of the hundreds of films discussed in the two volumes, it is not common but it does happen that one can detect an inaccuracy in what Deleuze describes, but there is never an apology for lack of adequate memory. Indeed, for detailed commentary accomplished before the advent of readily available video copies of films, how much the accounts attest keen insights and solid memory is consistently impressive. The sentences in this passage about *Willard* in *A Thousand Plateaus* do not read like Deleuze. The conceptualisation is clunky and dependent upon simplistic associations with psychological behaviour. Perhaps the mention of Godard, but only in passing, was Deleuze's addition to Guattari's exposition of a favourite film, or perhaps it was Guattari's insertion by way of differentiating this discussion from the cinema books. Without trying to speculate too much on the genesis of this brief discussion during the collaboration between Guattari and Deleuze, we can at least see that this is not the sort of film discussion that was typical of Deleuze.

Deleuze's discussion of Robert Bresson's *Au hasard Balthazar* (1966) in *Cinema 1: The Movement-Image* identifies the donkey as 'a fifth type of character ... the beast possessing the innocence of him who does not have to choose', absorbing the wounding effects of human actors, and without being able to reach beyond those effects (1986: 119). Other passages from both volumes elaborate Bresson: his actors are pure automatons, 'bereft of ideas and feelings', revealed in medium shots of 'fragmented, disconnected visual space' (Deleuze 1989: 12, 172; 1986: 112).

Bresson's medium-distance shots in *Au hasard Balthazar* situate a normal visual standpoint at donkey height. The realm of action and drama is thus defined as within the donkey's existential terrain, although the camera never represents the donkey's POV precisely, with the exception when Balthazar is within sight of circus animals chained up in cages. Though the eye-line match is not unambiguous, it is clear that the animals are within view of each other, well enough to demonstrate implicitly their reciprocal cognisance that shackled donkey and caged animals are equally humiliated in their iron constraints. The movement and compositions in the film are horizontal – gentle, slow, cyclical reverberations reflective of the donkey's inscrutable swaying back and forth. The region in which the Bressonian automaton human models act is also the bordering region of the animal who is at once innocent and ineffectual but also the receptacle of affect. This is the realm – donkey height, equal to the middle of the human torso, the gut, as its centre – where transactions are consummated. It is where deeds are done, where people inflict and receive harm, despair, manipulation, suffering, neglect, cruelty, brutality, sexual aggression, isolation, malevolence, hatred, and so on. Balthazar is impervious to most of it – the donkey understands pain, terror, abuse, and also nurture, caring and affection. He catches the surplus antagonism that otherwise does not find sufficient channel for expiation among people. It is when there is no opposite flow – towards love and caring – that the donkey no longer has a place, and he perishes from hopelessness.

Even without the donkey there to witness it, this realm of impassive, unconscious transactions in deprivation of human soul pervades Bresson's cinema. This realm thus pinpoints a rare confluence of the discourse on capitalism and schizophrenia and the discourse on the movement-image and time-image. It will be that instance where the narrative entertains sorcery, where cinema is becoming-animal, which is hardly the same thing as an animal movie. It is, rather, a realm where the region of becoming-animal is inhabited by an animal who is there to monitor the progress of the narrative. Even in the absence of the donkey, this is the realm of becoming-animal in subsequent Bresson films. As rich as Bresson's cinema is, so has it engendered a rich legacy of scholarly commentary. But aside from the exploration of Bresson's assimilation of the art of painting (Watkins 2012), and aside from how *Au hasard Balthazar* foregrounds the presence and plight of the animal per se (Burt 2002: 191; Pick 2011: 188–93), this film realises a realm for the unfolding of a narrative centred within the cognisance of the animal.

Deleuze and Guattari have many things to say about becoming-animal, and, as is typical of Deleuzian terminology, it's not a term that is simply defined in a certain way and then applied so much as simply used repeatedly, for which the accumulating contexts delineate a rhizomatic spreading of improvisational signification. For it *not* to 'consist in playing animal or imitating an animal', or anthropomorphising the animal, 'the becoming-animal of the human being . . . is simultaneously an animal peopling', in which what matters aren't the characteristics of the animal, but 'modes of expansion, propagation, occupation, contagion, peopling' of the animal in human reality (1987: 238–9, 242). We can see these modes defining the narrative form of *Au hasard Balthazar*, and hence to exemplify *becoming-animal cinema narrative*. Four significations of becoming-animal apply well in the current context. First, 'writers are sorcerers because they experience the animal as the only population before which they are responsible in principle' (240). Although Balthazar inhabits the realm of the film's sorcery, the sorcerer is Bresson, not Balthazar, or any other character in the film.

Second, 'the one who is tortured is fundamentally one who loses his or her face, entering into a becoming-animal, a becoming-molecular, the ashes of which are thrown to the wind' (1987: 116). Balthazar retains his face, in spite of multiple torments, but the orientation is within that realm at donkey-height, where people see what their hands do but do not return the look. Marie is tormented and ultimately turns away, hiding her face, submitting to having been forced into becoming the animalised female flesh. Ben, in *Willard*, realises this sense of losing face only by having become anthropomorphised, which isn't the same thing as becoming-animal. Thus as Willard assimilates Ben, it is not Ben as animal other but as anthropomorphised human Other that Willard absorbs. The becoming is thus doubly transcendent, which is to say, religious transformation that is equivalently secular, in the guise of horror science-fiction fantasy. By contrast, Balthazar remains a donkey, and it is the *cinema narrative* – Bresson's sorcery – that engulfs becoming-animal.

Third, 'a becoming-animal always involves a pack, a band, a population, a peopling, in short, a multiplicity. We sorcerers have always known that' (1987: 239). Balthazar isn't part of a pack, but becomes the centrepoint around which the pack of human automaton model actors connect centripetally.

Fourth, Deleuze and Guattari associate anomalousness with becoming-animal as the 'phenomenon of bordering' the animal as pet, bordering the animal as reducible to its mythical attributes, and the animal as 'demonic . . . sorcerers . . . at the edge of the field or woods. They haunt the fringes' (1987: 240–1, 245, 246). The sorcerer forges an alliance with the exceptional individual in the pack, Balthazar for Bresson, or Moby-Dick for Ahab, and, better, for Melville. The bordering is a bordering for both the animal and for the sorcerer. In *Au hasard Balthazar*, the bordering is that donkey-height realm where desires find passionless modes of hand transactions.

Bresson's *Au hasard Balthazar* exemplifies these four aspects of becoming-animal. More recent instances include, though with different creations of the sorcerer haunting the fringes, Michelangelo Frammartino's *Le Quattro Volte* (2011), Bela Tarr's *The Turin Horse* (2011), and Ang Lee's *Life of Pi* (2012).

Tarr's eponymous Turin horse struggles to maintain a pace through the on-coming heavy, dusty wind. The man in the wagon the horse pulls exerts himself nearly as much as the horse – holding the reins, encouraging the horse forward and also himself leaning into the wind. There is a single pole attached to the wagon for the horse to pull on slightly from the side. So this struggle continues at an angle, with a significant amount of the work expended not serving to pulling the wagon directly forward. It renders the horse's gait awkward and stumbling. This goes on a long time during the continuous eight-minute-long take. Bela Tarr's camera keeps the struggling horse within the frame of action, and eventually drifting down in front, slightly from the side. This is the position where we can best understand the horse, whose head is bowed from the struggle to keep pulling the burden. It's where we look up slightly into the horse's face. It's a level lower than head-height for humans, even lower than midriff. So, actually, lower than where Bresson's camera gravitates to for Balthazar. This is the old worn-out and pathetic horse that Friedrich Nietzsche embraced once he saw its owner beat it cruelly on a street in Turin. Nietzsche soon fell into a catatonic collapse from which he never recovered. This film is about the horse, whose unchanging daily life consists of being fed where she is housed in the weathered barn next to the hovel of a house where the man lives with his grown daughter. Every morning the man and his daughter strap the harness on the horse and connect the harness to the wagon. It's an elaborate process, consisting of several dozen very specific tasks, which the man and his daughter perform in exact sequence, collaborating without a word on those tasks that require both their hands. He is hampered by the lack of use of his right arm. As regimented and mundane as is the horse's routine, so is theirs. They are as much harnessed by this quotidian procedure as the horse is. They hardly speak the live-long day. That night, in the dark, she wonders what it all means. He says he doesn't know. The incessant gale winds howl. The intermittent nondiegetic music soundtrack repeats a dour motif endlessly – enough so that not getting it out of your head later will ruin your mood.

The next day, after they have gone through the elaborate steps harnessing the horse, the horse refuses to pull the wagon, no matter how much the man yells and slaps the horse with the reins. So they reverse the elaborate procedure and put the horse and then the wagon back in the barn. Inside, following an equally elaborate procedure and still wordlessly, she helps her father out of his work clothes and into his more rugged home clothes. She cooks two potatoes. They each eat one, peeling the still hot potato with their fingers and eating pieces gingerly. They don't eat it all, though two meals of one potato each comprise all of their daily nutritional intake.

The next day the horse won't eat, and both the man and his daughter show more diminishment of their appetite. A neighbour comes by to resupply his brandy and rambles on about how everything in the world is degraded, for which the incessant gale is just a reminder. The man of the house calls his rant rubbish. The next day the well goes dry, and the man and his daughter can hardly eat. But their countenance hasn't changed – it could not be more dour than it was at the outset. So they pack up the essentials among their possessions into a handcart. There is nothing in the house that serves as anything other than pure utilitarian value. Nothing is special, nothing is decorative, nothing is frivolous, nothing is so much as embellished. For the sake of what value they have, they could be no worse or no better than the crude implements, furniture and clothing that they have. But at this point, their rough-hewn table and stools can't be taken with them, but clothing and bags of potatoes can. They bring the horse out and tether it to the back of the hand cart. The daughter pulls the cart from the front handle, and the man pushes from the one side with his good arm. They leave with the cart before the horse. They make their way to the top of the low ridge beyond the well, and disappear behind it – but only temporarily. They come back and return to the house and unpack the handcart. During that aborted trek away from the house, Tarr has his camera dangling low and off to the side in front of the daughter, just as it had been for the horse in the opening scene. This positioning now dominates even more.

The next day it is clear that the horse is ill, probably dying. The wind stops, but then it becomes inexplicably dark. They light the lanterns, but the flames go out and won't be rekindled. The embers in the stove also go out. The next day they try eating raw potatoes, but it's too much. They sit opposite at the table and stare at nothing, heads slightly bowed, like that of the horse. It has also been their common posture, but ever more so now.

Tarr composes the film in excruciatingly long takes – each one between five and ten minutes. Parts of these shots are stationary, and part travelling. The movement is smooth and unobtrusive, following the movements of the man and his daughter. Absolutely every single little movement in the tasks in their lives gets play. There is no cutaway, no jump-cutting to cut short an action. There is no continuity editing to smooth out our attention to a mode of presentation that downplays undramatic details and moments. This is a film – at 150 minutes – that intends to be excruciatingly tedious. As dulled as is the horse's temperament from a lifetime of cruel monotonous burden, so also are the lives of the man and his daughter. Contrary to what Nietzsche had challenged for the sake of a meaningful life, they are not the authors of their lives, no more than is the horse. And there is scant any more pleasure and purpose to their lives than what the horse enjoys. What governs their lives is the wind, the well, the marginal business for the man and his horse wagon in town, and the health of the horse. Same for the horse.

The man and his daughter are the tortured ones, who lose face though that's the least of what matters. They enter into a becoming-animal, but they have done so for so long that there is no more becoming to it. Certainly, their ashes are thrown to the wind, the gale wind that afflicts their world relentlessly. Together, the man, his daughter and the horse compose a herd, a multiplicity. Their lives are integrated completely and in detail every day. There is nothing that either the man or the daughter does that isn't connected with each other, or together with the horse. In this way their existence is a bordering – as much devoted and dependent upon the horse as the horse is upon her daily feed. The sorcerer, the one who constructs the world in which those who are becoming-animal inhabit and endure, is Bela Tarr, though his operatives lie within the story, which are the wind and the harness. For it is the wind that robs them of their appetite, their will to endure, that dries up the well, and which puts out the light. It is the harness that connects them inextricably with the animal that leads them in having-become-animal.

In *Le Quattro Volte*, an old goatherd dies alone and after a long decline. No one notices this in the small remote rural village where he had lived. But the man's dog and the goats know that they must go out to the pasture in the morning and return in the evening. Without anyone noticing, the dog figures out how to release the blocks in front of the wheels of a small truck, which then rolls down a short street and crashes open the gate to the goat pen. The dog then herds the goats out through the town and to the pasture. The continuous ten-minute-long take that captures this action is from a vantage point high above the street and goat pen. The dog runs deliberately from one point to another in its actions. But Frammartino's camera needs to adjust its angle only slightly. It is the dog's movements that dictate the camera's panning slightly back and forth. Like the man, his daughter and the horse in *The Horse of Turin*, the goatherd, the dog and the goats share a necessitating detailed quotidian routine that fills their day, with little else supplying meaning. And so they comprise a herd together, albeit with differing roles between man, dog and goats. Their simple, austere but gently bucolic life draws them into a bordering – both of the life of goatherd, dog and goats, and also relative to the separate goings-about of the town, for which the goatherd's business is effectively invisible. The goatherd is the tormented one, by illness and loneliness. He coughs his life away to the wind, and retrieves ashes – in the form of dust – from the sweepings of the village's church floor, from which he makes tea, believing it to be a curative. Finally, Frammartino surely is the sorcerer storyteller, but more than just his operative or just an accomplice, the dog is the sorcerer, telling the tale of the goatherd better than any alternative narrative could. Just as some films are actor's vehicles, where there isn't much more significance than what an actor's performance provides, in this film it is the dog that provides significance. So much and so palpably so, that a special award – the Palme Dog – was devised and awarded at the Cannes Film Festival.

The fixation evident in films in the recent revival of 3D cinema is to accentuate depth of field – particularly movement deep into the direction orthogonal to the screen, or in the opposite direction on the same virtual axis, deep into an audience's sense of real space. This becomes very quickly dull, and it will have been only a matter of time before some filmmaker did something more interesting with the form. Ang Lee has done so in his adaptation of *Life of Pi*. Lee effectively *bends depth*, *folding depths* of the sea in ever-shifting layers of movement, engendering that the sea seethes with a much richer topography of life and movement that can be seen from how we encounter its flat surface. Pi is the tormented one, heroic in his equanimity in the face of unimaginable hardship. The dwindling entourage of the tiger, the orangutan, the hyena and the zebra constitute a pack defined by their conflicting needs, which entail a reciprocal bordering amongst them, and an extreme bordering dividing them from the earthy environment normal to them. Ang Lee is certainly the sorcerer, the one who devises this cinema of the folding depths of the sea, but equally so is the novelist, who becomes translated into a character on the screen in the film. That novelist divines the substitutions in Pi's telling of the story years later. The zebra was the injured sailor, the hyena was the brutish cook, and the orangutan was Pi's mother. The tiger, though, was Pi – the ferocious animal he needed to become in order to deal with the hyena, not as his own form but as what accompanied him in the journey. The face of the tiger, submerged in the sea except for his piteous face staring up at Pi as the tiger clings to the life boat, tells that sharing of torment, which Pi in his effective and psychological ingenuity transforms into how he needs to be ferocious, and how he is also piteous just in having that need. So the story is about a fabulous sorcerer, with a sorcery greater than the novel, but for which Lee's inventive cinema in this film is the properly conceived form of cinema narrative.

With hints of the one who is tormented, herding, bordering and sorcery, we see filmmaking sorcery with, in order, a donkey as the on-screen operative, the wind as the sorcerer's operative, a dog as a sorcerer, and a young man who applies sorcery to himself and finds himself externalised in the accompanying tiger. The horizontal donkey-height gently swaying, the viewpoint from where a sway-back mare would be looking, from a height to follow a dog-sorcerer's methods, and the topology of the sea folded unfathomably, are the filmmakers' cinema sorcery to accompany the sorcerer's storytelling. The threshold of becoming-animal doesn't in these cases revert to anthropomorphism of the animal, humans becoming comically or magically animalistic, or by resorting to an animal's POV shot, which are all the cheap tricks of mainstream Hollywood film, certainly to include *Willard*.

In one of the more fascinating passages in the first volume of the film books, Deleuze builds a discussion of POV and shot-reverse-shot, beginning with a discussion of Christian Metz on these common compositional ingredients of filmmaking, and the conceptual inadequacy of the standard terms of subjective and objective views. This discussion then leads to Pier Paolo Pasolini's exploration of how cinema can effect the counterpart to free indirect discourse, which for Pasolini opens the opportunity for *free indirect cinema*, or *cinema poetry*, and specifically to embody cinematically the standpoint of social class and ethnicity. Deleuze, though, takes that idea further, to encompass how film artists can create a way of being appropriate to a film's subject and drama. Effectively, the film slides into that way of being, filling it up from the inside as formative of the representation rather than render the subject within the structure of representation. So that's what we have in these four films by Bresson, Tarr, Frammartino and Lee. Significantly, becoming-animal finds its best occurrence in cinema in these examples of free indirect cinema.

References

Burt, J. (2002), *Animals in Film*, London: Reaktion Books.

Deleuze, G. (1986), *Cinema 1: The Movement-Image*, trans. Hugh Tomlinson and Barbara Habberjam, Minneapolis: University of Minnesota Press.

Deleuze, G. (1989), *Cinema 2: The Time-Image*, trans. Hugh Tomlinson and Barbara Habberjam, Minneapolis: Univeristy of Minnesota Press.

Deleuze, G. and F. Guattari (1987), *A Thousand Plateaus: Capitalism and Schizophrenia*, trans. B. Massumi, Minneapolis: University of Minnesota Press.

Pick, A. (2011), *Creaturely Poetics: Animality and Vulnerability in Literature and Film*, New York: Columbia University Press.

Watkins, R. (2012), 'Robert Bresson's Modernist Canvas: The Gesture Toward Painting in *Au hasard Balthazar*', *Cinema Journal: The Journal of the Society for Cinema and Media Studies*, Vol. 51, No. 2, pp. 1–25.

Yin, J. (2013), 'Becoming-Animal: Becoming-Wolf in *Wolf Totem*', *Deleuze Studies*, Vol. 7, No. 3, pp. 330–41.

Chapter 14

Deleuze and Roxy: The Time of the Intolerable and Godard's *Adieu au langage*

Ronald Bogue

For Deleuze, the modern cinema is signalled by a crisis in the action-image and a concomitant confrontation with the intolerable, or that which exceeds absorption within the sensory-motor schema. In *Cinema 2*, Deleuze presents Jean-Luc Godard as one of the primary practitioners of the modern cinema, citing his films frequently to explicate various aspects of the time-image. Had Deleuze lived long enough to see Godard's 2014 3D film, *Adieu au langage*, he most certainly would have praised it as an exemplary exploitation and expansion of the possibilities of the time-image. He would also have seen in it a form of resistance to the intolerable brought forth through a becoming-animal, a becoming-dog that might well have surprised and amused him.

The time-image, for Deleuze, is an image steeped in crisis. In the closing chapter of *Cinema 1*, 'The Crisis of the Action-Image', Deleuze identifies five elements in postwar American cinema that signal a collapse of the commonsense spatio-temporal coordinates of the sensory-motor schema: the emergence of dispersive situations that replace the globalising or synthesising situations of the action-image; the deliberate weakening of linkages, connections and relations that provide continuity from one situation to another; the substitution of aimless wanderings, strolls and continual back-and-forth journeys for the goal-oriented plotlines of action-image films; the disenchantment of quotidian reality induced by an acute awareness of the world as a mere circulation of clichés; and the sense of the cliché-ridden image-world as an impenetrable conspiracy of control and manipulation (see especially Deleuze 1986: 205–11).

These symptoms of crisis in American film mark a partial collapse of the sensory-motor schema, but Deleuze finds the advent of its full collapse, and its positive exploitation, only in Italian Neorealism, the French New Wave and the films of Yasujiro Ozu. Here, amidst the breakdown of the sensory-motor schema, new images arise: opsigns and sonsigns,

signs of pure optic and sonic situations. Such signs emerge when characters suddenly experience their situation as intolerable. Deleuze explains
that the intolerable is not defined by some quantum of suffering, terror
or violence, but solely by the characters' inability to react to their situation within the structure of the sensory-motor schema. 'It is a matter of
something too powerful, or too unjust, but sometimes also too beautiful, and which henceforth outstrips our sensory-motor capacities ...
It can be a limit-situation, the eruption of a volcano, but also the most
banal, a plain factory, a wasteland' (1989: 18). In such moments of
crisis, when a coherent reaction to a situation becomes impossible, 'the
character or the viewer, and the two together, become visionaries' (19).
A 'seeing function' arises (19), *une fonction de voyance*, which makes
'pure vision a means of knowledge and action' (18, trans. mod.). The
clichéd images of the sensory-motor schema are shattered and opsigns
and sonsigns reveal things in themselves, 'literally, not metaphorically'
(20).

The vision of the intolerable is inherently political, in that the clichés
of the sensory-motor schema are shaped by 'our economic interests,
ideological beliefs and psychological demands' (1989: 20). To see the
intolerable is to protest that too much is tolerated, too much violence,
cruelty, ugliness and stupidity is assimilated within the quotidian sensory-motor schema. Foucault, says Deleuze, 'saw what was intolerable
in things' (1990: 103), and throughout his philosophy, he 'never stopped
being a *voyant*' (1988: 50). Likewise, 'the modern political cinema',
Deleuze argues, is 'no longer constituted on the basis of a possibility of
evolution and revolution, like the classical cinema, but on impossibilities, in the style of Kafka: *the intolerable*' (1989: 249).

The opsigns and sonsigns of the intolerable give rise to direct images
of time, as well as new relations between sight and sound and between
thought and image. The forces of opsigns and sonsigns 'enter into relation with yet other forces ... those of the time-image, of the readable image and the thinking image ... "chronosigns", "lectosigns" and
"noosigns"' (Deleuze 1989: 23). Chronosigns manifest themselves as
time-crystals, peaks of the present, sheets of the past, and the powers
of the false, which reveal 'temporality as a state of *permanent crisis*'
(112), a pure form or force of time that puts 'the notion of truth into
crisis' (130). With lectosigns, 'as the eye takes up a clairvoyant function
[*une fonction de voyance*], the sound as well as visual elements of the
image enter into internal relations which means that the whole image
has to be "read", no less than seen, readable as well as visible' (22). And
with noosigns, 'a camera-consciousness' emerges, one that is 'no longer

defined by the movements it is able to follow or make, but by the mental connections it is able to enter into' (23).

Godard's *Adieu au langage* could well serve as a textbook (or text-film) of the possibilities of chronosigns, lectosigns and noosigns.[1] For those who haven't seen the film, no synopsis can adequately convey a sense of the work. Perhaps best described as an essay collage, the seventy-minute film consists of roughly 370 shots, a few lasting from two to five minutes, most on the screen for less than half a minute, many for only a few seconds. If there is a central plot among the multiple scraps of incipient narrative (too numerous to detail here), it involves two couples, Josette-Gédéon and Ivitch-Marcus (played by actors remarkably similar in appearance), in both cases a married female and a male lover, who walk around naked or minimally clothed in what appears to be the same apartment. In separate scenes outside the apartment, a third man – presumably the husband – issues threats in German to each of the women, who in both cases respond, 'Ça m'est égal!' ('I don't care!'). The first couple picks up a stray dog at a gas station, and later they apparently leave the dog on a lakeside dock. The dog subsequently appears in the apartment of the second couple. But this parallel mirror-plot of the two couples and the dog and irate husband they have in common occupies only a small portion of the film, the action fragmented and intercut with diverse images and sounds that function as visual and sonic motifs rather than story elements. Well over half the script consists of citations from sociological, literary and philosophical works; the score is a collage of fragments from Alfredo Bandelli, Ludwig van Beethoven, Giya Kanchelli, Arnold Schönberg, Jean Sibelius, Valentin Silvestrov, Dobrinka Tabakova and Pyotr Tchaikovsky; and clips from various films are intercut or shown on a background TV screen in the couples' apartment: Alexander Aja's *Piranha 3D*, Artur Aristakisyan's *Ladoni*, Boris Barnet's *By the Bluest of Seas*, Howard Hawks's *Only Angels Have Wings*, Henry King's *The Snows of Kilimanjaro*, Fritz Lang's *Metropolis*, Rouban Mamoulian's *Dr Jekyll and Mr Hyde*, Jean-Pierre Melville's *Les Enfants terribles* and Robert Siodmak's *Menschen am Sonntag*.[2] The film also includes archival footage of Hitler, Nazi parades, Second World War bombers and bombs, helicopters, battle scenes and the Tour de France. Title cards and black screens punctuate the film, as do repeated shots of a ferry arriving and departing from a pier, shots of streets, houses, trees, rivers, lakes and clouds, and multiple clips of the dog Roxy.

The time of *Adieu au langage* defies any assimilation within a chronometric sensory-motor schema. Markers of the seasons – snow, autumn leaves, mature crops, early spring foliage – recur in random patterns. The central plot of the two couples implies the existence of parallel durations, unattached to any goal-driven narrative, and interconnected in ways that suggest numerous temporal bifurcations, loops and reiterations. The film's sonic and visual components possess the characteristic autonomy of lectosigns, each component exploring variations within its medium while intervening in the other. Voices overlap, shift from right to left channel, from live action stereo to full studio surround sound. Musical passages are cut at arbitrary places in the phrase and repeated in fragments of varying lengths. Off-camera sounds of gulls and a car crash have no visual justification, and off-camera gunfire is followed by images that only minimally integrate the sounds within an embryonic proto-narrative. The visual elements vary in texture from grainy cell-phone footage to high definition video, with a wide range of colour saturation, and the camera's presence is constantly asserted, through stuttered slow motion, hand-held camera jerks, diagonal and rotating framings, and so on. But perhaps most importantly, the film is in 3D, which Godard handles in a decidedly unconventional way. And if irrational cuts characterise noosigns, one could say that *Adieu au langage* is one giant noosign, each cut demanding that viewers puzzle out the mental relations that interconnect the film's images.

These chronosigns, lectosigns and noosigns are not mere formal inventions, but responses to the intolerable, both as articulated by the characters and as enunciated in the voice-overs. What is the intolerable in *Adieu au langage*? The list is long: consumerism, capitalism, colonialism, totalitarianism, the state, the society of the spectacle, Hitler, fascism, the holocaust and war in general. All these themes are addressed in Godard's preceding films, but here they are framed in terms of an additional intolerable element: what Primo Levi called the 'shame of being human' (a phrase Deleuze comments on in *Negotiations* (1990: 172)). Many critics argue that the film's star is Godard's dog, Roxy. And Roxy's function is to put into question human animality – to explore what humans and other animals have and don't have in common. In the film, humans are separated from animals by language, self-consciousness and war; what they share are sight, sound and bodies.

Images of war are scattered throughout the film: battle scenes, explosions, bombers, bombs falling in slow motion, and helicopters. From the onset, war and Roxy are juxtaposed. The film opens with six seconds of low-resolution, square-pixel war footage in saturated reds, blues, purples, oranges and yellows. Sounds of explosions, machine-gun fire and shouting voices accompany these arresting images. After a twelve-second clip from Hawks's *Only Angels Have Wings*, we see Roxy in close-up. The proximity of war and dog seems arbitrary at first, but gradually the significance of the association becomes clear. In one sequence, a male voice-over cites a passage from Cesar Pavese's *The House on the Hill*: 'Now that I have seen war, I know that if it ended everyone would ask, "What do we do with the bodies?" Perhaps only for them is the war over.' On the screen we see Roxy defecating, and then shots of Roxy calmly walking along the shore of Lake Geneva. The scene suggests that the dog, unlike the humans of Pavese's narrative, is free of the burden of endless war and at peace with the world around him. In another sequence, archival footage of a helicopter in a grey sky is followed by shots of a dark-green low-resolution close-up of a helicopter touching down, an explosion in the violent colours of the opening battle scene, and a close-up of a dog's head in a flaming pile of debris, moving only when two concussive blasts jolt the body. Here, war engulfs the dog; human violence brings death to the animal that throughout the film has been presented as serene and benign. Implicit in this juxtaposition of images is an animal indictment of human cruelty and brutality. At another point in the film, as the camera pans across an urban parking lot to a distant cityscape, a voice-over cites a passage from Clifford Simak's sci-fi tale of a posthuman world in which genetically enhanced dogs tell ancient tales of a vanished reality: 'The family makes a circle around the fire. The young pups listen without saying a word. And when the story is over, they ask many questions. What is man? Or, what is a city? Or, again, what is war?' In Simak's story, the pups have never seen humans, cities or wars, and they are mystified by the traditional legends of such creatures and their history. In the film, by contrast, the pups give voice to a larger question. What is it that connects Man, City and War? Why is human civilisation inextricably linked to war and violence? The answer comes in a shot of Josette in close-up, telling Gédéon an anecdote of the Nazi concentration camps. 'When he entered the gas chamber, a child asked, "Why" to his mother. And an SS shouted, "Hier ist kein Warum!" Pas de pourquoi.' Why war? Why cruelty and savagery? There is no reason. In the face of humble animals, we stand shamed. As Ivitch says at one point, God could not, or would not make us humble. 'So he made us humiliated.'

Only self-conscious beings can be humiliated, since their shame arises from awareness of themselves in the eyes of others. Animal humility, by contrast, stems from an absence of self-consciousness, and at several points in the film Godard explores the ramifications of human self-consciousness and its relation to canine consciousness. 'There is no nudity in nature', a voice intones over an image of Roxy. 'And the animal, therefore, is not nude because he is nude.' Josette, Gédéon, Ivitch and Marcus wander nude in their apartment, briefly don a robe or a raincoat, then strip naked again, without any particular motive for their actions. Gédéon sits on the toilet, comparing his posture to that of Rodin's Thinker, and as he defecates in Josette's presence he says that his position is that of true human equality and that here thought finds its place 'dans le caca'. Roxy also defecates on camera, but his act is no more remarkable than his nudity. What some critics label Godard's scatology is actually an inquiry into the problematic status of human animality, which Godard presents through images of the couple's unself-conscious nudity accompanied by intellectual commentary on art, social class, thought and shit. A zone of indiscernibility is opened in which the differences between humans and animals such as dogs are blurred. The gratuitous, desexualised treatment of clothing and the transgression of excretory proprieties force awareness of the corporeal realities humans share with other animals as well as the cultural norms that set humans apart.

Godard offers a more philosophical reflection on this theme when a male voice-over cites Paul Valéry: 'No one could think freely if his eyes were locked in another's gaze. As soon as gazes lock, there are no longer exactly two of us. It is difficult to remain alone.' At the beginning of these lines, Roxy's head appears in black-and-white profile against the background of a rushing stream. With the word 'freely' this shot is replaced by a colour stop-action image of Roxy's face in frontal view. Seven stop-frames of Roxy's face ensue, each closer to the camera, each focusing more fully on Roxy's gaze. When the voice-over completes the phrase 'As soon as gazes lock', Godard cuts to a twilight shot of Roxy in mid-distance walking in the shallow water of a lake, and then strolling on the shore. With this idyllic image before us we hear that 'It is difficult to remain alone.' Two minutes later, a male voice repeats the phrase 'It is difficult to remain alone.' This time we see Roxy standing in snow beside a rushing stream. In neither case does Roxy seem to find solitude difficult. When the camera fixes its gaze on Roxy's eyes, there is no question of Roxy losing his freedom when looking at the other. His animal gaze at the camera (and audience) is steady, alert and unperturbed.

The relation of human to animal freedom is framed in more complex terms in another sequence when a male voice-over cites Levinas: 'Only free beings can be strangers to each other. They have a shared freedom but that is precisely what separates them.' A shot of Roxy resting in a car precedes the quote. A black screen appears, the voice begins to speak, and a white dot forms in the middle of the screen. At the word 'precisely' Godard cuts to a mid-shot of Roxy against a background of grass, the footage overexposed with blue bands pulsing across the image. Over this image the voice-over stops. This overexposed image is then followed by a shot of Roxy walking a rock path beside a lake, the bulrushes tinted bright orange, red and green, the rocks a watery blue, and then a second shot of a vibrant harlequin green field of long grass, with Roxy barely visible in the distance, only his head and shoulders occasionally rising from the greenery. The lakeside shot is accompanied by the sound of wind gusts and Roxy's footsteps, the grass field by the sound of chirping birds. All the images suggest that Roxy is a free being, but nothing indicates that he is a stranger to others, nor that his freedom is predicated on a shared freedom that separates him from the other. Roxy's freedom is untroubled by the paradoxes of self-consciousness, which only knows freedom as a shared separation. Roxy's freedom is presented as an unrestrained movement through a vital and pulsating land- and soundscape, hyperreal in its chromatic intensity.

But more important is the animal's unselfconscious gaze as a challenge to human vision. With Roxy's head in close-up, a voice says, 'It is not the animal that is blind, but man, blinded by consciousness, and incapable of seeing the world. What is outside, wrote Rilke, can be known only via an animal's gaze.' Godard's response to intolerable visual clichés has always been to create new ways of seeing, but in *Adieu au langage* that response is situated in a becoming-animal that seeks images outside canine or standard human perception. Godard frames the problem in a voice-over citation of a passage on painting from Marcel Proust's *Jean Santeuil* (mistakenly attributed to Claude Monet by the narrator):

> When – the sun already setting – the river still sleeps in the dreams of fog, we do not see it anymore than it sees itself. Here it is already the river, and the eye is arrested, one no longer sees anything but a void, a fog which prevents one from seeing further. In that part of the canvas, one must paint neither what one sees, since one sees nothing, nor what one doesn't see, since one must paint only what one sees, but one must paint that one doesn't see.

In these sentences we find a visual version of the literary paradox faced by Kafka – which, for Deleuze, is central to understanding Kafka's art – the 'impossibility of not writing, the impossibility of writing in German, the impossibility of writing otherwise' (Deleuze and Guattari 1986: 16). And, we recall, Deleuze sees this paradox of impossibilities as central to political cinema, which is 'no longer constituted on the basis of a possibility of evolution and revolution, like the classical cinema, but on impossibilities, in the style of Kafka: *the intolerable*' (Deleuze 1989: 249).

Godard's response to this problem is not simply to show us that we do not see – that clichés keep us from directly viewing the world – but to invent a mode of vision that has never existed before. And it is in 3D that Godard finds such a genuinely new way of seeing.[3] In his 3D images, Godard creates a different kind of lectosign, one that brings the crisis of the intolerable within the sign. What must be read in each sign is not its relation to other signs, but the relation of its parts to one another. This reading has its own undetermined time – that of the eye's movement within the shot, as it shifts focus from one element to another.

Conventional 3D films, as many have remarked, are initially arresting, but soon the eye adjusts and the 3D effect almost disappears. Godard's use of the medium is such that the eye is never allowed to normalise the images. From time to time, Godard offers images that are easy to assimilate, such as a shot of a woman's hands in a leaf-strewn fountain. Framed in the shot are the woman's arms in the left foreground, the water surface delineated by the floating leaves, and the hands moving below the surface to the right. Here, 3D simply adds a conventional sense of depth, with arms, water-surface and hands forming a diagonal spatial continuum from the closest to the farthest elements of the image. But more often, Godard imposes conflicting demands on the eye. In a shot of blood being splashed into a bathtub, for example, a foreground scrub brush in the upper-right corner of the frame is a distraction, its sharp, focused delineation pulling the eye away from the primary event of splashes of blood striking the tub surface and running down the drain. A visual irritant, the too-present brush eventually forces the eye to shift its focus from the tub to the brush and back again. In several shots through a car windshield (a common motif in Godard), the foreground windshield is a more insistent irritant, making the images much more difficult to negotiate than the bathtub shot. In most of these shots, it is raining or snowing, and the water or snow on the windshield is in sharp focus, as are the windshield wipers sweeping the screen. The eye tries to see through the glass, but the surface has detail and precision that are compatible only with a foreground focus. As the eye strains to process the moving images beyond the windshield, the glass surface relentlessly impedes the gaze and forces a stuttering shift of focus from foreground to background. The difficulties of negotiating the image are further compounded in a spinning hand-held shot of autumn-leaved tree branches against a purple-and-blue sky. The multiple planes of the leaves at various distances allow no stable focal point and force the eye to wander haphazardly within the image until, at the close of the shot, leaves come into extreme close-up and give one the sensation of being poked in the eye.

And then there's what Calum Marsh (2014) called 'the shot of the year', the shot that brought spontaneous applause when the film was premiered at Cannes. In 2D, the shot is innocuous, but in 3D it is painful to watch. 3D movies are usually shot with two cameras side-by-side, a fixed distance apart. 'The shot of the year' opens with Davidson, an older professor and friend of Ivitch's, and Ivitch in the frame, but as Ivitch is dragged away from Davidson by her husband, the cameras separate from one another. The left camera remains stationary and focused on Davidson, while the right camera tracks the movements of Ivitch and her husband to the right. When Ivitch finally returns to Davidson, the right camera assumes its original position in alignment with the left camera. What one sees are superimposed, irreconcilable images. As Jacob Kastrenakes (2014) observes, 'At first, you have no idea what's going on – your eyes twist in pain, you lift your 3D glasses up in confusion.' He discovers that if you close one eye, 'you see 2D action of the character on the left; close the other eye, and you see 2D action of the character on the right'. But while this viewing strategy reveals the components of the image, it provides no means of reconciling the conflicting, superimposed images with both eyes open. In the shots of the bathtub, windshield and spinning leaves, the eye traverses the image, negotiating the conflicting levels of attention, following an undetermined time as the gaze moves from one element to another. In this shot, however, there is no negotiation. One sees a smear of time, an astonishing, exhilarating but almost unendurable stretch of temporal crisis. It is as if the film's new way of seeing, brought forth by the intolerable, were itself a nearly unbearable vision at the limits of the human capacity to see.

There is nothing specifically canine about Godard's 3D images. Rather, they are animal-induced images fashioned in an effort to follow Rilke's challenge to know the outside 'via an animal's gaze'. Geoffrey O'Brien (2014) observes that

> in Roxy, Godard finds a more heroic figure than has yet appeared in his films, a figure whose movements through the natural world, to the edge of the water, through the underbrush, do indeed reinvent a primal cinema at one with the world it represents. At some point the 3-D process becomes a metaphor for an animal perception of the world that we can only guess at.

O'Brien rightly senses the connection between Roxy and the 3D process, but the 3D image, far from being a metaphor, is itself an animal perception, albeit the perception of an indeterminate animal, neither human nor canine, a perception in passage between the two and towards something 'that we can only guess at'.

This animal-induced vision is nonlinguistic, and at a very simple level, it may be regarded as a vision in opposition to language. These title cards appear twice – 1 Nature; 2 Métaphore – and one might posit the 3D becoming-animal vision as Nature and the language-mediated gaze as Metaphor, thereby recalling Deleuze's remark that the time-image is literal, not metaphorical. As we recall, humans are 'incapable of seeing the world', and hence in need of an animal's gaze, because they are 'blinded by consciousness', and Godard makes clear that self-conscious-ness and language are inextricable. Marcus indicates as much when he entertains the hypothesis that 'the face-to-face invents language', and later he ties language to humans' troubled relationship with the Other. During the film's second disorienting split-camera blur shot, in which the left camera stays focused on Ivitch as the right camera tracks Marcus, Marcus says that 'With language, something's happening . . . There's something troubling our relation to the world . . . It acts against pure freedom.' And as he moves away from Ivitch, he adds, 'I speak – subject . . . I listen – object.' Ivitch responds, 'We need to get an interpreter . . . Soon, everyone will need an interpreter to understand the words coming from their own mouths.'

It would seem that the 3D seeing-via-Roxy requires an adieu to lan-guage. A male voice suggests as much when he cites Blanchot, 'I seek poverty in language', as does Josette when she exclaims, 'Words! Words! I don't want to hear them spoken anymore!' One way beyond language is through sound. When Marcus speaks of the 'face-to-face' of language, he slowly intones the phrase 'si le face-à-face invente le langage', and then repeats the first word: 'si . . . si . . .'. Ivitch responds, 'do re mi fa sol si', to which Marcus replies, 'la . . . la . . .'. Here, a conjunction gives rise to linguistic signs of musical sounds outside language. And then there are the two title cards that rewrite the film's title – AH DIEUX, OH LANGAGE. In the 'AH' and 'OH', both of which appear on separate title cards, language reaches its limits. This is no Fort-Da but an Ah-Oh of intensities, sonic expressions of affects beyond linguistic articulation. At this point, in this Ah-Oh of intensities, human and animal enter a zone of indiscernibility.

In the closing moments of the film, Godard evokes this sonic zone of indiscernibility, but in a complex sequence of sounds and images that requires further contextualisation to be fully appreciated. So, before examining the film's ending, a brief digression.

The title card '2 Métaphore' clearly points to the essentially metaphorical nature of language, but a second reading of the title is obliquely insinuated when Davidson responds to Ivitch's question, 'What difference is there between an idea and a metaphor?' His answer, 'Ask the Athenians when they take the tram', may seem a feeble etymological joke, but the film's images suggest otherwise. Metaphor comes from the Greek *metapherein*, 'to transfer, carry over', from *meta-*, 'over, across' + *pherein*, 'to carry, bear'. Nothing in the Greek suggests a literal mode of transport, but Davidson's wordplay invites speculation about the significance of the many images of vehicles in the film. Six shots of a ferry on Lake Geneva appear at regular intervals. Seven shots through a car windshield punctuate the film, one shot lasting over a minute, the others between ten and thirty seconds. There are several shots of passing cars and parked cars, airplanes, helicopters, and even four shots of bicycles. But most significant is a twenty-one second section that juxtaposes Roxy and a train entering a Metro stop. At one-second intervals, the approach of the train towards the camera in three-quarter view is intercut with four shots of Roxy's head against a speckled-black asphalt background. The fourth shot of Roxy is followed by a perpendicular view of Metro cars passing in a succession of three stuttered blurs. After a brief black screen, the blurred succession of cars continues for eight seconds, but this time with a black silhouette of Roxy's head and shoulders superimposed on the image, as if he were calmly contemplating the train from some unspecified outside location. The slow, meditative strains of the second movement of Beethoven's Seventh Symphony play throughout the sequence, reinforcing the sense that Roxy and the train belong to separate worlds.

Roxy's world is outside language, but also in some respects outside the entirety of urban civilisation, represented by the Metro and all the other images of 'metaphoric' modes of transport. Roxy passes through the modern human world, but he belongs to a natural world with which humans have lost touch. Early in the film, Godard calls attention to the difference between contemporary and traditional societies. The student Marie rails against the law: 'In fact, the law cheats. The law that denies its own violence, cheats. The law that denies what turns it into a state apparatus, cheats. And the law that deems itself self-legitimising, cheats twice.' Her friend Alain counters, 'I think that in primitive societies, this was not the case.' When Marie objects, 'And when one had a war?', Alain responds, 'It is a war, but of society against the State' (an allusion to Pierre Clastres familiar to any reader of Deleuze and Guattari).[4] Such traditional societies not only ward off the state, but also remain in close contact with nature, as Godard indicates when a male voice-over says, 'The Apache Indians, the Chiricahua tribe, they call the world: the forest.' The film is filled with images of the forest, but no humans are shown in that space – only Roxy. Clearly, the world of law and the state apparatus, of cities and Metros, is far removed from the forest, the animal world that Roxy inhabits.

Midway through the film, the Apaches are mentioned a second time when Marcus says to Ivitch, 'I don't know about you, but when I was a kid, we played Indians. The Apaches were my favourite. To say "the world", they said "the forest".' Implicit in this remark is a connection between children, the Apaches and the forest – and thereby, a connection with Roxy. At the close of a sequence of Marcus and Ivitch conversing in their apartment, Marcus says, 'We will have children.' Ivitch responds, 'No, not yet. A dog, if you want.' As this scene closes, the pensive opening measures of Schönberg's *Transfigured Night* begin. A fifteen-second shot of four hands playing a piano is then followed by a scene of a young boy and young girl walking through an orchard in early spring, the colours of the landscape and the children's clothing in enhanced, vibrant hues. In voice-over, Ivitch says softly and slowly, 'Imagine that you are still a little boy.' The film cuts to an image of clouds in a deep blue sky as Ivitch says, 'We looked at cloud shapes.' Two more shots of the boy and girl ensue as *Transfigured Night* continues to play. Over these images, Ivitch says, 'As a girl, I saw dogs everywhere.' Marcus asks, 'In the blue or the white?', to which she responds, 'We are together, both.' Marcus then says, 'We need to have children.' The idyllic images of the children stop and a black screen appears as Ivitch answers, 'Not certain.' The music ends, and she adds, 'A dog, yes!'

In this playful sequence, a choice between child and dog frames images of children in an orchard, a cultivated forest midway between the wild and civilisation. Ivitch evokes a consciousness that finds dogs in clouds – indeed, dogs everywhere. The dogs are in the blue and the white, inseparably together, as are the young boy and girl. Ivitch invites Marcus to participate in the enchanted childhood realm of imaginative interaction with nature, but he breaks the spell by reiterating adult concerns: 'We need to have children.'

And now to the conclusion of *Adieu au langage*. The last shot before the credits shows a foreground close-up of two bright-red poppies, rustling in the wind, and a car passing in the background. A black screen follows with sounds of a crying baby and a howling dog. These sounds stop after the first credit title card appears. With the second title card, we hear a reprise of a song that accompanied the film's opening credits,

'La caccia alle streghe' ('The Witch Hunt'), a song celebrating worker/student solidarity and their fight for revolution. As the final title card of the credits appears, the song is replaced by a din of crowd noises, amidst which a voice shouts the opening lines of a French nursery song (sung to the tune of 'For he's a jolly good fellow') that dates to the eighteenth century: 'Marlbrough s'en va-t-en guerre, / Marlbrough s'en va-t-en guerre, / Marlbrough s'en va-t-en guerre' ('Marlborough is going to war, / Marlborough is going to war, / Marlborough is going to war'). During the final shout of the sentence, the credits' black screen is succeeded by an image of Roxy walking a magenta path into a forest of green and blue leaves and black and orange-red trunks and branches. The sound stops, then four seconds later, in a startling high-volume blast, the shouting voice screams the closing line of the nursery song chorus: 'Ne sait quand reviendra' ('Doesn't know when he'll return'). Silence again, then a final image of Roxy running towards the camera along the same forest path.

First, then, we see nature (the poppies) in the foreground, the human tekhnē of a mode of transport in the background, the juxtaposition of the two emphasising the unresolved conflicts inherent in their co-existence. This is followed by the nonlinguistic sounds of the dog mingled with the prelinguistic sounds of the infant. This sonic zone of indiscernibility signals a becoming-dog and a becoming-child, an opening to intensities outside language and the human institutions and practices that modify nature. These sounds give way to a song of resistance and potential revolution, suggesting that the *fonction de voyance* engaged through a confrontation with the intolerable opens up possibilities of transformative thought, sensation and action. In the final images and sounds, however, we are reminded of the two divergent destinies that await baby humans and canines: that of the infant, who will soon sing nursery songs of war with no foreseeable end, and that of the dog, who will live among humans, but will be able to run back and forth through the forest, which is what the Apaches called 'the world'.

In *A Thousand Plateaus*, Deleuze and Guattari say, '*anyone who likes cats or dogs is a fool*' (1987: 240; emphasis in original). Donna Haraway especially has taken exception to this statement, devoting several pages of *When Species Meet* to a vituperative screed against Deleuze and Guattari's mocking remarks about doting dog owners.[5] But Haraway ignores Deleuze and Guattari's assertion that, even if one must distinguish pets from 'pack or affect animals that form a multiplicity', it is also possible 'for any animal to be treated in the mode of the pack or swarm . . . Even the cat, even the dog' (1987: 241). Dogs were the first animals to be domesticated by humans, and they have been selectively bred to prefer human company to the company of other dogs – something Godard reminds us of in *Adieu au langage* when a voice-over says, 'And Darwin, citing Buffon, affirms that the dog is the only being on earth that loves you more than it loves itself.'[6] Hence, there is an inbred tendency for human-canine bonds to reinforce cultural norms that subordinate dogs to humans and valorise the human over the animal. But the domestication of dogs represents a long process of co-evolution involving both dogs and humans, one that opens an area of proximity between humans and another life form that is unparalleled in human relations with any other species. The dog is itself a zone of indiscernibility, living both inside and outside the human world, inviting the most infantilising of human attachments, but also affording a means of engaging human animality and thereby undoing the category of the human.

For the most part, Godard shows Roxy in landscapes unmarked by human presence: amidst forests, beside rivers and lakes, in fields of grass and snow. At one point, Roxy walks through a gateway to a human habitation; at another, he stands on a railroad trestle; and in a few shots he paces the couples' apartment floor or rests on their couch. But nowhere is Roxy shown with a human being. His status as pet is virtually ignored. Throughout the film, he is presented as an autonomous being, a self-contained creature unselfconsciously moving within his surroundings. Only once does Godard anthropomorphise Roxy. While various images of Roxy by a river occupy the screen, a voice-over cites a passage from Clifford D. Simak's *Time and Again*, substituting the name Roxy for that of the novel's protagonist, Sutton:

> The water spoke to him in a deep and serious voice. Roxy began to think. It's trying to talk to me as it has always tried to talk to people through the ages. Dialoguing with itself when there is no one to listen. But trying. Trying always to communicate to people the news that it has to give them. Some of them have taken from the river a certain truth. But none of them . . .

This is Roxy, the Cynic dog-philosopher living according to nature, in Heraclitean contemplation of water and the flow of all things. The sounds of a choir singing Valentin Silvestrov's liturgical chant 'Lord God' play before, during and after this sequence, situating Roxy and the river in an aural realm that aspires to render sonorous the ineffable. The effect is not to humanise Roxy, but to derive from human thought a mode of contemplation that belongs neither to humans nor to dogs. The result is the evocation of 'a certain truth', but one that trails off into silence before it can be enunciated.

The implicit opposition of nature and culture, and the association of pristine wilderness with traditional peoples, children and animals, might suggest that Godard is simply reviving the clichés of Romanticism and repackaging them in a jumbled collection of disconnected fragments. Such is not the case, however. The film's seemingly Romantic elements have a polemical function. Roxy, children and the Apaches serve as vantages from which to confront the intolerable, as points of resistance to war, violence, cliché and the malaise of contemporary quotidian existence. Traditional peoples are invoked solely to indict state violence and the degradation of human relations with the environment. The brief images of the carefree children in a landscape of pulsating colour are in sharp contrast to the dark browns and blacks of Marcus and Ivitch's apartment, with the perpetual glow of the large-screen TV in the background, the two of them speaking in flat, inexpressive tones. Like Gédéon and Josette, Marcus and Ivitch show no joy or vitality, simply an anesthetised numbness. Hence, beneath Ivitch's amusing suggestion that they have a dog instead of children is an implicit refusal to perpetuate the melancholy world she inhabits. And as for Roxy, he has a certain nobility, yet not that of a canine noble savage, but that of a self-possessed, autonomous and inscrutable being whose mere presence brings into sharp relief the contours of human consciousness and behaviour.

Roxy initiates a becoming-dog, a becoming-other that seeks something beyond human words, thoughts and vision. This becoming-other, however, is not in service of a Romantic primitivism or the restoration of some lost paradise. Although Godard sees much that is intolerable in the modern technological world, he promotes no return to the past but seeks a future-oriented transformation of our world through a creative use of its potentials. The Nature Godard invokes in his title cards is a new nature, one that has never existed before. The film's images of the natural world are decidedly unnatural – the colours constantly altered, enhanced and distorted, the visual textures varying in clarity and resolution, and all within a 3D format that defamiliarises object relations and makes palpable an alien dimension within conventional space. Godard exploits all the technological possibilities of cinema – that most machinic of arts – to invent new ways of seeing, hearing and thinking that blur the lines between nature and artifice, the human and the nonhuman. Just as the film attempts to move beyond language through language, via citation after citation of sociological, anthropological, historical, philosophical and literary texts, so it seeks a vision beyond contemporary mediated vision through the media that now limit our seeing.

The modern cinema begins with the intolerable, with images that cannot be processed within the sensory-motor schema. The intolerable activates a *fonction de voyance*, a power of seeing that promotes the invention of new cinematic signs: chronosigns, lectosigns and noosigns. The modern cinema's aim is to create new ways of seeing and hearing, but its ultimate goal is to restore belief in this world. 'Only belief in this world can reconnect man to what he sees and hears . . . Restoring our belief in the world – this is the power of modern cinema' (Deleuze 1989: 172). The characters in *Adieu au langage* have lost faith in this world, as is so pointedly demonstrated when Ivitch opts to have a dog instead of children. But Godard's becoming-dog attempts to reconnect humans to what they see and hear by inventing a visual and sonic world beyond the grasp of our commonsense senses.

God is mentioned in several texts Godard cites in the film, but never gods. And yet he chooses to rewrite 'adieu' as 'AH DIEUX' ('OH GODS'). If AH DIEUX is opposed to OH LANGAGE as NATURE is opposed to MÉTAPHORE, then it is Nature that is the realm of the gods. What gods? Not transcendent deities, but the animistic, immanent powers of the natural world that Roxy contemplates by the riverside, when 'The water spoke to him in a deep and serious voice.' That nature, however, is a new nature, one that has never existed before. Late in the film, Godard in voice-over cites Dostoyevsky's *The Possessed*: 'It's what Kiriloff said: "Two questions, a big one and a small one."' A female voice asks, 'The small one?', to which Godard responds, 'Suffering.' 'And the big one?', she inquires. 'The other world, the other world.' The world of suffering: the world of the intolerable. And the other world? Not an afterlife, but this world made new, a world we can believe in.

Notes

1. A number of insightful commentaries on *Adieu au langage* have appeared. Especially helpful are Bordwell 2014a and 2014b. Also of interest are Brody 2014, Ehrlich 2014, Foundas 2014, Kastrenakes 2014 and Williams 2014.
2. Ted Fendt (2014) provides an invaluable resource for study of the film, cataloguing most of the film's textual references, with citations of the film passage in French and in English translation, as well as citations of the original passage, with translations when necessary. All my citations of Godard's textual references are taken from Fendt's catalogue.
3. For insight into the technical aspects of Godard's use of 3D, see Rivoz 2014, in which Rivoz talks with Godard's director of photography, Fabrice Aragno, about the conventions of 3D cinema and the deviations from those conventions that he and Godard employ.
4. For discussions of Clastres, see Deleuze and Guattari 1983: 148, 180, and 1987: 357–61.

5. See Haraway 2008: 27–30 for her critique of Deleuze and Guattari. For a detailed response to her attack, see Bogue 2015.
6. For 'evidence' of canine preference of human to canine company, see Tuber et al. 1996.

References

Bogue, R. (2015), 'The Companion Cyborg: Technics and Domestication', in H. Stark and J. Roffe (eds), *Deleuze and the Non-Human*, London: Palgrave, pp. 163–79.

Bordwell, D. (2014a), 'Adieu au langage: 2 + 2 x 3', *Observations on film art*, September 7, at http://www.davidbordwell.net/blog/2014/09/07/adieu-au-langage-2-2-2-x-3d (accessed 25 March 2015).

Bordwell, D. (2014b), 'Say Hello to Goodbye to Language', Davidbordwell.net, November 2, at http://www.davidbordwell.net/blog/2014/11/02/say-hello-to-goodby-to-language (accessed 25 March 2015).

Brody, R. (2014), 'Godard's Revolutionary 3-D Film', *The New Yorker*, 29 October, at http://www.newyorker.com/culture/richard-brody/jean-luc-godards-3-d-movie (accessed 1 April 2015).

Deleuze, G. (1986), *Cinema 1: The Movement-Image*, trans. H. Tomlinson and B. Habberjam, Minneapolis: University of Minnesota Press.

Deleuze, G. (1988), *Foucault*, trans. S. Hand, Minneapolis: University of Minnesota Press.

Deleuze, G. (1989), *Cinema 2: The Time-Image*, trans. H. Tomlinson and R. Galeta, Minneapolis: University of Minnesota Press.

Deleuze, G. (1990), *Negotiations: 1972–1990*, trans. M. Joughin, New York: Columbia University Press.

Deleuze, G. and F. Guattari (1983), *Anti-Oedipus: Capitalism and Schizophrenia*, trans. R. Hurley, M. Seem and H. R. Lane, Minneapolis: University of Minnesota Press.

Deleuze, G. and F. Guattari (1986), *Kafka: Toward a Minor Literature*, trans. D. Polan, Minneapolis: University of Minnesota Press.

Deleuze, G. and F. Guattari (1987), *A Thousand Plateaus: Capitalism and Schizophrenia*, trans. B. Massumi, Minneapolis: University of Minnesota Press.

Ehrlich, D. (2014), 'Goodbye to Language', *The Dissolve*, 28 October, at http://thedissolve.com/reviews/1177-goodbye-to-language (accessed 1 April 2014).

Fendt, T. (2014). '"Adieu au langage" – "Goodbye to Language": A Works Cited', *MUBI*, 12 October, at https://mubi.com/notebook/posts/adieu-au-langage-good-bye-to-language-a-works-cited (accessed 1 April 2015).

Foundas, S. (2014), 'Cannes Film Review: "Goodbye to Language"', *Variety*, 21 May, at http://variety.com/2014/film/reviews/cannes-film-review-goodbye-to-lan-guage-1201199140 (accessed 25 March 2015).

Haraway, D. (2008), *When Species Meet*, Minneapolis: University of Minnesota Press.

Kastrenakes, J. (2014), 'Somebody Finally Made a Truly 3D Movie', *The Verge*, 21 September, at http://www.theverge.com/2014/9/21/6563495/goodbye-to-language-godard-messes-with-3d-and-its-awesome (accessed 26 March 2014).

Marsh, Calum (2014), 'The Shot of the Year', *The Dissolve*, 19 December, at https://thedissolve.com/features/2014-in-review/866-the-shot-if-the-year (last accessed 2 April 2015).

O'Brien, Geoffrey (2014), 'Tree! Fire! Water! Godard!', *The New York Review of Books*, 3 November, at www.nybooks.com/daily/2014/11/03/tree-fire-water-godard (last accessed 2 April 2015).

Rizov, V. (2014), 'Goodbye to 3-D Rules', *Filmmaker*, 20 October, at http://filmmakermagazine.com/87878-goodbye-to-3-d-rules/#.VVU5aWAk--_ (accessed 2 April 2015).

Tuber, D. S., M. B. Hennesey, S. Sander and J. A. Miller (1996), 'Behavioral and Glucocorticoid Responses of Adult Domestic Dogs (*Canis familiaris*) to Companionship and Social Separation', *Journal of Comparative Psychology*, Vol. 110, No. 1, pp. 103–8.

Williams, B. (2014), 'Cannes 2014: Adieu au langage (Jean-Luc Godard, France)', *Cinema Scope*, at http://cinema-scope.com/spotlight/adieu-au-langage-jean-luc-godard-france (accessed 2 April 2015).

PART V

TRANSVERSE ANIMALITIES: ECOSOPHICAL BECOMINGS

Chapter 15

Drinking Animals: Sobriety, Intoxication and Interspecies Assemblages

Gary Genosko

I will focus on alcohol, as a transversal component, in both its distilled form and in its pure form of ethanol, as well as its imbibition by drinking animals. This transversality passes through anthropocentric and across multiple non-anthropocentric assemblages. Alcohol's relations of exteriority include organic plant matter, water, yeast and fermentation; in both controlled scientific experiments and naturally ordinary fermentations of rotting fruit, alcohol is seen as in some way transformative for specific animal species. However, I do not only intend to review the literature bearing upon the consumption of alcohol in fruit, sap and nectar in the nonhuman world, which is a wide-ranging subject of study (Dominy 2004), and boozy fruit is often seen as a deterrent to consumption, or at least not a preferred foraging cue, especially by primates; conversely, heavy consumers of fermented fruits and nectars with high alcohol concentrations like treeshrews and lorises appear to show no ill-effects from their chronic imbibition (Wiens et al. 2008). I will mention studies concerning nonhuman species such as fruit flies that seem capable of imbibing towards a drunkenness similar to that of humans including disorientation, lack of coordination and passing out (Phillips 1998). Wild birds like blackbirds are known to gorge on fermented berries before crashing to the ground in a stupor, some fatally poisoned (n.a. 2012). For my purposes, there is something a bit too seductive about these latter examples as they provide formally similar behavioural correspondences between animals and humans. While there is no doubting the journalistic charm of such multi-species displays of drunkenness, and even their wibberlee-wobberlee lines of flight (Lowry 1971: 120), they tend, as Deleuze (1990: 157–61) has argued, to harden and actualise, that is, 'imprison', the alcohol consumed. I also wish to avoid the disreputable thesis of Italian ethnobotanist Giorgio Samorini in *Animals and Psychedelics* (2002) about the evolutionary role of inebriation, a kind of Darwin-on-acid view of life, that would, if not for its absurdity, fly in the face of Deleuze and Guattari's (1987: 286) recourse to a kind of heightened or distilled sobriety as a favoured passage into immanence where 'drugs' – including decidedly non-pharmacological regimes like the pure brush-strokes of calligraphy – really get free-based. Recalling Deleuze's (2002: 50) comment on Jack Kerouac's phrases as 'pure lines' and as a writer possessing the 'soberest of means', such sobriety doesn't guarantee anything as the desiring flows put into circulation can easily get caught up with reformist constructions that are never unlocked from their actualisations, and thus lose what might be thought of as the sweetness of pure virtuality (Deleuze and Guattari 1977: 277–8). It is perhaps easier to understand Deleuze's sense of sobriety by beginning from the perspective of falling off the wagon into the compromises of otherwise transmutating impersonal flows, and then to revisit the difficulty of getting back on the wagon from a position of experiential abjection: 'it would take a true alcoholic to attain that degree of sobriety' (Deleuze 2002: 50). What is meant by a true alcoholic will include in this chapter a profligate sobriety that involves alcohol but not the typical symptoms of prolonged alcohol consumption.

Following what Félix Guattari called an 'ethological montage', I seek relatively mutual imbrications of animal becomings-human and human becomings-animal: a block of becoming that tries to seize both and is crossed transversally by alcohol. Further, it is the question of how to mutually share in an interspecies encounter the potential of alcohol that I will attempt to answer – beyond the lab and fieldwork proper. But in doing so the discussion moves from wild animals to domesticates and back again – those whose worlds are often cramped by the manicured spaces of human habitats and the breeding practices of the pets industry – and are referred to disparagingly as *Oedipal pets* (Genosko 1993) because they are not incapable of but find it difficult to join a multiplicity (with the proviso that the distinction between Oedipal, State and pack animals does not foreclose upon the treatment of Oedipal animals as a pack (Deleuze and Guattari 1987: 240–1)). There are no shortages of Oedipalised packs: a pack of dogs each of which is on a leash held by a dog walker is a sad sight indeed. If we listen to Ionesco (1960) in *Rhinoceros*, we hear that a multiplicity of rhinoceroses can be frightening for a drinking man and hence, alcohol itself disturbs such a human becoming-rhinoceros (Chaudhuri 2014).

Indeed, as I entertain more overtly human cultural examples, such as 'wine' for cats, a recent Japanese pet trend, but one not confined to that country, the metabolic communion of interspecies companionship requires that the material expressivity of the substance is overcoded because the 'wine' is only non-alcoholic liquid catnip in a 'wine' bottle flavoured with sugar and grape juice. Hence, 'wine' serves within a specific cultural context to further involute human and feline domestic assemblages, as if Internet memes did not satisfy this need, but with a well-known plant oil and the inherited genetic dispositions of certain cats rather than to a fermented grape as such (Ashcroft 2013). Such 'wine' is, after all, for cross-species 'sharing' (or something like parallel asynchronous drinking) on the occasion of celebrations like birthdays.

My primary points of discussion will be animal consumption of alcohol that both rescues us from the correspondences between multi-species drunkenness by two means: animal drinking that has no obvious effects; and animal drinking that involves no alcohol (and may not involve much mutual imbibition whatsoever). In short, I am advancing two strange species of sobriety.

In addition, however, two further constraints need to be identified.

Two Constraints

Any effort to investigate alcohol must face the challenge of repeated calls for sobriety in *A Thousand Plateaus*. Such sobriety is not strictly speaking of the on-the-wagon type, but instead refers to a high degree of refinement in gesture, calculation, and the valorisation of simplicity: it is a principle of perspecuity and selection that yields a richness of machinic effects, affects and microperceptions. One cannot help but align it with 'a kind of dryness', insists Anne Sauvagnargues (2013: 109), but not in a dichotomy with wetness as historians of alcohol might explain two different urban zones where alcohol was or was not available. A sobriety, instead, that deterritorialises matter and links the resulting molecules to cosmic forces. There are of course refrains that fall well below that benchmark of cosmic release, and Deleuze and Guattari (1987: 349) name one of them: drinking songs. It is not merely tautological to say that drinking songs lack sobriety. They are among the most common accompaniments of heavy boozing. Bad uses of such refrains are too closed and therefore untransformable. Drinking songs never really take off, never deterritorialise and get out of their particularisms. They might reaffirm an already given collective identity or allegiance (Massumi 2002: 253); they may bolster what anthropologists call 'constructive drinking', but the boundaries they lay down are thick and their entreaties formulaic, often sexist and racist, too. Tellurian, perhaps; but too local, too socially specific and with an emphasis on enclosures, exclusions, and not on prodigious lift-offs (Kasmir 2005). Drinking songs lack sobriety not because of the alcohol that fuels them, but due to their refrains' qualities. On the contrary, it is possible to get there, to a collective and boisterous singing aloud, without alcoholised-racialised performances of erzatz Irishness or interminable Oktoberfestivity or the supporter's rah-rah. Deleuze and Guattari's hopes remain intact: it may be possible to achieve the effects of drugs and alcohol without the use of these substances (Deleuze 1990: 161). It is really the converse that interests me here: it may be possible to maintain sobriety with the use of certain of these substances. And this hope can be respected without going completely dry. Indeed, the animal consumption of alcohol without effect and the social construction of feline tippling of 'wine' are the unusual varietals of sobriety I wish to discuss, without phantasising about a prodigiously anthropomorphised pet drinking buddy (pink elephants are no substitute for Pink Panthers in this respect).

I also want to acknowledge the important insight of anthropologist Eduardo Viveiros de Castro, whose reflections are particularly helpful in understanding drinking animals. In *Cannibal Metaphysics* (2014: 57–62), he advises us to pass through a Western into an Amerindian cosmology in which nonhumans, especially predatory animals like jaguars, see humans as nonhuman prey, and see themselves and their conspecifics anthropomorphically as humans. However, predators see what humans consider to be natural as cultural: 'jaguars see blood as manioc beer', that is as a cultural product fit for the persons they consider themselves to be. The problem is not that all beings have the ontological potential for humanness; mostly large predators and prey actualise this multiperspectivalism. The vision of prosopomorphism is often confined to shamen, but despite this restriction, it requires knowing who rather than what, getting at the social agency of objects: what we call a fact, scientifically explainable, like blood, is for the jaguar a cultural artifact, namely brewed cassava. On this view, since objects are 'ontologically ambiguous', we can also admit, in advance, that what a biologist might analyse as a naturally occurring fermented nectar is, for the animal guzzling it, a cultural drink akin to a bottomless cup of tea: 'What one side calls nature, then, very often turns out to be culture for the other', writes de Castro (2014: 62).

Multiperspectivalism complicates the question of animal desire by an inversion in which certain animals can see natural phenomena ('brute facts') as cultural artifacts, yet does not answer the question about how far this may be extended outside of specific relations between big predators and prey within Amerinidian worldviews. Indeed, it is not altogether obvious that the reverse applies that easily: that what humans regard as cultural objects like home brew are perceived as natural by animal predators who consider themselves as humans, yet surely the ontological ambiguity thesis vouchsafes it to some degree, and I will find it useful to consider throughout the remainder of this chapter, if only as a provocative question that complexifies the immanent heterogeneity of assemblages of animal-human desire even in the most carpeted of interiors among highly domesticated denizens where de Castro's (2014: 68) observation that the 'common condition of humans and animals is not animality but humanity' may be foiled by the facile estrangement of our pets from their mythical human origins, regularly contained in the injunction delivered to any dog: don't eat the human food; or, vice versa, unintentionally acknowledged in permitting dogs to consume scraps from the table.

The second constraint was placed by George Orwell on the traffic between human and animal becomings in *Animal Farm* (1971) by means of alcohol. The overt political message of Orwell's novel troubled the substance's transversality. The politics of alcohol consumption that marked Orwell's novel was initially based on a commandment of sobriety by the animal leadership, against the all-too-human practice of drunkeness by the deposed farmer. But by the novel's end, the successive self-serving qualifications of the decrees by a bovine leadership that had acquired not only a taste for whiskey, the experience of hangovers and drinking songs, but an interest in brewing and distilling, culminates in mutually implicative animal and human becomings through collective toasting rituals. The collusive intoxication that Orwell conjures entangles animal and human becomings in a toasting that expresses allegorically the failures of post-revolutionary politics. These entangled becomings are witnessed by the non-leadership caste, that is, by those led: barnyard animals other than pigs. Moreover, animal human becomings are linked to performances such as cheating at cards and empty speechifying; but the human animal becomings appear linked to a proliferation of chins and non-specific dewlaps, and the reduction of speech to angry noises.

At a more subterranean level, Orwell helped to expose the irruption of barley and perhaps other grains in the boars, the plants that already manifest themselves in drunkeness in humans, but shoot out a stem to these creatures as well (Deleuze and Guattari 1987: 11). The rhizome formed reterritorialises the boars through malted barley – the smell of cooking barley emanating from the farmhouse kitchen also attracts the attention of the barnyard animals and this olfactory shoot reaches far

– deterritorialising the neighbour farmer by transgressing the intoxication barrier – the so-called *drunk line* – traditionally erected between humans and animals (not to mention between settlers and indigenous peoples) and that is thought to be a traditional hallmark of uniquely human Dionysian excess (Roth 2005: 2). Alcohol may have been figured by Orwell as an opiate of any leadership, but in a Deleuzo-Guattarian spirit he followed plants from grain crops to kitchen still right into the rituals of 'another' species even if, trapped in an unambiguous anthropomorphism, the boars could only see whiskey as whiskey, as human culture, and mimic human drunken behaviour, trapped, bottled, and capped by it.

Transversal Components and Guattari's Critique of Ethology

Guattari abandoned the much too psycho-sociological conception of 'group' for the sake of the more abstract 'assemblage' (*agencement*) in order to avoid the confusing distinction between groups and individuals, and so as to add nonhuman animal and machinic elements into the mix. For Guattari (2011: 55), an assemblage is a collection of heterogeneous components from which subjectifications are assembled that engage in a variety of semiotic and machinic processes of enunciation. The enunciative components are collective – a 'non-totalizable intensive multiplicity' – and neither human nor molar essences (i.e. indexed to persons). The collective assemblage of enunciation consists, therefore, of multiplicities of molecular components that productively interact and in so doing articulate consistencies. The point at which different varieties of consistencies (molar, molecular and abstract machinic) cross is called by Guattari a nucleus (2011: 47 and 50), but any assemblage has a number of such foci whose formulae are metastable.

Guattari's intense typologising (delineating fields of consistency, for instance) during the period of *The Machinic Unconscious*, as well as his insistence on respecting the virtuality of the most abstract consistencies, gives way in *A Thousand Plateaus* to an explicit existential-territorial analysis in the description of how to make a territory using ethological materials – but also, how to escape from one territory into another. In addition to the descriptive detail of how assemblages contain and release components of passage that permit intra- and inter-assemblage transversal relations to take place, and how inter-assemblages remain open to new components of mutation and improvisation despite the tendencies to harden them (i.e. biologically, in 'ethological misunderstandings'), Guattari interpolates freedom and experimentation into closed behavioural sequencing, thereby deterritorialising a given functional space and time (i.e. like avian courtship rituals) and establishing new transversal co-relations between the most and least deterministic components of an assemblage: a transversal component, as Deleuze and Guattari define it, 'has taken upon itself the specialized vector of deterritorialization' (1987: 336). Those components that assist in the integration and/ or escape from an assemblage are closely scrutinised by the schizoanalyst; likewise, redundancies, disempowering and/or liberating black holes, resonance effects and molar formations that clog assemblages are carefully parsed and then erased, or reversed, redefined, and otherwise nourished for 'controlled' deterritorialisations (Guattari 2011: 188). A schizoanalytic metamodelling of ethology entails a critique of its mechanistic behaviourist assumptions and hierarchical arborescent logics by means of the insertion of transversal connections between otherwise hardened distinctions (like acquired vs. innate characteristics). Both linear causality (from higher to lower) and binarisms (such as inhibitors or innate releasing mechanisms) are criticised by utilising non-transcendent entanglements of components, therein complexifying ethological logic rather than simply reversing its priorities or substituting one hierarchy for another, as Manuel De Landa observes (2006: 19–21). The most well-known example is the wasp-orchid assemblage, a 'bio-ecological rhizome' that for Guattari marks a 'new symbiotic assemblage' (2011: 121–2). The hallmark of Guattari's critique of ethology is the mutually influential biological and semiotic components of rhizomatic entanglements that exhibit mutual dependencies, in terms of mixing innate and acquired traits and/or modification of a brain by a refrain (Deleuze and Guattari 1987: 332; Guattari 2011: 145). That a refrain can be a catalyst for neuronal rewiring is attested to by the kind of attention required by heavy cell-phone usage and the addictive qualities of checking, or at least trying to check, email and social media updates even when the network is down. The richness of the mutational component is expressed by Guattari as the 'surplus-value of code, i.e. a result that exceeds the simple totalization of the encodings involved (the sexual purpose of the orchid + the nutritional aim of the wasp)' (2011: 122). Hence, an assemblage is not a totality and a component is not reducible to its properties (De Landa 2006: 11). Surplus-value of code describes aparallel evolution: rhizomatic supplements in animal and human becomings, the mutual liberation of wasp and orchid.

Next, I want to turn to this 'surplus-giving relation' (Massumi 2002: 253) as a key to understanding alcohol's transversal excess.

Animal Desire

Guattari's insistence on 'animal desire' in *The Machinic Unconscious* does not find a place within the unity of becoming as a rhizomatic process that proceeds by transversal communications as it appears in *A Thousand Plateaus* in terms of neo-evolutionism. Even elegant recodings of the discussion of evolution in *A Thousand Plateaus* by philosopher John Protevi (2012: 252–4) in terms of strong novelty (non-filiative outcomes; niche construction as the evolutionary unit) and weak novelty (including organisms with descendants; serial endosymbiosis) within contemporary philosophy of biology do not really address the Guattarian proposition. While the polyvocality of evolutionary adaptive pathways is a given in Guattari's formulation, involving the exploration of potentialities within 'living rhizomes', the question of animal desire cannot be bracketed as if it were more 'fixed' or 'impoverished' than human desire. Guattari sought to build bridges between animal and human desire on the basis of 'intermediate behaviors' and 'relativized mechanistic encodings', having recourse to hybrid ethological-psychoanalytical parallels involving, for instance, *aphanisis*: desire losing its way and disappearing, citing the sudden breakdown and reversal of avian courtship rituals, and even the storage and retrieval of temporarily deferred assemblages: 'many assemblages that seem marginal in appearance vegetate as if waiting on the miraculous chance encounter of a line of deteritorialisation that would allow them to *set out again*' (Guattari 2011: 118), unfading or better de-lurking themselves from a rain check of sorts. The surplus-value of code presented by the mutant wasp-orchid 'species' evolves 'on its own account and redistribut[es] the genetic and semiotic components selected from both original species according to its own standards' (118). For Guattari, the sequencing of the phylogenetic tree may actually 'better dispose' the species to novel encounters stirring in latent – even the most deferred, suspended and wandering – rhizomatic potentialities.

In the example of the pentailed treeshrew, which sips betram palm nectar (which has a light beer-level alcohol content) many times each night during its year-round availablility, as it is non-seasonal, there is no field evidence that inebriation irrupts. Of all the creatures that help to pollinate the palm, including many non-flying mammals, birds and insects, the treeshrew derives the obvious benefits of widespread and constantly available nutrients and sugary energy in the nectar. It is suggested that the production of alcohol attracts pollinators; not all consumers will be unaffected by it. The palm flower-treeshrew assemblage operates without any evident negative effects of an alcoholic diet, which may include limiting the pollen vector's mobility and precipitating longer term pathologies in heavy drinkers or obvious signs of intoxication. However, it is supposed that this kind of consumption undoubtedly put adaptive pressure on the capacity to detoxify otherwise dangerously high levels of intake that researchers posit as long-term adaptive maintenance (Wiens et al. 2008: 10429).

Guattari asks us, however, to consider choice, discernment and pleasure in animal and human assemblages, as well as the potentialities of the alcoholic nectar. A treeshrew's selection of palm flowers actualises some of the alcohol's potential, but the tasting that takes place is not well understood. Does the treeshrew seek out higher or lower concentrations of alcohol, and how does this influence its movements, and the options it exercises? Is the nectar a natural or cultural object for a treeshrew? The connection between treeshrew and nectar is not influenced by specific sensations related to alcohol's typical effects, but by no particular effect, or unknown effects; this emphatically underlines a paradoxical sobriety. A treeshrew does not seek what it lacks; it does not expand its consciousness through inebriation; rather, the alcoholic nectar's pure potential, no pun intended, lies in not actualising drunkenness. The block of becoming of the palm flower and treeshrew is neither reducible to the adaptive features already noted nor to an analysis of the enzymes in the beery nectar. Instead, it is to be found in-between in a fog of haecceities in combination with the deterritorialisations of plants, and perhaps in the multiperspectivalism of the human desire of the animal not for a natural drink but for a cultural beverage: the world that the treeshrew sees may not be the one described by field ethology: 'the things *they see* when they see them *like we do* are *different*' (de Castro 2014: 71). Treeshrews may (not) be drinking light beer.

Wine for Cats

Veterinarians and animal protection organisations understand that for most domestic pets alcohol can be highly toxic. While dogs may display effects of inebriation similar to those of humans, the results may include respiratory and central nervous system problems leading to death. Drunken animals are not very funny. Of course, alcohol may be accidentally sourced from any number of common household products (Houston and Head 1993). Animal welfare advocates strongly condemn the provision of alcohol to pets and the testing of toxicity (including alcohol and alcohol-based products) on living animal models in laboratories as well. Providing alcohol to pets may be prosecuted as animal abuse in many jurisdictions. Thus, providing wine to cats would be an act of abuse if the product in question contained any alcohol. However, as our example does contain a very limited portion of grape juice, and such juice is recommended neither for cats nor dogs, it is not the kind of drink to which pets should be exposed. As the Nyan Nyan Nouveau (Meow Meow Nouveau, like its companion product, Wan Wan [woof woof] Beer, both manufactured in limited quantities by the same Japanese company and sold online) is mostly liquid sugar with a catnip bouquet, it is likely only a novelty item and not an attractive drink (as a sugary liquid that produces rather than quenches thirst). The American equivalent for dogs is Bowser Beer, which is a non-alcoholic malt barley and meat-based broth in a beer bottle that is sold in six-packs.

The metabolic communion that wine intensifies among human drink-ers is troubled here. In this cross-species scenario of celebratory 'drinks' together, cat and human caregiver do not really drink to one another's health. More than a few Internet trolls have pointed out that it would be abusive to give dogs and cats these beverages, at least from the perspec-tive of their human palettes. The construction of sociality suggested by wine for cats is supposedly a special event treat, with the proviso that sharing need not be consummated with imbibition. *Les vins primeurs* – fast wines for a fast capitalism – are heavily marketed and sold at high prices, not unlike our 'nouveau' for cats (and what better name than nyan cat, that Internet meme, repurposed for a niche market – not blowing a rainbow out its ass but vomiting up a grape-spiked beverage). This does not mean that such substances cannot under any circum-stances contribute to the formation of multiplicities across species; yet on this point they flirt with a product-focused mediator within what might be constructed as a preposterously neurotic apparatus with all the hallmarks of domesticity in the worst sense.

Is erzatz booze for pets the kind of component that might plot lines of escape towards new forms of interspecies sociality? Does pouring a so-called 'drink' for one's cat successfully stage new and strange encoun-ters? Wine for cats is so indeterminate as a beverage that if it is possible to melt the strictly capitalistic subjectification that it helps to construct, then it may transition into a component that nourishes the celebratory interspecies assemblage wherein animals symbolically join in the col-lective enunciations of holiday pleasure, having neither to tinkle (their glasses) nor tipple (their so-called 'wine'). As a component of passage wine for cats belongs to an interspecies companionship assemblage, and helps to modify the assemblage at specific festive moments; even though its material semiotic profile is meagre, this only makes rough its traversal of the assemblage as it is not tied down to genuine dangers and risks, for instance, presented both to humans and pets by 'real' alcohol, but stumbles over the dangers posed to cats by grape juice; for that matter, the semiotic scene of interspecies celebration is fraught with the dangers posed to curious dogs and cats by human party dregs and leftover food, among other unfortunate fallouts of human collective rituals of degradation. For the non-alcoholic 'alcohol' may exist alongside the 'real' alcohol in the social assemblage. The desire of the interspecies assemblage is supported by the transversal component of two wines – the one for cats, and the other for humans – only the latter contributing indirectly to a group's self-mutilation (Guattari 2003: 78), in the potential abuse of alcohol as the diffusion of stupidity. Yet it may be that 'wine for cats' is a factor of the interspecies assemblage's subjugation to the marketplace of pet products, and the phantasies it spins about interspecies communion at least for the human caregiver. Whither animal desire? It is not completely lost in the assemblage since the transversal potential of 'wine for cats' gives it expression, albeit in a jejune form. Yet it would be churlish to block the affects circulating among caregivers and their pets.

Conclusion

Great drinkers who do not become drunk are among our most cherished philosophers. The pintail treeshrew is just this kind of philosopher of the rainforest. Two domains were explored in this chapter, the first bearing upon wild animals and alcohol that alighted on a paradoxical sobriety, and the second, bearing upon domesticates and non-alcoholic drinks not necessarily meant to be drunk; the latter exposed one layer of the interkingdoms of alcohol at play across species. The complex alterities of an interspecies domestic assemblage, its 'multi-layered form[s] of relationality', as Rosi Braidotti (2012: 181) puts it, and affective landscapes of companionship and co-dependencies, are marked by transversal components that refresh the relations within the assemblage. My sense of sobriety has been to focus less on the discourses of alcoholism and drugs that cross the Deleuzo-Guattarian corpuses and the outright rejection of the animal drinker in literary analyses of drunkenness (perhaps the truly 'Orwellian' contribution), and more on the many constraints of interspecies imbibition, from fictional imaginaries and veterinary science. Sobriety is, then, a viable outcome of deterritorialisation without inebriation, with and without alcohol, but not imitative and with open lines of becoming.

As Donna Haraway taught us, companionship species are engaged in co-constitutive becomings, with the understanding that 'beings do not preexist their relatings' (2003: 6). To these beings Guattari would add a range of objects, ideologies, forces, flows, agencies and temporalities, that inform collective assemblages of enunciation and the nonhuman components of hybrid processes of subjectification. Just hanging out together is not risk free, especially when one among us is a pet.

Although the wasp-orchid false coupling is a key example of Deleuzo-Guattarian ethology, when Haraway writes of co-evolution among humans and dogs, she extends and widens the co-evolutionary hypothesis to a domesticated multi-species assemblage that is forever emerging. The assemblage she has in mind includes breeding, training, playing, working and the vast amount of goods and contexts that multi-species companions negotiate. Co-evolution is the rule (2003: 31). It is in this jumble of components that I have tried to situate wine for cats. Despite Deleuze and Guattari's bad attitude towards the Oedipal domesticate (and recall Deleuze's personal dislike of animals that rubbed up against him), there is room for an emergent experimentation within the interspecies assemblage at the level of choice (individual, collective) and symbolic exchange. Guattari insisted that novel semioticisations and creative assemblages were not free-floating but indexed to the digestive tracts involved, to which may be added particular places and times and companies. Interkingdoms in elaboration may be sober, but that does not exclude the presence of alcohol because the dyad dry/wet is too restrictive and unproductive.

Recent ethnographic fieldwork by Maan Barua, on illegally home-distilled alcohol made of fermented treacle in rural India and the ethologies of elephants, figures alcohol as a 'hidden actor' in animal-human ecologies. Within this inter-assemblage alcohol readies and sustains the bodies of villagers who guard their crops at night against elephant raids, and supplements their incomes when crops are damaged, and at the same time the odiferous stills activate the sweet-teeth of elephants that otherwise, in the wild, actively seek out and consume fermented fruits like durian. It is speculated that elephants use alcohol to cope with their own traumas brought about by shrinking territories, deforestation, ivory poaching, etc. The issue of animal desire is not left out of the account, as Barua writes:

> The tranquilizing and sedating effects of alcohol could, indeed, be what the creatures seek to cope with trauma. Foregrounding nonhuman rhythms

and lifeworlds alters explanations of the causes and consequences of conflict. The latter can be generated from the flows of nonhuman desire, the assemblages that result when elephants and alcohol recorporealize in response to each other. (2014: 1473)

Important as it is, animal desire is not the inviolable centre (actor) of an interspecies assemblage, and it cannot be isolated since desire perfuses the interacting components of assemblages. Desire flows as much as alcohol is said to within an assemblage and together they build complex relations and milieus, rearranging ethograms and ecologies across species, and helping to pose the question whether or not elephants experience the taste of sweet spring water in every home brewed concoction they sample.

Readers of *A Thousand Plateaus* are abundantly aware of the trinity of sobriety, caution and prevention, and how taken together they moderate becoming by injecting 'pragmatic concerns', as Isabelle Stengers (2011: 147–8) states, into the existential situation of a 'devastated world'. Any reader's refrain about prevention that marshalls prophylaxis against illusion and destruction, in the spirit of self-management, maybe even doing more with less (Gilson 2011: 80–1), needs to reckon with the prodigious desires of sober assemblages, especially those involving fermented beverages. Sharing a 'drink' among householders human and animal may invite a discourse of responsibilisation, regardless of what's in it. Stengers meets this challenge by turning to magic in her cat's cradle of Guattari and Haraway, regaining the goddess against the cyborg, for the sake of *respect* for the forces that can easily devour the witless. So, the emphasis becomes, then, more ontological and less overtly ethical, open to the perception of strange affinities between substances where every glass of wine for cats has the tang of a freshly killed mouse: nobody ever drinks a *drink-in-itself*, as de Castro (2014: 73) affirms, as substances communicate affinally such that every drink is onto-semiotically charged and finishes with divergent self-variations.

If it were not for the conceptual antipathy between de Castro and French anthopologist Philippe Descola, I would end by injecting the latter's trenchant comment that 'for anthropology, no ontology is better or more truthful in itself than another' (2013: 66), and fold back the lesson of the ontology I have just explored onto itself, requiring it to find its affinal other, but in the process risking absurdity and a hard-to-win conceptualisation of sobriety at once.

References

Ashcroft, B. (2013), 'Introducing Japanese "Wine" for, uh, Cats', Kotaku. com, 15 October, at http://kotaku.com/introducing-japanese-wine-for-uh-cats-1445498718 (accessed 10 October 2016).

Barua, M. (2014), 'Volatile Ecologies: Toward a Material Politics of Human-Animal Relations', *Environment and Planning A*, Vol. 46, No. 6, pp. 1462–78.

Braidotti, R. (2012), 'Nomadic Ethics', in D. Smith and H. Somers-Hall (eds), *The Cambridge Companion to Deleuze*, London: Cambridge University Press, pp. 170–97.

Chaudhuri, U. (2014), 'Becoming-rhinoceros: Therio-theatricality as Problem and Promise in Western Drama', in G. Marvin and S. McHugh (eds), *Routledge Handbook of Human-Animal Studies*, New York: Routledge, pp. 194–207.

de Castro, E. V. (2014), *Cannibal Metaphysics*, trans. P. Skafish, Minneapolis: Univocal.

De Landa, M. (2006), *A New Philosophy of Society*, New York: Continuum.

Deleuze, G. (1990), *The Logic of Sense*, trans. M. Lester, New York: Columbia University Press.

Deleuze, G. (2002), *Dialogues II*, with Claire Parnet, trans. H. Tomlinson and B. Habberjam, New York: Columbia University Press.

Deleuze, G. and F. Guattari (1977), *Anti-Oedipus: Capitalism and Schizophrenia*, trans. R. Hurley, M. Seem, H.R. Lane, New York: Viking.

Deleuze, G. and F. Guattari (1987), *A Thousand Plateaus: Capitalism and Schizophrenia*, trans. B. Massumi, Minneapolis: University of Minnesota Press.

Descola, P. (2013), *The Ecology of Others*, trans. G. Godbout and B.P. Luley, Chicago: Prickly Paradigm Press.

Dominy, N. J. (2004), 'Fruits, Fingers, and Fermentation: The Sensory Cues Available to Foraging Primates', *Integrative and Comparative Biology*, Vol. 4, No. 4, pp. 295–303.

Genosko, G. (1993), 'Freud's Bestiary: How Does Psychoanalysis Treat Animals?, *The Psychoanalytic Review*, Vol. 80, No. 4, pp. 603–32.

Gilson, E. C. (2011), 'Responsive Becoming: Ethics Between Deleuze and Feminism', in D. W. Smith and N. Jun (eds), *Deleuze and Ethics*, Edinburgh: Edinburgh University Press, pp. 63–88.

Guattari, F. (2003), *Psychanalyse et transversalité*, Paris: La Découverte.

Guattari, F. (2011), *The Machinic Unconscious*, trans. T. Adkins, Los Angeles: Semiotext(e).

Haraway, D. (2003), *The Companion Species Manifesto: Dogs, People, and Significant Otherness*, Chicago: Prickly Paradigm Press.

Houston, D. M. and L. L. Head (1993), 'Acute Alcohol Intoxication in a Dog', *Canadian Veterinary Journal*, Vol. 34, pp. 41–2.

Ionesco, E. (1960), 'Rhinoceros', *Plays*, Vol. 4, trans. D. Prouse, London: Calder & Boyars, pp. 3–107.

Kasmir, S. (2005), 'Drinking Rituals, Identity and Politics in a Basque Town', in T. M. Wilson (ed.), *Drinking Cultures*, New York: Berg, pp. 201–23.

Lowry, M. (1971), *Under the Volcano*, New York: Penguin.

Massumi, B. (2002), *Parables for the Virtual*, Durham, NC: Duke University Press.

n.a. (2012) *British Medical Journal* (BMJ), 'Young birds can get "drunk" on fermented berries: Effects similar to those of people, only drunk birds have much further to fall', *Science Digest*, 2 November, at https://www.sciencedaily.com/releases/2012/11/121102205132.htm (accessed 10 October 2016).

Orwell, G. (1971), *Animal Farm: A Fairy Story*, Harmondsworth: Penguin.

Phillips, H. (1998), 'News: Inebriated insects', *Nature*, 2 July.

Protevi, J. (2012), 'Deleuze and Life', in D.W. Smith and H. Somers-Hall (eds), *The Cambridge Companion to Deleuze*, Cambridge: Cambridge University Press, pp. 239–64.

Roth, M. (2005), *Drunk the Night Before: An Anatomy of Intoxication*, Minneapolis: University of Minnesota Press.

Samorini, G. (2002), *Animals and Psychedelics*, South Paris, ME: Park Street Press.

Sauvagnargues, A. (2013), *Deleuze and Art*, trans. S. Bankston, London: Bloomsbury.

Stengers, I. (2011) 'Relaying a War Machine?', in E. Alliez and A. Goffey (eds), *The Guattari Effect*, London: Bloomsbury, pp. 134–55.

Wiens, F. et al. (2008), 'Chronic Intake of Fermented Floral Nectar by Wild Treeshrews', *Proceedings of the National Academy of Sciences of the United States of America*, Vol. 105, No. 30, pp. 10426–31.

Chapter 16

Becoming-Wolf: From Wolf-Man to the Tree Huggers of Turkey

Serazer Pekerman

> Bacon creates the painting of the scream because he establishes a relationship between the visibility of the scream (the open mouth as a shadowy abyss) and invisible forces, which are nothing other than the forces of the future . . . the diabolical powers of the future knocking at the door. Every scream contains them potentially. (Deleuze 2008: 43)

In February 2012, at a meeting of the youth wing of the Justice and Development Party, then Prime Minister Recep Tayyip Erdoğan declared that he wanted to raise pious and vengeful generations. His vengeful scheme has been unfolding for quite some time. As a result, the summer of 2013 saw the largest anti-government movement in the recent history of Turkey: the Gezi Protest. At the beginning of the protest, it seemed as though it was exactly what had been needed. The people were right, the government was wrong, and there was hope for change. However, it seems like this has not yet happened. Today, a few years after the initial protest, Erdoğan is far more powerful than before and the people are even less free. The main reason behind this is the fact that Erdoğan disrupted and diverted the conversation by making false accusations about the protesters. Some protesters felt the need to defend themselves. Once this started, Erdoğan had already won, because in order to defend themselves they had to stop protesting against the government and start criticising each other. Even though their innocence was immediately proven, the protesters were divided. Criticising the protests was deemed more important than protesting, especially among intellectuals. Not only did this undermine the commitment of the protesters, it also changed the way they were perceived. Had this not been the case, things could have been different.

This chapter will elaborate on the Gezi protests from a lycanthropic perspective, reconsidering people as pack animals, like wolves. During the protests, there were several blame-defence incidents among the body of protesters, triggered by Erdoğan. In this chapter, however, I shall particularly focus on feminist groups. After explaining how the feminist front of Gezi was destroyed, I shall draw an analogy between mainstream werewolf characters and the protesters. Then I shall comment on the fears that caused the werewolf to deny its own nature. I shall examine this in relation to the Wolf-Man, a patient of Freud's, also mentioned by Deleuze and Guattari in connection with becoming-wolf. In order to elaborate on the becoming of a protester, I will make use of the Deleuzo-Guattarian concepts of *assemblage* and the *paranoid subject*. These concepts will elucidate how and why some actions of the defending-protesters made the group dysfunctional.

The Gezi protests eventually spread to the whole country, but the movement is still widely known as the Gezi Park Protest because it began in a central park called 'Gezi' (which means 'journey' in Turkish) in Taksim Square in Istanbul. The park was to be destroyed with the intention of rebuilding Taksim military barracks (originally built in 1806). This project was one of Erdoğan's numerous attempts at creating a *New Turkey* that would revive the alleged glory of the Ottoman Empire. In this 'new' country Erdoğan promised that he was going to bring back all the good things that 'evil' secularism had taken away. It is also known that an infamous pro-sharia protest started in these barracks (31 March Incident, 1909). Today, after the Gezi protests, the area has acquired a certain worldwide fame that obviously has no resemblance to what Erdoğan and his devoted followers had in mind. The cry from Gezi was heard all around the world, before it was brutally silenced. This was a long-awaited uprising because Erdoğan had already made his radical Islamist intentions clear from the beginning of his political career. With every electoral victory, he increased the level of oppression and took away more liberties. As time went by, he seemed less and less willing to soften his fundamentalist agenda and showed no tolerance for any opinion other than his own. His oppressive manner has been internalised by most of his followers, even by most of the opposition and intelligentsia, and has invaded not only all public places but also the private spheres of individuals. At this stage, the timing of Gezi has turned it into an important last testament, constructed by the peoples of Turkey, even though it does not seem to have had a positive outcome for the country just yet.

The Gezi movement began with trees and it became a symbol of hope and a desire to reconnect with nature. The reconstruction project for the old barracks had no legal permit. Despite this, it began with the cutting down of trees in the park. The core protesters were a small number of civilians from the neighbourhood who simply went to the park and stayed there, hoping to stop the construction workers. The protesters were exercising their fundamental rights as stated in the Turkish constitution. As more people joined them, they started to put up tents, sit under the trees, hug them, or tie themselves to them in the hope of saving one of the very few remaining green areas from demolition. However, early one morning the police attacked these protesters in their sleep, burnt their tents and backpacks, pepper-gassed and, apparently, 'cleaned' the whole park. Later, on 24 June, Erdoğan admitted that he gave this 'cleaning' order to 'his' minister, because apparently 'he could not sit and watch some invaders'. That morning, after the police attack, thousands of people gathered around the park and, despite the police, the park was re-occupied in a few hours by civilians who had by then multiplied in numbers and determination. This small victory gave hope to literally millions of people who kept occupying parks, streams, olive groves and walking the streets throughout the country for weeks and weeks to come, despite the unceasing brutal police attacks, assaults, injuries and deaths. The movement was no longer only against illegal construction and the destruction of greenery. The protesters wanted a different future. From the smallest village to the capital city Ankara, people were calling for the government to resign.

It would not be wrong to say that the movement (colloquially, the 'Gezi spirit') still carries on in peaceful environmentalist and feminist protests and has won some victories, albeit very small ones, in some corners of Turkey. Up close, it seems as if the protests melted away with no tangible results, and it feels like whatever one does, one can only help Erdoğan and his gang to reinstate their omnipotence, which was recently crowned by his victory in the presidential elections. However, the big picture shows that he had long since lost his reliability and his status outside his close circle. Through the world media the whole world was made aware that at least half the country sees his acts as anti-democratic and illegal, though this has been less apparent in the Turkish media, probably because it has also been 'cleaned' systematically during Erdoğan's regime. Gezi was an unprecedented protest for Turkey. Firstly, it brought together various groups, political and apolitical alike, hand in hand for the first time, helping each other not only against a common threat, but also for a common hope. Also, fortunately, despite police provocation and imaginative defamation efforts, its peaceful, environmentalist and feminist core remained visible.

Not surprisingly, throughout the protests Erdoğan acted like an angry father figure who blames his children for his own mistakes. He always trades on this kind of familiarity, hoping to provide a fake feeling of security for the masses. He openly favours and forgives his pious children, who vote for him, and explicitly punishes the ones who do not. Also, he occasionally invites his favourite children to punish these 'infidels'. That summer, unusually even for him, every sentence that came out of his mouth seemed to be constructed to create enmity between the veiled and unveiled, pro-sharia and secular, Alewi and Sunni, Turkish and Kurdish – all of whom were out on the streets, protesting against him. Instead of explaining his extremely violent acts, and instead of answering the questions the protesters asked, Erdoğan made up stories of violence allegedly committed by the protesters. Two of his slanders brought him the closure he hoped for by occupying the whole media coverage of Gezi from the moment they were uttered: Erdoğan claimed that some protesters were 'drinking beer and peeing in a mosque' (although the imam of the mosque who was with the protesters said they did no such thing), and that some protesters were 'beating up one of his veiled sisters/daughters' (although there was security camera footage proving that no such incident happened, a veiled woman was falsely witnessing for him). Once again he hid behind the shield of the religious sensitivities that he made up for 'his own' people. Both alleged incidents were easily disproved because there was ample evidence, but Erdoğan has not yet admitted that he lied. As more evidence has been revealed, proving that none of it actually happened, he has elaborated his blatant lies even more because they kept bringing him success.

At this point I'd like to visit the mainstream werewolf narratives, underlining the similarities between their stories and those of the Gezi protesters. The mainstream werewolf's story commences like a typical hero/heroine story. The characters take action, listening to a call that no one else seems to hear. In the werewolf's case the call comes from nature; the call of the neglected, hurt and hungry animal inside. Typical mainstream heroes and heroines are initially perceived as guilty and are blamed for taking action. Their happy closure usually comes after the proof of their innocence. However, in the werewolf's case, unlike a typical hero, it remains impossible for them to ascertain their own innocence, let alone prove it to anyone else. In this sense, the Gezi protesters were sharing the destiny of a mainstream werewolf character. Werewolves, just like a body of protesters in a large group, are not entirely sure what 'the animal inside' (and all the other protesters) did the previous night. They typically find themselves experiencing regret, worry, guilt, mostly under a tree, naked, bruised, traumatised, covered in blood, early in the morning with no memory of the previous night.

They are destined to hear about their terrible deeds from other characters. Unlike typical heroes/heroines, werewolves do not find resolutions
for the obstacles they meet. Once they meet an obstacle (the alleged evil
deeds that they are told they might have committed), they leave everything else behind and devote their lives to self-defence, even when they
are innocent. This defensive mood changes how they are perceived by
others, even their loved ones. The self-defence of an innocent brings
inevitable self-destruction. Thus, although they set off like everybody
else, they never get a happy ending.

The Gezi protesters were actually in a better situation than a werewolf
to begin with. Everybody knew that they were right in their actions and
they were innocent of the charges. They did not have to defend themselves. Even if they could not follow the world media, they certainly
knew that at least half the country was proudly supporting them intel-
lectually, if not physically. However, despite all this, no one managed to
publicly ask Erdoğan the only necessary question: if someone had actually peed in a mosque, would this have given him the right to kill and
torture everyone on the streets? Instead, some protesters felt the need to
defend themselves, just like the mainstream werewolf. They allocated all
their time to arguing that the protest was not against religion. This may
have had some truth in it. However, when some started campaigning for
the freedom to wear the veil to prove their point, they could not have
been any further from the meaning of the protests. It must be stated that
in certain ways the protest was against religious oppression, and some
protesters believed that the veil was one of the tools of this oppression,
functioning as a discriminatory and sexist device. These discussions, or
the lack of a proper discussion, ruined the feminist expansion of the
uprising because, once again, women were forced to talk about the veil
– a sectarian religious garment – instead of trying to regain their most
basic human rights. Moreover, they were forced to publicly support the
so-called 'freedom' to use these garments in non-religious public indoor
places, in order to fulfil the sudden need for innocence.

The headscarf, used by Sunni Muslim women, has been transformed
into a symbol for Erdoğan's idea of freedom and has always been the
strongest 'Trojan horse' for his fundamentalist politics. He kept abusing
the issue without referring to the facts. Actually, his main claim that
headscarves were forbidden in Turkey was not true. The headscarf, like
some other accessories, was supposed to be taken off in public buildings
like schools and governmental offices. This was not simply a rule about
dressing though. It also underlined the Turkish Republic's message that
women were already safe in these places and did not need to cover

themselves as stated in the Holy Koran. However, none of this was discussed. The issue was handled in an extremely emotional and biased manner. Anyone who tried to point out the logical fallacies was labelled as a public enemy and excluded from most of the respectable intellectual circles out of fear. These circles felt safe and secure if, and only if, they systematically published materials that harshly criticised Mustafa Kemal Atatürk, the secular republic, and the secular army, as well as continually asking for more privileges for allegedly oppressed Sunni Muslim minorities; in doing so, they made use of preposterous lies and irrational or irrelevant theories and opinions. Empowered by these notions, the Islamist government has gradually been enforcing its own agenda by attacking republican ideals. According to the Islamists, one of the most disturbing legacies of the republic was the presence of independent, educated women. Consequently, while the Islamist government was attacking women from all walks of life, for example by in effect banning abortion, feminism in Turkey was diminished into a defence of headscarves. This carried on until the Gezi protests, which saw thousands of people marching for and reclaiming the rights of women – rights which had been bestowed by the republican revolutions almost a century ago. However, in the name of women the only outcome of the protests ended up being the freedom to wear headscarves. How did this happen?

Just like sad and lost werewolves, who try to defend themselves instead of their forest, a group of female public figures associated with the Gezi protests tried to prove innocence where no such proof was needed. They started a campaign, a 'Call for Freedom of Headscarves', the only 'feminist' campaign that was allowed in the media. They called themselves 'Unveiled Women for Veiled Women' (UWVW) and campaigned for 'the pious women's right to wear headscarves in the parliament'. They claimed that Gezi Park was their inspiration and that they wanted to see veiled MPs, totally ignoring the lack of connection between the two. The media loved this 'decent' story; it was a successful example for Erdoğan's brand-new state-feminism. Meanwhile on the streets, for trying to protect all women's most fundamental rights (from abortion to education), thousands of unveiled women were beaten and sexually assaulted by Erdoğan's police (and also by some of his followers). No one talked about any of this. Needless to say, none of the Gezi feminisms was about the freedom to wear any piece of clothing. Gezi was a collective voice against the normalisation of the extremely misogynist culture that has occupied public and private spheres from classrooms and courts to homes. Gezi was about the freedom of all peoples and universal human rights, which have been insidiously eroded by the radical Islamist government. Whereas, in the aftermath of the veil campaign of the UWVW, all these voices were silenced, losing any hope of being acknowledged. Different groups were even more polarised than before. The limits of feminism were, once again, drawn by Erdoğan, the omnipotent father, who always protects good girls who obey him.

The persistent allegations about the protesters and the truth being ignored stirred up deep emotions in everyone. Lying about the protests that were taking place in front of the world had a larger impact than lying about the distant past or promoting a rotten theory. However, the truth could not change the destiny of the protester who was found guilty for doing what seems like the only right thing to do. This is because the mainstream cannot reconcile the two faces of the werewolf. The good human and the bad wolf – the advocate who defended his people's rights and the disrespectful thug who peed in the mosque – should not and could not be perceived as one. It is believed that the wild wolf comes out uncontrollably and harms the innocent human and others. Therefore they must be separated or terminated even in cases where their fight is perfectly legitimate. Werewolves' deeds will be disproportionately punished just to be on the safe side, even when the characters are totally innocent except for answering nature's call. Strangely, werewolves themselves mostly seem to be convinced that they must be stopped by any means necessary. From *The Wolf Man* (dir. George Waggner, 1941) to *The Wolfman* (dir. Joe Johnston, 2010), and in various supporting roles, their stories end with their being willing to die, or killing their wolf-half in order to be tamed to fit in with the norms of society. They do not claim unconditional love from the audience or seek to be forgiven or even to be punished proportionately. The only way the mainstream accepts a werewolf as a good character, as seen in the film series *The Twilight Saga* (2008–12), is after stripping them of any connection with the myth and the lore. Werewolf characters represent humans' fear of their own instincts, of any large-scale change, and they remind the audience all the 'shameful quirks' humans share with animals, such as hunger, sexual desire, love of life and passion for nature.

In *Werewolf Complex*, Denis Duclos says that 'the werewolf is a raw image of the mad warrior at once human and animal' (1998: 83). He explains how the audience finds werewolf-like cult heroes sympathetic despite their unjustifiable violence, such as Robert de Niro in *Taxi Driver* (1976) and Michael Douglas in *Falling Down* (1993) (1998: 13). Duclos has a valid point when it comes to individual heroes – especially strong star personas like the given examples – whose madness might be tolerated and forgiven as a disconnected episode and may be perceived as temporary. They obviously do not experience an extreme bodily trans-formation, neither do they forget who they are. In the true werewolf's case, however, wolf and human do not resemble each other at all and do not use the same memory bank. This endangers the sense of identity, wholeness and reliability of character. Noël Carroll clarifies the function of shape-shifting as follows: 'A character ... is multiplied into one or more new facets each standing for another aspect of the self, generally one that is either hidden, ignored, repressed, or denied by the character' (1981: 21). Therefore the audience's reaction actually depends on the nature of this previously hidden part and how it unfolds. When De Niro is framed with a Mohawk haircut, whatever he does, the audience might still be ready to try to understand and forgive him more than they would a scary-looking wild beast. However, even among shape-shifters the werewolf has a uniquely unwanted position. From vampires to super-heroes, werewolf identity retains a unique shame due to its extreme shift. They are neither cool nor good, and they cannot have a happy ending no matter how hard they try. For example: they can never be accepted and loved as trigger-happy criminals like the vampires.

Phillip Bernhardt-House claims that the werewolf's power, unlike that of many other shape-shifters, is almost always a curse and not a gift. The werewolf is perceived as 'a human divided against itself, unable to control its emotions or its body' (2008: 165). 'Lycanthropy appears like a step not only backward but downward in the evolutionary scale ... the werewolf's form changes constantly and unexpectedly, thus were-wolves are a great threat to any enduring sense of identity' (163). This threat is typically conveyed in the transformation scenes of the films. The audience is invited to share the pain of the human while a certain beast comes out of him. On the other hand, how the human comes back after the episode is hardly an interesting moment to frame. It would be unusual to see the reverse transformation. The human, or what is left of her, is typically found where the beast finally leaves her. Once the beast destroys their sense of identity, this will always be perceived as a permanent threat both by themselves and their society. Even though the audience knows that the beast and human are one and the same, the expectation will always be that the beast-half who appears and ruins everything will ultimately be destroyed. Thus, following the normative society, the suicidal werewolf sacrifices herself for the closure of her own story.

In this sense werewolves and the Gezi protesters share a common burden by embodying a curious contradiction. The werewolf's bodily transformation is a perfect visualisation of becoming-animal, but it fails to let go of a fixed sense of identity; thus, it also fails in its becoming in a Deleuzo-Guattarian sense. In Gezi, the street protests proved that there was an assemblage on the streets, changing and evolving together, but it was not reflected in the media, thus losing support and potential. Like the mainstream werewolf, UWVW, by shifting their target from protest to defence, destroyed the feminist uprising of Gezi. Once the protest turned into a defence, the public was forced to change perspective and suddenly each and every one of the protesters was expected to prove their total innocence before they could demand their most basic rights. This gave control of the conversation to Erdoğan, who did not have to answer any further questions. No one was repeating the questions; they were too busy with self-defence. This weakened and ended the move-ment. The becoming-wolf of the mainstream werewolf had failed, again. At this point, I will focus on becoming-animal, in order to observe how it functions and when and how it fails.

Becoming is the Deleuzian response to a fixed identity, to being. Being assumes an unchanging position. On the other hand, becoming perceives identity as an experience, a process of moving with, understanding, changing and being changed by people, opinions, events and so on. In *A Thousand Plateaus*, the concept appears very often, always explained in terms of the individual's connection with the masses. Becoming starts with the attraction of becoming one among many: 'A becoming-animal always involves a pack, a band, a population, a peopling, in short a multiplicity' (Deleuze and Guattari 2007: 264). Becoming also neces-sitates another ingredient: *a loner*. The loner is not a guide or a leader. 'Wherever there is multiplicity, you will also find an exceptional indi-vidual, and it is with that individual that an alliance must be made in order to become-animal' (268). Throughout *A Thousand Plateaus*, Deleuze and Guattari quite often elaborate on the characteristics of wolves as loners and wolf packs as multiplicities, thus, becoming-wolf has a special place in any becoming-animal.

> In becoming-wolf, the important thing is the position of the mass, and above all the position of the subject itself in relation to the pack or wolf multiplicity: how the subject joins or does not join the pack, how far away it stays, how it does or does not hold to the multiplicity. (32)

In becoming, 'multiplicities form a single assemblage and operate in the same assemblage' (38). The assemblage is more than a simple uni-fication, it works like a specific kind of merging process that creates a unique new entity out of its various ingredients, not necessarily like any of them. In *A Thousand Plateaus*, it is mostly used in order to explicate a multiplicity in the process of becoming as opposed to a hierarchical unity that submits its absolute power to a leader or a group of privileged individuals. 'Assemblage' is a schizoanalytic term. An assemblage's function is to end the duality between the one and the multiple; also, between a leader and his mass. An assemblage, once constructed, carries on changing people and the relationships between people. It works exactly like the Gezi Park street protests: creating invisible ties between all the protesters, creating a 'we' or 'they', beyond class, age, gender, or ethnic background, a 'we' who are against Erdoğan and his oppressive regime, even if this certain 'we' could not physically be together or agree on any other matter. Therefore, an assemblage might have an intense, challenging and even threatening dynamic for its ingredients' individual identities. While some may not be concerned by this threat, others might become frightened and fall out of the assemblage.

Deleuze and Guattari make a distinction between two positions of a subject: the schizo position, the occupant of which would not be concerned by this threat, and the paranoid position. In the paranoid position, individuals feel threatened because they are identified with the group, and 'the group with the leader, and the leader with the group; [and one is expected to be] securely embedded in the mass, get close to the centre, never be at the edge except in the line of duty' (2007: 38). Consequently, the paranoid position would insist on keeping everyone in the centre and could not allow individuals to express their independent views. Any deviation from the norm would be perceived as extreme or marginal and therefore scary and dangerous. Paranoid subjects are prone to escape to a familiar territory due to fear of change. They might reunite with the oppressive regime simply because it is familiar. Deleuze and Guattari call this a dark-assemblage (38, 267). This is what ends the process of becoming. For example, in the case of Gezi, the headscarf campaign not only separated the UWVW from the rest of the protesters, but also, by imitating Erdoğan and protecting the 'good' veiled sisters only, it destroyed the assemblage. This self-proclaimed feminist group made their dark-assemblage with the only option they thought they had: the military and religious organisation of Erdoğan's omnipresent fundamentalist state.

Focusing on the section devoted to 'becoming-wolf', '1914: One or Several Wolves', will further illustrate this situation. Deleuze and Guattari choose to explain 'becoming-wolf' following an arrested (failed) becoming of one of Sigmund Freud's patients, nicknamed Wolf-Man. The Wolf-Man (Sergei Pankejeff 1886–1979) was the son of a rich Russian businessman. When he met Freud, he was 'entirely incapacitated and completely dependent upon other people' (Freud 1971: 154), suffering from severe depression and a bowel problem that obliged him to use an enema in order to defecate. He was given the nickname by Freud because of a dream he had when he was four or five years old. This dream remained at the centre of Freud's analysis (140). Like Gezi Park, the Wolf-Man's adventures begin around a tree:

> I dreamt that it was night and that I was lying in my bed. . . . Suddenly the window opened of its own accord, and I was terrified to see that some white wolves were sitting on the big walnut tree [there was an actual tree where he dreamt] in front of the window. There were six or seven of them . . . They had big tails like foxes and they had their ears pricked like dogs when they pay attention to something. In great terror, evidently of being eaten up by the wolves, I screamed and woke up . . . The only piece of action in the dream was the opening of the window; for the wolves sat quite still and without making any movement on the branches of the tree . . . and looked at me. It took quite a long while before I was convinced that it had only been a dream; such a clear and life-like picture. (Freud 1971: 172)

At this point it is important to note that when asked to draw the same dream, he only drew a tree and five wolves, not 'six or seven' (174). In 1914 – the year in the relevant chapter title in *A Thousand Plateaus* – Freud terminated the treatment and wrote about the case of the Wolf-Man in his 'From the History of an Infantile Neurosis' (153). Freud initially handled the case as a peculiar independent experience, but concluded that it was compatible with his analyses of previous cases (158). He reflected on the number of wolves in relation to several fairy tales such as 'The Wolf and the Seven Goats' (although, there is only one grey wolf in that story). He concluded that the wolves represented the patient's anxiety; the fear of being devoured/castrated and the fear of his authoritarian father. While the Wolf-Man himself focused on the realness of his dream, and looked for an answer in the stillness and attentive staring of the wolves, Freud limited himself by approaching the existence of the animals as symbolic and as distant as possible, as mere representations. He found relief in the fact that the wolves had some dog-like parts (ears), and this gave him enough confidence to domesticate the wolves, to reduce their number and to claim that the nightmare might have been inspired by the Wolf-Man's seeing the primal scene, his parents having sexual intercourse (probably doggy style), although the patient claimed that this was not possible. Freud's strong assertion turned the animals into mere representations rather than a pack of (six or seven) white wolves. According to him the wolves embodied the patient's fear of (and infantile sexual desire towards) his father, and this also explained his 'ambivalent attitude towards every father-surrogate' all his life (176). The Wolf-Man always loved and trusted Freud. His situation became considerably better after starting to work with him, but he never fully recovered. They remained friends.

The Wolf-Man's case and dream also attracted Deleuze and Guattari's attention. They described the dream as a particularly good image of the schizo position: 'To be fully a part of the crowd and at the same time completely outside it, removed from it: to be on the edge' (2007: 33). They do not share Freud's views on the case. Firstly, they have a fundamental disagreement with psychoanalysts on how to interpret animals in dreams. '[The psychoanalysts, even Jung] see the animal as a representative of drives, or a representation of the parents. They do not see the reality of a becoming-animal, that it is affect in itself, the drive in person, and represents nothing' (2007: 286). They criticise Freud for reducing everything to the possibility of the Wolf-Man's seeing his parents having sex. They believe that Freud does not understand the symbolic meaning of wolves for children. He domesticates the call of nature and cuts the main connection in the dream: 'Freud obviously knows nothing about the fascination exerted by wolves and the meaning of their silent call, the call to become-wolf' (32). This brings us to Deleuze and Guattari's general concern about Freud's analyses. They think that Freud does not explain to his patients that the norm is an external, hostile construct and neither does he invite them to rebel against it. Freud seems to help his patients to cope with the norm; Deleuze and Guattari, on the other hand, invite them to embrace change through becoming. According to them, 'the wolf-man says ... I feel myself becoming a wolf, one wolf among others, on the edge of the pack ... Freud hears: Help me not become wolf' (35).

Deleuze and Guattari claim that the Wolf-Man was one of the wolves in his dream – the one that was not drawn on paper – or else he wanted to be one of them. They also take into account when and where the Wolf-Man lived. This dimension, which was missing from Freud's analysis, gave them additional layers of connections to work on. The Wolf-Man saw the most important event of the turn of the century up close: he was contemporary with the Bolsheviks (a Russian word literally meaning 'majority' or 'one of the majority') in his homeland. Consequently, Deleuze and Guattari continue to interpret the same dream from a wider perspective: The pack of wolves might be the Bolsheviks for the Wolf-Man, who was a Russian aristocrat and probably very scared of the wild crowd on the streets; but at the same time he might have wanted to be a part of this monumental event (33). This wider picture does not, of course, eliminate the possibility that Wolf-Man was scared of his authoritarian father and was feeling guilty for wanting to be a part of the revolution, knowing that it was literally against his rich father. Actually, Deleuze and Guattari do not openly disagree that the Wolf-Man was scared of his father. They see his only cure in becoming-wolf, which was probably stopped by the fear of his father in the first place. This bring us back to the burden of the werewolf, who embodies a perfect becoming but fails to rebel against the expectations of the father/leader/state/family/norm.

The Gezi protests provide an interesting example of how a similar fear actually stopped becoming, produced the paranoid subject, and tore apart the assemblage. During Gezi, even though everybody knew Erdoğan was lying, his words were perceived as being much more important than any evidence. The paranoid subjects, exemplified by a self-proclaimed feminist group from Turkey (UWVW), were afraid to lose their established connections with him. Each needed to align themselves with what they believed was the centre (i.e. Erdoğan and the current Islamisms in Turkey). In all its absurdity, by choosing to side with the authority the UWVW were given enough power to present Gezi feminism as promoting the 'freedom' of a discriminatory and sexist piece of clothing. The women on the streets were silenced, their assemblage was torn apart, and they lost the creative potential they built up in the streets.

One may not foresee such dire consequences. But positively discriminating in favour of one group, for example veiled women, among the multiplicity unsettles any assemblage, where nobody should be interested in being the father's favourite child. This is especially true in a case like Gezi, where the group in question was an imaginary group of angelic women such as Erdoğan's 'veiled sisters'. It should not come as a surprise that dividing women into decent and indecent groups – this, in practice, is what a headscarf does – and favouring the decent group, puts any feminist movement in danger, because a certain right is given out as a privilege to a state-approved minority. Consequently, the father approves or disapproves of one's pain and suffering, he alone knows what sort of freedom one needs. The women of Turkey apparently deserve to be free to cover their hair, wherever they want to. This discrimination tells the rest of the multiplicity that they need to suffer more and come back some other time; or they need to find better fathers to defend themselves; and most importantly, it tells all the unveiled women that they are not as worthy as their veiled friends. This simple action might return all the protesters to their paranoid positions by stripping everyone of their fundamental rights, and introduces the concept of deserved privileges instead. The wolf becomes a State-fed dog. The timing of the headscarf campaign turned basic human rights into something one is given by an authority, and given only if one is 'decent' enough to deserve it, preferably after a kind of suffering that can be acknowledged by the same authority. Thus, absolute power was submitted back to Erdoğan and he successfully played his part as protector of religious 'freedoms'.

After focusing on the dynamics of this dark assemblage and failed becoming, it is worth taking a look at the tangible outcome of the headscarf campaign from the veiled women's perspective. In the first days of UWVW's campaign, even though their petition was announced on the front pages of several newspapers, it was signed by a negligible number of people. Meanwhile, a link to the campaign was shared on the community pages of various Muslim social networks, such as the Facebook page 'I put on a headscarf, I am happy – *Tesettürlüyüm Mutluyum*', and the page administrators tried to defend themselves for sharing these 'indecent unveiled women's deeds'. During those days it appeared that most veiled women did not trust unveiled women. For the majority of the community, it appeared that it was more important who said and did something rather than what was said and done. They were explaining their reasons on social media: Veiled women believed that unveiled women were not 'sincere in their hearts', because if they were, they would have put on a veil themselves and would have 'already chosen the right path'. Some even claimed that the campaign had to be for the campaigners' personal benefit. Consequently, they agreed that this was a trap, and even if it was not, they did not need 'some indecent women's help'. After realising what was happening, the UWVW changed their methods. Pictures (though not the names) of the unveiled women who started the campaign were removed from the campaign pages. Their faces were replaced by pictures of familiar veiled columnists and other veiled public figures who were then invited to join the campaign. The UWVW's cause was intensely advertised once again, this time with the familiar veiled faces, and they collected a few more signatures. Not long after, Erdoğan ended the suffering with his infamous September 2013 'Democracy' Package which stated that veiled women were now free to enter non-religious indoor public places without having to remove their religious garments. Erdoğan became the self-proclaimed hero for solving a made-up problem.

In Gezi more than half the protesters were women and most of them, including a small number of veiled women, were trying to attract attention to the culture of misogyny. But that culture, once again, silenced them. In short, the werewolf was sacrificed to conform to the society's norms and values. The weak human was left at war with its instincts, hanging on to strong leaders out of fear, just when it most felt like breaking free. There is still a lot to learn from thinking about the human as a pack animal, as Deleuze and Guattari suggest.

References

Bernhardt-House, P. (2008), 'The Werewolf as Queer, the Queer as Werewolf, and Queer Werewolves', in Noreen Giffney and Myra J. Hird (eds), *Queering the Non/Human*, Farnham: Ashgate.

Carroll, N. (1981), 'Nightmare and the Horror Film: The Symbolic Biology of Fantastic Beings', in *Film Quarterly*, Vol. 34, No. 3, pp. 16–25.

Deleuze, G. (2008), *Francis Bacon: The Logic of Sensation*, London and New York: Continuum.

Deleuze, G. and F. Guattari (2007), *A Thousand Plateaus: Capitalism and Schizophrenia*, trans. B. Massumi, London and New York: Continuum.

Duclos, D. (1998), *Werewolf Complex: America's Fascination with Violence*, Oxford and New York: Berg.

Freud, S. (1971), *The Wolf-Man*, ed. M. Gardiner, New York: Basic Books.

Notes on Contributors

Joanna Bednarek is a philosopher, translator and writer. She is the author of *Politics Beyond Form: Ontological Determinations of Poststructuralist Political Philosophy* (2012) and *Lines of Femininity: How Sexual Difference Transformed Literature and Philosophy* (2016). She has translated (among others) Rosi Braidotti, Donna Haraway and Karen Barad. She is a member of the editorial board of the journal *Praktyka Teoretyczna*, and collaborator on 'Krytyka Polityczna' in the years 2006–9. Her fields of interest are poststructuralism, feminism, autonomist Marxism and literature.

Ronald Bogue is both a Distinguished Research Professor and a Josiah Meigs Distinguished Teaching Professor. He retired in 2014, continuing to both conduct research as well as serve on graduate committees. His areas of research include literary theory and the comparative study of the arts. His books include *Deleuze and Guattari* (1989), *Deleuze on Literature* (2003), *Deleuze on Cinema* (2003), *Deleuze on Music, Painting, and the Arts* (2003), and *Deleuze's Wake* (2004).

Edward Campbell is Senior Lecturer in Music at the University of Aberdeen and co-director of the university's Centre for Modern Thought. He specialises in contemporary European art music and aesthetics including historical, analytical and aesthetic approaches to European modernism, the music and writings of Pierre Boulez, contemporary European opera and the interrelation of musical thought and critical theory. He is the author of the books *Boulez, Music and Philosophy* (2010), *Music After Deleuze* (2013), and the co-editor of *Pierre Boulez Studies* (2016). He is currently editing *The Cambridge Stravinsky Encyclopedia* for publication in 2018 and working on a monograph provisionally titled *Colonising the Sound of an Empire: Music in France from Debussy to Dufourt*.

Colin Gardner is Professor of Critical Theory and Integrative Studies at the University of California, Santa Barbara, where he teaches in the departments of Art, Film & Media Studies, Comparative Literature, and the History of Art and Architecture. Gardner has published two books in Manchester University Press's 'British Film Makers' series: *Joseph Losey* (2004) and *Karel Reisz* (2006). His most recent book is *Beckett, Deleuze and the Televisual Event: Peephole Art* (2012), a critical analysis of Samuel Beckett's experimental work for film and television and its relation to the philosophical writings of Deleuze and Guattari.

Gary Genosko is Professor at the University of Ontario Institute of Technology. He is the co-editor, translator and contributor to *Machinic Eros: Félix Guattari's Writings on Japan* (2015), co-editor and contributor to *The Deleuze and Guattari Dictionary* (2014), the author of *When Technocultures Collide: Innovation from Below and the Struggle for Autonomy* (2013) and *Remodelling Communication: From WWII to the WWW* (2012), and has published extensively on Deleuze and Guattari.

renée c. hoogland is Professor of English at Wayne State University in Detroit, where she teaches Literature and Culture after 1870, Critical Theory, Visual Culture, Cultural Studies, and Queer Theory. She is the editor of *Criticism: A Quarterly for Literature and the Arts*, and senior editor in chief of *MacMillan Interdisciplinary Handbooks: Gender*. hoogland's most recent book is *A Violent Embrace: Art and Aesthetics After Representation* (2014).

Zach Horton is currently completing his PhD in English at the University of California, Santa Barbara. He is also a filmmaker, and most recently worked for over four years as the director of a collaborative science-fiction film titled *Swerve*, about the entanglement between the virtual and the actual in a nano-contaminated dystopia (see www.swerveinterface.com). Horton's interdisciplinary research is situated at the intersections of literary theory, media theory, technology studies and the environmental humanities. His current project focuses on technologies and discourses that mediate our access to objects, such as atomic structures and the Earth, that occupy radically disparate scales. See www.zachhorton.com.

Gregg Lambert is Dean's Professor of the Humanities and Director of the Central New York Humanities Corridor at Syracuse University. He is the author of *In Search of a New Image of Thought: Gilles Deleuze and Philosophical Expressionism* (2014), *On the (New) Baroque*, Vol. 12 in 'Critical Studies in the Humanities' (2009), *Who's Afraid of Deleuze and Guattari?* (2008), *The Non-Philosophy of Gilles Deleuze* (2002), and numerous articles and monographs.

Patricia MacCormack is Professor of Continental Philosophy in English, Communication, Film and Media at Anglia Ruskin University, Cambridge. She has published extensively on Guattari, Blanchot, Serres, Irigaray, queer theory, teratology, body modification, posthuman theory, animal rights and horror film. Her work includes 'Inhuman Ecstasy' (*Angelaki*), 'Becoming-Vulva' (*New Formations*), 'The Great Ephemeral Tattooed Skin' (*Body and Society*), 'Necrosexuality' (*Queering the Non/Human*), 'Unnatural Alliances' (*Deleuze and Queer Theory*), 'Vitalistic FeminEthics' (*Deleuze and Law*), and 'Cinemasochism: Time, Space and Submission' (*The Afterimage of Gilles Deleuze's Film Philosophy*). She is the author of *Cinesexuality* (2008) and *Posthuman Ethics* (2012), the editor of *The Animal Catalyst: Toward Ahuman Theory* (2014), and the co-editor with Ian Buchanan of *The Schizoanalysis of Cinema* (2008).

John Ó Maoilearca is Professor of Film and Television Studies at Kingston University, London. He has also taught philosophy and film theory at the University of Sunderland, England, and the University of Dundee, Scotland. He has published ten books, including (as author) *Bergson and Philosophy* (2000), *Post-Continental Philosophy: An Outline* (2006), *Philosophy and the Moving Image: Refractions of Reality* (2010), and (as editor) *Laruelle and Non-Philosophy* (2012) and *The Bloomsbury Companion to Continental Philosophy* (2013). His most recent book is *All Thoughts Are Equal: Laruelle and Nonhuman Thought* (2015). In 2014 his name reverted from the English 'Mullarkey' to the original Irish, 'Ó Maoilearca', which ultimately translates as 'follower of the animal'.

Nur Ozgenalp teaches film at Aki-ArtEZ Enschede and SAE Amsterdam, and other courses at Amsterdam University College. She is a doctoral researcher at the Amsterdam School for Cultural Analysis, where she studies cultural and political transformations by examining storytelling elements of serial television fiction in relation to Deleuzo-Guattarian theories. She has directed short films as part of her bachelor's degree in Cinema and Television from Mimar Sinan University. Her MA thesis focused on film theory and psychoanalysis, and she taught film and media at Academy Istanbul and Izmir University of Economics from 2008–12.

Serazer Pekerman is a writer and part-time tutor in Film Studies at the University of St Andrews. She holds a BArch degree from METU, Turkey, and a PhD in Film Studies from the University of St Andrews. She lives in Scotland.

Laurence A. Rickels taught for thirty years at the University of California, and is now Professor in art and theory at the Academy of Fine Arts Karlsruhe as successor to Klaus Theweleit. He is the author of numerous publications on unmourning, as he terms it, as well as on the cultural study of occult and technical media. His works include *SPECTRE* (2013), *I Think I Am: Philip K. Dick* (2010), *The Devil Notebooks* (2008), *Ulrike Ottinger: The Autobiography of Art Cinema* (2008), *Nazi Psychoanalysis, 3 Volumes: Only Psychoanalysis Won the War, Crypto-Fetishism, Psy-Fi* (2002) and *The Vampire Lectures* (1999). For more information please visit: www.larickels.com

Dennis Rothermel is Professor Emeritus in Philosophy at California State University, Chico. He has co-edited a volume of essays on peace studies published by Rodopi. A co-edited collection of theoretical essays in film and media theory, *A Critique of Judgment in Film and Television*, was published by Palgrave Macmillan in 2014, and includes his chapter, 'The Tones of Judgment in Local Evening News'. He is working on a monograph on Westerns, and another on Gilles Deleuze's cinema books.

Charles J. Stivale is Distinguished Professor of French at Wayne State University, Detroit. He is the author of numerous journal articles and books, including *The Art of Rupture, Narrative Desire and Duplicity in the Tales of Guy de Maupassant* (1994), *The Two-Fold Thought of Deleuze and Guattari, Intersections and Animations* (1998), and *Gilles Deleuze's ABCs: The Folds of Friendship* (2008). He is the translator (with Mark Lester) of Deleuze's *The Logic of Sense*, and (with Giuseppina Mecchia) *Félix Guattari: Thought, Friendship, and Visionary Cartography*, by Franco Berardi (Bifo). He is the editor of two editions of *Gilles Deleuze: Key Concepts*, *Modern French Literary Studies in the Classroom: Pedagogical Strategies*, and *Gilles Deleuze: Image and Text* (co-edited with Eugene W. Holland and Daniel W. Smith).

Index